Critical Acclaim for
Complete Maya Programming!

David Gould is an expert at using, programming, and teaching Maya, and it shows. People who need to program Maya will find this book essential. Even Maya users who don't intend to do extensive programming should read this book for a better understanding of what's going on under the hood. Compact yet thorough, it covers both MEL and the C++ API and is written to be informative for both novice and expert programmers. Highly recommended!

—**Larry Gritz,** Exluna/NVIDIA

This book should be required reading for all Maya programmers, novice and expert alike. For the novice, it provides a thorough and wonderfully well thought out, hands-on tutorial and introduction to Maya. The book's greatest contribution, however, is that David shares his deep understanding of Maya's fundamental concepts and architecture so that even the expert can learn to more effectively exploit Maya's rich and powerful programming interfaces.

—**Philip J. Schneider,** Disney Feature Animation

Having provided a technical review of David Gould's *Complete Maya Programming,* I must say that this book is the definitive text for scripting and plug-in development for Maya. Never before has there been such a concise and clearly written guide to programming for Maya. Any user smart enough to pick up this book would be better off for it.

—**Chris Rock,** Technical Director at a Large Animation Studio in Northern California

If you ever wanted to open the Maya toolbox, this is your guide. With clear step-by-step instructions, you will soon be able to customize and improve the application, as well as create your own extensions, either through the MEL scripting language or the full C++ API.

—**Christophe Hery,** Industrial Light + Magic

COMPLETE
MAYA PROGRAMMING

An Extensive Guide to MEL and the C++ API

The Morgan Kaufmann Series in Computer Graphics and Geometric Modeling

Series Editor: Brian A. Barsky, University of California, Berkeley

Complete Maya Programming:
An Extensive Guide to MEL and the C++ API
David A. D. Gould

Real-Time Shader Programming
Ron Fosner

MEL Scripting for Maya Animators
Mark R. Wilkins and Chris Kazmier

Texturing & Modeling:
A Procedural Approach, Third Edition
David S. Ebert, F. Kenton Musgrave,
Darwyn Peachey, Ken Perlin, and Steven Worley

Geometric Tools for Computer Graphics
Philip Schneider and David Eberly

Understanding Virtual Reality:
Interface, Application, and Design
William Sherman and Alan Craig

Jim Blinn's Corner: Notation, Notation, Notation
Jim Blinn

Level of Detail for 3D Graphics: Application and Theory
David Luebke, Martin Reddy, Jonathan D. Cohen,
Amitabh Varshney, Benjamin Watson,
and Robert Huebner

Digital Video and HDTV Algorithms and Interfaces
Charles Poynton

Pyramid Algorithms: A Dynamic Programming
Approach to Curves and Surfaces for Geometric
Modeling
Ron Goldman

Non-Photorealistic Computer Graphics:
Modeling, Rendering, and Animation
Thomas Strothotte and Stefan Schlechtweg

Curves and Surfaces for CAGD: A Practical Guide, Fifth
Edition
Gerald Farin

Subdivision Methods for Geometric Design:
A Constructive Approach
Joe Warren and Henrik Weimer

Computer Animation: Algorithms and Techniques
Rick Parent

The Computer Animator's Technical Handbook
Lynn Pocock and Judson Rosebush

Advanced RenderMan:
Creating CGI for Motion Pictures
Anthony A. Apodaca and Larry Gritz

Curves and Surfaces in Geometric Modeling:
Theory and Algorithms
Jean Gallier

Andrew Glassner's Notebook:
Recreational Computer Graphics
Andrew S. Glassner

Warping and Morphing of Graphical Objects
Jonas Gomes, Lucia Darsa, Bruno Costa,
and Luiz Velho

Jim Blinn's Corner: Dirty Pixels
Jim Blinn

Rendering with Radiance:
The Art and Science of Lighting Visualization
Greg Ward Larson and Rob Shakespeare

Introduction to Implicit Surfaces
Edited by Jules Bloomenthal

Jim Blinn's Corner: A Trip Down the Graphics Pipeline
Jim Blinn

Interactive Curves and Surfaces:
A Multimedia Tutorial on CAGD
Alyn Rockwood and Peter Chambers

Wavelets for Computer Graphics:
Theory and Applications
Eric J. Stollnitz, Tony D. DeRose,
and David H. Salesin

Principles of Digital Image Synthesis
Andrew S. Glassner

Radiosity & Global Illumination
François X. Sillion and Claude Puech

Knotty: A B-Spline Visualization Program
Jonathan Yen

User Interface Management Systems:
Models and Algorithms
Dan R. Olsen, Jr.

Making Them Move: Mechanics, Control, and
Animation of Articulated Figures
Edited by Norman I. Badler, Brian A. Barsky,
and David Zeltzer

Geometric and Solid Modeling: An Introduction
Christoph M. Hoffmann

An Introduction to Splines for Use in Computer Graphics
and Geometric Modeling
Richard H. Bartels, John C. Beatty,
and Brian A. Barsky

COMPLETE MAYA PROGRAMMING

An Extensive Guide to MEL and the C++ API

David A. D. Gould

MORGAN KAUFMANN PUBLISHERS

AN IMPRINT OF ELSEVIER SCIENCE

SAN FRANCISCO   SAN DIEGO   NEW YORK   BOSTON
LONDON   SYDNEY   TOKYO

Publishing Director	Diane D. Cerra
Publishing Services Manager	Edward Wade
Project Management	Yonie Overton
Editorial Coordinator	Mona Buehler
Cover and Text Design	Frances Baca Design
Cover Illustration	Sean Platter
Composition	Proctor-Willenbacher
Technical Illustration	Dartmouth Publishing, Inc.
Copyeditor	John Hammett
Proofreader	Sharilyn Hovind
Indexer	Richard Evans, Infodex Indexing Services, Inc.
Interior Printer	The Maple-Vail Book Manufacturing Group
Cover Printer	Phoenix Color Corporation

Microsoft® and Windows NT® and Windows 2000® are registered trademarks of Microsoft Corporation in the United States and/or other countries. Maya® is a registered trademark of Alias | Wavefront. IRIX® is a registered trademark of SGI. All other product names mentioned are trademarks or registered trademarks of their respective holders.

Designations used by companies to distinguish their products are often claimed as trademarks or registered trademarks. In all instances in which Morgan Kaufmann Publishers is aware of a claim, the product names appear in initial capital or all capital letters. Readers, however, should contact the appropriate companies for more complete information regarding trademarks and registration.

Morgan Kaufmann Publishers
An Imprint of Elsevier Science
340 Pine Street, Sixth Floor
San Francisco, CA 94104-3205
www.mkp.com

07 06 05 04 03   5 4 3 2 1

Library of Congress Control Number: 2002111021
ISBN: 1-55860-835-4

This book is printed on acid-free paper.

To my father, for instilling in me a love for the written word

CONTENTS

PREFACE

Maya is, undisputedly, a very powerful tool for creating computer graphics. However, it must also be stated that learning Maya is a daunting task. Its sheer depth and breadth of features alone make it a formidable package to learn, let alone master. There was probably never a time when this was more apparent than the day you first opened it up. I'm sure that it felt as if you were at the foot of a mountain, about to start a long climb. You will be pleased to know that the journey can be made easier. Maya can be customized and extended in ways that you never thought possible. A great many of your daily tasks can be automated or greatly simplified. You can create tools that not only increase your productivity but also give you far greater control. All this, and more, can be achieved through Maya programming.

For many, the mere mention of programming provokes fear and trepidation. This is understandable, since many programming books make extensive assumptions about the reader's existing programming expertise. This book assumes that you have no prior programming experience and, as such, will dispel the myth that only professional programmers can program Maya. With a solid understanding of the basic concepts, anyone can begin harnessing the level of control that only programming offers. What would once have seemed a daunting undertaking will be shown instead to be an enabling and empowering experience.

With an experienced and patient guide, any journey is made easier. As such, this book endeavors not to lecture but to guide you gently through an understanding of how Maya works at its most fundamental level. Starting with an exploration of the very heart of Maya, you will learn how data is maintained and processed. This knowledge is critical, since it is the foundation on which all of Maya's functionality is built. Using Maya's easiest programming language, MEL (Maya Embedded Language), you will begin to learn how to control Maya and automate many operations. The C++ application programming interface (API) is then presented. With a basic understanding of the C++ language, you'll quickly learn how to develop your own custom tools and features. As each real-world example is presented, you'll gain a further understanding of just how Maya's features can be accessed and controlled. By using MEL and C++, in combination, you'll soon be able to gain complete control over every aspect of Maya and extend it to suit your every need.

In addition to teaching the specifics of Maya programming, this book focuses on *why* something is designed in a particular way. Programming often affords an unlimited number of possible ways for solving a problem. However, it is important to understand that Maya has its own particular design philosophy. This book presents a set of guidelines for designing your programs so that they will integrate and work seamlessly within Maya. With an understanding of why a particular approach is used, you'll be able to extrapolate the underlying idea to solve your own problems. It is my goal that when you finish reading this book you will not only be inspired to imagine new and exciting possibilities but you will also have the necessary skills and knowledge to turn them into reality.

SOURCE FILES

Please note that all the files used in this book are available at *www.davidgould.com*. A list, though not exhaustive, of the information available at the site includes

♦ MEL scripts and C++ source code for all the examples in the book

♦ Additional examples of MEL scripts

♦ Additional examples of C++ API source code

♦ Errata for this book

♦ Continually updated glossary

♦ Updated list of other relevant websites and online resources

CHAPTER 1

INTRODUCTION

In terms of change, it would be safe to say that no other industry is as dynamic as the computer graphics industry. While still relatively young, it has already spread into many different and diverse areas. These include modeling, animation, and rendering. Each distinct area continually pushes forward with greater improvements and advancements. As a result, never before have such images of breathtaking realism and believability been produced as those seen today. Never before have there been scientific simulations of such complexity. Never before have there been interactive games with the depth of engagement as right now. Never before, that is, until tomorrow!

If one thing is sure in the computer graphics industry, it is that change is not only inevitable but that it is continuing at an ever quickening pace. The steady progress of the past pales in comparison to the speed with which new inventions and ideas are both conceived and implemented right now. The driving force behind this progress is the public's insatiable appetite for images and experiences of greater depth and complexity. With no foreseeable end to this appetite, the computer graphics industry has been continually pushing forward in pursuit of the "ultimate" experience.

Alias | Wavefront has consistently been at the forefront of this continual wave of change. Its commitment to long-term research and development has lead to some of the most advanced tools and technology currently available. One such technology is Maya. Since its release in 1998, Maya has become the computer graphics package of choice among the world's best animation studios and companies. With an extensive toolset, covering such areas as modeling, dynamics, animation, and rendering, it is used for all aspects of production work.

In order to keep up with the rapid pace of change, Maya is continually being updated and improved. Even with its extensive feature set, the designers of Maya recognized that they will never be able to provide all the features and functionality that every user could possibly want. Nor could they design it to cater to the preferred workflow of each individual. As a result, they designed it so that users are free to customize and extend the package as they need. Users are free to mold and change Maya to fit their particular production environment and workflow. From changing the main graphical user interface to seamlessly adding new features, users are free to turn the package into something entirely different.

In fact, Maya can be considered an open architecture for doing computer graphics. Think of it as a framework in which you have a host of 3D components (objects, animations, dynamics, and so on) that can be repurposed for your own custom applications. For example, you could use Maya to do custom simulations or real-time interactive tasks. A good demonstration of the extent to which Maya can be repurposed is by Mike Taylor, an Alias | Wavefront engineer. Through the use of some simple scripts he was able to turn Maya into a 3D tetris game. The final interface and interactivity were so different that it was hard to believe that it was actually Maya.

As you gain a greater understanding of the degree to which Maya can be customized and extended, you will soon realize that there are very few limitations on what you can do. The flexibility offered is matched only by your imagination.

1.1   MAYA'S PROGRAMMABILITY

So what exactly can be programmed in Maya? This section covers some of the major areas of Maya's functionality that can be directly accessed and controlled using the programming interfaces.

1.1.1   Customization

The entire Maya graphical user interface (GUI) is written and controlled using MEL, the Maya Embedded Language. The creation, editing, and deletion of all the graphical user interface elements is done using the MEL language. It then follows that you too can control the Maya interface by using MEL. In fact you can entirely replace the standard Maya interface by using your own MEL scripts. There is often a need for specialized customization of parts of Maya's interface. For instance, you may want to develop a particular interface that allows animators to set keys without their having to learn the **Channel Box** or other **Graph Editor.** You can also hide or remove a lot of the Maya interface elements to reduce the complexity of the interface for certain users.

In addition to the user interface, you can customize Maya's internal settings. Using MEL you can make changes to Maya's settings on a per project or on a systemwide basis. For instance, you can ensure that all users consistently use the same time, angle, and linear units. Alternatively, any users that open a particular project can have specific settings applied at that time.

1.1.2 Integration

Often Maya isn't the only package used in a production environment. Only some of its features may be used, while other packages are used for specific tasks. Therefore, there is a need to pass data into and out of Maya from these external packages. While Maya comes standard with features to export and import certain data formats, the programming interfaces allow you to write custom *data exporters* and *importers.* These are also known as *translators,* since they translate data from one package into a form that is understandable to another. Since Maya provides access to the entire scene and all its data, you can output this data in any form you require. A common require-ment, for a games company, is to take the Maya assets (models, animation, and so on) and convert them into a form that is readily usable by a given games engine.

Maya's functionality can also be compiled into a stand-alone application. This way you can use a mix of Maya and custom programming code to provide a com-plete application solution.

1.1.3 Automation

Many tasks are often continually repeated. Programming is well suited to automat-ing repetitive tasks. Rather than have the user repeat the task each time by hand, a MEL script can be written that completely automates it. Whether it be the applica-tion of a shading network, the positioning of objects, or just about any task that is completed more than once, it can be automated. In fact with the generalization that programming offers, you can have your script perform different tasks depending on the current context. For instance, a series of objects can be made to stick on top or bottom of another automatically without requiring the user to manually position each object individually.

1.1.4 Extensions

While Maya boasts a very extensive feature set, there will always be a need for custom tools and features. Fortunately Maya allows you to add your own features and functionality. These features can also be made to work seamlessly with the rest of Maya. From the user's perspective, the tools that you create appear no different from the standard Maya tools. Using MEL and C++ you can create large and exten-sive extensions to the Maya package.

There are few limits on what functionality you can extend. Maya allows you to create custom shaders, dynamics, particles, deformers, and animation controllers, to name a few. In fact the extensions you create can be integrated directly into the Dependency Graph, the very heart of Maya. Once integrated, the functionality can be accessed in the same manner that standard Maya features are accessed.

1.2   PROGRAMMING INTERFACES

Artists typically complete their work in Maya by using its graphical user interface. The interface includes menus, dialog boxes, buttons, and so on to give users a visual means of performing actions. There is another way to perform these same actions. Maya programming allows users to complete the same tasks by writing and executing a program. This program can be developed using one of Maya's two programming interfaces: MEL or C++.

1.2.1   MEL

MEL is an acronym for Maya Embedded Language. This is a custom programming language designed specifically to work inside Maya. Due to its simpler structure and syntax, it is easier and more widely accessible than the C++ programming interface. One of MEL's great strengths is that it is an *interpreted language.* While typical programming languages require that you compile and then link your source code, an interpreted language can be executed immediately. This ability to immediately execute your instructions means that MEL is particularly well suited to rapid prototyping. You can more readily design and implement new ideas, since the compile-link step isn't needed. In fact, MEL can be written, debugged, and tested entirely within Maya. There is no need to use external compilers or debuggers.

Since MEL is an interpreted language it does have a downside: it can run a lot slower than an equivalent C++ program. A C++ program is compiled from the source code to generate actual native machine instructions, and it runs very fast. An interpreted language has the source code interpreted on the fly. As Maya encounters a MEL instruction, it must be interpreted and then finally converted to the native machine instruction. Even though Maya does a great job of speeding this up, there are many times when MEL lags far behind C++ in terms of speed. That being said, there are many cases in which the added advantage of rapidly creating and executing a MEL program far outweighs the setup, complexity, and compile costs of a C++ program. It all depends on the type and complexity of the task you want to undertake.

1.2.2 C++

Maya can be programmed using the standard C++ programming language. While daunting for users who don't know the language, it is by far the most powerful means of extending Maya. Using C++ you can create native Maya plugins that work seamlessly with the rest of the package.

Programming access is provided through the C++ API (application programming interface). This interface consists of a series of C++ class libraries. To create a plugin you simply write a C++ program that uses and extends the basic Maya classes. As such, the process of learning C++ API programming involves learning what the various classes are and how to use them. Fortunately the classes are designed in a consistent manner, so having learned some of the simpler classes helps when you learn some of the more advanced. While the number of classes may at first seem daunting, a typical Maya plugin will use only a small portion of them. Generally, only about a third of the available classes are used regularly. Some of the more esoteric classes are rarely used.

1.2.3 MEL or C++?

Given the two options for programming Maya, you are now left to decide which one to use. In choosing which programming inteface to use, it is important to weigh both equally in light of your particular needs. The final choice may depend on outside factors such as a tight deadline or specific speed requirements. Generally, MEL provides you with all the programming functionality you need. It allows a great deal of access to Maya's functionality without the need to use C++. When the C++ programming interface is used, it is typically for specific functionality that can't be found in the MEL interface.

It is also important to understand that chosing one doesn't automatically exclude the other. The C++ interface isn't a superset of the MEL interface; that is, the C++ interface doesn't contain everything the MEL interface has and more. There are some features you'll find in the MEL interface that aren't available in the C++ interface, and vice versa. As such, some problems can be solved only by a combination of the two. As you gain greater proficiency and experience developing for Maya, a good understanding of both MEL and the C++ API will give you the greatest leverage in coming up with the best solution to a given problem. With a better understanding of both programming interfaces, you will be able to recognize when one is better suited for a given part, and thereby create the best mix.

EASE OF USE

The choice of which programming interface to use may simply be determined by your programming proficiency. While MEL bears a remarkable similarity to the C programming language, it is sufficiently different to make it easily accessible to less experienced developers. The removal of such constructs as pointers and memory allocation and deallocation makes MEL far easier to use and understand. While MEL doesn't provide the low-level access offered by C, there is rarely a need for this when you are programming Maya. Also, not having these constructs also prevents some of the more common causes for program crashes and general instability.

MEL scripts, as they are closer to *pseudocode* than other languages, tend to be easier to read. MEL is also more forgiving in that it doesn't enforce as much type checking. This means that you can quickly write scripts without having to worry about what types your variables are. This can be both a blessing and a curse, since it can result in subtle bugs that may be hard to find later. Fortunately you can choose to improve the type checking by explicity declaring the type of the variable when it is defined.

If you are more experienced with C++, you may want to use the C++ API. Maya's C++ class hierarchy provides access to a great deal of Maya's functionality. However, you will inevitably need to do some MEL programming, even if you intend to write everything in C++. A good understanding of C++ will most certainly aid in also learning MEL, since its syntax is very similar to C. Appendix B explains the important differences between C and the MEL programming languages.

If the programming task requires complex data structures, you will most likely need to use the C++ API. MEL contains a limited set of different variable types and doesn't allow you to define your own data structures.

SPECIFIC FUNCTIONALITY

It is easy to assume that since the C++ API is more complex than MEL it must give the greater level of access and control. This assumption is partly right. Using the C++ API, you can create plugins and write software that allows you a tighter level of integration with the core Maya package. However it is wrong to assume that the C++ API is a superset of the MEL functionality. In fact they are complementary.

There is certain functionality that you can access from MEL that you can't access from the C++ API, and vice versa. So in order to perform certain tasks you have no choice but to use a combination of both. In fact, it is quite common to see a C++ plugin with sprinklings of calls to MEL commands. Most commonly, however, MEL provides enough functionality that writing a C++ plugin is unnecessary.

This may not always be the case. The C++ API provides certain features that are simply impossible to replicate with MEL. Only through the C++ API can you create your own nodes. Creating your own nodes allows you to create custom tools, deformers, shapes, shaders, locators, manipulators, and so on. Also MEL doesn't allow you to create custom commands, although you can create MEL procedures that act similarly to certain commands.

Irrespective of which programming interface you decide on for developing your core functionality, when you begin dealing with any graphical user interface issues you will have to use MEL, as it is the sole means of controlling the interface. Fortunately it is possible to execute MEL commands from the C++ API.

CROSS-PLATFORM PORTABILITY

Given Maya's widespread deployment on multiple platforms, it is important to decide whether portability is an important consideration. If you need to develop for only one platform, then this becomes less of an issue. However, with the increasingly widespread use of mixed platforms for both data processing and rendering, it may be prudent to consider the potential consequences of your decision now.

Since MEL is a scripting language, it has been designed to be easily portable to other platforms. MEL contains little platform-dependent functionality. In fact almost all commands work without regard to which particular platform they are running on. This means deploying a MEL script on multiple platforms is typically easier since it has less dependency on platform-specific features. Since MEL is used for all the graphical user interface functionality, you never have to be concerned with the specifics of the different windowing systems. Using MEL you can develop the interface on one platform and know that it will appear and operate similarly on other platforms.

Developing cross-platform C++ software has been notoriously difficult for a variety of reasons. The problems start with different C++ compilers having their own incompatibilities. They also have varying degrees of *ANSI* C++ language conformance. Finally, not all compilers use the same standard C libraries. Using just the Maya C++ classes and libraries with little dependency on other external libraries and advanced language features should ease any cross-platform development effort.

In cases in which cross-platform compatibility is an important issue, attempt to write as much of the functionality in MEL as possible. Use C++ only when it is absolutely necessary.

SPEED

Since MEL is an interpreted language, it is likely to be slower than C++. This is not always the case, however, and the speed depends largely on the complexity of the program. For certain tasks, the speed difference may not be significant enough to warrant the extra effort to write it in C++. For truly time-critical and complex operations there is no question that the C++ program will run faster. In fact the speed gain can be tenfold. This is an important consideration when large and complex geometry is used in a scene. The extra C++ programming effort can reap large rewards in general user interactivity and overall productivity.

DISCLOSURE

There may be occasions when you'd like to release some functionality to an outside party but not disclose exactly how it was implemented. This often means a script or plugin that contains some proprietary algorithm or technology. You would like to protect this information while still allowing others to use the resulting functionality.

Since a MEL script is both the source code as well as what is finally executed, there is no way to separate the two. In order for users to run the script, they will need the MEL script. Since they will have the script, they can see exactly how it works by opening it in a text editor. A C++ plugin, on the other hand, is in machine code. It is the end result of compilation and linking. Since the final result is in machine code, it isn't obvious to the user how the actual program was written. This effectively protects the methods and algorithms used to write the program.

So if you do mind that the user of your MEL scripts can see exactly how they work, it is best to write the functionality as a C++ plugin with additional scripts used sparingly. Note that it is still possible for your C++ plugin to make calls to MEL commands.

CHAPTER 2

FUNDAMENTAL MAYA CONCEPTS

Any structure is only as strong as its foundation. This principle is equally applicable to Maya programming. A solid foundation in the fundamental Maya concepts will greatly ease your development efforts. Since you will be working within the framework of the Maya system, it is important to understand how this system works. Any system imposes a set of constraints on what it is you can and cannot do. While Maya is, undoubtedly, extremely flexible in terms of what you can achieve, there are some fundamental rules that simply must be learned and adhered to.

While you may feel pressed to skip this section and begin the actual programming, I caution you about doing so. Although they get the job done, I've seen many Maya developers who have been using the product for years but who have simply ignored or not learned some of the fundamental Maya concepts. As a result their applications don't fully exploit all of Maya's power. Many times the developers were essentially trying to shoehorn their approach into the Maya framework. Unfortunately, with this approach they always inevitably lose. With the small amount of education given in this chapter, developers could finally grasp some of Maya's governing rules and thereby create better and faster applications.

This situation also underlies another point; Maya allows you to "do it the wrong way." Since the Maya framework is extremely flexible, it rarely places strict guidelines on how you should achieve a particular task. This is extremely attractive, since almost any problem can be tackled from a variety of different angles. The disadvantage of this open flexibility is that sometimes it allows the misinformed developer to create applications that don't really fit properly into the framework. This often results in long agonizing hours spent debugging and testing scripts and plugins that simply don't work or behave erratically. In this book you have the first steps to building the necessary foundation of knowledge.

Much of the material presented in this chapter gives a broad overview of how Maya works internally. This material is equally applicable to artists and developers alike. While this chapter contains no specific programming per se, it is vital to gaining a better understanding of the Maya system and will help you to write better programs later. The later chapters on MEL and the C++ API cover in great detail exactly how to program Maya.

2.1   MAYA ARCHITECTURE

If you had experience using another 3D package before using Maya, you'll recall that you had to make a mental switch from what you were accustomed to with the other package to how Maya works. While most 3D packages ultimately attempt to accomplish the same overall tasks, the approach they take can be quite different. The steps that you must perform in order to complete a particular operation are often unique to a given package and therefore impose a certain predefined structure to your workflow. Fortunately, Maya has a very flexible workflow that doesn't impose very many constraints. For the most part there is more than one way to approach a particular problem. This means that you can use whichever approach is most suited to your needs. In time, you will learn how to create your very own custom workflows.

2.1.1   Overview

Taking the entire Maya system and breaking it down into its major components results in the schematic diagram shown in Figure 2.1.

As a Maya user, you will interact with the Maya GUI. You will select menu items, change parameters, animate and move objects, and so on. When you interact

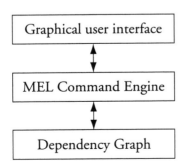

FIGURE 2.1   Maya system

with the user interface, Maya is actually issuing MEL commands. These commands are sent to the Command Engine where they are interpreted then executed. As you may know, it is possible to run Maya in batch mode. In this mode there is no GUI, so MEL commands are sent directly to the Command Engine to be executed.

The majority of the MEL commands operate on the Dependency Graph. The reason for this is that the Dependency Graph can be intuitively thought of as the entire *scene*. The scene is all the important data and information that make up the 3D world, including the objects, animation, dynamics, materials, and so on. Not only does the Dependency Graph define what data is in the current scene, its very structure and layout define how data is processed. The Dependency Graph is really the heart and brains of Maya. Given its importance, you will now explore it in greater detail.

2.2 THE DEPENDENCY GRAPH

2.2.1 3D Application Design

In order to gain a better understanding of how the Maya architecture differs from other 3D applications, it is important to highlight how most "typical" 3D applications are designed. Understanding what makes Maya's approach different will have a definite impact on how you design your plugins.

PAST APPROACHES

Generally, a 3D application provides a given set of tools to perform the tasks of modeling, animating, lighting, and rendering. It is clear that these tasks are quite different from one another. The operations that you perform when modeling are quite different from those when you render. The information and data created, manipulated, then stored when modeling are also very different from that when rendering.

Since each area has its own particular set of data and operations, it follows logically that each area can be designed and implemented separately. In fact, each area can be defined by a distinct, and separate, module. Each module stores and operates on a given type of data. The modeling module, for instance, would operate on the geometric and modeling data. A separate module would be created for each of the tasks: modeling, animating, lighting, and rendering. Within each of these tasks, a well-defined set of functionality would be implemented. The result is a clean programming interface to each module.

Ironically enough, it is the very clarity these interfaces provide that prevents them from being truly flexible. Say you designed a 3D application that had a modeling system. Once you had modeled an object in its static form, it could then be animated by passing it to the animation module. The animation module would allow it to move about in space. The rendering module would then take the animated object from the animation module and render it to the screen. Since each of the modules has a precise interface, it knows exactly how to communicate to other modules. Well, what happens if you wanted to include a deformation system that took animated objects and deformed them? Since the rendering module knows how to talk only to the animation module, you'd either have to change it and adapt it to include the new functionality or create a new module. In any event the need to add this new functionality would mean that the animation and rendering module would need to be updated. So the simple inclusion of a new feature could have a rippling effect on the entire system resulting in many revisions. The downfall of this design is that it doesn't easily let you add new functionality without making changes to all the affected modules. What is needed is a more general and flexible design.

MAYA APPROACH

Ultimately you would like to add new features and functionality without needing to touch any of the existing modules. You would also like to change the functionality or interface in a given module without having to manually update all the dependent modules.

In order to find a better solution you need to ask yourself: at a fundamental level, what are 3D applications really trying to achieve? At their most fundamental level, they are simply creating some data that is then manipulated through a series of operations. For instance, the end result of these data-creation and manipulation steps could be a final polygonal mesh or a series of pixels in an image. The steps that take a piece of data from its inception to its final result can be easily identified as a series of sequential operations. The result of one operation is then fed into the next and so on. Each operation modifies the data in some way then passes it on to the next operation for further modification. So the whole process can be thought of as data entering one end of a series of operations and exiting the other end edited in some way. This is commonly referred to as the *data flow model*. Data appears to be flowing through the operations.

When you consider what a 3D application is trying to do, you can see that each of the distinct modules can really be broken down into smaller operations. These smaller operations can operate on the data and then pass it on to the next operation. So at the very fundamental level, all the functionality provided by the separate modules can be encapsulated in a series of interconnected operators. These operators take data in and produce some data as output. Connected up sequentially, these operators can be thought of as a pipe or *pipeline*. Data is fed into the first operator in the pipeline and then comes out of the final operator at the other end, processed in some way. With the right set of operators, you can place a 3D model in one end of the pipeline and end up with a series of pixels at the other end. Generalizing this even further, you can simply have any data go in one end and any data come out the other. In fact, there is no need to even enforce that the data be related to 3D. It would be possible to place a text file in one end and have a series of edited characters result at the other.

Alias | Wavefront implemented Maya's core using this data flow paradigm. This core is physically embodied in the Dependency Graph.[1] For simplicity, I will refer to the Dependency Graph by its abbreviation, DG. Before continuing I must note that, technically, the DG is based on a *push-pull model* and not on a strict data flow model. I will explain later, in fine detail, the distinction between the two, but for now the data flow paradigm provides an intuitive framework for understanding how Maya works.

The DG is really the heart of Maya. It provides for all the fundamental building blocks just mentioned. It allows you to create arbitrary data that is fed into a series of operations and that results in some processed data at the other end. The data and their operations are encapsulated in the DG as *nodes*. A node holds any number of slots that contain the data used by Maya. Nodes also contain an operator that can work on their data and produce some other data as a result.

The common 3D tasks can be completed by connecting a series of nodes together. The data from the first node is fed into the next, and it processes it in some way or creates some new data that is then fed into the following node. So the data is fed through the network of nodes from the very first to the last. Along the way the nodes are free to process and edit the data in any way they please. They can also create new data that can then be fed into other nodes. Each type of node is designed to perform only a small, restricted set of different operations. A node for orienting an object to point at another object will provide only that specific functionality. It won't, for instance, deform the object. A deformation node will be designed for that task. By designing the nodes to perform specific unitary tasks, they can be kept simple and more manageable.

In order to perform some complex modification to some data, you'd create a network of these simple nodes. There is no restriction on the number of nodes and

---

[1] The Dependency Graph technology is covered by the U.S. patents #5,808,625 and #5,929,864.

how they are connected, so you can create networks of arbitrary complexity. Much as a series of simple Lego blocks can be combined to created complex structures, so can Maya nodes be connected to create complex data flows.

A testament to the flexibility of the DG is that all data (modeling, dynamics, animation, shading, and so on) in Maya is created and manipulated through nodes. This approach of building complexity from simpler building blocks gives Maya its real power and flexibility. Whereas previous 3D application designs called for separate modules, Maya provides an extensive set of different nodes. With enough of these nodes connected in a given network, you can complete almost any computational task. All the modeling, dynamics, shading, and rendering functionality is provided as a network of interconnected nodes. Given their generality, it is easy to see that future features can be easily integrated since there is no fixed set of interfaces nor the concept of separate modules.

In order to add new functionality to Maya, you simply need to create a new node. Since you can create it so that it appears as a native node, it can be seamlessly inserted into the DG. This, combined with the ability to define your own commands, affords you practically unlimited possibilities when it comes to extending Maya. With the addition of the powerful MEL scripting language, there is almost no area of Maya you can't extend or customize.

2.2.2 The Scene

The *scene* is the common term for describing the entire 3D graphics state for a given 3D application. The scene comprises all the models, their animation, and textures, as well as all the lights, cameras, and any other supplemental information such as rendering options and so on. In Maya, the scene *is* the DG. They are one and the same. When Maya stores or loads the scene from disk, it simply stores or loads the DG. The DG defines the entire scene through its network of interconnected nodes.

In a typical application, all the information that makes up the scene would be stored in separate, specific data structures. These structures would commonly reside in a central database. Since the DG is a set of interconnected nodes, and these nodes keep their data internally, the scene is effectively stored not in a central location but as a distributed network. All the nodes collectively form a distributed database. Since new nodes can be added to and removed from the network, it is highly dynamic in structure.

With the data being distributed among all the connected nodes, how do you retrieve a particular piece of data? Since other systems have their data stored in a central database, it is easy to query a particular piece of data. It is easy, for instance, to ask the scene for a list of all the lights in the scene. Since all data is stored in a network of nodes, this type of query could be difficult. Fortunately Maya shields you from the internal workings of the DG and provides you with convenience functions to access the scene as if it were a central repository of data. The programming interface to the DG doesn't require you to know its underlying layout and structure. For instance, you can quickly and easily obtain a list of all objects of a given type without knowing where in the network they are located.

Even though the various programming interfaces hide much of this complexity, it is important to understand what is really going on underneath. There will be many times when a deeper understanding of how Maya really stores the scene will help you develop more robust and faster applications.

2.2.3 Visualizing the Dependency Graph

Following is a snapshot of the Hypergraph. The Hypergraph is the visual window in the DG, the very core of Maya. Figure 2.2 shows the result of just a few modeling operations. You can see that the number of nodes and their connections quickly increase even after just a few operations.

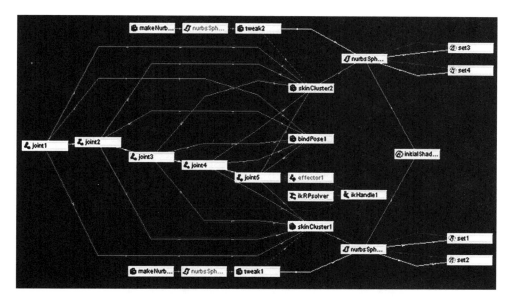

FIGURE 2.2 Example of the Dependency Graph

While at first glance the DG may appear daunting, with the knowledge gained in the following chapters you will be able to quickly decipher what each node is and how it is connected to the others. Already you'll note that there are different types of nodes: joints, sets, tweaks, and so on. These nodes are connected to other nodes. The lines show the connections between the nodes, and the arrows show the direction the data is flowing.

If you aren't very familiar with the Hypergraph, I'd strongly suggest that you complete the Maya tutorials and study the associated reference documentation. You will use the Hypergraph countless times during your programming work, so a firm understanding of how it works is very important.

2.2.4   Data Flow

The following isolates a smaller DG and studies it in detail. Figure 2.3 shows a simpler DG that demonstrates some of the common functionality seen in all node networks. Larger, more complex networks are simply the result of adding more nodes and connections. The fundamental means of creating nodes and connecting them remains the same.

This particular configuration of nodes is very common, and you will undoubtedly see it quite often. This configuration is how values are typically animated in Maya. This DG consists of just three nodes. The first is a *time node,* the second is a *curveAnim* (animation curve) node, and the final node is a *transform* (transformation) node. As you become more familiar with the different types of nodes, you'll most likely want to know more about their inner workings. The MEL and C++ API chapters describe where to find information on all the possible types of nodes and their respective data attributes.

Following the lines connecting the nodes in the direction of the arrows, you see that the **time1** node connects into the **nurbsSphere_translateX** node, which then connects to the **nurbsSphere1** node. Intuitively you can see that time feeds into the animation curve, which then feeds into the transform. This diagram shows that the output of **time1** feeds into the input of the animation curve. The output of **time1** is

FIGURE 2.3   Typical DG animation configuration

simply the current time. As such, every scene has a **time1** node. Given the current time, the animation curve generates an output value. This output value is the result of evaluating the animation curve at the given time. So as the time changes, the animation curve is evaluated at different times. If the curve is varying, the resulting value also varies, resulting in an animated value. This value is fed into the transform's **translateX** value. This is the position of the object along the x-axis. As this value changes, the **nurbsSphere1**'s position along the x-axis changes. So, in summary, the sphere's x position results from the evaluation of the animation curve at the current time. Changing the current time causes the nodes to recompute their values, and as a result the sphere moves along the x-axis. Intuitively you can think of the data starting out at the first node on the left and being processed as it goes until it arrives in the final node on the far right. The flow is essentially from left to right in the direction of the connected arrows.

2.2.5 Nodes

Since nodes are really the fundamental building blocks of Maya, it is important to present them in further detail. In order to understand what they contain and how they work, I will be presenting them in a schematic form. Figure 2.4 shows a generic node.

Each node has one or more properties associated with it. These properties are commonly referred to as *attributes*. An attribute is a particular property of a given node. A **transform** node, for example, has a **translateX** attribute that holds the current position of the object along the x-axis. Nodes of type, **makeNurbSphere**, each have a **radius** attribute in addition to many others. In this example the node has two attributes, **input** and **output**. Conceptually, each node stores its attribute data internally. The C++ API chapter goes into further detail on exactly how node data is stored.

In addition to attributes, all nodes contain a *compute function*. While you won't see this displayed visually in Maya, you can assume that each node contains one. The

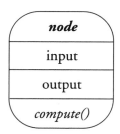

FIGURE 2.4 Generic node

compute function is assigned the task of taking one or more input attributes and producing one or more output attributes. As mentioned before, the main purpose of a node is to store data and possibly modify it in some way. The data itself is simply stored in the node's attributes. It is the compute function that does all the work of modifying the data. It knows how to create the resulting output data from the input data.

With an understanding that the scene is really just the DG, and the DG is a series of interconnected nodes, an interesting logical conclusion can be made about the compute function. The individual compute functions can be considered the "neurons" in the network of nodes that ultimately make up Maya's "brain." Conceptually Maya's brain isn't unlike a human brain. Whereas in our brains it is the neurons that connect together in a network through dendrites, in Maya's brain it is a series of nodes that connect together and, through their individual compute functions, cause data to flow and be modified from one node to the next.

The "intelligence" of Maya is the direct result of the combination of all the compute functions. Since the DG can consist of many different nodes, you can effectively create different "brains" that create and process data. By creating your own nodes and their corresponding compute functions, you can effectively add your own component into this machinery. Your custom node can be added to one or more places in the DG. It can then contribute its own particular functionality to the overall data processing.

2.2.6 Attributes

As mentioned earlier, all the data is stored in each node as an attribute. An attribute is simply a placeholder in a given node to store some particular information. An attribute will have a name and *data type*. The name is used to provide a short description of the attribute and is used later to refer to it. For instance the name **radius** is given to the **makeNurbsSphere** node's attribute for controlling the radius of the sphere. The data type defines what kind of data the attribute can hold. If, for instance, an attribute is of type long, then it can hold an integer value. Alternately, if it is of type float, it can hold a fractional value. These two types are referred to as *simple data types* since they can hold only a single value. A nonexhaustive list of some of the simple data types includes boolean, byte, char, short, long, float, double, and so on. These types correspond to the basic numeric types available on computers. The node in Figure 2.5 has a single attribute named **size** and it is of type float.

More complex data types are also supported. An entire geometric mesh or nonuniform rational B-splines (NURBS) surface can be stored as an attribute in a node. In fact all data, whether it be simple or complex, is stored as an attribute. The ability to have an attribute contain either simple or complex data results in a great deal of flexibilty.

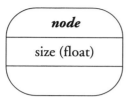

FIGURE 2.5 Simple node

node
pointA (compound)
x (float)
y (float)
z (float)

FIGURE 2.6 Node with compound attribute

Maya also allows you to combine the simple data types into more complex structures. For example, if you take three *floats* you can define a position (point) in 3D space. The point would consist of three attributes named **x**, **y**, **z** of type float. The point itself can be considered the *parent attribute* of the *child attributes* **x**, **y**, **z**. Since the parent is itself an attribute, you can refer to the parent and indirectly its children, or you can refer to the children individually. In Figure 2.6 the node has a **pointA** attribute that consists of three **x**, **y**, **z** attributes.

Maya refers to the attribute **pointA** as a *compound attribute* since it is the result of combining the other attributes. The **pointA** attribute is considered the parent while the **x**, **y**, **z** attributes are considered the children. There is no limit to how many children an attribute has or what type they are. You can therefore create arbitrary "trees" of attributes.

In addition to creating compound attributes, you can also create *arrays* of attributes. An array attribute is an attribute that contains a sequence of one or more other attributes. For example, you may want to store an array of points that define the positions of a series of particles. The node in Figure 2.7 contains an attribute named **points**. This attribute is an array of point attributes. The **point** attribute is a compound attribute containing three child attributes **x**, **y**, **z**. This simple example effectively creates a relatively complex quantity and hierarchy of attributes.

So an attribute is a very flexible means of storing arbitrary data. Attributes can store simple data or a more complex combination of simple data. Since attributes allow you to create a parent-child relationship, you are free to create hierarchies of arbitrary complexity. Combining this with the ability to store arrays of hierarchies, you can almost always represent any complex data structure using Maya attributes.

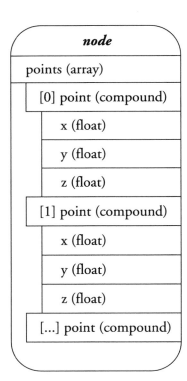

FIGURE 2.7   Node with array of compound attributes

2.2.7 Compute Function

As mentioned earlier, the compute function is really the brains of the node. The attributes hold the node data, but they don't do anything else. In order to do something useful, the node data must be processed in some way. For instance, to make a character walk, you'd like it to move as time changes. The muscles and skin of the character should change over time. Starting from a character in a static pose, the system should modify and deform the character as time changes. At each frame the character should be deformed differently. The result of the deformation at each frame is the result of putting the static character in one end of the DG pipeline and having the fully deformed character come out the other end.

At its most basic level, the compute function takes one or more input attributes and generates a result in an output attribute. As a programming function, the compute function can be considered as follows:

output = compute(input0, ..., inputN)

Since the inputs and outputs are attributes and since attributes can take many different forms, the compute function can operate on a wide variety of data. It can for instance take a NURBS surface as input and generate a new NURBS surface as output. It could take the input surface and calculate some measure of the surface and output a single value representing, for instance, the area of the surface. So the flexibility afforded by the generality of attributes means that the compute function can generate arbitrarily complex data as well as take arbitrarily complex data as its input.

It is very important to note that both the input and output attributes that the compute function uses are local to the node. As such, the compute function needs to look only at its own attributes in order to perform its task. It never takes information from other nodes or from other places. The data that it uses in its computation must all come from itself and nowhere else. This very important constraint will be repeated several times throughout this book, since it's fundamental to designing "well-behaved" nodes.

Internally the compute function is free to do whatever it pleases to generate its final output. The exact specifics of how it calculates the output are never known or exposed to Maya. The compute function can be effectively thought of as a *black box*. There is no way to determine from its output exactly how it went about creating its result. The advantage of this approach is that you never have to know exactly how a node works internally in order to use it. The node that goes about blending two faces together could be internally quite complex, but you'll never have to know this.

When using it, all you need to know is that given a set of input shapes the `compute` function generates an output shape.

From the point of view of the outside world, a node exposes just the attributes it uses: its input and output attributes. These attributes effectively define the *interface* to the node. When using a node, you access it by getting and setting its attributes. You don't ever have direct control over its compute function. A **makeNurbSphere** node will generate a NURBS surface in the form of a sphere given its input attributes, **radius**, **start sweep**, and so on. You control how the node generates the NURBS surface by changing its input attributes. To make the sphere larger, you would simply increase the **radius** attribute's value. The node would then generate a larger sphere. The node generates the sphere surface without your ever needing to know how it did it.

The advantage of this design is that if, for instance, you created your own **makeMyNurbsSphere** node you are free to implement the surface generation method however you like. If you later decide on a more efficient method, you are free to implement it without breaking the DG and its network. All that matters is that your `compute` function generate a surface. How it goes about this is entirely up to you.

DEPENDENT ATTRIBUTES

It is very important to note that while I've described attributes as being either input or output attributes, Maya doesn't make any such distinction. To Maya there is no such thing as an input or output attribute. All attributes simply hold data.

However, it is necessary to logically classify attributes to be either input or output. An input attribute is one that is fed into a node's compute function. An output attribute is one that results from taking one or more of the input attributes and calculating its value using the `compute` function. The node, **sphereVolume**, will be used to demonstrate how a node could compute the volume of given sphere. The node is shown in Figure 2.8.

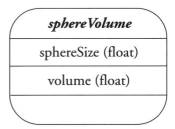

FIGURE 2.8   **sphereVolume** node

It has two attributes, **sphereSize** and **volume**, each stored as a `float` value. As always, the attributes simply hold values. There is no consideration as to which is an input or which is an output attribute.

You know that the volume of a sphere is dependent on the sphere's size, so you can quickly conclude that the **volume** attribute's value must depend on the **sphereSize** attribute's value. The **volume** attribute therefore depends on the **sphereSize** attribute. The **volume** attribute can be considered the output attribute and the **sphereSize** attribute the input attribute. The actual calculation of the **volume** attribute's value is the responsibility of the `compute` function. The calculation of the volume can be written schematically as follows:

volume = compute(sphereSize)

Notice that you didn't define how that volume was calculated. As with any node, it isn't important to know how its `compute` function works. In order to use any node, you simply need to know what input and output attributes it has. The `compute` function takes care of the rest.

It is clear that you have now set up an intrinsic relationship between the two attributes. The **volume** attribute is the result of the `compute` function that takes the **sphereSize** as input. If the **sphereSize** changes, then the **volume** needs to be recomputed. You need a mechanism to define this dependent relationship between the **sphereSize** and the **volume** attributes.

It is up to the individual nodes to define this dependency relationship. Internally, this is done using the C++ API `attributeAffects` function. This function tells Maya that a given attribute affects another, which effectively sets up this dependency relationship between the two attributes. In this example the function call would take the following form:

```
attributeAffects( sphereSize, volume );
```

This specifies that the **sphereSize** attribute will affect the value of the **volume** attribute. This single function call has defined two important states. First it informs Maya that the **volume** is the result of a computation, that is, its value will always come from the result of the `compute` function. Second it informs Maya that the **sphereSize** should be used as input to the `compute` function when the **volume** is being calculated.

Setting up this dependency relationship for all output attributes defines how the node generates data. Whenever the value of the **volume** attribute is requested, it computes the value from the **sphereSize**. Whenever the **sphereSize** changes, the **volume** attribute is also computed.

Note also that I didn't mention how the node actually goes about computing the volume. Internally it could use any algorithm to derive this value. In order to use the node, you won't ever have to know how the attributes are calculated. You can simply ask the node for the value of the **volume** attribute, and it goes away and computes it, then returns you the result. If you intend on writing your own Maya nodes, you can begin to see where most of your development time will be spent: writing the compute function.

While this simple example had just a single input attribute that produced a single output attribute, in practice the compute function can calculate any number of output attributes from any number of input attributes. A dependency relationship simply has to be defined between the input attributes and a given output attribute. This same scheme is applied to different output attributes. It is also possible for the output attribute to be used as an input.

Define a node, **boxMetrics**, that takes a box as input and generates the surface area of its top as well as its volume. Figure 2.9 shows a diagram of the node. The box is defined by its **width**, **height**, and **depth** attributes.

The node's attributes are all defined as float and there is, as yet, no intrinsic relationship between any of them. They are all simply slots that hold a single floating-point value.

boxMetrics
width (float)
height (float)
depth (float)
areaOfTop (float)
volume (float)

FIGURE 2.9 **boxMetrics** node

The following formulas are going to be used to calculate the metrics:

areaOfTop = width × depth
volume = areaOfTop × height

Since you are operating on a box, the area of the top is effectively the same area as the bottom. So expressing this in terms of your `compute` function, you have:

areaOfTop = compute(width, depth)
volume = compute(areaOfTop, height)

Notice that in order to calculate the **volume** you need to compute the **areaOfTop** value. The **height** value is used directly. So the computation of the **volume** value depends on the computation of the **areaOfTop**. How do you define this relationship in Maya? The dependent relationship of the **areaOfTop** attribute is completed as follows:

```
attributeAffects( width, areaOfTop );
attributeAffects( depth, areaOfTop );
```

The dependent relationship of the **volume** attribute follows similarly:

```
attributeAffects( areaOfTop, volume );
attributeAffects( height, volume );
```

There is no need to do anything special for the **volume** attribute. You simply need to specify which attributes it depends on as before. Maya automatically ensures that the **areaOfTop** is computed before passing it in to the computation of the **volume**.

When the value of the **width** or **depth** changes, the **areaOfTop** value is recomputed. Since the **areaOfTop** also affects the volume, Maya recomputes the value of the **volume**. Likewise if the **height** changes, then the **volume** is recomputed. Since the **areaOfTop** doesn't depend on the **height**, it won't be affected if the **height** changes.

TIME

Before continuing it is important to note that a node doesn't necessarily compute something. It is totally valid to have a node that simply holds one or more attributes. These nodes act as simple data repositories. The **time** node is a perfect example. The current time is stored in Maya in a **time** node named **time1**. The layout of the **time** node is displayed in Figure 2.10.

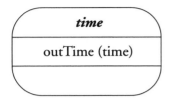

FIGURE 2.10 Time node

The **time** node simply holds a time value in the **outTime** attribute. When you move the frame slider or click on **Play**, Maya simply sets **time1** node's **outTime** value to the current frame. The **time** node doesn't compute anything. This isn't to say that it doesn't contain a compute function. All nodes have a compute function. Since you have not set up any dependency relationship between any attributes, the compute function isn't ever called.

2.2.8 Connecting Nodes

You now know what a node is and what purpose it serves. While a node can compute just about anything from a set of input values, a node in isolation doesn't provide you with much. The real ability of nodes to perform complex calculations comes when they are connected into networks. Each of the nodes then performs its computation as before, but now the results of those computations are fed into other nodes that then also perform their own computations. By connecting nodes, you can create a chain of computations that produce a final result. The final results are the output attributes of the nodes at the very end of the chain.

Referring back to the original example of the animation DG, you can delve deeper and see how nodes are actually connected to one another. Figure 2.11 shows the original DG node configuration.

Schematically this DG can be presented as in Figure 2.12. You can now see clearly each node's attributes and how they are connected. The **time** node contains a

FIGURE 2.11 Node configuration for animation

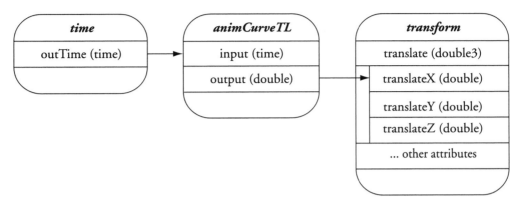

FIGURE 2.12 Schematic view of DG

single value, **outTime**, which is set to the current time. This time value feeds into the **input** attribute of the **animCurveTL** node. This node contains an animation curve. This is the curve that you edit in the Graph Editor in order to animate a value. This node computes the **output** attribute that is fed into the **translateX** attribute of the **transform** node. The **transform** node is quite a large node with a lot of attributes. For simplicity only the **translate** attribute and its child attributes, **translateX, translateY,** and **translateZ,** are shown.

It is clear from this diagram that the process of connecting nodes consists of connecting a node's attributes. The flow of data and information happens from an attribute in one node to another attribute in another node. Notice that an attribute can connect only to another attribute of the same type. The **time** node's **outTime** is of type `time`. It is possible to connect it to **animCurveTL** node's **input** attribute since it is also of type `time`. However, it wouldn't be possible to connect the **outTime** attribute to the **transform** node's **translateX** since it is of a different type, `double`. Without going into specifics, Maya does provide mechanisms for converting from some specific types to other different types.

It is important to note that a node is never "aware" that is it connected to other nodes. It never has any knowledge of which other nodes it is connected to or where it sits in the DG network. In fact the node is aware only of its own input and output attributes. It doesn't know if they are connected or not. Maya handles the flow of data from one node to the next, so a node simply computes its output attributes as before. By forcing this "local knowledge only" constraint on all nodes, you can use them as true building blocks. Nodes never have to know what context they are being used in.

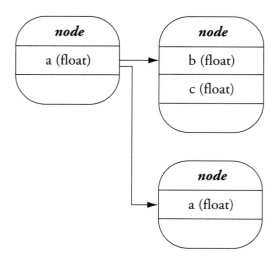

FIGURE 2.13   Single attribute connecting to multiple destinations

One attribute can be connected into many other attributes. The attribute's value feeds into all the connected attributes of the other nodes. An example of this configuration is shown in Figure 2.13.

It is illegal, however, to have multiple attributes feed into a single attribute, as shown in Figure 2.14. This constraint is understable since the attribute holds just a single value and you've provided it with multiple connections so it can't know which of the connections to use for its value. What is the value of the **a** attribute in this configuration? Is it **b** or **c**? There is no correct answer.

When an attribute isn't the destination of a connection, it stores a value in the node. When a connection is made so that another attribute connects into the attribute, its value comes from the attribute that provides that connection. The internal value that it had previously is thrown away and it takes the value of the incoming connection. Similarly when a connection is broken between two attributes, the value stored in the previous destination attribute is the last value it had before the disconnection. So if the value it was fed from the connected attribute was 1.23 and then you remove the connection, the attribute retains the value of 1.23. Since the connection has now been broken and the source attribute changes, the now-isolated attribute remains unaffected.

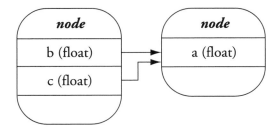

FIGURE 2.14 Illegal connection

2.2.9 DAG Nodes

Up to this point, nodes have been described in general terms. Nodes in the DG are more precisely referred to as *dependency nodes*. Since they are nodes in a dependency graph, this is a logical naming. Nodes can be added and removed from the graph as needed. Any of the node's attributes can be connected to any other node's attributes so you can have a simple or complex network of interconnected nodes. Since you can connect nodes freely, the structure of the network can be arbitrary.

This provides a great deal of flexibility; but what if you want to impose some logical structure to some of the nodes? The concept of a hierarchy is often used in computer graphics to define a parent-child relationship between 3D objects. For instance you may want to build a car model and then have the wheels as children. Wherever the car goes, the wheels will follow. The DG doesn't allow you to specify this relationship.

To resolve this, special DAG, or directed acyclic graph, nodes are used. *Directed acyclic graph* is essentially a technical term for a hierarchy in which a node can't be both a parent and child in the same lineage. It is important to understand that a DAG node *is* a DG node. A DAG node exists in the DG like all other nodes. It is just specialized to provide a logical parent-child relationship with other nodes.

The relationship between DAG and DG nodes can be confusing to most users. The main reason is that Maya doesn't provide any visual means for seeing their true relationship. The Hypergraph allows you to see the nodes in their DAG hierarchical form (Scene Hierarchy) *or* as the dependency graph nodes (Up- and Downstream Connections), but it doesn't allow you to see them *both* at the same time. If it could, the relationship may look something similar to Figure 2.15.

The **transform** and **shape** nodes are DAG nodes and will be introduced in greater detail shortly. For the moment it is simply enough to understand that they

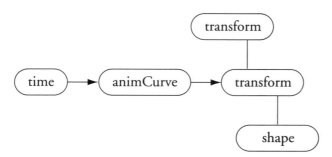

FIGURE 2.15 DAG and DG nodes

provide a parent-child relationship. There is a **transform** node that has another **transform** node as its child. This child **transform**, in turn, has a **shape** node as its child. The nodes, **time** and **animCurveTL**, are standard DG nodes. The arrows show, as before, how attributes are connected between the different nodes. The vertical lines joining the DAG nodes show their parent-child relationship.

The DAG nodes impose a top-down hierarchy due to the resulting tree structure that their parent-child relationships create. At the same time, other dependency nodes can have their attributes connected to any of the nodes in the DAG hierarchy. Thus the DG can be "read" in two directions: top to bottom from the root of the DAG nodes down through all the transform and shape nodes, and left to right from the leftmost node following all the connected nodes horizontally.

Above all it is very important to understand that DAG nodes are simply DG nodes. They just provide a means of defining parent-child relationships that ordinary DG nodes don't have. In all other respects they operate and function in exactly the same way.

TRANSFORMS AND SHAPES

In Maya, when you create a 3D object, it is actually the combined result of two DAG nodes. The first node is the object's **transform** node and the second is the object's **shape** node. Maya makes available a wide variety of **shape** nodes including meshes, NURBS curves and surfaces, springs, cameras, lights, particles, and so on. The parent-child relationship between the **transform** node and the **shape** node is shown in Figure 2.16.

The **transform** node defines where in space the object should be placed, and the **shape** node defines the actual form of the object. Setting up this relationship is

FIGURE 2.16 The **shape** node's child relationship to the **transform** node

important for both modeling and animating. The Hypergraph shows this relationship when you select the Show Hierarchy option. The hierarchy for a NURBS sphere is shown in Figure 2.17.

The **nurbsSphereShape2 shape** node contains the NURBS surface. The node's attributes hold the actual surface data. The node above it, **nurbsSphere2**, is the **transform** node. Its purpose is to take the NURBS surface and transform it. Typically a **transform** node takes the shape, which is intrinsically defined in object space, and transforms it into world space. This simple explanation assumes the **transform** node doesn't have another **transform** node as its parent. Parenting will be discussed shortly. It is very important to understand that a **shape** node *can't exist* without a **transform** node. This is understandable, since without a **transform**, Maya can't know where to place the shape in 3D space. If you want to leave the shape in object space, simply set the **transform** node's transformation to *identity* so it doesn't have any effect.

Any object that wants to display itself in 3D space needs to be built using this transform-shape structure. Locators are a prime example. While they don't define a physical object that can be rendered, they do provide a visual guide for other operations. Locators are defined using a special *locator* **shape** node. The **shape** node simply

FIGURE 2.17 Hierarchy for NURBS sphere

draws the locator in the 3D viewport. Like other **shape** nodes, it has as its parent a **transform** node that defines where it will be positioned and oriented in the scene.

Both the **transform** and **shape** nodes are DAG nodes: a specialization of the common dependency node to support this parent-child relationship. As mentioned ealier, DAG is an abbreviation of directed acyclic graph. The *directed acyclic* part essentially means the node can't exist in two places in the hierarchy if you walk down it from the root to the given node. This prevents a cyclic relationship in which a node could be both a child and indirect parent of a given node. The *graph* part refers to the fact that the hierarchy isn't strictly a *tree*. In a tree, each child has only one single parent. In a graph, it is legal for a child to have multiple parents, as is the case for instancing. In a Dependency Graph that has instanced nodes, there will be multiple paths from the root to the instanced node. Each of these paths represents a unique hierarchy. There are as many possible hierarchies as there are separate parents.

PARENTING

In the previous example the NURBS sphere had just one parent, its **transform** node. What if you wanted to have it transformed by other **transform** nodes? You might even want to place these transforms into a hierarchy so that children are transformed by their parents. This would define a *transformation hierarchy.* The shapes themselves still exist under their immediate parent transforms. It is the parent transforms themselves that can be made children of other transforms. This allows you to create an arbitrary hierarchy of **transform** nodes. Conceptually this can be thought of as a tree. Figure 2.18 shows a **transform** hierarchy for a simple humanoid robot.

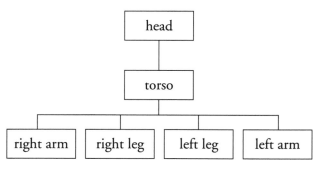

FIGURE 2.18   Humanoid hierarchy

The hierarchy isn't a physical one. The robot isn't physically laid out in 3D space as the diagram shows. In the physical model, the head could be in front of the torso. The same hierarchy as displayed in the Hypergraph is shown in Figure 2.19.

Under each of the transforms is its associated shape. From the top down, following the gray lines connecting the nodes, you can see that the hierarchy defines the root of the tree as the **head transform** node. Under it is the **torso transform** node. Under this node are four **transform** nodes, **leftArm**, **rightArm**, **leftLeg**, and **rightLeg**.

When you have multiple parent transforms, the final position of the shape in world space is no longer defined solely by its immediate parent's **transform** node. The transformation from object to world space is the result of all the **transform** nodes that lie above a given shape. These define a *transformation path*. To determine the final object to world space transformation, start from the shape's immediate parent transform and then collect all the transformations that you pass on your way up to the root

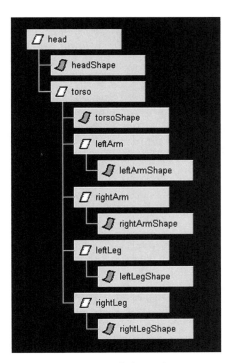

FIGURE 2.19 Node hierarchy

node. As each transform is collected, its *transformation matrix* is postmultiplied with the current transformation matrix. In the case of the **rightLegShape** node, its final transformation is:

final transformation matrix = rightLeg matrix × torso matrix × head matrix

This final **transform** matrix is applied to all the points in the **rightLegShape** shape in order to transform them from object to world space.

In this particular example, all the **transform** nodes had a **shape** node as a child. It is also possible to have a **transform** node without a **shape** node. In fact, Maya's *grouping* functionality is implemented just using **transform** nodes. When you group a series of objects, Maya simply creates a new **transform** node and places all the selected objects as children under it.

DAG PATHS

The tree structure of the DAG hierarchy means that each DAG node exists as a *leaf* in the tree. There are many times when you'll want to refer to a specific node in the hierarchy. Maya provides *DAG paths* as a means of referencing a specific node. A DAG path is a precise description of how you would get from the root node to the specific node by traveling down through the intervening nodes in the tree.

If you were to start at the very top of the tree and walk down through the nodes, noting which ones you'd visited, until you arrived at the node you're interested in, the list of nodes in your notes would define a path to that node. So what is the DAG path for the **leftLegShape** node? The nodes along the path would be **head**, then **torso**, then **leftLeg**, then **leftLegShape**.

Maya uses a particular notation for defining the path to a given node. Each of the node names is separated with a vertical line character (|). So the DAG path of the **leftLegShape** node, written in Maya's notation, would be:

| head | torso | leftLeg | leftLegShape

Notice that there is an empty parent above the **head** node. This defines the root node of the scene, which is the parent of all scene nodes. It doesn't transform any of the shapes under it but provides a global root node from which all objects in the scene are children. Next follows the **head** node and so on.

THE UNDERWORLD

A little known and easily misunderstood concept is that of the *underworld*. Unlike its dark and sinister name suggests, it is really just another type of geometric space in which to position your objects. The position of an object is typically given as a point with Cartesian coordinates (x, y, z). This point can exist in any number of conceptual spaces such as object, parent, world, and so on, but it is still just a point.

It is also possible to think of the surface of some objects as a space. How this space differs is that it is defined using two coordinates (u, v), which define a point in *parametric space*. Not all objects have parametric space. A typical object that does have a parametric space is a NURBS surface. A NURBS surface is a patch that can have positions varying in parametric space from $(0, 0)$ in the lower-left corner right up to $(1, 1)$ in the upper right. While this is the most common, it is possible to have other parametric extents for a patch. Positions across the surface have (u, v) coordinates that vary between 0 and 1. For example, the center of the parameteric space has coordinates $(0.5, 0.5)$. Figure 2.20 shows the parametric space and how this projects onto the NURBS patch.

Since the object still needs a 3D position in order to be displayed, the surface is evaluated at the parametric coordinate (u, v), which results in a 3D position. The object is drawn at that position. The advantage with parametric coordinates is that they "ride" along with the surface. If you change the surface shape, the position remains relative to the surface. You can also slide the object across the surface by

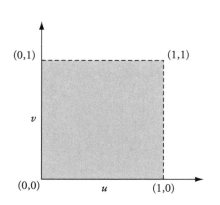
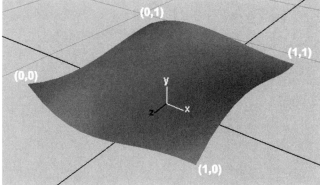

FIGURE 2.20 Parametric space

changing its parametric coordinates, since the point is always guaranteed to be on the surface. This is why trim curves for NURBS surfaces are defined in parametric space, since they will always stick to the underlying surface.

In the following example, a NURBS plane is created. It is then made *live*, by selecting it then choosing **Modify | Make Live** from the main menu. A curve was then drawn on the surface. Since the NURBS plane was live, the curve drawn was actually specified in parametric space, so the curve is automatically defined in the underworld. A Hypergraph view of this configuration is given in Figure 2.21. Note that there is a dotted line connecting the **curve1 transform** node to the **nurbsPlaneShape1 shape**

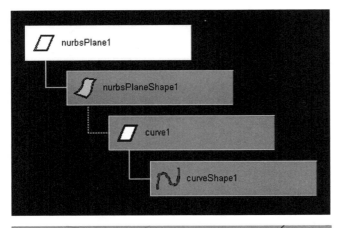

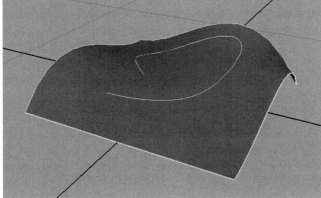

FIGURE 2.21   Hypergraph view of NURBS plane with attached curve

node. This indicates that the object under the NURBS shape is in the underworld and is therefore positioned in parametric space.

Since the underworld is, in essence, just another coordinate space in which to position your objects, Maya makes it a part of the DAG. In fact, there is only a small difference in the notation for defining a DAG path to an object in the underworld. An arrow (->) is used instead of the vertical line (|). Whenever you encounter an arrow in a DAG path, you know that you are moving down into the underworld. This effectively means that you are going from the object's local 3D space into 2D parametric space. For the current example, the complete DAG path to the **curve1 shape** node would be:

| **nurbsPlane1** | **nurbsPlaneShape1** -> **curve1** | **curveShape1**

You may wonder if there are other spaces in which an object can be positioned. The standard Cartesian (*x, y, z*) and parametric (*u, v*) spaces are really the only two. A slight variation on the parametric space happens when you attach an object to a motion path. Its position is defined in a one-dimensional parametric space (U) along the curve path.

INSTANCES

A very important, but sometimes misunderstood, feature of Maya is *instances*. Instances become very useful when you want a large number of exact copies of a given object. With instances, when you change the original object, all the other copies are immediately updated.

The following is an example of when you may want to consider using instances. If you were to model an apple tree fully laden with apples, you would most likely create a single apple model and replicate it many times along the tree branches. You could potentially create 1,000 duplicate apples. With 1,000 apples you have created 1,000 times the amount of original geometry of the initial apple. This results in a lot more memory used and increases the scene file size. It also means that Maya has to do more processing, since each apple is a distinct separate object. Also, any changes to one apple would be retained only by that single object. All the other apples will remain unchanged.

What if you wanted to make a change to the original apple and then have all the other apples reflect that change? What if you wanted each of the apples to retain the form of the original apple but be slightly smaller or oriented differently? Instances provide this capability. When you create an instance of a given shape, you are creating a new **transform** node that directly references the original shape. When displayed in the viewport, the object has the same shape but is transformed (translation, scale, rotation) differently by the new **transform** parent.

The Hypergraph view in Figure 2.22 shows a NURBS sphere, **nurbsSphere1**, that has been duplicated resulting in **nurbsSphere2**. It is clear that the second sphere, **nurbsSphere2**, has its own unique **shape** node, **nurbsSphereShape2**. Changing the **nurbsSphereShape2** shape won't have any effect on the original shape, **nurbsSphereShape1**.

In the second example, shown in Figure 2.23, the first sphere is instanced, resulting again in the **nurbsSphere2 transform** node, but this time you'll note that it doesn't have its own **shape** node. Instead it is referencing the original **shape** node, **nurbsSphereShape1**, so any changes to it will be reflected immediately in the second instance.

An instance is just a new **transform** node that refers to a shared **shape** node. Since it is a **transform** node, you can transform the new instance as you please.

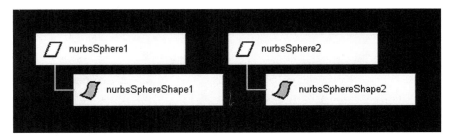

FIGURE 2.22   After duplication

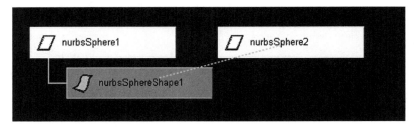

FIGURE 2.23   After instancing

The advantage of using instances is that memory usage is reduced, since only a single copy of the shape is used. All instances share this single shape. This can provide significant savings for very large and intricate models. For example, a battle scene with many infantry soldiers could take up a great deal of memory if each soldier had its own unique **shape** node. Using instances ensures that only one soldier model, which is used by all the transformed instances in the scene, resides in memory.

Unfortunately, instances introduce a subtle twist when you use DAG paths. Note, in the instancing example, that you now have two **transform** nodes, **nurbsSphere1** and **nurbsSphere2**. What is the DAG path to the **nurbsSphereShape1 shape** node? You'll notice that since you used an instance, there are in fact now two possible paths from the root to the **shape** node. The two paths are as follows:

| nurbsSphere1 | nurbsSphereShape1
| nurbsSphere2 | nurbsSphereShape1

It is very important to keep in mind that when referring to any node, there may be multiple paths to it if instancing is being used. The consequence of this is that you can't simply reference a node directly by name. You need a complete path to the node in order to define exactly which instance you are referring to.

Instancing can also be extended to the **transform** nodes themselves. In the Hypergraph view shown in Figure 2.24, a more complex example of instancing is shown.

Taking the previous example in which the first sphere, **nurbsSphere1**, was instanced to create **nurbsSphere2**, the original **nurbsSphere1** transform was grouped. This created the **group1 transform** node as its parent. This **group1** transform was then instanced, which resulted in the **group2 transform** node. Note how the **group2** transform references the **transform** node of **group1** and *not* the **shape**

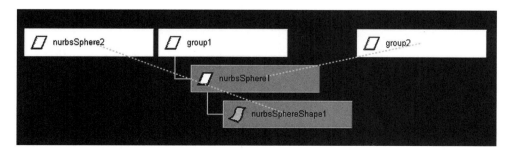

FIGURE 2.24 Complex instancing

node. This demonstrates that you can instance other types of DAG nodes, in this case **transform** nodes.

This last example adds further importance to always taking instancing into consideration when designing your applications. Remembering that there may be multiple DAG paths to a given node ensures that you don't fall into the trap in which you reference the correct node but go down the wrong path. This can result in hard-to-find bugs, since these kinds of mistakes are often replicated throughout the code. Fortunately, both MEL and the API provide functions to determine if a given node is instanced or not, and these should be used liberally throughout your code.

2.2.10   Dependency Graph Updating

With a firm understanding of how the various components of the DG are used, it is now possible to cover the most important and relevant topic: exactly how does the DG get updated when a value changes? The reason this topic is so important is that, if you don't understand it, you may never be able to track down the cause of typical node updating problems. The DG can often create subtle problems for developers, since it appears not to be updating as you might expect. This misunderstanding can lead to many hours, if not days, of lost productivity as you attempt to track down why your application isn't working.

The main reason this whole area causes so much confusion is really quite simple. The nodes you create have absolutely no control over when or how they will update. Maya has complete and final control over this. A node is simply a bit player in a larger story. A node at its most fundamental is really just the compute function. It is asked to compute some output values given some input values. A node is never aware of why it is being asked to compute these values, it just does. So as a developer you really have no control over when and how your nodes will update. Bearing this in mind, now delve deeper into the very core of the DG and discover exactly how it goes about updating.

PUSH-PULL APPROACH

As mentioned earlier, the DG operates, at least in a conceptual sense, like a data flow model. It would appear that data is fed into one end of the machine and some processed data comes out the other. While this mental model makes it easier to understand how all the nodes could be connected to create a machine capable of processing data, the actual implementation of the DG is more subtle.

The DG is, in fact, based on a *push-pull model*. This model defines that certain information can be *pushed* through the network. Also information can be *pulled*

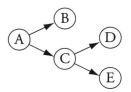

FIGURE 2.25   Connected nodes

through the network. The difference between the two is that when you push something you begin at a given node and it propagates to all the nodes connected as outputs. When you pull information from a node, it propagates that request through all the nodes that provide input connections to the node. The need to make a distinction between the two modes of information flow is for efficiency. The push-pull model allows for a much more efficient updating mechanism than if a pure data flow model were used.

In Figure 2.25 there are five interconnected nodes. Each of the nodes can process data coming into it, producing some resulting data that is then output. In this example, node **A** generates some data that is then passed to its output connections, nodes **B** and **C**. Node **C** doesn't generate any data directly but takes the input data from node **A** and processes it before passing the result to both nodes **D** and **E**.

To demonstrate the difference between a data flow approach and a push-pull approach, start with some data at node **A** and see how it propagates through this simple node network.

Using the data flow approach, you start at node **A**, where some data is generated. It is then fed into nodes **B** and **C**, which further process it. Node **C** passes the result of its processing to nodes **D** and **E**, which in turn perform their own processing. From this description it is clear that data starts from the leftmost node and propagates through the network, with each node doing some form of data processing along the way. When node **A** generates new data, the entire network updates. When the processing is complete, the nodes **B**, **D**, and **E** contain the final results.

Now imagine that the processing done by each node was extremely complex. Say, for instance, that it took roughly an hour for each individual node to process its input data and then generate its output data. This means that if node **A** generated some new data, it would take a total combined time of four hours before all the end nodes (**B**, **D**, **E**) had their results.

Updated   Needs updating

FIGURE 2.26 Node states

What if, instead of wanting the results for **B**, **D**, and **E**, you wanted only the result of node **B**? Unfortunately, under this model all data is propagated through all the nodes. This means that even though you may just want the results of node **B**, you still have to wait for all the nodes to complete their processing. The node network in this example is purposely simplified, but you could easily imagine a more complex network and the performance problems that this approach will create.

Ideally you would like to pick a given node and have the network do the minimum amount of work in order to update that node. This is where the push-pull model becomes very useful. This model breaks the network updating into two distinct steps. The first step is the propagation of a status flag, and the second step is the actual processing of the data. The first step is the push, and the second step is the pull.

Imagine that each of the nodes contains a flag. This flag, which you can call the **needsUpdating** flag, indicates that the output of the node is no longer valid and therefore needs updating. If the flag is set, then the node recomputes its output. If the flag is not set, then it just passes on its current output value without doing any recomputation. The use of this flag brings an immediate gain in speed. When a node doesn't need updating, all its processing can be circumvented and its current result passed on to the next node. Since the network updating happens in two stages, the nodes in the diagrams will be drawn in one of two states: updated or needs updating. Figure 2.26 shows how the nodes will be drawn in their different states.

The first step of the push-pull approach is the pushing through of the status flag to all the connected nodes. When node **A** generates a new value, data isn't sent on to the connected nodes, but the status flag is propagated instead. This status flag specifies that the nodes now need updating. Nodes **B** and **C** first receive this flag and update their status; then it is passed on. This step continues for all connected nodes. Finally, the nodes appear in their new state, as shown in Figure 2.27.

Notice that node **A** hasn't been flagged as needing updating. Since it generated the original data it holds the most current value for the data. It is all the other nodes that now contain potentially old data, since they depend, directly or indirectly, on node **A**.

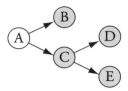

FIGURE 2.27 After node **A** changes

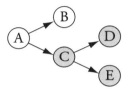

FIGURE 2.28 After node **B** is updated

Since you didn't do any processing of the data at each of the nodes, this step can be performed very quickly. At this point, the nodes remain unchanged until you make a request for their data. What if you wanted the resulting output of node **B**? Getting the result from node **B** is likened to pulling the information from the node. So the process of pulling is the same as asking the node for its output.

Asking a given node for its output, however, can indirectly result in a chain of node updates. This ensures that the result in the given node is correct. When node **B** is asked for its output, it checks its **needsUpdating** flag. Since it is set, it knows that its current output is old and therefore needs to be recomputed. It takes its input, in this case the output from node **A**, and then recomputes its output. Since the output is now updated, the **needsUpdating** flag is unset. This indicates that the node is currently holding valid output data. After this pull step, the graph appears as in Figure 2.28.

Notice that only node **B** was updated. Since you requested only its ouput, it alone was updated. Nodes **C**, **D**, and **E** did no processing, and their **needsUpdating** flags are still set. The push-pull model allowed you to choose a single node and request its result without having to update unrelated nodes. This approach of updating only nodes that contribute to the final output is what makes the push-pull model much more efficient than the data flow model.

Now look at what happens if you request the result of node **D**. The mechanism for its update is exactly the same as for node **B**, but with some additional requests. The step each node does to update itself is exactly the same as before. It checks

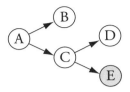

FIGURE 2.29   After node **D** is updated

whether its **needsUpdating** flag is set, and if so, it generates a new output. If this flag isn't set, it just passes on its current output. In this case the **needsUpdating** flag isn't set, so it can safely assume that its current output is the most recent and up to date. All nodes go through this simple process when asked for their output. Even in a longer chain of interconnected nodes, the same process is used.

When node **D** is asked for its output, it sees that it needs updating. It then requests the input data from node **C**. Node **C** in turn sees that it also needs updating. It then requests the input data from node **A**. Node **A** doesn't have its **needsUpdating** flag set, so it simply passes on its current output. Node **C** takes this input then updates itself. It then turns off its **needsUpdating** flag and passes along its new result. Node **D** then takes this new input and calculates its new output, after which its **needsUpdating** flag is also reset. At the end of the pull step, the graph appears as shown in Figure 2.29.

Note that node **E** hasn't been updated. Since it isn't directly or indirectly connected to node **D**, it doesn't get asked to update. On the other hand, node **C** has been updated, since it is connected to node **D** and needed updating.

When a node's output is requested, the node then requests its inputs. If the input nodes themselves need updating, this process continues. This can result in a chain of updates for some or all of the nodes in the chain.

UPDATING IN PRACTICE

Now look specifically at how Maya has implemented this push-pull approach. This section takes all the knowledge gained in the previous sections and provides a complete explanation of how the DG works internally. The DG presented earlier is shown in Figure 2.30.

Maya associates with each attribute a flag that works exactly like the **needsUpdating** flag discussed in the previous section. Maya refers to this flag as the *dirty bit*. The dirty bit is set when an attribute's value is old and needs updating. When the dirty bit is

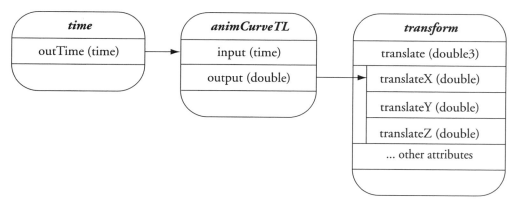

FIGURE 2.30 Dependency Graph nodes and connections

not set, the attribute contains the most up-to-date data and therefore doesn't need recomputing. When an attribute has its dirty bit set, it will be displayed, as in the previous diagrams, as shaded.

For argument's sake, assume that the DG has already been updated. This means that all the attributes hold their most recent results and no attributes have their dirty bit set. This is precisely the scenario represented in the diagram in Figure 2.30.

Now move the time slider to another frame. Since the **translateX** attribute is an animated value, you would assume that changing the current time will cause it to update, which is precisely what happens. How Maya goes about this isn't as easy as it may seem.

When the time slider was changed, the single global **time** node, **time1**, also changed. Its **outTime** attribute was updated to the new time. Notification of this change is propagated to all the attributes that are connected to **outTime** by setting their respective dirty bits. Note that the dirty bit of the **outTime** attribute won't be set, since Maya just set it to a new value. It contains the latest data, so it won't be marked dirty.

In this example, the **outTime** attribute is connected to the **input** attribute of the **animCurveTL** node. The dirty bit of this attribute is set. The next step is to see which attributes are then connected to the **input** attribute, since they will also need to be notified. The **input** attribute doesn't have any connections, so it isn't propagated further. However, the **input** attribute affects the **output** attribute. This relationship was defined when the node specified that the **input** attribute affected the

output attribute using the `attributeAffects(input, output)` function call. When the **input** attribute changes, the **output** attribute is affected and therefore needs to be recomputed, so the **output** attribute has its dirty bit set. All connections from the **output** attribute are then followed. The **translateX** attribute is connected to the **output** attribute, so its dirty bit is set. Since the **translateX** attribute isn't connected to any other attributes or doesn't affect other attributes within the same node, the propagation of the dirty bit has now finished. The push part of the process is now complete.

Figure 2.31 shows the state of the DG after this *dirty bit propagation*. At this point none of the attributes affected by the **outTime**'s change have been updated. They are all simply marked as dirty. Maya performs no further processing.

Under certain circumstances Maya asks the DG to update itself. Some example circumstances include the request for an attribute value, when rendering starts, or the Attribute Editor or Channel Box is displayed. There are many others, but the most common reason for the DG update is when the screen needs to be refreshed. An indirect result of moving the time slider is that a screen redraw request is sent to Maya. Before redrawing all the objects in the scene, Maya will ask the DG to update itself, since some of the objects may have been animated and will therefore appear different at the new time.

Maya tries to be as efficient as possible when updating the DG. It requests the latest values only from those nodes that really need to be updated. The update begins by starting at the root node of the DAG nodes. It then walks down the DAG node tree, depth-first, and asks each node if it is visible. If it isn't visible, then Maya ignores

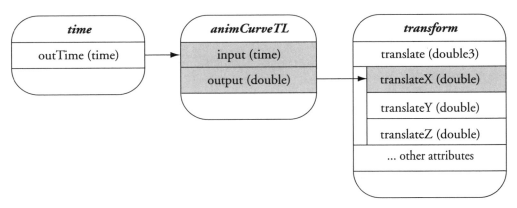

FIGURE 2.31   After dirty bit propagation

that node and all of its children since visibility is inherited. For those nodes that are visible, Maya asks them to update themselves. So when it reaches the **transform** node in the example, it attempts to update the transformation matrix so that it can place the shape in its correct position in world space. The request for the transformation matrix indirectly results in requests for the latest **translate, scale,** and **rotate** attribute values. When the value of the **translateX** attribute is requested, you begin the pull part of the update process. Since the **translateX** attribute has its dirty bit set, it must be updated.

Since the attribute gets its value from an input connection, it requests the value of that input. The **animCurveTL** node fields this request. It sees that the **output** attribute that is being requested is dirty and needs to be updated. Since its value is generated by the compute function, the function is called. The compute function then requests the value of the **input** attribute in order to complete its computation. The **input** attribute is marked dirty so that it needs to be updated. Its value comes from the **outTime** attribute that it requests. The **outTime** attribute looks at itself and sees that its dirty bit isn't set, so it simply returns the value it is currently holding.

The chain of requests now unrolls, and the series of requests is fulfilled from the last to the first. The **input** attribute takes the value from the **outTime** and resets its dirty bit. The compute function takes the **input** attribute value and computes the value of the **output** attribute. As always, the attribute's dirty bit is reset after the attribute is updated. The **output** attribute is then fed into the **translateX** attribute. The value of the **translateX** attribute is then returned fulfilling the original request.

This example demonstrates that a simple request to get an attribute's value can result in a potentially long chain of similar requests, each resulting in possibly further computations until the final result is known. The amount of work that each request requires is in direct proportion to the number of attributes further down in the chain and how many have their dirty bits set. If in the example the **translateX** dirty bit was reset, then none of this processing would have been done. In fact if you now requested the value of the **translateX**, it would simply return its stored value, since it is no longer dirty.

Outside of one of Maya's specific requests for the DG to update itself, it is possible for the DG to be partially evaluated by simply requesting the current value of an attribute. The propagation of updating proceeds exactly as previously described. Instead of requesting the **translateX**, you are just requesting another attribute from some other node. However the steps to get the latest value from the attribute are exactly the same.

KEYFRAME ANIMATION UPDATING

One of the interesting side effects of the push-pull model is that it allows you easily to build an interactive *keyframe animation system*. A keyframe animation system is one in which the animation of the objects is defined by a series of animation keys defined at different points in time. When no key exists for the given time, a new value is derived by interpolating from the key before and after the current time. Interestingly enough, it is the side effect of using dirty bits that allows you to interactively move or transform an object in 3D and then, when you are ready, set a keyframe to lock in that transform for the current frame. Such a feature is very important for interactively animating objects.

On first inspection this may not seem like a big deal, but when you consider that the **translateX** is being driven by the animation curve node, **animCurveTL**, further upstream, how is it that you can move the object at all without explicitly changing the animation curve? How is it possible to take an object that has already been keyframed and move it about interactively in the viewport? Shouldn't the value of **translateX** always come from the animation curve node it is connected to? Is the animation curve being deactivated during the interaction?

The answer is very simple and shows another somewhat subtle consequence of using the push-pull approach. In order to learn better what is actually going on behind the scenes, start with some interactive exercises in Maya.

1. Load the scene **SimpleAnimatedSphere.ma**.

2. Click the **Play** button.

    The sphere moves along the x-axis.

3. Press the **Stop** button.

4. Select the **nurbsSphere1** object.

5. Open the **Hypergraph**, and click on the **Up and Downstream Connections** button. The screen will resemble Figure 2.32.

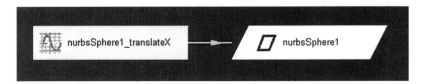

FIGURE 2.32 Hypergraph

The **nurbsSphere1_translateX** animation curve node is controlling the **translateX** attribute of the **nurbsSphere1 transform** node. This is why the sphere moves along the x-axis.

6. Close the **Hypergraph**.

7. Move the time slider to frame 27.

8. Ensure that the **Channel Box** is displayed.

9. Select the **nurbsSphere1** object, then select the **Move** Tool. Move the sphere somewhere along the x-axis.

   Look at the sphere's **Translate X** value as you move the sphere. How is this possible? The sphere's *x* translation is coming from the animation curve node, and yet you can interactively move it around. Somehow the sphere's transform is ignoring the animation curve.

10. Go to frame 28.

    The sphere pops back to its original animated position at frame 28.

11. Move to frame 27.

    The previous position to which you interactively moved the sphere has been lost. The sphere is now getting its **Translate X** value from the original animation curve.

12. Move the sphere along the x-axis to some new position. Press **Shift+w**.

    A keyframe is set at frame 27.

13. Click the **Play** button.

    The sphere animates as before but now moves to your new position at frame 27. Clearly the translation is coming from the animation curve. The keyframe you set is now being taken into account as you would expect.

What kind of magic is Maya doing behind the scenes so that you can interactively move the sphere even when its position is being controlled by the animation curve? Well the truth is, there is no magic. Maya is still doing the same DG update steps as mentioned before.

Now walk through the same steps, but this time note what is happening to each attribute in the DG. When the scene was loaded, Maya would immediately evaluate the DG. This results in all the attributes' dirty bits being reset after the update.

When the **Play** button was clicked, Maya incremented the current frame number. So at each new frame the **outTime** attribute would change and the dirty bits would be propagated to the other attributes as described earlier. At each frame the scene would need to be redrawn, so Maya would ask the DG to evaluate itself. The **translateX** value would be requested, and as a result it would indirectly cause a chain of updates for those nodes affected. This is exactly the process explained in the previous section.

The playback was stopped at frame 27, then the sphere was moved along the x-axis. This effectively sets the sphere's **translateX** attribute to the resulting value from the interactive move. Since this attribute, like **outTime**, was set directly, its dirty bit is automatically reset. This immediate resetting of the dirty bit is the key to understanding how it is possible to interactively move the sphere. The **translateX** attribute is now assumed to hold the current updated value, by virtue of its dirty bit not being set. Yes, it does hold the value given by the interactive move, but it really should have its value come from the animation curve's **output** attribute. Why won't it get that value? When the object is being moved around interactively, Maya is receiving a lot of screen refresh requests. As always, it asks the DG to update itself before redrawing. It walks down the DG, and once again the **translateX** value is requested. This time, however, the **translateX** attribute's dirty bit has been reset, so it doesn't go through the previous process of requesting the values of any attributes it takes as input. In this scenario, the animation curve is never asked for its output value, since the **translateX** attribute's current value, the result of the interactive move, is assumed to be the most current value.

You next moved the current frame to 28. The sphere suddenly popped back to its animated position controlled by the animation curve. What happened was that you indirectly changed the current time by moving to another frame. Like before, the **outTime** value was updated, and all the affected attributes, including the **translateX** attribute, had their dirty bit set as a result. Its value is now marked as dirty, so as happened originally, when the request came for its value, it had to get it through the other nodes, which instigated the usual series of attribute updates.

So the ability to interactively move an already animated object is a direct result of the dirty bit in the **translateX** attribute being reset. Since the dirty bit wasn't set, further updating wasn't needed, so the animated curve was never asked for its output value. The value it used is that set directly by the interactive move.

This example further emphasizes that under certain circumstances the DG may appear to behave unpredictably. In reality, the DG always follows the same procedure, thereby always behaving predictably. When a value is requested from an attribute, it looks at its dirty bit. If it isn't dirty, the current value it is holding is returned immediately. If the dirty bit is set, then it attempts to get the latest value.

This can result in the attribute getting recomputed by the `compute` function or simply getting the value from one of the other attributes it is connected to. This process can be repeated recursively for all affected attributes until the attribute returns its final value. When the new value is stored in the attribute, its dirty flag is reset so that if the value is requested again it can simply return the stored value and thereby avoid a lot of potential recomputation.

The push-pull approach is just one of many internal mechanisms that the DG uses to avoid doing unnecessary calculations. Some of the other less critical mechanisms are explored in future chapters. A firm understanding of how the DG updates by way of the push-pull approach will definitely help you to avoid a lot of potential Maya programming headaches.

CHAPTER 3

MEL

3.1 INTRODUCTION

The Maya Embedded Language (MEL) is Maya's most easily accessible programming interface. Without knowing it, you have been using MEL from the very moment you opened Maya. Selecting an object or displaying a dialog box is the direct result of a MEL command being executed. In fact, the entire Maya *graphical user interface (GUI)* is controlled by MEL. Almost all of Maya's functionality can be accessed through MEL. As you move through this chapter, you'll get a much better idea of how pervasive MEL is throughout Maya and thereby understand when and how you can access and control Maya's functionality.

Fortunately, MEL is a relatively simple programming language to learn. Following is an example of a MEL command to create a sphere:

```
sphere;
```

Since MEL is a *scripting language,* you can simply write a command and then immediately execute it. Scripting languages don't need to go through the usual *compile-and-link* step that is needed for other programming languages, like C and C++. This means that you can quickly begin experimenting and see immediate results. If the script doesn't work, it can be quickly changed and run again. The entire iterative process of implementing and testing your ideas becomes much faster and easier when you use MEL.

A MEL script can be as simple or as complex as you want. In order to complete a common task that you repeat frequently, a simple script can be written; then with the click of a button it can be executed. Scripts can also be written to perform very complex tasks, as well as to generate elaborate GUIs. The ability to tackle both simple and difficult problems without your having to learn another programming language is one of MEL's greatest strengths.

With a good solid foundation in MEL programming, you will be able to control almost any aspect of Maya and develop tools and features that will make your work faster and more productive. After a little experimentation, you'll find that even a little MEL greatly aids in your daily Maya tasks.

If you are familiar with the C programming language, refer to Appendix B, "MEL for C Programmers," for a complete list of differences between MEL and C. Fortunately the two languages have a lot in common, so a good grasp of the C language most definitely helps when you learn MEL.

3.1.1   Behind the Scenes

When you use the Maya interface, you are indirectly issuing MEL commands that in turn do the real work. Behind the scenes Maya is running MEL commands and scripts in response to your mouse clicks and selections. It is even possible to monitor these operations in the Script Editor.

Since all your interactions with the Maya graphical interface are done using MEL, it is logical to assume that you could automate many of your daily tasks by recording these operations then playing them back. While Maya doesn't directly provide a means of recording all your keystrokes and mouse clicks, it can display the resulting MEL commands in the Script Editor. From the Script Editor you can select the commands and then copy and paste them into your own scripts. As such, they can be used as the basis for your own customizations.

So what is Maya doing behind the scenes? Following is a look:

1.   Select **File | New Scene**.

2.   Open the **Script Editor**.

3.   From the **Script Editor's** main menu, select **Edit | Clear All**.

4.   From the Maya main menu, select **Create | Nurbs Primitives | Sphere**.

   A sphere is created in the scene, and the following line is displayed in the Script Editor:

```
sphere -p 0 0 0 -ax 0 1 0 -ssw 0 -esw 360 -r 1 -d 3 -ut 0 -tol 0.01
    -s 8 -nsp 4 -ch 1;
objectMoveCommand;
```

Selecting the menu item causes the preceding MEL commands to be executed. Two commands are issued; the first creates a sphere (with a given set of parameters) and the second sets the current tool to be the **Move** tool. As mentioned before, MEL is used for all the GUI interactions. The commands listed are those that were executed once the menu item was selected. But what about the MEL commands that performed all the user interface operations?

5. From the **Script Editor** menu, select **Edit | Clear All**.

6. Select **Script | Echo All Commands**.

7. From the Maya menu, select **Create | Nurbs Primitives | Sphere**.

   With all commands now being echoed to the Script Editor, a lot more commands are now displayed. All of the user interface operations you completed are now shown. Each of the menu selections resulted in a series of MEL commands.

```
editMenuUpdate MayaWindow|mainEditMenu;
CreateNURBSSphere;
performNurbsSphere 0;
sphere -p 0 0 0 -ax 0 1 0 -ssw 0 -esw 360 -r 1 -d 3 -ut 0 -tol 0.01
    -s 8 -nsp 4 -ch 1;objectMoveCommand;
// Result: sphere -p 0 0 0 -ax 0 1 0 -ssw 0 -esw 360 -r 1 -d 3 -ut 0
    -tol 0.01 -s 8 -nsp 4 -ch 1;objectMoveCommand //
autoUpdateAttrEd;
editMenuUpdate MayaWindow|mainEditMenu;
```

   While the exact details of the commands may not be easily understood, what is important to learn is that almost all of the operations you perform in Maya are in fact the end result of a series of MEL commands.

8. Select **Script | Echo All Commands** to turn command echoing off.

Using the Script Editor in this way, with **Echo All Commands** on, is a very good way of learning what MEL commands and procedures are being called when a given operation is performed. If you would like to do a similar operation in your own script, turn echoing on and see what MEL commands have been issued. These commands can then be copied and pasted into your script.

3.2 THE MEL PROGRAMMING LANGUAGE

This section provides an introduction to the programming language, as well as covering, in detail, the language's syntax and constructs.

3.2.1 Commands

When a MEL command is executed, what actually is happening is that one of Maya's C++ functions is being called. When you created the sphere from the user interface, you were indirectly calling Maya's sphere command, which actually created the sphere object. In the C++ API chapter, you'll learn how to create your own commands, but for the moment you focus on learning many of Maya's built-in commands.

ISSUING COMMANDS

Maya has quite a few different places where you can type and execute MEL commands. Depending on your needs, some are more convenient than others.

1. Select **File | New Scene** or press **Ctrl+n.**

    The **Command Line** is another place where you can execute MEL commands. It is a single-line text box. It is a great place to try single-line commands without having to open the Script Editor. The **Command Line** is located in the bottom left corner, as shown in Figure 3.1. If it isn't visible, select **Display | UI Elements | Command Line** from the main menu.

2. Click in the **Command Line**, then type the following text:

    sphere

    The default hotkey to place the cursor into the **Command Line** is the back quote (`) key.

FIGURE 3.I The **Command Line**

3. Press **Enter**.

A sphere, with default parameters, is created in the scene. To the right of the **Command Line** area is the **Command Feedback** area. It displays the result of the last command issued. In this case it displays the following text:

```
Result: nurbsSphere1 makeNurbSphere1
```

While the **Command Line** is ideal for issuing small, succinct commands, the Script Editor is where you typically do most of your experimenting, since you can issue a series of commands each on its own line. It is possible to do the same in the **Command Line**, but it can get confusing when more complex statements are used, since each statement is on the same line.

The Script Editor window consists of two main sections, as shown in Figure 3.2. The upper gray area, the **History Panel**, is where the results of MEL commands are displayed. The lower white area is the **Command Input Panel** and is where you type your commands. The window can be resized so you can see all the text.

1. Select **File | New Scene**.

2. Open the **Script Editor**.

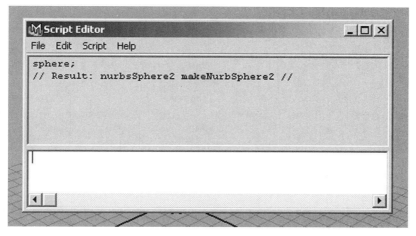

FIGURE 3.2 Script Editor

3. Ensure that **Echo All Commands** is off by selecting **Script | Echo All Commands** if its check box is set.

4. Click in the **Command Input Panel** (white area) of the **Script Editor**.

5. Type in the following text:

```
textCurves -t "Hello World"
```

6. Press **Ctrl+Enter**.

A text object is created in the scene with the letters "Hello World". Notice that the text you typed is moved into the Script Editor feedback area, and its result is listed below it.

```
textCurves -t "Hello World";
// Result: Text_Hello_World_1 makeTextCurves1 //
```

Pressing **Ctrl+Enter**, or alternatively just **Enter** from the numeric keypad, executes whatever text is currently in the Script Editor. Simply press the standard **Enter** key, and the cursor moves down to the next line when you are writing multiline commands.

Notice that Maya always prints the result of the command enclosed in the character (//). When you execute the text in the **Command Input Panel**, Maya executes all the statements it contains. It is possible to execute only some of the statements by using the cursor to highlight only those statements you want to execute and then pressing **Ctrl+Enter** or **Enter** (keypad). This method also prevents your statements from being automatically moved from the **Command Input Panel** to the **History Panel**.

You'd now like to make this MEL command available at any time. A good way of doing this is to create a shelf button that when clicked will execute the command.

1. If the **Shelf** isn't displayed, select **Display | UI Elements | Shelf** from the main menu.

2. In the **Script Editor's History Panel**, select the text:

```
textCurves -t "Hello World";
```

Be sure to include the semicolon (;). The semicolon is used to separate statements.

3. With the left mouse button, drag the selected text to the **Shelf.**

   A new shelf button is created. Alternatively you could have selected the text and then selected **File | Save Selected to Shelf...** from the **Script Editor** menu.

4. Select **File | New Scene.**

5. Click on the newly created shelf button.

   The "Hello World" text is created.

Using the shelf buttons provides a quick and easy means of executing MEL commands. The shelf buttons and the MEL commands they contain are stored when the shelf is saved. It is also possible to edit the MEL commands used by each shelf button.

The last, and most permanent, means of executing a series of MEL commands is to store it in a file. MEL commands stored in files are referred to as MEL *scripts.* MEL script files are simply text files with a file name extension of .mel. When Maya executes a MEL script, it opens the file and executes each command listed therein.

In order to differentiate where one command ends and the next begins, it is important to use the semicolon character (;) at the end of each command. In fact, it is a good programming practice to ensure that each of your commands end with a semicolon.

1. Select the following text from the **Script Editor's History Panel**. Again, be sure to include the semicolon in the selection.

   ```
   textCurves -t "Hello World";
   ```

2. From the **Script Editor** menu, select **File | Save Selected...**

3. Type in myscript.mel as the file name.

4. Click on the **Save** button.

   The command is now saved to the myscript.mel file. You can now execute the entire MEL script file.

5. Select **File | New Scene.**

6. In the **Script Editor's Command Input Panel**, type the following text:

   ```
   source myscript.mel
   ```

7. Press **Ctrl+Enter**.

The script is executed and the text "Hello World" is once again created in the scene. Sourcing a script file loads it into Maya, where it is then executed. The script could also be sourced by selecting **File | Source Script…** from the **Script Editor** menu.

It should be clear now that there are many different ways that you can execute MEL commands. The different methods, with details on when they may or may not be the most appropriate, are as follows:

♦ **Command Line**

Used to write and execute simple commands that are typically one line in length. It is possible to write more than one command in the **Command Line** using semicolons to separate each one, though in practice this becomes cumbersome for all but the simplest set of commands.

♦ **Command Shell**

The Command Shell is a window that operates like a Unix shell window. MEL commands can be executed from this window. Those familiar with Unix shells may be more comfortable using the Command Shell. To access it, select **Windows | General Editors… | Command Shell…** from the main Maya menu.

♦ **Script Editor**

The Script Editor allows you to write multiline scripts. Once executed, the script is listed in the **History Panel**. You can copy and paste the script back into the **Command Input Panel** for further editing and refinement. This is the main method of creating simple, yet functional scripts. Once they are tested and debugged in the Script Editor, they can then be saved to a script file for later reuse.

♦ **Shelf**

Once you have finished writing and testing your commands, they can be assigned to an item in the **Shelf** control. You can edit the commands for the item by using the Shelf Editor.

♦ **Script Files**

Saving your scripts to files is the main method for defining a series of commands that you want to keep between Maya sessions. Once stored to a script file, the commands can be used in different scenes and projects.

♦ **Others**

There are other ways of executing MEL commands including hotkeys, expressions, and Script Nodes. These are covered later in the chapter.

COMMAND ARGUMENTS

In the previous example, the `sphere` command was executed. This created a sphere object with a default size. It is possible to define, in advance, what size you would like the sphere to be. In order to do this, you simply need to include a specification for the sphere's radius when you call the `sphere` command. To create a sphere with a radius of two, you would use the following:

```
sphere -radius 2;
```

Following the `sphere` command is the radius argument: `-radius 2`. This argument includes which parameter is to be set and what its value should be. In this case the argument is `-radius`, and its value will be `2`. If you don't explicitly specify the argument, as you did with the radius, the parameter uses a default value instead. If the radius isn't specified when `sphere` is called, a default radius of 1 will be used.

1. Select **File | New Scene.**

2. In the **Command Line**, type the following:

    ```
    sphere
    ```

3. Press **Enter.**

    A sphere is created with a radius of 1.

4. Execute the following command by typing it into the **Command Line**, then pressing **Enter.**

    ```
    sphere -radius 2
    ```

    A larger sphere, with a radius of 2, is created.

    Almost all command arguments are of the following general form:

    -flag value

The flag is the particular parameter that you'd like to set. Following the parameter is the value that you'd like to assign to the parameter. It is possible to set multiple parameters.

1. In the **Command Line**, execute the following:

```
sphere -name MySphere -radius 3
```

A new sphere is created with a radius of 3 and the name **MySphere**. If you are using Maya interactively as you have just done, it would be nicer if you didn't have to type so much each time. Fortunately Maya provides a command's parameters in two forms: short name and long name. The short name consists of just a few characters so you can type it faster than the long name. A more succinct way of creating the previous sphere would be the following:

2. In the **Command Line**, execute the following:

```
undo; sphere -r 3 -n MySphere
```

The undo command removes the previous sphere. The new sphere is then created using the short form for the parameter names. Notice how a semicolon is used to separate the two commands.

While the short form is easier when you quickly write commands and execute them, they aren't as immediately obvious to understand as their long form. In particular, when you write scripts it is better to use the long name, since this gives the reader a clearer understanding of what is being done. The benefits of using the longer form can also be applied to scripts that only you will ever read. When looking at a script that was written some time ago, the longer parameter names make it clearer if you have forgotten what you originally intended. The longer form makes it immediately clear which parameter is being set and should therefore be used in preference to the short form.

COMMAND HELP

As just mentioned, the sphere command takes many different arguments. What other arguments can it take? Since this is a very often asked question, Maya provides the help command. The help command provides a brief listing of what arguments a command takes as well as a brief synopsis.

1. Open the **Script Editor**.

   The Script Editor will be used because the text that the `help` command will generate is longer than a single line; if the **Command Line** were used, you would see only the last line of the help text in the **Command Feedback** line.

2. Execute the following command:

   ```
   help sphere
   ```

   Remember that to execute the text in the **Script Editor**, either **Ctrl+Enter** or the **Enter** (numeric keypad) key can be used. The `help` command's text is displayed as its result.

   ```
   help sphere;
   // Result:

   Synopsis: sphere [flags] [String...]
   Flags:
       -e -edit
       -q -query
       -ax -axis                  Length Length Length
       -cch -caching              on|off
       -ch -constructionHistory   on|off
       -d -degree                 Int
       -esw -endSweep             Angle
       -hr -heightRatio           Float
       -n -name                   String
       -nds -nodeState            Int
       -nsp -spans                Int
       -o -object                 on|off
       -p -pivot                  Length Length Length
       -po -polygon               Int
       -r -radius                 Length
       -s -sections               Int
       -ssw -startSweep           Angle
       -tol -tolerance            Length
       -ut -useTolerance          on|off
   //
   ```

The `help` command provides a relatively brief overview of the given command. The synopsis lists the general form of the command including any optional flags and arguments you can specify. Afterwards, all the flags are listed with both their short and long names. Either name can be used. Following each flag is the type of values that can be assigned to the flag.

The `help` command is particularly useful when you know which command you want to use but have forgotten some of the parameters it takes. The most definitive guide to all built-in Maya commands is the Mel Command Reference. The reference contains a complete listing of all the MEL commands as well as a detailed description of their flags and other parameters. To access the Maya documentation complete the following:

1. In the **Script Editor**, select **Help | MEL Command Reference...**

    From this same Help menu, you can also access **Help on MEL...** as well as **Help on Script Editor...**

2. Click on the **s** link in the horizontal alphabetical list.

3. Locate the `sphere` command, then click on it.

    The complete reference for the `sphere` command is displayed. The format and layout of the page is the same for all MEL commands. In particular all the parameters are listed in the flags section with a complete description of each of the parameter's function. Also listed are their default values. While the rest of the page is fairly self-explanatory, it is important to note the Examples section. This section gives small examples of how the command can be used. This is particularly helpful when you aren't sure how the command would be used or how a particular parameter may be set.

    The MEL Command Reference is, by default, displayed with commands listed in alphabetical order. There may be times when you want to see all the commands associated with a particular function, for instance, creating user interface elements.

1. At the top right of the page, click on the **Sort By: Function** button.

    A listing of all the various MEL topics is displayed.

2. Click on the **NURBS** link under the **Modeling** topic.

    Among the many nurbs modeling commands, the `sphere` command is listed.

Since the MEL Command Reference is so useful when writing MEL scripts, it should always be kept open. In fact, it may be worthwhile to create a bookmark to it in your browser. Another method of looking up a particular command is by using the search mechanism.

1. At the top of the page, click the **Search** link.

2. Click in the **Search In:** combo box, then select **Maya Commands** from the drop-down list.

3. Type `sphere` in the search field, then click the **Search** button.

   A list of all documentation in which the `sphere` command is used is listed.

COMMAND QUERY

The result of the `sphere` command was a newly created sphere object. Using the same `sphere` command, you can query some of the properties of the sphere. As such, the `sphere` command serves the dual purpose of creating the sphere object as well as later retrieving its properties. Used in this way, the `sphere` command can be used on other sphere objects in the scene.

1. Select **File | New Scene...**

2. In the **Command Line**, execute the following:

   ```
   sphere -radius 1.5 -name MySphere
   ```

3. In the **Command Line**, execute the following:

   ```
   sphere -query -radius MySphere
   ```

4. The **Command Feedback** line displays the following result:

   ```
   Result: 1.5
   ```

Notice how the sphere's name had to be specified. When querying the property of a sphere, you must specify exactly which sphere object you are referring to. For this reason, the sphere was given a known name when it was created.

The first use of the `sphere` command created the **MySphere** sphere. This is an example of calling the command in *creation mode*. In creation mode the command generates a new object. In the second use of the `sphere` command, you used the `-query` flag. With this flag, the `sphere` command operates in *query mode* and retrieves the value of the parameter specified.

Almost all commands support the -query flag. To see if a given command supports querying, take a look at the MEL Command Reference. The type of value returned depends on the particular parameter being queried. In the previous example, a floating-point number was returned since you requested the radius of the sphere. When executing a command in query mode, you can retrieve the value of only one parameter at a time. To query several parameters, simply run several query commands in succession.

COMMAND EDIT

In addition to the creation and query modes, a command can also operate in *edit mode*. In edit mode, a command can change a given property of an object.

1. In the **Command Line**, execute the following:

```
sphere -edit -radius 3 MySphere
```

The sphere now has a radius of 3.

Like the query flag, the edit flag, -edit, is used to specify which parameter is being operated on. However, unlike the query flag, which allows only a single value to be queried at a given time, the edit flag allows multiple parameters to be edited at once.

2. In the **Command Line**, execute the following:

```
sphere -edit -radius 4 -degree 1 MySphere
```

The sphere is now larger and has a faceted surface.

Changing the degree made the sphere a linear surface rather than the smooth cubic surface it was previously. As with the query mode, the name of the sphere had to be given so that Maya knew which sphere you wanted to edit.

COMMAND MODES

From the previous few examples, it is now clear that a command can operate in a total of three different modes; *create, query,* or *edit*. Unless you explicitly specify the query or edit mode, the command operates in create mode. When -query or -edit is specified in the command's arguments, then the appropriate mode is used. Some examples of the sphere command, executing in its different modes, are as follows.

```
sphere -name Sphere01; // Create mode
sphere -query -radius Sphere01; // Query mode
sphere -edit -radius 2 Sphere01; // Edit mode
```

It is important to note that the different modes can't be mixed in a single call to the command. You can't, for example, create a sphere and query it at the same time. In order to do this, simply break it down into two calls to the sphere command. The first would create the sphere, and the second would query it.

Not all commands support the various modes. Take a look at the MEL Command Reference documentation for details on which modes each command supports. The documentation lists each flag with the various command modes it supports. These are denoted with the **C**, **Q**, **E**, and **M** icons, for creation, query, edit, and multiple-use, respectively. The multiple-use option is for flags that you can use multiple times in the same command.

3.2.2 Variables

All programming languages provide a means of storing values that can later be reused. These are known as *variables*. The next example shows how to get the results of a MEL command and place them in a variable.

1. Open the **Script Editor**.

2. Type the following into the **Command Input Panel**:

```
$rad = 2;
sphere -radius $rad;
```

3. Press **Ctrl+Enter** to execute the commands.

   A sphere with a radius of 2 is created.

Rather than specify the sphere radius explicitly to the sphere command, a variable was used instead. The first line defines a variable named $rad to which the value of 2 is assigned. All variables in MEL begin with a dollar sign ($). When the sphere command is called, it uses the value stored in the $rad variable to set the radius parameter.

Other than some minor restrictions, a variable can have any name. Variables can't contain whitespace (spaces, tabs, and so on) or other special characters. Variables can't have names that start with a number, though numbers can be used after the first character. Variable names are also *case sensitive*. Case sensitive means that whether you use upper- or lowercase letters in the name matters. So in MEL, the variable names $RAD, $rad, and $Rad all refer to different variables.

VARIABLE TYPES

MEL provides a limited set of variable types: int, float, string, vector, and matrix. They are sufficient, however, for the scripting needs of a majority of users. If a variable's type is given but no initial value is provided, the variable is assigned its default value.

Ints

The int type is used to hold whole integer numbers. This type can't hold decimal digits.

```
int $a = -23;
int $b = 100;
int $c = 270038;
```

The actual number of bits used to store an int is platform dependent. Though it is generally safe to assume that an int is at least 32 bits in size, and therefore has a range of possible values from −2,147,483,648 to 2,147,483,647, some platforms may store the int as 64 bits or higher, thereby providing a greater range. The default value for an int variable is 0.

Floats

The float type is used to hold real numbers. These numbers can have decimal digits.

```
float $a = 10002.34;
float $b = 1.0;
float $c = -2.35;
```

As with an int, the number of bits to store a float is platform dependent. It is the equivalent of the double data type in C. For most platforms this means that floats are represented with 64 bits. As such they can hold a very wide range of values: 2.2250738585072014e−308 to 1.7976931348623158e+308. They maintain 15 digits of precision. The default value for a float is 0.0.

Strings

A `string` variable is used to hold a series of text characters. String variables can be initialized to some text as follows:

```
string $txt = "Hello there";
```

If a string isn't explicitly assigned a value, it uses the default value of an empty string. This is a string with no text.

```
string $txt; // Empty string
```

You can explicitly make a string into an empty string as follows:

```
$txt = "";
```

A common operation performed on string variables is to concatenate (join) them. This is done using the plus sign (+) as follows:

```
string $name = "David";
string $txt = "My name is " + $name;
print $txt; // Result = My name is David
```

To count the number of characters in a string, use the `size` command.

```
string $welcome = "Hi";
int $numChars = size( $welcome );
print $numChars; // Result: 2
```

It is important to understand that MEL preprocesses each string and substitutes special characters wherever it sees a backslash character (\). A special character is one that is often impossible to enter manually into a text editor but exists in the *ASCII* table. They are also referred to as escape characters. To have a string that contains a newline character, simply use the character sequence: \n. This sequence of characters is replaced by the ASCII character equivalent for new lines. The following example prints out part of the text on one line, then the rest on the following line:

```
print "Hi there\nBob";
```

The result is:

```
Hi there
Bob
```

Other special characters include the following:

```
\t      tab
\r      carriage-return
\\      backslash character
```

Notice that to actually have a backslash character (\) in a string, you need to specify it as \\. If this isn't done, MEL tries to substitute a special character any time it sees a backslash character. This can be particularly problematic under Windows when you give the complete path to a file, since backslashes are used to separate directories. The following string:

```
"c:\maya\temp"
```

is processed by MEL, resulting in the final string:

```
"c:maya    emp"
```

This character string contains two escape sequences; the first is the \m and the second the \t. The \m isn't a valid escape sequence and is therefore deleted. The \t sequence is replaced with a tab character. To ensure that the backslash remains, you need to use \\. The original string should therefore be written as follows:

```
"c:\\maya\\temp"
```

The final string, after MEL's automatic substition, will be as originally intended:

```
"c:\maya\temp"
```

The amount of text you can store in a string is limited only by the available memory, though the hard upper limit is set by the maximum int value.

Vectors

Vector variables allow you to store three floating-point values. Vectors are typically used to store positions and directions.

1. In the **Script Editor**, type the following commands:

```
sphere;
vector $p = << 10.0, 5.0, 2.5 >>;
move -absolute ($p.x) ($p.y) ($p.z);
```

2. Press **Ctrl+Enter** to execute them.

   A sphere is created and then moved to the position ($x = 10$, $y = 5$, and $z = 2.5$).

The individual vector components x, y, z are accessed using $p.x$, $p.y$, and $p.z$, respectively. It is important to note that to access the vector components they must be enclosed in parentheses. The following example demonstrates the problem of not using parentheses:

```
vector $p = << 10.0, 5.0, 2.5 >>;
print $p.x; // Error
print ($p.x); // Result: 10.0
```

Another idiosyncrasy of the MEL language is that you can't directly assign a number to a vector's component. The following code, for example, results in an error:

```
$p.x = 3.0;    // Error
($p.x) = 3.0; // Error
```

In fact there is no direct way to assign a value to a vector's component. Instead, this has to be done indirectly by creating another vector and assigning it to the original vector. The purpose of the following code is to assign $p.x the value of 3.0:

```
vector $p = << 10.0, 5.0, 2.5 >>;
$p = << 3.0, $p.y, $p.z >>;   // Assign 3.0 to just x
print $p                      // Result = 3 5 2.5
```

If a vector isn't explicitly assigned a value, it will use the default value <<0.0, 0.0, 0.0>>.

```
vector $p; // Automatically initialized to default <<0.0, 0.0, 0.0>>
```

Arrays

There will be many times when you'll need to store a series of variables. MEL allows you to define an *array* of variables. Often it isn't known ahead of time how many elements will be in an array, so MEL allows the number of elements to increase automatically, as needed. The following shows some examples of arrays:

```
int $values[] = { 2, 5, 7, 1 };
string $names[3] = { "Bill", "Bob", "Jeff" };
vector $positions[2] = { <<0.5,0.1,1.0>>, <<2.3,4.0,1.2>> };
float $scores[]; // Empty array
```

When defining an array, the square brackets ([]) must be used. To access an individual element of the array, its index must be given between the brackets.

```
int $values[4] = { 2, 5, 7, 1 };
print ( $values[0] ); // Result: 2
print ( $values[3] ); // Result: 1
```

Indices are base 0, so the index of the first item in the array is 0, the second is 1, and so on. The total range of indices of the array ranges from 0 to (*number of elements* −1). To find the total number of elements in an array, use the size command.

```
int $values[3] = { 4, 8, 9 };
int $numElements = size( $values );
print $numElements; // Result: 3
```

A typical operation is to append an element to an existing array. To do that, use the size command in the following way:

```
int $values[2] = { 5, 1 };
$values[ size($values) ] = 3; // Append 3 to the array
print $values;                // Result: 5 1 3
```

It is also possible to add an element by directly referring to it.

```
int $values[];   // Empty array
$values[0] = 2;  // First element set to 2
$values[2] = 7;  // Third element set to 7
print $values;   // Result: 2 0 7
```

The array was initially empty, so it contained no elements. By directly assigning a value to the first element (index 0), the array was increased in size to accommodate the new element. The array, at this point, had just one element. The next line sets the third element (index 2), so the array size is increased to hold three elements. Since you gave a value for the third element, it was set to 7. Notice that you didn't give a value for the second element (index 1). When Maya increases the size of an array, it assigns the default value to all elements that aren't explicitly initialized. Since it is an array of integers, the second element is automatically assigned the default value for integers: 0.

As elements are added to an array, the array takes more space in memory. For large arrays that contain many elements, this can result in a lot of memory allocated. If the elements of an array are no longer needed, it is best to remove them to free up memory. The clear command removes all the elements in an array and frees any memory it used.

```
int $values[4] = { 6, 9, 2, 1 };
print $values; // Result: 6 9 2 1
clear( $values );
print $values; // Result:
```

Unfortunately there is no direct way to remove elements from an array. Instead you must create a new array with the elements you want to retain and then copy this back into the original array. The following example demonstrates this method by removing the third element (index 2) from an array.

```
int $values[] = { 1, 2, 3, 4 };

// Remove the third element
int $temp[];
int $i;
for( $i=0; $i < size($values); $i++ )
  {
  if( $i == 2 ) // Skip the third element(index 2)
    continue;
  $temp[size($temp)] = $values[$i];
  }
$values = $temp;

print $values;
// Result 1 2 4
```

Note that arrays can be only one dimensional. For two-dimensional arrays of a fixed size, use the `matrix` type, described next. For dynamic multidimensional arrays, you need to pack them into a single-dimensional array. Assume in the following example that you want to create a two-dimensional array; that is, you can access it using row and column indices. The following example creates a single-dimensional array that holds the two-dimensional data. It has two rows and four columns. The first row 1, 2, 3, 4 is followed by the second row 5, 6, 7, 8, in a single-dimensional array.

```
int $pixs[] = { 1, 2, 3, 4, 5, 6, 7, 8 };
```

To find out what the single array index is that corresponds to a given row and column, the following formula is used:

index = row × number_of_ columns + column

Remember that all indices are base 0. So to access row 1 (second row), column 3 (fourth column), you would do the following.

```
int $nCols = 4;
int $index = 1 * $nCols + 3;
print $pixs[$index];
// Result: 8
```

This formula for accessing the elements can be generalized into a procedure that can access the array at any row and column. Procedures are explained in a later section.

Matrices

A matrix is very similar to an array except that it has two dimensions. While an array can be considered a single row of elements, a matrix has both rows and columns of elements. Unlike arrays, however, matrices can't be resized once they have been defined. As such, it isn't possible to add additional elements to a matrix. Also a matrix can hold only `float` values.

A matrix is defined with the number of rows and columns it will support.

```
matrix $m[2][1]; // Set dimensions of matrix to 2 rows and 1 column
```

If the dimensions of the matrix aren't explicitly specified, an error results.

```
matrix $m[2][]; // ERROR: size not specified
matrix $m[][]; // ERROR: size not specified
```

Matrices are initialized using a syntax similar to that used for vectors. Matrix elements are defined in a row order. So in the following example, the first row of the matrix consists of values 3, 4, 6, 7 while the second row consists of values 3, 9, 0, 1.

```
matrix $m[2][4] = << 3,4,6,7; 3,9,0,1 >>;
```

The elements of the matrix are accessed in a similar manner to arrays, except that a column index has to be given.

```
matrix $m[2][4] = << 3,4,6,7; 3,9,0,1 >>;
print( $m[0][0] ); // Result: 3
print( $m[1][3] ); // Result: 1
```

Since a matrix has a fixed number of rows and columns, if you attempt to access an element outside of the range of possible indices, an error is displayed.

```
matrix $m[2][4] = << 3,4,6,7; 3,9,0,1 >>;
print ( $m[2][0] );
// Error: line 2: Index value of 2 exceeds dimension limit (2) of $m. //
```

If a matrix isn't explicitly assigned values when it is defined, each of its individual elements is automatically initialized to 0.0.

```
matrix $m[2][1]; // Automatically initialized to <<0.0; 0.0>>
```

AUTOMATIC VARIABLE TYPES

Unlike stricter programming languages, MEL doesn't require you to give a variable's type when you define it. MEL determines what type of variable it is by the value you assign to it.

```
$rad = 2.1;
```

Since the value 2.1 could be represented only as a floating-point value, the $rad value is made to be a float variable. A direct consequence of this is that it's important to understand how Maya differentiates different variable types. Take the following example:

```
$a = 2;
$b = 2.0;
```

Even though both of these values could be stored as the integer value 2, since the second value is 2.0 the variable $b is made a float. This automatic behavior can cause some subtle bugs in your scripts. With a box object at position (3.43, 0, 0), executing the following statements gives an unexpected result:

```
$i = 5;
$i = `getAttr box.translateX`;
print $i;
// Result: 3
```

When a result of 3 is given, the correct value for the box's x position is 3.43. There are a couple of reasons why this was the result. The $i variable is created and assigned the value of 3. Since you didn't explicitly specify the type of the variable, Maya assumed that it was an integer, since the value 5 is clearly an integer. In the next statement, you ask for the box's x position. Maya returns the correct value of 3.43; however, this value is being stored in the $i integer variable. Given that $i is an integer, it can't store all the decimal digits but only the whole value. So the value of 3 is ultimately stored in $i.

What was really intended was for $i to be a float variable so that it could hold all the digits in the x position. As a general rule, it is best to explicitly declare the type of a variable when it is defined. This ensures that you aren't depending on Maya to automatically determine the variable type for you. The previous statements should now read:

```
float $i = 5;
$i = `getAttr box.translateX`;
print $i;
// Result: 3.43
```

Since this can lead to some confusion and hard-to-find bugs, it is best to explicitly define the type of the variable when it is declared. The following examples illustrate this:

```
float $a = 34; // set to 34.0
int $b = 2.3; // set to 2
```

Since a float can hold any real number, including decimal points, it easily holds the number 34. An int, on the other hand, can't hold decimal point values. It can hold only the whole part, so it drops the .3 and stores just the value 2.

Once a variable's type is set, either explicitly or implicitly, it can't be changed. In the following example, the variable $a is made a float implicitly by assigining it 2.3. From then on the variable $a can hold only float data. When you assign it a non-float value, Maya attempts to convert it to a float. Assigning the $a variable a string sets it to a value of 0, since there is no reasonable conversion from a string to a float. Fortunately Maya warns you about such conversions.

```
$a = 2.3;      // Implicitly make $a a float
$a = "notes"; // Attempt to make $a a string
// Warning: $a = "notes";
//
// Warning: Line 3.13 : Converting string "notes" to a float value of 0.//
```

It is important to understand what possible values each type of variable can store. As a general rule, floats should be used for all numbers since that is the format that Maya typically uses. When doing counting or iterating over lists, then the int type can be used.

AUTOMATIC TYPE CONVERSIONS

Another even more esoteric cause for problems in your scripts is the automatic conversion of types. The reason they can be difficult to locate is that they require you to understand the exact mechanisms of how one variable's data type is converted to and from another's. This understanding is based on a knowledge of how each data type holds its particular information. Take, for instance, the following statements:

```
int $i = 7.534;
print $i;
// Result: 7
```

As mentioned earlier, the int data type can hold only whole integer values. If you attempt to give it a value of 7.534, it simply truncates the fractional part and just stores the whole part. As a result, the value of 7 is stored. Unfortunately Maya does not warn you about such potentially dangerous conversions.

Seemingly simple statements can evaluate incorrectly simply because of the different ways data types operate. These statements result in 0 being printed:

```
float $i = 1 / 3;
print $i;
// Result: 0
```

Shouldn't the value be 0.333...? The reason this didn't work was that the initial calculation was done with integer arithmetic. Maya assumed the 1 and 3 in the first statement were integers. As such, it used integer arithmetic to calculate the division; 1/3 is normally 0.333... but since you are using integers, the whole part of the division is 0 and this is all that is stored. Now if the statement were formulated as follows, it would have worked:

```
float $i = 1 / 3.0;
print $i;
// Result: 0.33333
```

Why does it now calculate correctly? Maya looked at the operands to the division as follows. The 1 was interpreted as an int. The 3.0 was intepreted as a float. Internally Maya doesn't do operations on mixed data types; instead it makes them all the same type and then does the operation. Since a float is more precise than an integer, Maya will promote the integer to a float and then do the operation with floating-point values, and the result is therefore more precise.

It may be clear that the whole topic of automatic type conversion is rather tricky and complex. It isn't necessary to understand all its intricacies in order to program well. However it may be important when you are debugging scripts that don't behave quite as expected even though you've checked everything and there are no syntax or logic errors. It may be that automatic type conversion is to blame. If you suspect this to be the case, then print the values of each of the calculations to check their results. If they are incorrect, break the calculation down into smaller pieces and check their individual results. Eventually you will uncover the offending statements. As a general rule, unless explicitly needed otherwise, do all mathematical calculations using the float type.

From Type	To Type	Example	Issues
int	float	`float $i = 3;` `// Result: $i = 3.0`	exact
int	vector	`vector $v = 3;` `// Result: $v = <<3.0,3.0,3.0>>`	exact
float	int	`int $i = 3.45;` `// Result: $i = 3`	whole part only
float	vector	`vector $v = 3.45;` `// Result: $v = <<3.45,3.45,3.45>>`	exact
vector	int	`int $i = <<1,2,3>>` `// Result: $i = 3`	whole part only of magnitude
vector	float	`float $i = <<1,2,3>>` `// Result: $i = 3.741657`	exact length of vector

TABLE 3.1 AUTOMATIC VARIABLE TYPE CONVERSIONS

Table 3.1 lists how Maya automatically converts different types. It should offer a general guide as to how the values in the different types are interpreted and then stored.

3.2.3 Comments

It is possible to annotate your scripts by adding comments. Sometimes it isn't obvious by simply looking at a script how it works or why it was designed in a particular way. To explain this, it is best to add comments. This enables another person to better understand what you intended. Comments can also be an important reference for the original developer, since it is often easy to forget why a particular piece of code was designed in a given way.

MEL supports two types of comments. The first is the single-line comment. It starts with two forward slash characters (//). All text following these characters, until the end of the line, is treated as a comment.

```
int $avg; // Average number of particles in the scene
```

The second type of comment is the multiline comment. To have a comment that spans more than one line, simply enclose it with characters (/*, */).

```
/*
This script is part of the advanced visualization package.
Copyright (c) 2002 Smarty Pants Inc.
*/
```

It isn't possible to nest multiline comments. This is where you have one comment including another comment. The following would cause a syntax error:

```
/*
int $avg;
/*
The average is calculated using the sum
of all the spheres in the scene.
*/
$avg = average( $input );
*/
```

Comments can be very handy for turning on and off different sections of a script. If, for example, you were developing a script to perform a given task and then you'd like to modify the script and add some enhancements, it is a generally good practice to copy the original sections of code and put them in a comment. This way you can restore your original code later if needed.

The main purpose of a comment is to explain to the reader the "why" and "how" of what you are doing. It isn't important to detail the "what," since that is evident from looking at the code. In the following example, the comment is redundant since you can deduce what is happening from simply looking at the statement:

```
$total = $total + 1; // Add one to total
```

It would be better to explain why this was done, as follows:

```
$total = $total + 1; // Increase total to include the current year
```

3.2.4   Operators

With a better understanding of what different data types MEL supports, you now look at what operations you can perform on these data types.

ASSIGNMENT OPERATOR

The most common operator is the assignment operator (=). It is used to assign a value to a variable as follows:

```
int $score;
$score = 253;
```

ARITHMETIC OPERATORS

The arithmetic operators perform all the basic mathematical operations on numbers, including addition (+), subtraction (–), multiplication (*), division (/), and others.

Addition and Subtraction

Addition and subtraction work as they should for numerical types.

```
int $a = 3;
int $b = 5;
print ($a + $b);            // Result: 8

float $a = 2.3;
print (4 - $a);             // Result: 1.7

vector $va = <<1,2,3>>;
print ($va + <<0.5,0.5,0.5>>); // Result: 1.5 2.5 3.5

matrix $m[2][1] = << 3; 5 >>;
matrix $n[2][1] = << 2; 1 >>;
print ($m + $n);            // Result:  << 5; 6 >>
```

As mentioned earlier, the addition operator (+) has a different meaning when used with string variables. Adding together two strings results in a string that is a combination of both strings; the second string is appended to the first.

```
string $a = "Hi ";
string $b = "there";
print ($a + $b); // Result: Hi there
```

Addition is the only arithmetic operator that has an effect on strings. You can't, for instance, use subtraction to remove one string from another.

Multiplication

Multiplication works on all numerical data types.

```
float $v = 8.2;
print ($v * 2); // Result: 16.4
```

Multiplying two matrices together results in a single matrix that adheres to standard matrix multiplication rules.

When the multiplication operator (*) is used on two vectors the result is the *dot product* of the vectors. This is the equivalent of multiplying each component together then summing the result.

dotproduct(a,b) = a.x × b.x + a.y × b.y + a.z × b.z

For instance:

```
vector $a = << 1, 2, 3 >>;
vector $b = << 6, 2, 1 >>;
print ($a * $b); // Result: 13
```

Unfortunately, you can't multiply a matrix by a vector to transform it. MEL doesn't support this operation. Instead you must explicitly define the operation as a series of multiplications and additions.

Division and Modulus

Division works on all the numerical types. The result of the division is exactly as you would expect, except with integers. Since an integer is a whole number and can't contain a fractional amount, any division that results in a remainder can't be fully represented by an integer. The result of the division with two integers is the whole amount of the division.

```
int $a = 12;
print ($a / 3); // Result: 4

int $a = 12;
print ($a / 5); // Result: 2 (the precise answer is 2.4)
```

While the division operator gives the whole amount of the division, the modulus operator (%) can be used to get the fractional remainder of the division.

```
int $a = 13;
print ($a % 5); // Result: 3
```

It is possible to use the division and modulus operators on a `matrix`. The only condition is that the right side of the operator be a single value of type `int` or `float`.

```
matrix $m[2][3] = << 3, 6, 8; 4, 8, 2 >>;
print ($m / 2); // Result: << 1.5, 3, 4; 2, 4, 1>>
```

Cross Product

For vectors, the cross-product operator (^) is used to calculate the *cross product* of the two vectors. The cross product of two vectors is a vector that is perpendicular (normal) to the two original vectors. The equation for the cross product is as follows:

$$\text{crossproduct}(a,b) = (\ a.y \times b.z - a.z \times b.y,$$
$$a.z \times b.x - a.x \times b.z,$$
$$a.x \times b.y - a.y \times b.x\ )$$

In some languages, the ^ operator is used to raise a number to a given exponent. In MEL, the `pow` command is used to do this.

BOOLEANS

Before learning about relational and logical operators, it is important to understand what a *boolean* is. A boolean can be in one of two states: `true` or `false`. It is therefore used when making comparisons. When something is determined to be `true`, you can perform some action. Likewise, you may want to perform an action when something is found to be `false`.

In MEL a boolean is actually stored as an `int`. The integer values for `true` and `false` are 1 and 0, respectively. The following statement demonstrates this:

```
$a = true;
$b = false;
print ($a + ", " + $b);
```

Result: 1, 0

The additional keywords `yes` and `on` can be used in place of `true`. Likewise, the keywords `no` and `off` can be used in place of `false`. The complete list of boolean values is given in Table 3.2.

TABLE 3.2 BOOLEAN KEYWORDS	
Boolean	**Integer value**
true, yes, on	1
false, no, off	0

While the constant `true` has an integer value of 1, any integer value that is not 0 is considered to be true, in the logical sense. The following example demonstrates this:

```
int $a = 5;
if( $a )
   print "a is true";
```

The result is:

```
a is true
```

Since any integer value that isn't 0 is considered true, it is important to be careful when doing comparisons against the constant `true`, which has an integer value of 1.

```
int $a = 3;

if( $a )
  print "a is true";

// Fails since comparison expands to 3 == 1 which is false
if( $a == true )
  print "a is true";
```

RELATIONAL OPERATORS

A very common programming task is to compare two variables. For instance you may want to perform an action if the distance of an object exceeds a given limit. This would be described in pseudocode as follows:

if distance is greater than limit then
   perform action
end

In MEL this can be written as follows:

```
if( $distance > $limit )
  action();
```

If the statement inside the if (...) is true, the statement under it is executed. If the statement is found to be false, the preceding statement is skipped. So, the if statement allows you to perform one action if the comparison statement evaluates to true or another action if it evaluates to false. This is further demonstrated as follows:

```
int $a = 10;
if( $a == 10 )
  print "a is 10";
else
  print "a is not 10";
```

The statement following the else is executed if the comparison is false. If the action includes more than one statement, it has to be enclosed in braces ({, }). This groups the statements together into one logical block. The following code demonstrates this:

```
int $a = 10
if( $a == 10 )
  {
  print "a is 10";
  int $b = $a * 2;
  }
```

```
else
  print "a is not 10";
```

It is also possible to nest if statements. Nesting the if statement means including another if statement inside the original if.

```
int $a = 10;
if( $a < 11 )
  {
  if( $a > 5 )
    print "a is between 6 and 10";
  else
    print "a is less than 6";
  }
else
  print "a is greater than 10";
```

This is no limit to the number of if statements you can nest. There also exists the else if statement, but it can lead to more obfuscated code and so should be avoided in preference to creating nested if statements with enclosing braces.

As always, the result of a relational operator is a boolean value. Therefore each comparison will have a result of either true or false. The complete set of relational operators is listed in Table 3.3.

TABLE 3.3 POSSIBLE COMPARISON OPERATORS		
Relation	Symbol	Example
less than	<	a < b
less than or equal to	<=	a <= b
greater than	>	a > b
greater than or equal to	>=	a >= b
equal to	==	a == b
not equal to	!=	a != b

Following are some example uses:

```
$homeTeam = 234;
$visitingTeam = 123;
if( $homeTeam > $visitingTeam )
    print "Home team won!";
if( $homeTeam < $visitingTeam )
    print "Visting team won";
if( $homeTeam == $visitingTeam )
  print "Tie";
```

Notice that the symbol for comparing whether two variables are equal is two equal signs (==) and not just one (=). Recall that the single equal sign is used for assignment. If you did the following, variable $a would be assigned the value of 2, rather than being compared against 2:

```
$a = 5;
if( $a = 2 )
    print "Second";
```

To prevent this assignment, the code should be changed to:

```
$a = 5;
if( $a == 2 )
  print "Second";
```

This is a *very* common mistake, and what's more, Maya won't warn you against making such an error. The best method to prevent this is to put the literal value on the left of the comparison.

```
if( 23 == $score )
    ....
```

If you then make the mistake of doing an assignment, MEL displays an error, since you are trying to assign a value to something that isn't a variable.

```
if( 23 = $score )
    ....
// Error: Line 2.2: Syntax error //
```

LOGICAL OPERATORS

Sometimes you'll want to compare more than two variables in combination and then perform some action. For example:

```
float $result = 2.9;
float $worldRecord = 2.87;
float $firstPlace = 2.9;
float $personalBest = 2.8;

if( $result == $firstPlace && $result > $worldRecord )
   print "Winner and beat world record";

if( $result < $firstPlace && $result > $personalBest )
   print "Lost race but beat personal best";
```

Using logical operators, you can combine multiple comparisons and then perform some action. The complete list of logical operators is given in Table 3.4.

TABLE 3.4 LOGICAL OPERATORS		
Logical Operator	Symbol	Example
or	||	a || b
and	&&	a && b
not	!	!a

When using the or operator (||), the result is true if either a *or* b are true; otherwise it is false. The following examples demonstrate this:

```
int $a = 10;
int $b = 12;
if( $a > 3 || $b > 5 ) // true or true = true
   print "yes"; // Is printed

if( $a == 5 || $b == 12 ) // false or true = true
   print "yes"; // Is printed

if( $a == 3 || $b == 2 ) // false or false = false
   print "yes"; // Doesn't get printed
```

When using the and operator (&&), the result is true only if both a *and* b are true; otherwise it is false.

```
int $a = 10;
int $b = 12;
if( $a == 10 && $b == 12 ) // true and true = true
   print "yes"; // Is printed

if( $a == 10 && $b == 2 ) // true and false = false
   print "yes"; // Doesn't get printed

if( $a == 3 && $b == 2 ) // false and false = false
   print "yes"; // Doesn't get printed
```

The not operator (!) switches the result of the comparison. If the result was true, then it becomes false and vice versa. Consider the following:

```
int $a = 10;
int $b = 12;

// Comparison is true, but not (!) flips meaning so result is false
if( !($a == 10 && $b == 12) )
   print "no";  // Never printed

// Comparison is false, but not (!) flips meaning so result is true
if( !($a > 10) )
   print "a is not greater than 10"; // Is printed
```

The following two statements are equivalent:

```
int $a = 0;
if( $a == 0 )
   print "a is false";

// The not operator (!) flips the logical meaning of $a
// It flips 0, which results in 1, which is true
if( !$a )
   print "a is false";
```

OPERATOR PRECEDENCE

It is very important to understand the precedence of a given operator. Not knowing the order in which an expression will be evaluated can cause obscure bugs. The code looks right and runs just fine, but the end result is wrong. The cause is often an incorrect assumption about the order in which operators are evaluated. Take the following piece of code:

```
int $a = 10 + 2 * 5;
```

From mathematics you know that the multiplication should be evaluated first then the addition, resulting in 20. If the multiplication didn't have precedence over the addition, the result would be 60. An operator's precedence defines whether it is evaluated before or after another operator, so the precedence defines the order in which the expression is evaluated.

While the precedence of arithmetic operators is well known to most users, this isn't the case for other MEL operators. What is the precedence of the following operators, and subsequently what is the order of their evaluation?

```
$height > 2 || $width == 1
```

Without knowing the precedence, you'd most likely evaluate them left to right in the order they appear. Using parentheses to group the operators, this would result in:

```
((($height > 2) || $width) == 1)
```

This may not be what you had intended. In reality the > operator has the greater of the precedences, so it is evaluated first. The == equality operator comes next, followed by the || or operator, resulting in the following grouping:

```
(($height > 2) || ($width == 1))
```

The complete lists of operators and their precedence is given in Table 3.5. The operators with the highest precedence are listed first, followed by operators of a lower precedence.

Where operators with the same precedence are encountered in a statement, they are grouped from left to right in the order they appear. For instance both addition and subtraction have the same precedence and so are evaluated left to right in the following code.

```
int $a = 2 - 3 + 4; // Result 3
```

There may be times when you need to override the default precedence of an operator. This can be done using the grouping operator (). As in mathematics, it has the highest precedence and therefore overrules the precedence of any other operator. For instance, the grouping operator can be used to ensure that the addition happens before the subtraction in the previous code.

```
int $a = 2 - (3 + 4); // Result -5
```

When in doubt about an operator's precedence, always use the grouping operator to explicitly define the order in which you want the expressions to evaluate. The grouping operator also helps to state your intentions clearly to other people who may be reading your code.

TABLE 3.5 PRECEDENCE OF OPERATORS
Operator Precedence
(), []
!, ++, --
*, /, %, ^
+, -
<, <=, >, >=
==, !=
&&
||
?:
=, +=, -=, *=, /=

The grouping operator can be used to ensure that an entire expression is evaluated before it is passed to a command. The following causes a syntax error:

```
int $a = 2;
int $b = 1;
print $a + $b;
// Error: print $a + $b;
//
// Error: Line 4.10: Syntax error //
```

The reason for this is that the last statement is actually evaluated as follows:

```
(print $a) + $b;
```

Maya is attempting to add the result of the print command to the $b variable. This is clearly not what was intended. To make your intentions explicit, the grouping operator is used.

```
print ($a + $b);
```

3.2.5 Looping

When you need to perform the same task multiple times, you need a *loop*. The following language constructs provide this functionality.

FOR

Given an array of numbers, how would you calculate their sum? Logically, the process would be to keep a running total and add each number in the array to this total. In order to visit each element in the array, a for loop is used. The following example also illustrates how to calculate the product of all the elements:

```
float $nums[3] = { 2, 5, 6 };
float $sum = 0;
float $prod = 1;
int $i;
for( $i = 0; $i < size($nums); $i = $i + 1 )
  {
  $sum = $sum + $nums[$i];
  $prod = $prod * $nums[$i];
  }
```

```
print $sum; // Result: 13
print $prod; // Result: 60
```

The for loop statement is composed of four parts:

for (execute_first; test_condition; execute_each_loop)
   operation;

The **execute_first** statement is called once, before the loop is started; The **test_condition** statement is used to determine whether the loop should terminate. If this statement ever results in false, the loop is terminated. This statement is run and tested once before entering the loop and at the end of each full loop. This **execute_each_loop** statement is executed at the end of each loop. For each loop, the **operation** statement is executed.

WHILE

Another alternative to the for loop is the while loop. It is composed of just two parts:

while(test_condition)
   operation;

The while loop continues executing the **operation** statement as long as the **test_condition** evaluates to true. The while loop is exactly the same as the for loop except that it doesn't have the **execute_first** or **execute_each_loop** statements. The preceding for loop can be reformulated using a while loop as follows:

```
float $nums[3] = { 2, 5, 6 };
float $sum = 0;
int $i = 0;
while( $i < size($nums) )
  {
  $sum = $sum + $nums[$i];
  $i = $i + 1;
  }
```

DO-WHILE

The last looping method is the do-while statement. Like the while statement, it is composed of just two parts.

```
do
  {
  operation;
  } while( test_condition );
```

The do-while statements operate exactly like a while loop except that the **operation** statement is run once before the first **test_condition** statement. This allows you to do at least one entire loop before testing whether to terminate.

INFINITE LOOPS

For all the looping methods it is very important to correctly code the **test_condition**. It is quite possible that a badly formulated **test_condition** or **execute_each_loop** statement could create an infinite loop. This happens when the **test_condition** never evaluates to false, so the loop never terminates. At that point the only alternative is to kill the Maya process and start it again. For this reason alone, it is important that you save the current scene and any scripts you are working on before executing them.

CONTINUE

The continue statement allows you to skip the remainder of the statements in the current loop and start the next one. The continue statement can be used in all the different types of loops. An example use of continue in a for loop follows:

```
string $names[] = { "Jenny", "Bob", "Bill", "Paula" };
int $i;
for( $i=0; $i < size($names); $i = $i + 1 )
    {
    if( $names[$i] == "Bill" )
        continue; // Don't print out Bill

    print ($names[$i] + "\n");
    }
```

Result:

```
Jenny
Bob
Paula
```

BREAK

The break statement is used to exit immediately out of a loop. It can be used in any of the loops. In this next piece of code, you want to terminate the while loop the moment one of the numbers in the array is greater than 10.

```
int $nums[] = { 2, 4, 7, 12, 3, 10 };
int $i = 0;
while( $i < size($nums) )
   {
   if( $nums[$i] > 10 )
      break;

   print ($nums[$i] + " ");

   $i = $i + 1;
   }
```

Result:

```
2 4 7
```

The break statement is particularly useful if you are in a series of nested conditional statements and want to break out of the enclosing loop.

3.2.6 Procedures

Once you start writing longer MEL scripts, it becomes harder to manage all the complexity that soon results. One easy approach to handling complexity is to break it down into smaller, more manageable parts. While the overall system may be quite complex, the individual parts that make it up can be easily understood. This approach to dividing up a computer programming task into smaller pieces is known as *structured programming*.

The principle of structured programming is that the programming task is broken into small units based on their functionality. If you were to develop a program that makes cakes, you'd probably develop it in two pieces. The first piece would handle making the cake mixture. The second piece would then handle baking the cake. If you later decided to create a system for making biscuits, there is a good chance that you could reuse a lot of the "baking" piece.

The goal of structured programming is to divide your program into smaller functional pieces that can be reused. MEL provides a means for doing this through *procedures*. A procedure is like a command, in that you call it in your script and it performs some operation. A procedure can take any number of variables as input. It can also produce some output. A procedure can be thought of as a machine into which things get fed and which processes them to produce a result.

Following is a very simple procedure that prints your name:

1. Open the **Script Editor.**

2. Type the following text into the **Command Input Panel.** Substitute your name in place of David.

```
proc printName()
{
print "My name is David";
}
```

3. Press **Ctrl+Enter** to execute it.

   Nothing happens. What you have done is simply define the procedure. In order to execute it, you must call it.

4. Type, then execute, the following text:

```
printName;
```

   The result is:

```
My name is David
```

While this procedure works just fine, what happens if you want to print someone else's name? What if you didn't know the person's name in advance? In that case you design the procedure to take the name as input. You can then print it out.

5. Type, then execute, the following:

```
proc printName( string $name )
{
print ("My name is " + $name);
}
```

Maya emits the following warning:

```
// Warning: New procedure definition for "printName" has
    a different argument list and/or return type. //
```

Maya is simply warning you that the new version of the printName procedure that was entered will override the previous one.

6. Type, then execute, the following:

```
printName( "Bill" );
```

The result is:

```
My name is Bill
```

The new procedure takes a string variable, $name, as input. When it is called this time, the value "Bill" is given as input. This input is assigned to the $name variable. The procedure then prints out the value of this variable.

A procedure can take an unlimited number of variables as input. A procedure can also produce an output. In the next exercise a procedure named sum is defined that adds two numbers together and then returns the result.

7. Execute the following:

```
proc int sum( int $a, int $b )
{
int $c = $a + $b;
return $c;
}

int $res = sum( 4, 5 );
print $res;
```

The result is:

9

The sum procedure takes two integer input variables, $a and $b, and produces a single output integer value.

The sum procedure is a good example of the general form of a procedure.

proc return_type procedure_name(arguments)
{
statements;
return_result;
}

When defining a procedure that returns a result, the type of result must be specified in the **return_type** statement. If the procedure doesn't return a value, then **return_type** can be left blank. The **procedure_name** can be any name. There cannot, however, be any whitespace in the name, and the first letter musn't be a number. The procedure can take no input variables or as many as needed. The type and name of the variables are listed in the **arguments** statement. If the procedure returns a result, then it must contain at least one **return_result** statement. If it doesn't, Maya will warn you. This statement doesn't necessarily have to be at the end of the procedure, but the procedure cannot exit without having returned a result. If the procedure doesn't return a result, then the **return_result** statement can be omitted.

It isn't possible to define a procedure within another procedure.

3.2.7 Scope

It is important to understand that all variables and procedures have a clearly defined *scope*. The scope of a variable defines its accessibility from other scopes. It also indirectly defines the *lifetime* of the variable. Each variable has a defined period in which it is accessible. Outside this period, the variable doesn't exist and is therefore inaccessible. The easiest way to look at scopes is to consider them as a block. A section of code that is enclosed in braces ({, }) is considered a block. The following is a block:

```
{
int $a;
$a = 3 + 5;
}
```

A new block of code can be created at any time by simply putting braces around it. All the variables defined within a given block exist only for the length of that block. When the block ends with a closing brace, all the variables it defined are removed. The variables are therefore no longer available. So when the closing brace is reached in the preceding code, the variable $a is removed. It is also possible to create blocks inside other blocks.

```
// Block 1
{
int $a = 12;

  // Inner Block 2
  {
  int $b = 10;
  print $a;
  }

print $b;
}
```

When this is executed, the following error is displayed:

```
// Error: print $b;
//
// Error: Line 7.9: "$b" is an undeclared variable. //
```

The reason variable $b is undeclared is that it is inside an inner block that ended. Variables created in a block are also available to inner blocks. So in this case the variable $a, while defined in Block 1, is available in Inner Block 2. However variables created in inner blocks aren't available to their outer blocks for the simple reason that when the inner block ends all its variables are removed, so the outer block never gets the chance to access them. So when, in Block 1, you tried to print the value of the $b variable, it failed. At this point the inner block has terminated and therefore variable $b no longer exists.

GLOBAL AND LOCAL

Variables $a and $b are considered *local* to their particular blocks. Being local means that they are accessible only within their block and any inner blocks they may have defined. Sometimes you'll want to have a variable that you can share with other blocks defined outside. For example, you may want to store the name of the current user and make this accessible to all your scripts. A special scope has been created for this very purpose, the *global* scope. Once a variable is defined as global, it is accessible anytime and anywhere throughout Maya. Defining a global variable involves putting it in the outermost scope (not inside any braces) and including the `global` keyword.

```
global string $currentUserName;
```

To access the global variable inside a block, you need to tell MEL that you want to refer to it.

```
global string $currentUserName;

{
global string $currentUserName;
$currentUserName = "John Doe";
}
```

What would happen if you didn't explicitly declare that you wanted to use the global variable?

```
global string $currentUserName;

{
$currentUserName = "John Doe";
}
```

MEL creates a new local variable named `$currentUserName` inside the block, and it is used instead. By explicitly declaring that you want to reference the global variable, MEL knows which one you want to use. The assumption is always that you want to use the local variable unless explicitly told otherwise.

INITIALIZATION OF GLOBALS

It is important to understand how initialization of a global variable is done. Like all variables, unless you explicitly initialize them, they take the default value. The following variable, `$depth`, since it is an `int`, is initialized to the default 0:

```
global int $depth;
```

An explicit value for the variable could also be specified. It is always preferable explicitly to initialize your variables. This makes it immediately clear what value it should have.

```
global int $depth = 3;
```

It is important to understand that a global variable is initialized only *once*. This happens when the statement is first encountered by MEL during compilation (refer to section 3.3.4 for complete details about script compilation). After compilation, any statements that initialize the global variable are ignored.

```
proc go()
{
global int $depth = 3;
print ("\n" + $depth);
$depth = 1;
print (" " + $depth);
}

go();
go();
```

This prints out the following:

```
3 1
1 1
```

When the go procedure was first called, it needed to be compiled, so the global variable $depth was intialized to 3. When the go procedure is called again, it already resides in memory, so a recompilation isn't needed. The procedure is simply called. This time the $depth value is used with its current value and isn't reinitialized. If the go procedure needed to be recompiled, then the global variable would once again be initialized.

Another small difference needs to be noted about how global and local variables are initialized. Since all the variables in a block are created when the block is entered, the local variables are created and initialized at that time. For instance:

```
{
int $b; // Defaults to 0
int $a = 3 * $b;
}
```

A global variable is created and initialized before any other code. As such it can only be initialized using constant values. It can't, for instance, be initialized to the result of a procedure call.

```
global int $a = 23; // OK
global int $b = 1.5 * screenSize(); // Error!
```

CONFLICTS

Since all global variables exist in the same space (scope), it is possible that two users, unknowingly, use the same name for a global variable. The first person would use the variable in his or her scripts and the second person would also use the same variable in his or her scripts. Neither will know that the variable can now be changed outside his or her scripts. One user may set it to a given value, then another user may set it to another value. The first user assumes it has his or her value, when it now doesn't. It is easy to see the problems that having both users changing the same variable can cause.

It is possible to get a list of all the current global variables by using the env command. Even if your variable isn't in the list, this doesn't mean there won't be a conflict later. If another user loads a script that has a global variable with the same name, there will be a conflict.

The best solution to prevent any conflicts is to ensure that your variables have a unique name. At Alias | Wavefront, programmers prepend all their global variables with the lowercase *g*. For instance:

```
$gScaleLimits
```

Therefore, when you name your variables it is best not to use this coding convention. A better choice is to prepend two or three characters to the name that are unique to you, your company, or your project. For instance, all code developed for your Maya programming projects could be prepended with mp:

```
global string $mpUserName;
```

There is no guarantee that someone else won't use the same name, but it should reduce the likelihood considerably.

Once a global variable is defined, there is no way to remove it later. The reason for this is that some other script somewhere may depend on that variable existing. Therefore, all global variables defined during a Maya session exist until the session is terminated. If you want to remove some global variables, the only way to do this is to exit Maya, then restart it.

As mentioned earlier, to get a list of all the current global variables, use the `env` command. To test whether a given variable name is an existing global variable, use the following procedure:

```
global proc int isGlobal( string $varName )
{
string $vars[] = `env`;
for( $var in $vars )
  {
  if( $var == $varName )
    return yes;
  }
return no;
}
```

This procedure can then be used as follows:

```
if( isGlobal( "$myGlobal" ) )
   ... do something
```

As a general programming practice, you should avoid using global variables unless absolutely necessary. Since they are shared by *all* scripts and MEL code, they can introduce hard to find bugs. It is far better to keep variables local to a given script so that there is no potential for conflict.

GLOBAL PROCEDURES

Like variables, it's possible to define procedures to be either local or global. Unless specified otherwise, a procedure is local. A local procedure is one that is accessible only in the script in which it is defined. All procedures in the script can access the local procedure, but procedures outside the script can't. This allows you to create self-contained scripts that won't cause any potential conflict with other scripts that may use the same procedure name. To define a procedure as global, simply prepend it with the `global` keyword.

```
global proc printName( string $name )
{
print $name;
}
```

This procedure can now be called from anywhere in Maya. Like global variables, global procedures share the same *namespace,* so there is nothing stopping another script from also defining the same procedure. The last-sourced procedure overrides any previous procedure definition. To reduce the possibility of this happening, try to create unique names for your procedure. For instance, rather than printName, use dgPrintName. While there is no guarantee that another procedure with that name doesn't exist, it does reduce the possibility. Also bear in mind that once a global procedure is sourced it remains resident in Maya's memory. By reducing the number of global procedures, you reduce Maya's memory usage. In general, try to limit the number of global procedures in your scripts to the very minimum possible.

MEL has a particular mechanism for searching for global procedures if they aren't already loaded into memory. When MEL sources a script and encounters a procedure that isn't already known, it attempts to find it. If, for example, a call is made to the procedure createSpline() and it wasn't already defined in the current script or already sourced as a global procedure, then Maya attempts to look for a script file named createSpline.mel. It searches through all its script paths attempting to find it. If the file is found, then it is sourced.

SCRIPT EDITOR

It is important to bear in mind that when using the Script Editor all variables and procedures you define are *automatically* global. This happens even if you don't include the global keyword. This may not always be what you intended, especially when you are experimenting in the Script Editor. Fortunately there is a way to circumvent this. Recalling that any variables defined within a block are immediately removed when the block ends, you can create a section of code that removes everything it defines. So when developing code in the Script Editor, simply enclose it in braces to create a block.

For procedures, this isn't possible. Since the procedure is being defined in the Script Editor, there is no concept of a local script. As such, all procedures defined in the Script Editor are automatically global, and there is no avoiding this.

3.2.8   Additional Execution Methods

MEL commands can be executed using a variety of mechanisms. The following example demonstrates how the same command can be executed in different ways:

1. `currentTime -query;`

2. `` `currentTime -query`; ``

3. `eval( "currentTime -query" );`

It is important to understand that the command still performs the same action, irrespective of how its execution is instigated. The different execution methods are provided simply to give you more control. In the first case, the command is executed but the result isn't returned. This is the most typical execution method. In the second case, the entire command is enclosed with back quote characters (`` ` ``). The command is executed as before, but this time its result is returned. In the last case, the command is called with the `eval` command. The `eval` command allows you to pass in a series of MEL statements, as a string, and execute them. It also returns the result.

COMMAND RESULTS

There is an important distinction to be made about how the results of a command are retrieved. Getting the return values from a procedure is very straightforward. If, for instance, you had a procedure `getUserName()` that returned the current user name, you could call it as follows:

```
$userName = getUserName();
```

The procedure's return value would be assigned to the `$userName` variable. Commands, however, can't be called directly when you want their return value. The `currentTime` command can be used to query the current time. Using it directly, as follows, causes an error.

```
$time = currentTime -q;
```

The command has to be enclosed with the back quote character (`` ` ``) as follows:

```
$time = `currentTime -q`;
```

Maya then evaluates everything in the quotes, finally returning the result. This result can then be assigned to the `$time` variable.

A common mistake is to accidently enclose the statement with the apostrophe or single quote character (') rather than the back quote character (`` ` ``). Using the apostrophe causes a syntax error.

EVAL COMMAND

The MEL language has a very powerful but little known feature: the eval command. It allows you to construct a series of commands on the fly and then have Maya evaluate them. This means that your MEL script can generate statements that can then be executed. In other noninterpreted languages, there is no way to do this. Instead you would have to write the code then go through the usual compile-and-link step to make that new code available. Consider the following statement, which adds two numbers together:

```
float $res = 1 + 2;
print $res;
```

Now what if you wanted to let users define their own calculations? Since you don't know in advance what they could possibly want, you can't write it directly into the script. However you could use the eval command to evaluate the users' statements at run time. The following procedure, which takes a statement as input then evaluates it, is defined:

```
global proc calc ( string $statement )
{
float $res = eval("float $_dummy = " + $statement);
print ("\n" + $statement + " = " + $res);
}
```

Now users can type the following statements into the Script Editor and execute them:

```
calc( "1 + 2" );
calc( "10 * 2 / 5" );
```

The procedure prints out the following results:

```
1 + 2 = 3
10 * 2 / 5 = 4
```

The statements were generated on the fly then executed. As such you can write your own script to generate programming instructions on the fly and execute them at run time. While this is a very simple example, there is no limit to the complexity of the statements that can be evaluated. It is even possible to have one script generate an entire program, as a series of MEL statements, then execute it using the `eval` command.

3.2.9 Efficiency

Since MEL is an interpreted language, it must interpret the script instructions in real time. As such this interpretation overhead can make it slower than compiled languages. There are, however, some programming practices that you can adhere to that can increase the speed of your MEL scripts.

EXPLICIT TYPE DECLARATION

First, declare the variable's type when defining it. So rather than define a variable like this:

```
$objs = `selectedNodes`;
```

explicitly specify the type of the variable:

```
string $objs[] = `selectedNodes`;
```

This speeds up MEL, since it doesn't have to determine the variable type based on what it is being assigned. This also means it can do better type checking.

ARRAY SIZES

When you use arrays it is more efficient if you specify the number of elements they will contain when they are defined. This avoids MEL having to resize them later. Even if you don't know in advance the exact number of elements in an array, it is still worthwhile to make a rough guess. This guess is likely to be closer than MEL's default array size of 16. The default is 16 elements, since this is how many floating-point numbers there are in a transformation matrix (4 × 4). For instance if you know that there are roughly a maximum of 50 elements, then specify that size.

```
int $nums[50];
int $avgs[]; // Defaults to 16 elements
```

Setting the size of an array doesn't prevent you from adding elements later. The efficiency gained by giving an initial size is due to the fact that MEL doesn't have to perform as many memory resizing operations as elements are added, thereby speeding up the execution.

3.2.10 Additional Constructs

The following MEL programming constructs, operators, and statements aren't absolutely necessary to writing fully functional MEL scripts; however, you may encounter them in other scripts, so it is worthwhile to familiarize yourself with them. Many are included simply because they make some statements more succinct, but there is nothing that they do that can't be achieved with the programming constructs already presented.

ASSIGNMENT CHAINING

It is also possible to assign more than one variable the same value by chaining the variables together as follows:

```
int $score, $results;
$score = $results = 253; // Same as $score = 253; $results = $score;
```

IN-PLACE ARITHMETIC OPERATORS

When using the basic arithmetic operators on variables that will also hold the result, the following operators can be used. To add a value to a variable and store the result in that same variable, write it using the addition-and-assignment operator.

```
$score += 3.2; // Same as $score = $score + 3.2
```

The other arithmetic operators use a similar form:

```
$score *= 2;
$score -= 4;
$score /= 1.3;
$score %= 3;
```

INCREMENT AND DECREMENT OPERATORS

When doing simple counting, 1 is added to or subtracted from a variable. This can be written more succinctly using the increment and decrement operators.

```
$score++; // Same as $score = $score + 1
$score--; // Same as $score = $score - 1
```

It is also possible to use these operators in their *pre* and *post* forms. There are different assignment side effects depending on which one you use. Rather than cause confusion, it is best not to rely on these side effects.

CONDITIONAL OPERATOR

The conditional operator (?:) can be used to reduce a syntactically longer statement into a shorter one. The following code:

```
int $a = 3;
if( $a > 1 )
  $score = 100;
else
  $score = 50;
```

can be reduced to this simple statement using the conditional operator:

```
int $a = 3;
$score = ($a > 1) ? 100 : 50;
```

The variable on the left side is assigned the value following the ? character if the comparison yields a true result. If the result is false, then the variable is assigned the value to the right of the : character.

SWITCH STATEMENT

The switch statement is used to turn what would previously have been a series of if statements into a more succinct and easily read form. Take the following series of if statements:

```
int $a = 3;
if( $a == 1 )
  print "a is 1";
else
  {
  if( $a == 2 )
    print "a is 2";
  else
    {
    if( $a == 3 )
      print "a is 3";
    else
      print "a is another number";
    }
  }
```

These statements are all comparing the original $a variable against some known value. A switch statement makes this type of coding easier to read and understand. This same code can be rewritten using a switch statement as follows:

```
int $a = 3;
switch( $a )
  {
  case 1:
    print "a is 1";
    break;

  case 2:
    print "a is 2";
    break;

  case 3:
    print "a is 3";
    break;

  default:
    print "a is another number";
    break;
  }
```

The value of $a is compared just once. Depending on the variable's value, one of the later case statements is executed. Each case statement defines which values it handles. The first case statement, case 1, is executed when $a is equal to 1.

At the end of each case statement is the break statement. The break statement is included to prevent execution continuing into the next case statement. The break effectively jumps the execution out of the switch statement.

The last case is the catch-all case, and is denoted by default. This contains the statements that are executed if the value doesn't match any of the other case statements.

There may be times when you want to omit the break statement for a given case statement. This happens when different values should all be handled the same. In the following example, when $a is either –1 or –2, the print "below zero"; statement is executed. For values of 1 or 2, the print "above zero"; statement is executed.

```
int $a = 2;
switch( $a )
   {
   case -1:
   case -2:
      print "below zero";
      break;

   case 0:
      print "zero";
      break;

   case 1:
   case 2:
      print "above zero"';
      break;
   }
```

FOR-IN STATEMENT

The for-in statement is provided as a shorthand way of iterating over elements in an array. Whereas iteration of an array is performed with a for loop:

```
int $nums[4] = { 4, 7, 2, 3 };
int $elem;
int $i;
for( $i = 0; $i < size($nums); $i++ )
   {
   $elem = $nums[$i];
   do something with $elem
   }
```

with a for-in loop, this can be reduced to just this:

```
int $nums[4] = { 4, 7, 2, 3 };
int $elem;
for( $elem in $nums )
   {
   do something with $elem
   }
```

3.3   SCRIPTING

For all but the simplest tasks, you'll need to write more than one MEL statement. While the Command Line is ideal for issuing short statements and the Script Editor is well suited to issuing several statements, there comes a point at which you need to write more complex MEL statements. At that point, it is best to save your statements into a MEL script. A MEL script is simply a text file containing all your statements. Once the statements are saved in a file, they can be recalled as many times as needed without the need to retype them each time. Scripting also opens up the possibility of using more MEL functionality, including the definition of your own procedures.

3.3.1   Text Editor

Since MEL scripts are plain ASCII text files, you can use almost any text editor to write and edit them. It is important, however, that the editor create only plain text. Applications such as Microsoft Word automatically put formating and other "hidden" information in the resulting file. Your editor must be able to write simple plain ASCII text, without any formatting information.

If possible, choose an editor that displays the current line and column position of the caret or cursor. When MEL finds an error in your script, it can give you the line and column number of the offending statement. You can then quickly go to this line and column in your editor if it supports this feature.

Also ensure that the text editor is using a monospaced font. This means that the width of each of the characters is the same. If not, it becomes hard to define a consistent layout for your statements, as some characters will be thinner or wider than others.

If don't have a text editor, it is possible to use the Script Editor, though I recommend this only for the simplest scripting. You can type the commands into the Command Input Panel then execute them. Since the executed commands are immediately put into the History Panel, they can be copied then pasted into the Command Input Panel to be run again. This can be tedious, to say the least. Also, many of the Script Editor's hotkeys (copy, cut, paste, and so on) are different on different platforms. Given this and the fact that the Script Editor's text editing capabilities are fairly limited, it may be best to learn to use another editor.

3.3.2   Storing Scripts

Scripts are most commonly stored in a text file with a .mel file extension. While it is possible to use any file extension, it is best to use the .mel extension. If a file name has no extension, then Maya will assume it has a .mel extension.

DEFAULT SCRIPT DIRECTORIES

Assuming you've created a script file, it needs to be placed in a directory where Maya can find it. Maya looks for user-defined scripts in a few different places. The root path that Maya uses to begin looking for your scripts is based on the user's login name. Under Unix this is just the *username*, while under Windows it is the name used to log in with. In the following example, the *user* is the directory in which the user settings are stored. The *disk_letter* denotes the letter of the hard disk where the settings are stored. The combined result is the *user path*, as follows:

```
Windows 2000:
    disk_letter:\Documents and Settings\user\

Windows NT:
    disk_letter:\winnt\profiles\user\

Unix\Linux:
    ~

Mac OS X:
    ~/Library/Preferences/
```

Underneath the *user path*, Maya will have created its maya directory and subsequent subdirectories. For all versions of Maya there is a common scripts directory. This directory is where scripts you use for *all* installed versions of Maya reside. If you have scripts that operate irrespective of the version of Maya running, then you'll want to place them there. Only if you are confident that your scripts can run under any version of Maya, and this may include future versions, should you place it in this directory. For the different platforms, this common scripts directory location is as follows:

```
Windows 2000:
    disk_letter:\Documents and Settings\user\My Documents\maya\scripts\

Windows NT:
    disk_letter:\winnt\profiles\user\maya\scripts\

Unix\Linux:
    ~/maya/scripts/

Mac OS X:
    ~/Library/Preferences/AliasWavefront/maya/scripts/
```

In general, you'll want to store your scripts in the `scripts` directory for the current version of Maya you'll be running. This is the directory that includes the explicit version number, for example, `maya\4.0\scripts`. Having your scripts in a version-specific directory ensures that you won't have incompatibilities with older or future versions of Maya. The version of Maya that you are using is denoted as *x.x* in the following examples:

```
Windows 2000:
    disk_letter:\Documents and Settings\user\My Documents\maya\x.x\scripts\

Windows NT:
    disk_letter:\winnt\profiles\user\maya\x.x\scripts\

Unix\Linux:
    ~/maya/x.x/scripts/

Mac OS X:
    ~/Library/Preferences/AliasWavefront/maya/x.x/scripts/
```

When Maya is asked to execute a script, it begins by looking in the version-independent `\maya\scripts` directory followed by the version-dependent `\maya\x.x\scripts` directory.

To get the current user's `script` directory, use the `internalVar` command.

```
string $dir = `internalVar -userScriptDir`;
```

CUSTOM SCRIPT DIRECTORIES

If you'd like to have your scripts stored in a custom directory, then you simply need to set the `MAYA_SCRIPTS_PATH` environment variable. While the concept of environment variables exists on all platforms, the exact implementation and methods for using them often differs. If, for example, you had your scripts in the `c:\myScripts` directory, then the environment variable can be added to the script path as follows:

```
set MAYA_SCRIPTS_PATH=$MAYA_SCRIPTS_PATH;c:\myScripts
```

When Maya looks for a script, it looks through all the scripts listed in the `MAYA_SCRIPTS_PATH` variable before looking in the default locations previously mentioned.

You can also set this environment variable by placing the following line into your `maya.env` file. Note that on Mac OS X, the file name is `Maya.env` with an uppercase *M*.

```
MAYA_SCRIPTS_PATH=custom_script_directory
```

If the `maya.env` file doesn't exist, then simply create it. The file should be stored in the user's main `maya` directory for the current version of Maya being run. This directory is as follows:

```
Windows 2000:
    disk_letter:\Documents and Settings\user\My Documents\maya\x.x\

Windows NT:
    disk_letter:\winnt\profiles\user\maya\x.x\

Unix\Linux:
    ~/maya/x.x/

Mac OS X:
    ~/Library/Preferences/AliasWavefront/maya/x.x/
```

To get the location of the current `maya.env` file from within Maya, use the `about` command.

```
string $envFile = `about -environmentFile`;
```

AUTOMATIC STARTUP

It may be necessary to run a series of commands or statements each time Maya is started. To do this, create a `userSetup.mel` file and place this in your `scripts` directory. When Maya starts, it executes all the commands listed in the file.

It is important to note that the Maya scene is cleared after the `userSetup.mel` script is run. Therefore any changes you made to the scene using the script won't be maintained.

3.3.3   Development Preparation

Unfortunately Maya doesn't provide any sophisticated IDE (integrated development environment) for developing scripts. However, it is possible with a little preparation to create a custom development environment that automates many of your development tasks. This initial setup is well worth the effort when it comes to working on many scripts.

Be sure to complete the steps in this section, since the resulting development environment is used in subsequent chapters.

The first step is to automate the process of opening a MEL script so that it can be edited.

1.   Select **File | New Scene**.

2.   Open the **Script Editor**.

3.   Enter the following text:

```
string $scriptsPath = `internalVar -userScriptDir`;
chdir $scriptsPath;
```

4.   Depending on which operating system you are using, add the following line:

```
Irix/Linux:
system( "editor learning.mel >/dev/null 2>&1 &" );

Windows:
system( "start editor learning.mel" );

Mac OS X:
system( "open -e learning.mel" );
```

Substitute *editor* with the name and path of your text editor. For instance, under Windows, you could substitute *editor* with notepad.exe.

There should now be three lines of text in the Script Editor.

5.   Press **Ctrl+Enter** to test the commands.

If everything went well, the text editor should start. Depending on your editor, it will ask to create the learning.mel file.

6. Save the empty file, then close the text editor.

7. From the **Script Editor's History Panel**, select the text of the two commands just executed.

8. With the left mouse button, drag the text to the **Shelf**.

   A shelf button is created containing the selected text.

9. Click on the newly created shelf button.

   The text editor starts, then opens the `learning.mel` script file. This shelf button allows you to quickly open and begin editing the script. From now on, this will be referred to as the **Edit Script** button.

10. Set the `learning.mel` script file to the following text:

```
sphere;
move 1 0 0;
```

11. Save the script file.

12. In the **Script Editor**, type the following:

```
source learning;
```

   A script can be sourced without giving the extension `.mel`. Maya automatically looks for a file with the complete name: `learning.mel`. Sourcing is explained shortly.

13. Press **Ctrl+Enter** to execute the command.

   A sphere is created and then moved one unit along the x-axis.

14. In the **Script Editor's History Panel**, select the previously executed command.

15. With the left mouse button, drag the text to the **Shelf**.

   A new shelf button is created, containing the text for the command. This shelf button loads the script and executes it. From now on, this will be referred to as the **Execute Script** button.

16. Select **File | New Scene**.

17. Click on the **Execute Script** button.

   The `learning.mel` script is loaded then executed. As a result, the sphere is created, then translated.

Even though this took a little time to set up, you can now quickly load, edit, and execute your script with just a few mouse clicks.

3.3.4 Sourcing

In the previous example you sourced the learning.mel script. Understanding exactly how *sourcing* a MEL script works is very important. A MEL script exists as a text file on the hard disk and isn't available in Maya until you source it. When a file is sourced, the following happens:

♦   All the MEL commands are executed in the order listed.

♦   All the global procedures are loaded into memory. They aren't executed unless explicitly called.

Once sourced, the MEL script file is no longer used or referred to. Maya has executed everything in the script file and now holds all the global procedures in its memory. One of the most common mistakes is to assume that if you now change your script and save it, Maya will automatically recognize those changes. It isn't until you source the script that Maya executes it and loads it into memory, thereby replacing any older version it may have. As such, it is important that once you change a script you immediately source it. If you don't source the newly changed script, then Maya continues to use the older script that it has loaded in memory.

The usual development cycle proceeds as follows. First create a script and then source it. Test the results of the script. Edit the script file then save the changes. Source the script file again and then test the result. Continue editing then re-sourcing until your script has been completely debugged and tested.

It is important to bear in mind that a script isn't automatically sourced when a scene that uses it is loaded. Unless you explicitly source the script file, the commands and procedures it defines won't be accessible.

If the script you want to source is in one of the known MEL script directories (see 3.3.2, "Storing Scripts"), then simply use its name.

```
source learning.mel;
```

In general it is best to always enclose the script file name in double quotes ("). This ensures that file names that contain a complete path or have spaces are correctly located.

```
source "learning.mel";
```

If the script is a directory not known to Maya, then its complete path must be specified.

```
source "c:\\myScripts\\learning.mel";
```

If the script file name doesn't include an extension, then Maya automatically adds the .mel extension.

3.3.5 Debugging and Testing

Unfortunately Maya doesn't come equipped with an interactive debugger. However, there are a few different options that assist in tracking down syntax and logic errors in your scripts.

SAVE BEFORE EXECUTING!

Before executing a script, or any MEL commands for that matter, be sure to save the current scene and any other relevant Maya files. There is no way to interactively terminate the execution of a script or series of MEL commands. If the script has entered an infinite loop or is performing a long process, it can't be cancelled. The only way to stop it is to kill the entire Maya process. At that point there will be no opportunity to save the current Maya scene, so any unsaved changes will be lost.

If the script completes but produces incorrect results, you could attempt an undo. However, the script may have called certain operations that don't support undo, so there is no way to roll back to the original scene. However, if the scene is saved beforehand, it can simply be reopened and the script reapplied.

An even better approach is to save a copy of the current scene, then apply your script to it. This way the original scene is never touched and therefore can't be inadvertently changed. Only when the script has been verified to work correctly should it be applied to the original scene.

SHOWING LINE NUMBERS

Unless you are the world's luckiest programmer, not all your scripts will compile and execute the first time without error. The most common errors are syntax errors. These are errors in which the text you've typed doesn't make sense to the interpreter, so it displays an error, then stops. The steps to locate and correct syntax errors are now covered.

1. Click on the **Edit Script** button.

2. Remove the semicolon from the `sphere` command so the file now appears as follows:

```
sphere
move 1 0 0;
```

This has clearly introduced a syntax error, since there is no semicolon separating the two commands.

3. Save the script file.

4. Click on the **Execute Script** button.

The Command Feedback line displays the following text. The text is drawn against a red background to indicate an error.

```
// Error: No object matches name: move //
```

Since you didn't include the semicolon, Maya assumed that the `move` command is being called as one of the arguments to the `sphere` command. This particular problem is fairly easy to debug since your script is so small. In a much larger and more complex script that contained many more lines, the error would be harder to locate. Fortunately Maya provides a way of indicating on which line the syntax error occurred.

5. From the **Script Editor** menu, select **Script | Show Line Numbers**.

6. Click on the **Execute Script** button.

```
// Error: No object matches name: move //
// Error: file: D:/Documents and Settings/davidgould/My Documents/maya/
4.0/scripts/learning.mel line 2: No object matches name: move //
```

This time a more complete error message is generated. In addition to the line number of the offending statement, Maya also lists the exact path to the script file.

The **Show Line Numbers** feature also includes the column number of the line in which the error occured. Take, for example, an error message with the following line reference, `line 12.31`. This error refers to line 12 and column 31. With this additional information, you can more precisely pinpoint the location of the error. Maya stores the setting of **Show Line Numbers** between sessions, so it will be active in future sessions.

TRACING SCRIPT EXECUTION

In Maya, there is a variable watch window so that you can see the current value of a variable during the execution of a script. It is not possible to set a breakpoint, then see the current value of a variable at that given point in the execution. Instead the old, tried-and-tested method of printing out explicit diagnostics has to be used. Depending on whether you want the diagnostics to be displayed in the main Maya window or to standard error (**Output Window** under Windows) you can use either print or trace, respectively.

The print command can print out the values of variables of different types, as well as arrays. As such, there is no need to use the string formatting specification as you would in C.

```
int $i = 23;
print $i; // Result: 23
vector $b = << 1.2, 3.4, 7.2 >>;
print $b; // Result: 1.2 3.4 7.2
int $nums[3] = { 3, 6, 7 };
print $nums; // Result: 3 6 7 (each on a new line)
```

With the added advantage of simple string concatenation, you can quickly develop a series of diagnostic outputs.

```
int $i = 23;
print ("\nThe value of $i is " + $i );
string $name[] = `cone`;
print ("\nThe name of the cone is " + $name[0] );
```

The trace command is used to output a string to the standard output. Under Windows the standard output is displayed in the **Output Window**. Under other platforms, it is possible to redirect this output to a file by launching Maya from a command line. In the following example, the standard output is redirected to the stdout.txt file:

```
maya > stdout.txt
```

Using this method, you can store a complete log of your script's execution by including trace statements throughout your script. For Windows users, simply right-click in the **Output Window**, then select **Select All**. Copy the text and paste it into a file.

The trace command works the same as the print command.

```
trace "\nAt the start of printName";
int $a = 33;
trace ("The value of $a is " + $a);
```

Another advantage of the trace command is that it can display the file name and line number of the script that issued the trace call. This makes locating the trace statement far easier. If, for example, the learning.mel script contained the following statements:

```
int $a = 65;
trace -where ("The value of $a is " + $a);
```

the trace command would print out:

```
file: D:/Documents and Settings/davidgould/My Documents/maya/4.0/scripts/
    learning.mel line 3: The value of $a is 65
```

This makes it far easier to locate which particular trace call printed out the information.

DISPLAYING WARNINGS AND ERRORS

To signal when a warning or error occurs, use the warning or error commands, respectively. As a general convention, warning is used when a nonfatal error is encountered and the script can continue execution. When a fatal error has occurred and the script can't continue execution, and therefore must be terminated, error is used. Both these commands print a message to Maya's command window. When Maya is running in batch mode, both types of messages are printed to standard error. This is typically the shell or command window that launched Maya.

The warning command prints the given message after the text "Warning: ". The Command Feedback line also displays the text in magenta.

```
warning "Incorrect size given, using default.";
```

Result:

```
Warning: Incorrect size given, using default.
```

The error command prints the given message after the text "Error: ". The Command Feedback line displays the text in red.

```
error "Unable to load image.";
```

Result:

```
Error: Unable to load image.
```

When the error command is called, execution of the script stops immediately, then an exception is thrown. The complete execution stack is then unrolled.

It is also possible to have the complete path to the script file and line number of the command call displayed. This is mainly for debugging purposes.

```
warning -showLineNumber true "Missing data file";
```

Result:

```
// Warning: file: D:/Documents and Settings/davidgould/My Documents/maya/
    4.0/scripts/learning.mel line 3: Missing data file //
```

The -showLineNumber option can also be used for your final scripts, which are released to users. When there is a problem, the end user can provide you with this extra information, thereby making your task of tracking down the problem that much easier. This option is also available for the error command.

RUNTIME CHECKING

Since your scripts may depend on many other scripts and commands in order to function, there may be a need to test before calling a procedure or command to see if it exists. The exists command is designed to test whether a procedure or command is available. If it returns false, you can then take appropriate action.

```
source simulation.mel
if( !`exists startSimulation` )
  error "Please reinstall the simulation software";
```

DETERMINING TYPES

If you are unsure about the type of a given variable, procedure, or other MEL statement, use the whatIs command. In this example, the whatIs command is used to determine what $a is.

```
$a = 23;
whatIs "$a";
// Result: int variable //
```

This example shows that arrays of variables can also be identified.

```
$objs = `ls`;
whatIs "$objs";
// Result: string[] variable //
```

The whatIs command can be used to determine if a function call is to a built-in command.

```
whatIs sphere; // Result: command
```

It can also be used to determine whether the statement is a procedure and where the source code for the procedure is located. If you execute these commands from the Script Editor:

```
proc printName() { print "Bill"; };
whatIs printName;
```

the following results:

```
// Result: Mel procedure entered interactively. //
```

If you have written a printResults global procedure in the learning.mel script:

```
whatIs printResults;
```

the following results:

```
// Result: Mel procedure found in: D:/Documents and Settings/davidgould/
    My Documents/maya/4.0/scripts/learning.mel //
```

whatIs can be used to determine if a statement refers to a script file. If it does, the complete path to the script is given.

```
whatIs learning;
// Result: Script found in: D:/Documents and Settings/davidgould/
    My Documents/maya/4.0/scripts/learning.mel //
```

3.3.6 Versioning

If your scripts have to run under different versions of Maya, you'll be pleased to hear that the majority of the MEL commands work without change. If you want to use a feature that isn't supported in a particular version, then you could possibly provide an alternative.

To determine which version of Maya is running, use the about command.

```
about -version;
// Result: 4.0 //
```

The following example shows how a script that supports only Maya 4.0 can stop execution if an older version of Maya is being run:

```
float $ver = float(`about -version`);
if( $ver < 4.0 )
    error "Only supports Maya 4.0 or later";
else
    print "Supports this version of Maya";
```

The about command can also be used to determine the current operating system.

```
about -operatingSystem;
// Result: nt //
```

If you need to load operating-system-specific scripts, you can do this by first querying the about command.

```
if( `about -operatingSystem` == "nt" )
  source "c:\\myScripts\\start.mel";
else
  source "~/myScripts/startX.mel";
```

3.3.7 Deployment

If you are the only person who will use your scripts, then leaving them in your local scripts directory is just fine. If you need to make your scripts available to a larger number of users, then you need to decide on a deployment scheme. The following instructions describe one way of deploying your scripts to a wider audience. Depending on your circumstances, another method may be necessary.

1. If you have a work environment in which all the users can access a central server, the task of deployment is greatly simplified. Simply create a shared directory on the server, for example:

    ```
    \\server\mayaScripts
    ```

    This example uses the UNC (Universal Naming Code) format. You'll use what path format your network system requires.

    If you don't have a central server but instead each user has his or her own local machine, then create a directory on each machine, for example:

    ```
    c:\mayaScripts
    ```

    Whether it be on a server or a local hard disk, this directory is referred to as the *script_directory*.

2. Copy the completed MEL script files to the *script_directory*.

3. On each of the users' machines set the MAYA_SCRIPTS_PATH environment variable to include the path to the script's directory.

    ```
    set MAYA_SCRIPTS_PATH=$MAYA_SCRIPTS_PATH;script_directory
    ```

    Alternatively, you could update each users' maya.env file to contain the environment variable setting.

    ```
    MAYA_SCRIPTS_PATH=$MAYA_SCRIPTS_PATH;script_directory
    ```

It is possible, but it isn't advisable, to store your scripts directly in the following directory:

Mac OS X:

```
/Applications/Maya x.x/Maya.app/Contents/scripts/
```

All Others:

```
maya_install\scripts\
```

It is always best to keep your scripts separate from the standard Maya scripts. This prevents your accidently overriding one of the standard Maya scripts with your own. It also helps simplify updating.

UPDATING

If users are already running Maya when you deploy your scripts, they won't automatically use the latest version. To do this they need to quit Maya then restart it. Alternatively, they could simply source the scripts. In both cases, this ensures that they are using the latest versions of your scripts.

3.4 OBJECTS

MEL is most commonly used to create and edit objects. This section covers the variety of commands devoted to objects. As mentioned earlier, all Maya objects are actually Dependency Graph nodes, so the process of creating and manipulating objects really involves creating and manipulating nodes. Fortunately you don't have to know the exact details of each object or node in order to use it. There are a lot of MEL commands designed specifically to access objects without your knowing their inner workings. Some commands can also operate on a variety of different objects.

3.4.1 Basics

The following covers some of the basics of object creation and manipulation using MEL:

1. Open the **Primitives.ma** scene.

    The scene contains three NURBS primitives: a cone, a sphere, and a cylinder. A very common operation is to get a complete list of objects in the scene.

2.   Open the **Script Editor.**

3.   Execute the following:

```
ls;
```

The complete list of objects in the scene is printed.

```
// Result: time1 renderPartition renderGlobalsList1 defaultLight ...
```

To get a list of just the surface shapes, execute the following.

```
ls -type surfaceShape
```

The result is as follows:

```
// Result: nurbsConeShape1 nurbsCylinderShape1 nurbsSphereShape1 //
```

You often want a list of the currently selected objects.

4.   Select the **nurbsCone1** object.

5.   Execute the following:

```
ls -selection;
```

The result is:

```
// Result: nurbsCone1 //
```

To delete an object, use the delete command.

6.   Execute the following:

```
delete nurbsCone1;
```

Alternatively, to delete the currently selected objects, simply use delete without any arguments. To rename an object, the rename command is used.

7.   Execute the following:

```
rename nurbsSphere1 ball;
```

The **nurbsSphere1** object has been renamed to **ball**. To determine if an object with a given name exists, use the `objExists` command.

8. Execute the following:

```
if( `objExists ball` )
   print( "ball does exist" );
```

Each object has a particular type. The `objectType` command is used to determine the type of a given object.

9. Execute the following:

```
objectType ball;
```

The **ball** object is of the `transform` type. This means that it is a **transform** node.

LISTALL SCRIPT

This script demonstrates how to iterate over all the objects in the scene and display their names as well as their types.

```
proc listAll()
{
print( "\nNodes..." );
string $nodes[] = `ls`;
for( $node in $nodes )
  {
  string $nodeType = `objectType $node`;
  print ("\nNode: " + $node + " (" + $nodeType + ")");
  }
}


listAll();
```

The procedure, `listAll`, is first defined. This procedure doesn't take any parameters or return any values.

```
proc listAll()
{
```

Having printed out the text, Nodes..., on a new line, the next step is to get the complete list of nodes in the scene. The result of the ls command is stored in the $nodes array. Notice that you had to enclose the ls command with the single back quotes (`) in order to get its return value.

```
string $nodes[] = `ls`;
```

You then iterate over every item in the list.

```
for( $node in $nodes )
  {
```

For each node you then get its type using the objectType command. The resulting type is stored in the $nodeType variable.

```
string $nodeType = `objectType $node`;
```

Finally, the node's information is then printed out. The information is the result of concatenating a series of literal strings as well as the string variables you stored earlier. It is very important that you enclose the entire statement in parentheses before calling the print command.

```
print ("\nNode: " + $node + " (" + $nodeType + ")");
```

When run, inside the **Primitives.ma** scene, the script generates the following output:

```
Nodes...
Node: time1 (time)
Node: renderPartition (partition)
Node: renderGlobalsList1 (renderGlobalsList)
Node: defaultLightList1 (defaultLightList)
Node: defaultShaderList1 (defaultShaderList)
Node: postProcessList1 (postProcessList)
Node: defaultRenderUtilityList1 (defaultRenderUtilityList)
Node: lightList1 (lightList)
Node: defaultTextureList1 (defaultTextureList)
Node: lambert1 (lambert)
... continues
```

3.4.2 Hierarchies

All surface shapes have a parent **transform** node. The surface **shape** node is therefore considered the child of the **transform** node. It is possible to have a **transform** node as the parent of another **transform** node. In fact you can create an arbitrary hierarchy of nodes with any number of children. Each of these children, in turn, could have their own children.

MEL provides several commands to create and navigate an object's hierarchy.

1. Open the **Primitives.ma** scene.

2. In the **Script Editor**, execute the following:

```
group -name topTransform nurbsSphere1;
```

The `group` command is used to create a new **transform** node. In this case it is named **topTransform** and has the **nurbsSphere1** added as a child. The `parent` command can be used to make a given node a child of another node.

```
parent nurbsCone1 topTransform;
```

The **nurbsCone1** node is now a child of the **topTransform** node. The hierarchy now appears as shown in Figure 3.3.

If the **topTransform** node is moved, scaled, or rotated, all the children are affected. Execute the following:

```
move -relative 0 3 0 topTransform;
```

Both the cone and sphere are moved upwards. To not have the parent's transform affect a child, use the `inheritTransform` command to turn this off.

```
inheritTransform -off nurbsCone1;
```

The cone returns to its original position. Moving the **topTransform** from now on has no effect on the cone, but it does affect the sphere. To see a list of the children of a node, use the following:

```
listRelatives topTransform;
```

The result is:

```
// Result: nurbsSphere1 nurbsCone1 //
```

To get a complete list of all children, including grandchildren, use the -allDescendents flag. To get a list of all shapes under a node, use the -shapes flag, as follows:

```
listRelatives -shapes nurbsSphere1;
```

The result is:

```
// Result: nurbsSphereShape1 //
```

Given a node, it is also possible to get its parents as follows:

```
listRelatives -parent nurbsSphereShape1;
```

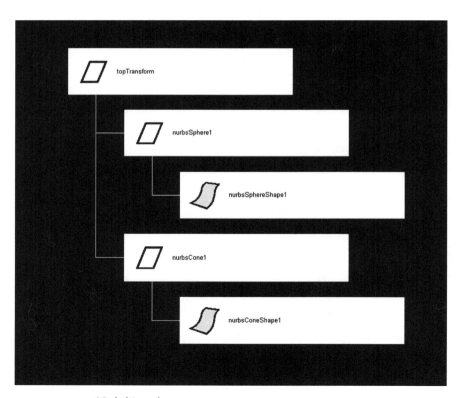

FIGURE 3.3 Node hierarchy

The result is:

```
// Result: nurbsSphere1 //
```

If the object was instanced, getting all the possible parents can be done using the -allParents flag. To change the order of the *siblings* use the reorder command. Use the following to put the nurbsCone1 first:

```
reorder -front nurbsCone1;
```

Reordering siblings doesn't have any effect on their parent-child relationship but simply changes their order in the list of children. To disconnect a child from its parent is the equivalent of making it a child of the world. The world is the topmost parent of all nodes. To disconnect the **nurbsCone1** transform, use the following:

```
parent -world nurbsCone1;
```

The ungroup command could also have been used. The equivalent would have been ungroup -world nurbsCone1.

3.4.3 Transforms

Almost all the objects in a scene (cameras, lights, surfaces, and so on) are stored as DAG nodes. The majority of these DAG nodes consist of a **shape** node with a **transform** node as the parent. The **transform** node defines the position, orientation, and scale of their child nodes.

1. Open the **Primitives.ma** scene.

2. In the **Script Editor**, execute the following:

```
move -relative 3 0 0 nurbsSphere1;
```

While it may appear that the **nurbsSphere1** node has moved, it is in fact the **nurbsSphereShape1** that has. The **nurbsSphere1** node simply holds the information needed to move its children. This information is stored in a transformation matrix. This matrix is then used to transform the children to their new position. So in this case, the surface **shape** node (**nurbsSphereShape1**) is transformed by the matrix resulting in its new position along the x-axis.

3. Execute the following:

```
scale -absolute 1 0.5 1 nurbsSphere1;
```

The sphere is now scaled down the y-axis. Rotating objects can be done using the `rotate` command.

```
rotate -relative 45deg 0 0 nurbsSphere1;
```

Alternatively the translation, rotation, and scale can all be applied at once by using the `xform` command. Execute the following:

```
xform -relative -translation 0 -2 3 -scale 0.5 1 1
    -rotation 0 0 10deg nurbsSphere1;
```

The `xform` command can also be used to perform a shear.

```
xform -shear 1 0 0
```

TRANSFORMATION MATRICES

While you interact with the transform by changing its individual components (scale, translation, rotation), the final result is a transformation matrix. This matrix encodes all these operations into a single structure. Transformation matrices have four rows and four columns: 4×4. To transform a point, postmultiply it by the matrix.

point' = point $\times$ matrix

The **transform** node holds the current transformation matrix. You can ask that Maya give you different types of matrices depending on which *space* you want to work in.

SPACES

When a position is defined, it is automatically relative to the origin (0, 0, 0). Such a position is said to be in *local space*. This is the space in which the point first exists and in which it hasn't undergone any transformations. All shapes have their points defined in this space.

Each shape has a transform node whose job is to transform the shape to *world space*. World space is the final space in which the shapes are drawn. When a shape has only one transform, this transform implicitly defines the local-to-world-space transformation. Take for instance a shape, **fingerShape**, that has a single parent **transform** node, **finger**.

finger | fingerShape

To transform a point in the **fingerShape** to world coordinates, simply multiply the point by the finger transformation matrix.

worldPoint = point × fingerTransform

When a shape's transform has other transforms as parents, then to calculate the final local-to-world transformation, all the parent transformations must be concatenated. Consider that the **finger** transform has other parents such as **hand**, then **arm**.

arm | hand | finger | fingerShape

Now to transform a point from the local space to world space, you need to concatenate all the parent transforms.

finalTransform = fingerTransform × handTransform × armTransform
worldPoint = point × finalTransform

Notice that the matrices are postmultiplied. This means that any new matrix is multiplied on the right of the existing matrix: **existingMatrix × newMatrix**.

1. Open the **Primitives.ma** scene.

2. In the **Script Editor**, execute the following:

```
xform -query -matrix nurbsSphere1;
// Result: 1 0 0 0 0 1 0 0 0 0 1 0 0 0 0 1 //
```

The transformation matrix for the **nurbsSphere1** is returned. Now try storing this matrix. Execute the following:

```
matrix $mtx[4][4] = `xform -query -matrix nurbsSphere1`;
```

Unfortunately this generates an error.

```
// Error: line 1: Cannot convert data of type float[] to type matrix. //
```

The problem is that rather than return a matrix [4][4], the xform command returns a single array of 16 floats. So the correct way to retrieve the matrix is as follows:

```
float $mat[] = `xform -query -matrix nurbsSphere1`;
```

The array returned is the result of flattening the two-dimensional matrix into a single-dimensional array. The following is a matrix with four rows and four columns:

```
[ a b c d ]
[ e f g h ]
[ i j k l ]
[ m n o p ]
```

Converting this to a single array results in the following:

```
[ a b c d e f g h i j k l m n o p ]
```

Each row is simply placed one after another. To access the single array using row and column indices, simply use this conversion:

```
arrayIndex = rowIndex * numberOfColums + columnIndex;
```

While it is possible to query the current transformation matrix, you can't set it using a matrix that you precomputed. The transformation matrix can be changed only indirectly by changing the **transform** node's **scale**, **rotate**, and **translate** values.

By default the xform command returns the **transform** node's current transformation. To get the local-to-world transformation matrix, use the following:

```
float $mat[] = `xform -query -worldSpace -matrix nurbsSphere1`;
```

OBJTOWORLD SCRIPT

The following script can be used to convert a point in a shape's local space to its final position in world space:

```
proc float[] transformPoint( float $pt[], float $mtx[] )
{
float $res[] = { 0.0, 0.0, 0.0 };

if( size($pt) != 3 && size($mtx) != 16 )
  {
  warning "transformPoint proc: pt must have three elements and
          matrix must have 16 elements";
  return $res;
  }

$res[0] = $pt[0] * $mtx[0] + $pt[1] * $mtx[4] +
          $pt[2] * $mtx[8] + $mtx[12];
$res[1] = $pt[0] * $mtx[1] + $pt[1] * $mtx[5] +
          $pt[2] * $mtx[9] + $mtx[13];
$res[2] = $pt[0] * $mtx[2] + $pt[1] * $mtx[6] +
          $pt[2] * $mtx[10] + $mtx[14];
return $res;
}


proc float[] objToWorld( float $pt[], string $transformNode )
{
float $mtx[16] = `xform -query -worldSpace -matrix $transformNode`;
float $res[] = transformPoint( $pt, $mtx );
return $res;
}
```

Unfortunately the MEL language doesn't provide for matrix multiplication of transformation matrices and vectors. Combined with the problem that transformation matrices are given as a single array, this means that you need to do this yourself.

The transformPoint procedure is designed to transform a point by a transformation matrix. The point ($pt) is given as an array of 3 floats. The matrix ($mtx) is given as an array of 16 floats. The procedure returns the resulting transformed point as an array of 3 floats.

```
proc float[] transformPoint( float $pt[], float $mtx[] )
{
```

It is important to note that the procedure assumes that the matrix defines an *affine transformation.* This is a transformation that consists of only a scaling, rotation, and translation. The scaling can be nonuniform. Since the transformation matrix is affine, the last column of the matrix is assumed to be [0 0 0 1].

The resulting point is defined and initialized.

```
float $res[] = { 0.0, 0.0, 0.0 };
```

The sizes of the $pt and $mtx arrays are then checked. If they aren't the right size, then a warning is issued and the procedure returns.

```
if( size($pt) != 3 && size($mtx) != 16 )
  {
  warning "transformPoint proc: pt must have three elements and
          matrix must have 16 elements";
  return $res;
  }
```

The point is then transformed using matrix multiplication. The resulting point is then returned.

```
$res[0] = $pt[0] * $mtx[0] + $pt[1] * $mtx[4] +
          $pt[2] * $mtx[8] + $mtx[12];
$res[1] = $pt[0] * $mtx[1] + $pt[1] * $mtx[5] +
          $pt[2] * $mtx[9] + $mtx[13];
$res[2] = $pt[0] * $mtx[2] + $pt[1] * $mtx[6] +
          $pt[2] * $mtx[10] + $mtx[14];
return $res;
```

The objToWorld procedure takes a point defined in the shape's local space and transforms it to world space. It takes a point ($pt) as an array of three floats and the name of the **transform** node ($transformNode). The resulting point in world space is returned as an array of 3 floats.

```
proc float[] objToWorld( float $pt[], string $transformNode )
{
```

First, the local-to-world-space transformation matrix is retrieved.

```
float $mtx[16] = `xform -query -worldSpace -matrix $transformNode`;
```

The point is then transformed by this matrix and returned.

```
float $res[] = transformPoint( $pt, $mtx );
return $res;
}
```

Following is an example use of this procedure:

```
float $pt[] = { 1.0, 2.0, 3.0 };
$pt = objToWorld( $pt, "nurbsSphere1" );
print $pt;
```

SPACETOSPACE SCRIPT

The following is a more sophsticated script that can convert a point from one space to another:

```
proc float[] transformPoint( float $pt[], float $mtx[] )
{
... same as before
}

proc int getInstanceIndex( string $nodePath )
{
string $paths[] = `ls -allPaths $nodePath`;
int $i;
for( $i=0; $i < size($paths); $i++ )
  {
  if( $paths[$i] == $nodePath )
    return $i;
  }
return -1;
}
```

```
proc float[] spaceToSpace( float $pt[],
                           string $fromSpace, string $fromNode,
                           string $toSpace, string $toNode )
{
float $res[] = $pt;
float $mtx[];

// Convert pt to world space
if( $fromSpace == "local" )
   {
   $mtx = `xform -query -worldSpace -matrix $fromNode`;
   $res = transformPoint( $res, $mtx );
   }

// Convert pt to destination space
if( $toSpace == "local" )
   {
   int $inst = getInstanceIndex( $toNode );
   string $attr = $toNode + ".worldInverseMatrix[" + $inst + "]";
   $mtx = `getAttr $attr`;
   print "\nInverse: ";
   print $mtx;
   $res = transformPoint( $res, $mtx );
   }

return $res;
}
```

The getInstanceIndex procedure returns the instance index of a given node. The complete DAG path to the object is given as $nodePath.

```
proc int getInstanceIndex( string $nodePath )
{
```

The complete list of all possible paths to the given node is retrieved.

```
string $paths[] = `ls -allPaths $nodePath`;
```

Each of these paths is then iterated over.

```
int $i;
for( $i=0; $i < size($paths); $i++ )
   {
```

If the path matches the given path, then you return its index. This is the instance index.

```
   if( $paths[$i] == $nodePath )
       return $i;
   }
```

If the path to the node isn't found, then −1 is returned to indicate that the function failed.

```
return -1;
}
```

The spaceToSpace procedure takes the point to be transformed, $pt, as an array of three floats. The possible spaces are local or world. The $fromSpace variable specifies the space in which the point is defined. The $fromNode variable specifies in which node the point is defined. The $toSpace and $toNode variables define the target space and node, respectively.

```
proc float[] spaceToSpace( float $pt[],
                           string $fromSpace, string $fromNode,
                           string $toSpace, string $toNode )
{
```

The resulting point, $res, is initialized to the original point.

```
float $res[] = $pt;
```

The point is transformed into world space so that it exists in a single common space. If the $fromSpace is already world then you don't have to do this transform; otherwise the point must be defined in local space, so it needs to be transformed to world space.

```
if( $fromSpace == "local" )
   {
```

The local-to-world-space transformation matrix is retrieved for the $fromNode.

```
$mtx = `xform -query -worldSpace -matrix $fromNode`;
```

The point is then transformed.

```
$res = transformPoint( $res, $mtx );
}
```

With the point now in world space coordinates, you transform it to the destination space. If the $toSpace is world, then you are finished. If it is local, then you need to convert the world point to the local space of the destination node.

```
if( $toSpace == "local" )
  {
```

Get the instance index of the destination node. It is important to use this since an instanced node can have different paths. You need the path index of the destination node to ensure that you get the correct transformation matrix.

```
int $inst = getInstanceIndex( $toNode );
```

The world-to-local transformation matrix is then retrieved for the destination node. This is the **worldInverseMatrix** attribute. This attribute is an array of matrices, one for each of the possible instance paths. You use the instance index to get the relevant matrix.

```
string $attr = $toNode + ".worldInverseMatrix[" + $inst + "]";
$mtx = `getAttr $attr`;
```

The point is then transformed by this matrix to put it into the local space of the destination node.

```
$res = transformPoint( $res, $mtx );
}
```

The resulting point is then returned.

```
return $res;
}
```

The spaceToSpace procedure can be used as follows:

```
float $pt[3] = { 1.0, 2.0, 3.0 };
$pt = spaceToSpace( $pt, "local", "nurbsSphere1", "local", "nurbsCone1" );
print ("\n From nurbs to cone: " + $pt[0] + ", " +
        $pt[1] + ", " + $pt[2]);
```

To transform a point in local coordinates to world coordinates, use the following:

```
$pt = spaceToSpace( $pt, "local", "nurbsSphere1", "world", "" );
```

To transform a point from world coordinates to local coordinates, use the following:

```
$pt = spaceToSpace( $pt, "world", "", "local", "nurbsCone1" );
```

3.4.4 Attributes

Since all of the scene data is stored in each node's attributes, you very often need to access and edit attributes. In order to get and set the various attributes of an object, MEL provides the getAttr and setAttr commands respectively.

1. Open the **Primitives.ma** scene.

2. Open the **Script Editor.**

3. Execute the following:

   ```
   $rad = `getAttr makeNurbCone1.radius`;
   print ("\nRadius: " + $rad);
   ```

   The result is:

   ```
   Radius: 1
   ```

4. Execute the following:

   ```
   setAttr makeNurbCone1.radius 2.5;
   $rad = `getAttr makeNurbCone1.radius`;
   print ("\nRadius: " + $rad);
   ```

   The cone is now larger, and the result is printed.

   ```
   Radius: 2.5
   ```

Notice that the call to setAttr wasn't enclosed in back quotes (`). Since you weren't interested in the return value of the setAttr command, you could call it directly.

5. Execute the following:

```
float $s[] = `getAttr nurbsSphere1.scale`;
print $s;
```

Since the **scale** attribute is of type double3, you needed an array of floats to store it. To set a more complex attribute's values, you need to separate it into separate setAttr calls.

6. Execute the following:

```
vector $sc = << 1.5, 2.3, 1.4 >>;
setAttr nurbsSphere1.scale ($sc.x) ($sc.y) ($sc.z);
```

The sphere's scale is set to the $s variable's components. It may seem more intuitive to simply call setAttr as follows:

```
setAttr nurbsSphere1.scale $sc;
    // Result: Error while parsing arguments
```

Unfortunately this causes an error. The components of the scale, or any other complex attribute, must be specified separately.

In the previous example, you knew the name of the object you wanted to get the radius from. What if you wanted to get or set an attribute of the currently selected objects?

1. Select all the primitives.

You will attempt to scale the height of all the objects by half.

2. Execute the following:

```
$objs = `ls -selection`;
for( $obj in $objs )
  setAttr ($obj + ".scale") 1 0.5 1;
```

The selected primitives' height is reduced.

DYNAMIC ATTRIBUTES

Each node comes with a predefined set of attributes. A **transform** node for instance has a variety of attributes for defining the translation, scale, and rotation of a transformation. Additional attributes can be added to a node. These may be used to attach custom data to a given node. For instance, a game may classify different objects in the scene as being either a weapon, potion, or obstacle. Associated with each object is the number of points it adds to the player's total as well as whether the object can be renewed.

1. Open the **Primitives.ma** scene.

2. Select the sphere object, **nurbsSphere1**.

3. Execute the following:

```
$objs = `ls -selection`;
for( $obj in $objs )
  {
  addAttr -longName "points" -attributeType long int $obj;
  addAttr -longName "renewable" -attributeType bool $obj;
  addAttr -longName "category" -attributeType enum
          -enumNames "Weapon:Potion:Obstacle" $obj;
  }
```

The attributes are added to the **nurbsSphere1** node.

4. Open the **Attribute Editor.**

5. Click on the **nurbsSphere1** tab.

6. Click on the **Extra Attributes** button to expand it.

The three new attributes just added are displayed.

If an attribute exists and you attempt to add it again, an error occurs. To prevent this, use the attributeExists command to determine if the attribute is already in the node.

```
if( !attributeExists( "points", $obj ) )
    addAttr ...;
```

This same command can be also used for preexisting node attributes.

In order to display the dynamic attributes in the Channel Box, the attribute must be made keyable. This means that the attribute can be keyframed. To change the **points** attribute to be keyable, use the following:

```
setAttr -keyable true nurbsSphere1.points;
```

Note that the order in which the attributes are displayed in the Channel Box is the order in which they were added. It isn't possible to change the ordering afterwards, so be careful about the ordering if this is important.

To delete a dynamic attribute, use the deleteAttr command.

```
deleteAttr nurbsSphere1.points;
```

A dynamic attribute can also be renamed.

```
renameAttr nurbsSphere1.points boost;
```

It isn't possible to delete or rename preexisting node attributes. These commands apply only to dynamic attributes.

ATTRIBUTE INFORMATION

What are all the available attributes of a given node? The listAttr command can be used to get a complete list of a node's attributes.

```
listAttr nurbsSphere1;
```

The listAttr command returns an array of strings (string[]) that hold the attribute names. The following example shows you how to iterate over the individual names and print them out:

```
string $attrs[] = `listAttr nurbsSphere1`;
print ("\nAttributes...");
for( $attr in $attrs )
    print ("\n" + $attr);
```

It is also possible to use filters to restrict the listing to particular types of attributes. To see only the dynamic attributes, use the following:

```
listAttr -userDefined nurbsSphere1;
```

All keyable attributes can be listed by using:

```
listAttr -keyable nurbsSphere1;
```

For all Maya's internal nodes, there is a complete reference document listing the nodes as well as all their attributes. Select **Help | Nodes and Attributes Reference...** from Maya's main menu to access this documentation.

To get general information about an attribute, use the getAttr command.

```
getAttr -type nurbsSphere1.points;    // Result: long
getAttr -keyable nurbsSphere1.points; // Result: 0
```

To get other information about an attribute, use the attributeQuery command.

```
attributeQuery -node nurbsSphere1 -hidden points;      // Result: 0
attributeQuery -node nurbsSphere1 -rangeExists points; // Result: 0
```

3.5 ANIMATION

MEL provides a lot of commands for creating and editing animations. Also many of the commands can be very useful for automating a lot of the typical animation tasks. While it is usually the task of an animator to define all the keyframes for an object, using MEL, it is also possible to create, edit, and delete keys. By programmatically generating keyframes, you can create complex animations that would be impossible or simply impractical through more traditional methods. It also possible to use a MEL script that takes a series of hand-animated keyframes and modifies them in some way. MEL can relieve the animator from a lot of the more mundane and tedious tasks thereby allowing more time for more creative work.

3.5.1 Time

Any discussion of animation must start with an exact definition of time. This is particularly important in Maya, since time can be defined in many different units, including frames, fields, seconds, minutes, and so on. Internally, Maya stores time in seconds, but it can display it in any convenient format. For example, time can be displayed as frames, even though it is being stored internally in seconds.

The current time unit is defined in the Preferences settings. Select **Window | Settings/Preferences | Preferences....** Click on the **Settings** category. The **Working Units** will be displayed. By default the time unit is **Film[24fps]**. Changing the time unit scales the current animation to match the new unit. For instance, if you had a key on frame 12 when the time unit was **Film[24fps]**, then changed the unit to **NTSC[30fps]**, the key moves to frame 15, since this preserves its relative location in time. At frame 12, using film units, it was at 0.5 seconds. Under NTSC it has to be moved to frame 15 to ensure that it maintains it location at 0.5 seconds.

Use the following command to determine what the current time unit is:

```
currentUnit -query -time;
```

To set the current time unit, use:

```
currentUnit -time "min"; // Set time unit to minutes
```

By default, Maya adjusts all the keyframes relative to the new unit so that the relative times of keyframes are maintained. To set the current time unit without automatically changing the location of any keys, use the following:

```
currentUnit -time "min" -updateAnimation false;
```

It is important to understand that all MEL commands operate using the current working time unit. If the time unit is set to **Film[24fps]**, the time is specified in frames. If it is set to **milliseconds**, it is specified in milliseconds. When writing MEL scripts, never assume that you know in advance what the working time unit is. The `currentTime` command is used to set the current time. It does not have the same result if the working time units are different.

```
currentTime 10;
```

If the time unit were set to **Film[24fps]**, this would set the current time to frame 10. If the time unit were in **milliseconds**, this would set the current time to 10 milliseconds. If you need to specify absolute times, irrespective of the current unit, you can append this to the time value. For example, the following command always sets the current time to 2 seconds:

```
currentTime 2sec;
```

You can use any of the following units after the value: `hour`, `min`, `sec`, `millisec`, `game`, `film`, `pal`, `ntsc`, `show`, `palf`, `ntscf`. Setting the current time to 1¼ hours can be done as follows:

```
currentTime 1.25hour;
```

The units that don't correspond to standard time value are given in frames per second (fps), as shown in Table 3.6.

TABLE 3.6 TIME UNITS		
Unit	Description	Frames per second
game	Games animation speed	15
film	Standard motion picture film	24
pal	PAL video format (frames)	25
ntsc	NTSC video format (frames)	30
show	Show format (frames)	48
palf	PAL video format (fields)	50 (2 × frame rate)
ntscf	NTSC video format (fields)	60 (2 × frame rate)

To be more precise, NTSC actually plays at 29.97 fps, so rendering at 30 fps requires you to drop frames in the final composite or edit. If outputting to SECAM, simply use the PAL setting, since they both have the same speed.

When you ask for the value of a given attribute, it will, by default, get the value at the current time.

```
currentTime 5;
getAttr sphere.translateX; // Get attribute at time=5
```

It is possible to use getAttr with an alternative time.

```
currentTime 5;
getAttr -time 10 sphere.translateX; // Get attribute at time=10
```

This feature can be particulary handy when you are getting the values of attributes from different objects at different times. You aren't forced to set the currentTime beforehand. Unfortunately not all commands provide this. The setAttr command, for instance, allows you to set an attribute's value only at the current time. Since changing the current time causes the entire scene to update, this can be expensive if you just want to change the time, apply some commands, then return to the previous time. Fortunately it is possible to change the current time without updating the scene. The following example changes the current time, sets a value, then returns to the previous time. Simply use -update false flag to prevent the update of the scene.

```
float $cTime = currentTime -query; // Get the current time
currentTime -update false 10; // Go to frame 10 but don't update the scene
setAttr sphere.translateX 23.4;    // Set the attribute value at frame 10
currentTime -update false $cTime;  // Restore the previous time
```

3.5.2 Playback

Maya provides a variety of commands to directly control the playback of the current animation. These options define the playback in Maya's viewports and not the speed of the final animation. This is considered the interactive real-time playback speed, since Maya is calculating the animation at each frame and then displaying it. The speed at which the animation is displayed in the interactive viewports is dependent on many factors including the speed of your machine, the complexity of the scene, and the 3D graphics card used.

1.   Open the **SimpleAnimatedSphere.ma** scene.

2.   Click on the **Play** button.

     A sphere moves from left to right across the screen.

3.   Execute the following in the **Script Editor**:

```
play;
```

     The animation is played. The `play` command is used to play the animation. It is possible to control the direction of playback and other options. Without stopping the playback, complete the following.

4.   Execute the following in the **Script Editor**:

```
play -forward false;
```

     The animation is now played backwards.

5.   Execute the following in the **Script Editor**:

```
play -query -state;
// Result: 1 //
```

     The state of the `play` command returns 1 if the animation is currently playing and 0 otherwise.

6. Execute the following in the **Script Editor**:

```
play -state off;
```

The animation stops.

The current playback options define the range and speed of playback. Using the playbackOptions command, you can alter these. It is important to understand the difference between the animation range and the playback range. The animation range is the total length of your animation. The playback range can be either the entire animation or a smaller subset. When working on a particular action, it is often best to reduce the playback range to the action while leaving the total animation range untouched.

1. Execute the following in the **Script Editor**:

```
playbackOptions -minTime 12 -maxTime 20;
```

The playback range is set to 12, 20. The animation range remains at 0, 48. Use the -animationStartTime and -animationEndTime flags to set the animation range.

2. Execute the following in the **Script Editor**:

```
undo;
playbackOptions -loop "oscillate";
play;
```

The animation now oscillates between playing forward and playing backwards.

3. Execute the following in the **Script Editor**:

```
playbackOptions -query -playbackSpeed;
// Result: 1 //
```

The playback speed is at 100%. To play back the animation at half its normal speed, use the following:

```
playbackOptions -playbackSpeed 0.5;
// Result: 0.5 //
```

It is important to understand that the playback speed is just a guide. More often than not, final playback speed won't match the current time unit setting. To see the actual speed at which the animation is being played, you need to display the frame rate in the **Heads Up Display**. To do this, turn on the menu option **Display | Heads Up Display | Frame Rate**. You'll notice that the rate varies. This is because the speed at which Maya can play back the animation is dependent on the complexity of the scene and its animation. If the scene is complex, Maya may have to drop frames in order to maintain the desired frame rate. Because it is continually evaluating and estimating how many frames need to be dropped, the result is an erratic final frame rate.

4. Shrink the current viewport to display all the viewports.

5. Execute the following in the **Script Editor**:

```
playbackOptions -view "all";
```

The animation is played back in all the viewports instead of just the current one. Certain playback options are stored in your preferences and so will be kept between sessions. The playback speed, loop, and view are some of those. To restore them to their default values, use the following:

```
playbackOptions -loop "continuous";
playbackOptions -playbackSpeed 1;
playbackOptions -view "active";
```

6. Click the **Play** button to stop the animation.

The playblast feature can also be controlled using MEL. In a playblast, Maya plays the current animation, storing each frame into an animation file for later playback. Since Maya actually captures the screen at each frame, it is important that the current viewport be exposed during the entire capture period. The following command does a playblast then puts the result in the test.mov file.

```
playblast -filename test.mov;
```

3.5.3 Animation Curves

FUNCTIONS

At its most fundamental, animation in Maya is simply the result of an attribute whose value changes over time. As you play back the animation, the value of an attribute is determined at each time instant. If an attribute is animated, its value varies from one time to another. The value that varies is said to depend on time. This relationship between a given time and another value can be defined using a mathematical function. In fact, other packages refer to animation curves as function curves. A function is defined as follows:

$$y = f(x)$$

This notation basically specifies that the function (f) takes an input value (x) and then generates a resulting output value (y). The function itself can be very simple or very complex. For this discussion it isn't important how the function generates its value. What is important is to understand that the function produces one value given another. Say you had a function that simply added 2 to the x value. This function would be written as:

$$y = x + 2$$

Given an arbitrary set of values for x, put them into your function and see what numbers pop out. Given a set of x values (0, 1, 2, 3) the resulting y values are (2, 3, 4, 5). If you put each x value with its resulting y value, you can create a point (x, y). Figure 3.4 shows the result of plotting these points on a graph.

Now if you draw a line through the points, you end up with a straight line. So the function $y = x + 2$ defines a straight line. Depending on the equation for the function, a different set of points will be generated, and when a line is drawn through them, different curves result. For instance, a smooth sine curve results if you set the function to be $y = \sin(x)$.

Now consider the x value to be time. As a new time value is put into the function, a different y value results. This is precisely how values are animated. By defining a function that takes time as input and pops out a resulting value, you get a series of varying values.

With this understanding, you can see that, conceptually, all of Maya's animation curves can be considered mathematical functions. For a given x value, they compute

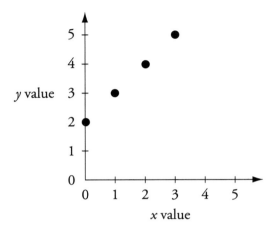

FIGURE 3.4   Plot of the *x* and *y* values

a resulting *y* value. When you create a series of keyframes, you are, in essence, defining a mathematical function. The advantage is that rather than write this as an equation, you can do it visually by adding and manipulating keyframes. Using Expressions, which are covered in a later section, you can actually define your own mathematical functions to animate values.

Another way of expressing this relationship is to consider that mathematical functions define a mapping from one set of values (*x*) to another set of values (*y*). Since animation curves are functions, they also provide this mapping. When creating a time-based animation, you are defining a mapping between time and some attribute's value. If you are animating the **translateX** attribute, for instance, you are defining how values of time are mapping to **translateX** values. A key defines this mapping explicitly. A key has an input and output value:

key = (input value, output value)

For instance, to define a key that, given an input value of 3, you'd like mapped to a value of 2, you'd create the key (3, 2). If you create a key for every input value, you would have directly defined the mapping from *x* to *y*. Alternatively you could define just a limited number of keys and have the computer determine the mapping where keys don't exist through interpolation. This is exactly how keyframe animation curves work.

In Maya, it is possible to map any value to another. In time-based animation you'll want to map time to some floating-point value. For instance, when you animate the translation of an object, you are defining a mapping from time to distance. The keys are of the following form:

key = (time, distance)

When animating a rotation, you are defining a mapping from time to angle, so the keys are of the following form:

key = (time, angle)

A *driven key* is simply a mapping from one value to another.

key = (input value, output value)

The driver attribute is fed into the input value and the driven attribute is set to the resulting output value. Understanding that time-based animation and driven animation are conceptually no different opens up a great deal of possibilties. You can map any input to any output. For instance you could map an angle to time. This would produce a given time value for an input angle.

key = (angle, time)

You could then feed this resulting time into some other animation curve that used time as input. There is no limit to the ways you can combine different types of mappings.

KEYFRAMING

An animation curve consists of a set of control points (keys) and their associated tangents. The control points define the keys of the animation. The tangents define how values between keys are interpolated. This interpolation can be defined in a variety of ways, including linear, stepped, spline, flat, and so on.

The process of creating an animation curve is greatly simplified by using Maya's various curve editing tools. These tools allow you to create and manipulate the curve points, tangents, and segments interactively. As well as using MEL to create curves interactively, it is also possible to use MEL to create and edit animation curves.

When an attribute is animated using keyframing, Maya automatically creates an animation curve and connects it to the attribute being animated. Animation curves are stored as nodes in the Dependency Graph. To get a complete list of all the animation curve nodes associated with a given node, use the keyframe command as follows:

```
keyframe -query -name ball;
// Result: nurbsSphere1_translateX ball_scaleX //
```

This shows that the node named **ball** has two animation nodes, **nurbsSphere1_translateX** and **ball_scaleX**. To get the animation curve node for a given attribute, use the following:

```
keyframe -query -name ball.translateX;
// Result: nurbsSphere1_translateX //
```

To determine if a given node is an animation curve, use the isAnimCurve command. The following example gets the animation curve node associated with a node's attribute, then determines if it is an animation curve:

```
string $nodes[] = `keyframe -query -name ball.translateX`;
if( isAnimCurve( $nodes[0] ) )
  print( "is animation curve" );
```

To determine if a node is animatable, use the listAnimatable command.

```
listAnimatable -type ball;
// Result: transform //
```

Alternatively you can determine which of a node's attributes can be animated by using the following:

```
listAnimatable ball;
// Result: ball.rotateX ball.rotateY ball.rotateZ ball.scaleX ball.scaleY
    ball.scaleZ ball.translateX ball.visibility //
```

The listAnimatable command can be used on the currently selected nodes by not explicitly specifying a node. In the previous examples, simply remove ball from the statements.

EVALUATION

To get the value of an animated attribute, simply use the `getAttr` command. This returns the attribute's value at the current time. This command could indirectly result in any input connections to the animation curve node being updated.

If you'd like to evaluate the animation curve in its current state, then use the following statement:

```
keyframe -time 250 -query -eval ball.translateX;
```

Using the `-eval` flag, you can quickly sample the animation curve at different times without causing the typical Dependency Graph update on all the curve's input connections. For animation curves that use driven keys, simply use `-float` in place of the `-time` flag.

INFINITY

The valid range of the animation curve is defined by the first and last keys. If your first key is at frame 10 and your last key is at frame 25, the valid range is 10 to 25. Any attempt to evaluate the curve outside that range will result in the animation curve's infinity value. A curve has a *preinfinity* and *postinfinity* setting. Preinfinity is to the left of the first key, and postinfinity is to the right of the last key. They can have one of the following settings:

```
constant, linear, cycle, cycleRelative, oscillate
```

By default all curves have preinfinity and postinfinity set to `constant`. When `constant` is used, the value is that of the next closest key. For preinfinity, this is the value of the first key, and for postinfinity, the value of the last key. To query the current infinity settings, use the `setInfinity` command with either the `-preInfinite` or `-postInfinite` flags.

```
setInfinity -query -preInfinite ball.translateX;
// Result: constant //
```

To set the infinity settings, use the following:

```
setInfinity -preInfinite "cycle" ball.translateX;
setInfinity -postInfinite "linear" ball.translateX;
```

KEYS

This section covers the creation, editing, and querying of keys on an animation curve.

Creating

1. Select **File | New Scene...**

2. In the **Script Editor**, execute the following:

    ```
    sphere;
    rename ball;
    ```

    You now create some keys for the ball's *x* translation.

3. Execute the following:

    ```
    setKeyframe -time 1 -value -5 ball.translateX;
    setKeyframe -time 48 -value 5 ball.translateX;
    ```

    A key is created at frames 1 and 48. When setKeyframe is called on an attribute that isn't already animated, an animation curve node is automatically created and connected to the attribute. To see which animation curve node is now controlling the **translateX** attribute, use the following:

    ```
    keyframe -query -name ball.translateX;
    // Result: ball_translateX //
    ```

4. Click the **Play** button.

    The ball now moves across the screen.

5. Select **Window | Animation Editors | Graph Editor...**

    The animation curve for the ball's **translateX** attribute is shown. You'd like to have the ball's translation control its *x* scaling. To do this you need to create a driven key.

6. Execute the following:

    ```
    setDrivenKeyframe -driverValue 0 -value 0 -currentDriver
        ball.translateX ball.scaleX;
    setDrivenKeyframe -driverValue 5 -value 1 ball.scaleX;
    ```

First, a driven key is created so that the ball's **translateX** becomes the driving attribute and the ball's **scaleX** becomes the driven attribute. At the same time, a key is created so that when the **translateX** value is 0, the **scaleX** value is also 0. Another driven key is then created. This key is set so that when the **translateX** value is 5, the **scaleX** value is 1.

7. Click the **Play** button.

The ball is flat while the *x* translation is less than 0. As the ball moves towards the *x* position 5, it expands gradually. Why does the ball stay flat until it reaches position 0? Since the range of the driven animation curve is from time 0 to 5, when an attempt is made to evaluate the curve outside this range, the preinfinity and postinfinity values are used. Since they are constant by default, the **scaleX** uses the value of the first keyframe, which is 0.

Now delete the driven animation curve.

8. Execute the following:

```
string $nodes[] = `keyframe -query -name ball.scaleX`;
delete $nodes[0];
```

The first statement retrieves the name of the animation curve node. The second deletes it.

Now insert a key in the **translateX** animation curve. Execute the following:

```
setKeyframe -insert -time 24 ball.translateX;
```

A new key is inserted between the two existing ones. Using the -insert flag, a new key is inserted without changing the overall shape of the curve.

Editing

1. Open the **SimpleAnimatedSphere.ma** scene.

2. Select the **ball** object.

3. Select **Window | Animation Editors | Graph Editor...**

The animation curve for the sphere is displayed. Currently only the **translateX** attribute is animated. In Maya, all keyframe animation is stored in an animation curve node. This node holds a list of keys. For time-based animation, each key consists of a time and float value. You will now use MEL to query and edit the keys in the animation curve.

4. Execute the following in the **Script Editor**:

```
keyframe -query -keyframeCount ball.translateX;
// Result: 2 //
```

Using the -keyframeCount flag, you can determine the number of keys in the animation curve.

5. In the **Graph Editor**, select the last key, at frame 48.

6. Execute the following:

```
keyframe -query -selected -keyframeCount ball.translateX;
// Result: 1 //
```

This returns the number of currently selected keys. To determine the time of the selected keys, execute the following.

```
keyframe -query -selected -timeChange ball.translateX;
// Result: 48 //
```

To get the actual value of the selected keys, use this statement:

```
keyframe -query -selected -valueChange ball.translateX;
// Result: 1.64126 //
```

To do the same operations but on all the keys, use the same statements but without the -selected flag. You'll now start moving the keys around. To choose a key to edit, you must specify its time. Execute the following:

```
keyframe -edit -time 48 -timeChange 20 ball.translateX;
```

This moves the key at frame 48 to frame 20. As always, you can specify time using any unit by appending it with the appropriate time-unit specification. For instance to edit the frame at 1.5 seconds simply use -time 1.5sec. By default, time changes are considered absolute. It is also possible to move keys by relative amounts. Execute the following:

```
keyframe -edit -time 20 -relative -timeChange 5 ball.translateX;
```

This moves the key at frame 20 to the right by 5 frames. The key is now located at frame 25. Movements to the left can be done by using a negative time change, for example, −5. To change the actual value of a key, execute the following:

```
keyframe -edit -time 25 -valueChange 2 ball.translateX;
```

The ball now moves 2 units along the x-axis at frame 25. As with time changes, it is possible to move a key's value by a relative amount. Using -relative in the previous example would have increased the existing value by 2.

If you don't know the exact time of a given key but do know its relative position in the list of keys, you can use the -index flag. Indices are 0 based, so the first key is at index 0, the second at index 1, and so on. Execute the following to move the first key to the left.

```
keyframe -edit -index 0 -relative -timeChange -5 ball.translateX;
```

More than one key can be operated on at a time by specifying multiple keys, using either the -time or -index flag. To move the first and second keys 10 frames to the right, execute the following:

```
keyframe -edit -index 0 -index 1 -relative -timeChange 10
    ball.translateX;
```

It is also possible to apply an operation to a range of keys. The range can be given either in time units or in indices. To increase the value of all keys between time 0 and time 12 by 5 units, execute the following:

```
keyframe -edit -time "0:12" -relative -valueChange 5 ball.translateX;
```

The only key in that time range is the first key. Its value is increased by 5. Using the range notation you can also specify just one of the bounds. To operate on all the keys before time 20, for instance, simply use -time ":20". Since the beginning isn't specified, the first key will be used. Note that the bounds are inclusive, so they include any keys on the range's boundary. Alternatively, to specify a time range starting at time 20 and including all following keys, use -time "20:". It logically follows that to select all keys using this notation, you'd use -time ":". Execute the following to move all the keys 3 frames to the left:

```
keyframe -edit -time ":" -relative -timeChange 3 ball.translateX;
```

This same range notation can be applied to indices. To change all the keys from index 1 to 20, so that they all have a value of 2.5, you'd use the following:

```
keyframe -edit -index "1:20" -valueChange 2.5 ball.translateX;
```

In addition to explicitly setting the time and value of a key, it is possible to scale the values. To scale all the key's values, execute the following:

```
scaleKey -time ":" -valueScale 0.5 ball.translateX;
```

A key's time can also be scaled using the -timeScale flag. The following scales all the key's time by half:

```
scaleKey -timeScale 0.5 ball.translateX;
```

Scaling happens about a pivot point. This is the origin used for the scaling. To use a different pivot point for time, use the -timePivot flag. To scale the keys about their center, execute the following:

```
float $times[] = `keyframe -index 0 -index 1
                          -query -timeChange ball.translateX`;
scaleKey -timePivot (($times[0] + $times[1])/2)
         -timeScale 2 ball.translateX;
```

The -valuePivot and -floatPivot flags can be used for using a different value and float origin, respectively. As a result of moving keys around it is possible that some keys don't fall on exact frame numbers. Currently the two keys are located at –2.752 and 26.248, in time. To put them back on whole frame numbers, execute the following.

```
snapKey -timeMultiple 1 ball.translateX;
```

The snapKey command can also be applied to individual keys by specifying them explicitly or using a range. The -timeMultiple flag doesn't have to be a whole number. For instance, you may want to have the keys snapped to half-second intervals. In that case simply use -timeMultiple 0.5sec.

Breakdown Keys

In Maya, there are two types of keys: normal and breakdown. The difference between the two is that a breakdown key's time is relative to the keys surrounding it. Unlike a normal key, which remains fixed unless you explicitly move it, a breakdown key attempts to maintain its relative time to the surrounding keys if they are moved.

To determine if a key is a breakdown key, use the -query and -breakdown flags.

```
float $isBreakdown[] = `keyframe -time $keyTime
    -query -breakdown $nodeAttribute`;
if( $isBreakdown[0] )
    ... // do something
```

To change a key into a breakdown key, use:

```
keyframe -time $keyTime -breakdown true $nodeAttribute;
```

Tangents

The direction of the curve as it comes into and out of a key is defined by its *tangent*. Figure 3.5 shows an animation curve with its tangents.

Each key has an *in* and *out tangent*. The in tangent is to the left of the key and the out tangent to its right. Tangents have the following properties: type, angle,

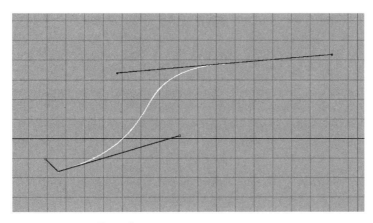

FIGURE 3.5   Example tangent types

weighting, and locking. The type of tangent defines how it interpolates values. Which tangent type is used determines how values are interpolated between keys. A step tangent, for instance, holds a value constant between keys. A spline tangent offers a smoother transition from one key to the next.

The angle of a tangent defines its direction. Weighted tangents allow you to move the end points of the tangents to get complete control over the tangents. Tangents support two types of locking. The first is general locking, in which the angle and length of the in and out tangents can't be changed. The tangents can be rotated, but they can't change angles individually. Also, their lengths remain fixed. Tangents also support weight locking. This is when the tangent weights are fixed so the tangent end points can't be extended or retracted. The tangents can be rotated however.

1. Open the **SimpleAnimatedSphere.ma** scene.

2. Select the **ball** object.

3. Select **Window | Animation Editors | Graph Editor...**

4. Press the **f** key in the **Graph Editor** to frame the current animation curve.

   The current curve is a straight line between the two keys.

5. Execute the following:

```
keyTangent -index 0 -outTangentType flat ball.translateX;
```

If the animation is played, the ball would start out slowly then speed up towards the end. If you want the ball to make a sharp jump from one position to the next, execute the following:

```
keyTangent -index 0 -outTangentType step ball.translateX;
```

The ball stays at its first position, then jumps abruptly to its second position at the end of the animation. Execute the following to restore the tangent to its original type:

```
keyTangent -index 0 -outTangentType spline ball.translateX;
```

The tangents at the first key are broken. Setting some tangent types causes both the in and out tangents to be affected. To change back, it may be necessary to change both tangents. Execute the following:

```
keyTangent -index 0 -inTangentType spline ball.translateX;
```

Now rotate the first tangent to 45 degrees:

```
keyTangent -index 0 -inAngle 45 ball.translateX;
```

All angles are relative to the horizontal x-axis and continue in a counterclock-wise direction. Tangents rotate since they are automatically angle-locked because the "spline" tangent type is being used. Rotations can also be relative.

```
keyTangent -index 0 -relative -inAngle 15 ball.translateX;
```

The in tangent angle has been increased by 15 degrees. To get the direction of the out tangent as a unit vector (length of 1), use the -ox and -oy flags.

```
float $dir[] = `keyTangent -index 0 -query -ox -oy ball.translateX`;
print $dir;
```

Result:

```
0.153655
0.988124
```

The same statement, but using -ix and -iy, gives the in tangent direction. Now unlock the in and out tangents so they can rotate independently.

```
keyTangent -index 0 -lock false ball.translateX;
```

In the Graph Editor, the two tangents are now drawn in different colors. Rotat-ing the out tangent should no longer affect the in tangent.

```
keyTangent -index 0 -outAngle 15 ball.translateX;
```

In order to give tangents a weighting, the entire animation curve must be con-verted to use weighted tangents.

```
keyTangent -edit -weightedTangents yes ball.translateX;
```

The curve now has weighted tangents. The tangent end points are now dis-played differently in the Graph Editor. It is important to know that the curve can become distorted when you convert a curve to use weighted tangents and then attempt to convert them back to unweighted tangents. An unweighted tangent loses its weighting information, so the curve is almost always different. Changing the tangent weighting of the second key can be done as follows:

```
keyTangent -index 1 -inWeight 20 ball.translateX;
```

Since the weights of both tangents are locked by default, you need to unlock them to have them weighted separately. You need to unlock the tangents as well as their weights.

```
keyTangent -index 1 -lock false -weightLock no ball.translateX;
```

You can now change the weight of one without it affecting the other.

```
keyTangent -index 1 -inWeight 10 ball.translateX;
```

The in tangent's weight has now changed without affecting the out tangent's weight.

When an attribute is first animated, Maya creates an animation curve. As you add keys, the tangent type and weighting are determined automatically by the **Tangents** setting in the **Window | Settings/Preferences | Preferences... | Keys** section. By changing this, you can ensure that all keys created from then on use the new setting. To query the current settings, use the following:

```
keyTangent -query -global -inTangentType;    // Query in-tangent type
keyTangent -query -global -outTangentType;   // Query out-tangent type
keyTangent -query -global -weightedTangents; // Query automatic weighting
```

To set the default in tangent, type the following:

```
keyTangent -global -inTangentType flat;
```

To set it so that all new animation curves automatically have weighting, use the following:

```
keyTangent -global -weightedTangents yes;
```

Key Clipboard

Keys can be cut, copied, and pasted. Maya has a clipboard into which the cut and copied keys are placed temporarily. From the clipboard, they can be pasted into the same animation curve at a different time or into another animation curve. An entire sequence of keys can be copied to the clipboard.

1. Open the **SimpleAnimatedSphere.ma** scene.

2. Select the **ball** object.

3. Execute the following:

```
copyKey -index 0 ball.translateX;
// Result: 1 //
```

The first key is copied to the clipboard. Now paste it to another time location.

```
pasteKey -time 12 -option insert ball.translateX;
```

The first key is inserted into the curve at frame 12.

The key's value is scaled by half. To remove a key and put it in the clipboard, use the cutKey command.

```
cutKey -index 1 -option keys ball.translateX;
```

To remove a key without putting it into the clipboard, use the cutKey command with the -clear flag.

```
cutKey -index 1 -clear ball.translateX;
```

EXAMPLES

The next few examples demonstrate how to create and edit keyframe animation curves.

PrintAnim Script

A common task is to iterate over all the animation curves and get their keys. This script defines the printAnim procedure that prints out the animation information for the currently selected nodes. When asked to print detailed information, it also prints the type of key as well as its tangent information.

```
proc printAnim( int $detailed )
{
print "\nAnimation...";
string $animNodes[];
float $keytimes[];
string $sel[] = `ls -selection`;
for( $node in $sel )
   {
   print ("\nNode: " + $node);
   $animNodes = `keyframe -query -name $node`;
   for( $ac in $animNodes )
      {
      print ("\nAnimCurve: " + $ac );
      $keytimes = `keyframe -query -timeChange $ac`;
      print ("\n" + size($keytimes) + " keys: " );
      for( $keyt in $keytimes )
         {
         $keyv = `keyframe -time $keyt -query -valueChange $ac`;
         if( $detailed )
            {
            float $isBd[] = `keyframe -time $keyt -query -breakdown $ac`;
            print ("\n" + ($isBd[0] ? "Breakdown" : "Normal") + " Key:" );
            }

         print (" [" + $keyt + ", " + $keyv[0] + "]");

         if( $detailed )
            {
            print ("\nTangent: ");
            $keyinT = `keyTangent -time $keyt -query -inTangentType $ac`;
            $keyoutT = `keyTangent -time $keyt -query -outTangentType $ac`;
            $keyinA = `keyTangent -time $keyt -query -inAngle $ac`;
            $keyoutA = `keyTangent -time $keyt -query -outAngle $ac`;
            print ("("+ $keyinT[0] + " angle=" + $keyinA[0] +
                    ", " + $keyoutT[0] + " angle=" + $keyoutA[0] + ")");
            }
         }
      }
   }
}
```

After you've defined the procedure, the first step is to get the list of selected nodes. You then iterate over every node in the list.

```
string $sel[] = `ls -selection`;
for( $node in $sel )
    {
```

Using the `keyframe` command, you can get a list of all the animation curve nodes associated with a given node. You can then iterate over the animation curves.

```
$animNodes = `keyframe -query -name $node`;
for( $ac in $animNodes )
    {
```

Get a list of all the key's times for the current animation curve.

```
$keytimes = `keyframe -query -timeChange $ac`;
```

The number of keys is the size of the $keytimes array.

```
print ("\n" + size($keytimes) + " keys: " );
```

With the list of key times, you then iterate over all the keys, since you can index the keys by time. It would also have been possible to index the keys by their order.

```
for( $keyt in $keytimes )
    {
```

Get the value of the current key. It is important that you specify the target key, in this case, using `-time $keyt` before you use the `-query` flag. If you don't do it in this order, the command will fail.

```
$keyv = `keyframe -time $keyt -query -valueChange $ac`;
```

When printing out detailed information, you print out the type of key. A key can be either a breakdown or a normal key.

```
if( $detailed )
   {
   float $isBd[] = `keyframe -time $keyt -query -breakdown $ac`;
   print ("\n" + ($isBd[0] ? "Breakdown" : "Normal") + " Key:" );
   }
```

The time and value of the current key is printed out.

```
print (" [" + $keyt + ", " + $keyv[0] + "]");
```

The tangent information is retrieved using the keyTangent command with the -query flag. Four different properties of the tanget are retrieved: inTangentType, outTangentType, inAngle, outAngle. The tangent types can be any of the following: spline, linear, fast, slow, flat, step, fixed, and clamped. The in and out angles define the angle of the tangents, which in turn define their direction.

```
if( $detailed )
   {
   print ("\nTangent: ");
   $keyinT = `keyTangent -time $keyt -query -inTangentType $ac`;
   $keyoutT = `keyTangent -time $keyt -query -outTangentType $ac`;
   $keyinA = `keyTangent -time $keyt -query -inAngle $ac`;
   $keyoutA = `keyTangent -time $keyt -query -outAngle $ac`;
   print ("("+ $keyinT[0] + " angle=" + $keyinA[0] + ", "
            + $keyoutT[0] + " angle=" + $keyoutA[0] + ")");
   }
```

The following is an example of the output generated by the printAnim procedure:

```
Animation...
Node: ball
AnimCurve: nurbsSphere1_translateX
2 keys:
Normal Key: [1, -5.3210074]
Tangent: (spline angle=8.426138245, spline angle=8.426138245)
Normal Key: [48, 1.641259667]
Tangent: (spline angle=8.426138245, spline angle=8.426138245)
AnimCurve: ball_scaleX
0 keys:
```

PrintTangentPositions Script

When Maya gives tangent information, it gives it as a direction and weighting. To determine the exact position of a tangent's end point, this information needs to be converted to Cartesian coordinates. The following script prints out the end positions of the tangents. It can output the tangents relative to their respective keys or as an absolute position relative to the origin.

```
proc printTangentPostions( string $animCurve, int $absolute )
{
print ("\nTangent Positions...");

float $ktimes[], $kvalues[];
if( $absolute )
  {
  $ktimes = `keyframe -query -timeChange $animCurve`;
  $kvalues = `keyframe -query -valueChange $animCurve`;
  }

float $xcomps[], $ycomps[], $weights[];
int $i, $j;
for( $i=0; $i < 2; $i++ )
  {
  string $xreq, $yreq, $wreq;
  if( $i == 0 )
      {
      $xreq = "-ix";
      $yreq = "-iy";
      $wreq = "-inWeight";
      }
    else
      {
      $xreq = "-ox";
      $yreq = "-oy";
      $wreq = "-outWeight";
      }

    $xcomps = `keyTangent -query $xreq $animCurve`;
    $ycomps = `keyTangent -query $yreq $animCurve`;
    $weights = `keyTangent -query $wreq $animCurve`;
```

```
    print ("\n");
    for( $j=0; $j < size($xcomps); $j = $j + 1 )
        {
        $xcomps[$j] *= $weights[$j];
        $ycomps[$j] *= $weights[$j];
        if( $absolute )
            {
            $xcomps[$j] += $ktimes[$j];
            $ycomps[$j] += $kvalues[$j];
            }

        print (" [" + $xcomps[$j] + ", " + $ycomps[$j] + "]");
        }
    }
}


proc testProc()
{
string $animCurves[] = `keyframe -query -name ball.translateX`;
printTangentPostions( $animCurves[0], true );
}


testProc();
```

The `printTangentPositions` procedure takes the name of the animation curve node ($animCurve) and whether you want to print out the absolute or relative positions of the tangents ($absolute).

```
proc printTangentPostions( string $animCurve, int $absolute )
{
```

If you need absolute tangent positions, you will need the positions of the keys associated with the tangents. All the keys' times and values are retrieved.

```
float $ktimes[], $kvalues[];
if( $absolute )
  {
  $ktimes = `keyframe -query -timeChange $animCurve`;
  $kvalues = `keyframe -query -valueChange $animCurve`;
  }
```

There are two tangents: in tangent and out tangent. You need to iterate over them both.

```
for( $i=0; $i < 2; $i++ )
    {
```

Depending on which tangent you need, you repair the command flags ($xreq, $yreq, $wreq) to retrieve their *x* and *y* vector components, as well as their weights. This could also have been written as a switch statement.

```
string $xreq, $yreq, $wreq;
    if( $i == 0 )
        {
        $xreq = "-ix";
        $yreq = "-iy";
        $wreq = "-inWeight";
        }
    else
        {
        $xreq = "-ox";
        $yreq = "-oy";
        $wreq = "-outWeight";
        }
```

The *x* component, *y* component, and weight of all the tangents are now retrieved.

```
$xcomps = `keyTangent -query $xreq $animCurve`;
$ycomps = `keyTangent -query $xreq $animCurve`;
$weights = `keyTangent -query $wreq $animCurve`;
```

You now iterate over every tangent.

```
for( $j=0; $j < size($xcomps); $j = $j + 1 )
    {
```

The *x* and *y* components make up the unit vector that points in the direction of the tangent. The weight defines the length of the tangent vector. By multiplying the unit vector by the tangent length, you get a vector that has the direction and length of the tangents.

```
$xcomps[$j] *= $weights[$j];
$ycomps[$j] *= $weights[$j];
```

At this point the vectors are relative to the key; that is, the vector is an offset from the key's position. If you want tangent positions relative to the same origin used for the keys, you need to add the tangent vectors to the key positions:

```
if( $absolute )
  {
  $xcomps[$j] += $ktimes[$j];
  $ycomps[$j] += $kvalues[$j];
  }
```

Print out the final position of the tangent's end point:

```
print (" [" + $xcomps[$j] + ", " + $ycomps[$j] + "]");
```

A small testing procedure, testProc, is created to test the printTangentPostions procedure. It prints the absolute tangent positions of the **ball** node's **translateX** animation curve.

```
proc testProc()
{
string $animCurves[] = `keyframe -query -name ball.translateX`;
printTangentPostions( $animCurves[0], true );
}
```

```
testProc();
```

Following is an example of the output from the script:

```
Tangent Positions...
[1.009253906, -5.311753494] [60.4534152, 14.09467487]
[32.76284582, 26.44183842] [8113845077, 34.77971043]
```

3.5.4 Skeletons

A skeleton is simply a hierarchy of joints. The joints simulate the internal bones of a character. Their hierarchical relationship (parent-child) is what defines the skeleton. By rotating the individual joints, a character can assume a given pose. Typically the model of a character is attached to the joints. This is done through a process of *skinning,* also known as *enveloping.* Now when the joints move, the model is affected. Each joint affects a portion of the model and causes it to deform as if the model were muscle and skin wrapped around the bones.

A skeleton is typically created by hand. This is because it is difficult to generate a skeleton for a given model automatically. Depending on the particular needs of the animation, the skeleton may require different joint configurations. For instance, a velociraptor model may need additional joints in the neck that a human model wouldn't.

In the event that you need to generate skeletons using MEL, use the `joint` command.

1. Select **File | New Scene...**

2. Activate the **top** viewport and maximize it.

3. In the **Script Editor**, execute the following:

```
joint;
```

A single joint, **joint1**, is created at the origin. Execute the following:

```
joint -position 0 0 10;
```

Another joint is created, **joint2**, and made a child under the first joint, **joint1**. Since the first joint was still selected, calling the `joint` command automatically adds the new joint as a child. You'd like to insert another joint between the current two:

```
insertJoint joint1;
```

A new joint, **joint3**, is inserted. It is now the child of **joint1** and a parent of **joint2**. The hierarchy of joints is now as follows:

> **joint1**
> **joint3**
> **joint2**

Notice that the new joint is located at the origin. Unfortunately the `insertJoint` command doesn't allow the specification of an initial joint position. To edit a joint's position after it is created, use the following:

```
joint -edit -position 0 0 5 joint3;
```

The joint, **joint3**, moved down. Its child, **joint2**, also moved by the same distance. Since joints have a parent-child relationship, wherever the parent moves, the child follows. Reposition the **joint3** node, and the **joint2** node follows. If you'd like to move a joint but not affect its children, then the `-component` flag can be used. Execute the following:

```
undo;
joint -edit -position 0 0 5 -component joint3;
```

The previous movement is undone, then the **joint3** node is moved but its child joints remain fixed. By default, all positioning is given in world space. It may be more convenient to specify a joint's position relative to its parent. Using the `-relative` flag enables this.

```
joint -edit -relative -position 5 0 0 joint2;
```

The **joint2** is now positioned 5 units to the right of its parent, **joint3**. You'll now cover some of the rotation options for joints. By default, a joint is created with three degrees of rotational freedom; that is, the object is free to rotate about the x-, y-, and z-axes. To get the current degrees of freedom use the following:

```
joint -query -degreeOfFreedom joint1;
```

The result is:

```
// Result: xyz //
```

This indicates that the joint is completely free. To reduce the possible rotations to just the y-axis, use the following:

```
joint -edit -degreeOfFreedom "y" joint1;
```

The new value for -degreeOfFreedom completely replaces any previous setting. Any attempt to rotate the joint about the x- or z-axis fails. It is also possible to limit the range of possible rotations on any given axis. By default there is no limit.

```
joint -edit -limitSwitchY yes joint1;
```

The rotational limits, for the y-axis, have now been activated. To query what the current limits are, use the following:

```
joint -query -limitY joint1;
```

The result is:

```
// Result: -360 360 //
```

Currently, the joint is free to move between −360 and +360 degrees. Limiting the range to 0–90 degrees can be done as follows:

```
joint -edit -limitY 0deg 90deg joint1;
```

Notice that the deg option was used for specifying the angles. Since you can't know in advance what the current angle unit is, it is best to specify the angle in the exact unit needed. Now rotate the joint beyond its limit:

```
rotate 0 200deg 0 joint1;
```

The joint rotates to a maximum of 90 degrees. To rotate a joint relative to its parent, use the following:

```
joint -edit -angleY 10deg joint3;
```

The **joint3** is rotated 10 degrees about the y-axis. It is important to note that all joint rotations using the joint command are relative. Only positioning of joints can be done in absolute coordinates. To query a joint's current rotation, use the following:

```
xform -query -rotation joint3;
```

The result is:

```
// Result: 0 10 0 //
```

To delete a joint, use the removeJoint command.

```
removeJoint joint3;
```

This command removes the joint, then automatically reparents any orphaned child joints to the deleted joint's parent. If the delete command has been used instead, the **joint3** node and all its child joints would have been deleted.

OUTPUTJOINTS SCRIPT

This script takes a hierarchy of joints and then outputs the position, rotation, and scale of the joints over a given time range. The output is stored to a file as well as being printed to the Maya window. This script works with skeletons that do and don't use inverse kinematic (IK) handles. As such, this script is particularly useful for exporting joint information to applications that don't support inverse kinematics. The joints' transformation can be output in local or world space.

```
proc writeArray( int $fileHnd, float $array[] )
{
float $v;
for( $v in $array )
    fwrite $fileHnd $v;
}


proc outputJoints( string $rootNode, string $filename,
                   float $startFrame, float $endFrame,
                   int $outputWS )
{
int $fileHnd = `fopen $filename w`;
if( $fileHnd == 0 )
  {
  error ("Unable to open output file " + $filename + " for writing");
```

```
        return;
      }

string $childNodes[] = `listRelatives -fullPath
                        -type joint -allDescendents $rootNode`;
string $rn[] = { $rootNode };
string $nodes[] = stringArrayCatenate( $rn, $childNodes );

float $cTime = `currentTime -query`;

string $spaceFlag = ($outputWS) ? "-worldSpace" : "-objectSpace";

print "\nOutputting joints...";
float $t;
for( $t = $startFrame; $t <= $endFrame; $t++ )
    {
    currentTime -update false $t;
    fwrite $fileHnd $t;
    print ("\nFrame: " + $t);

    for( $node in $nodes )
      {
      fwrite $fileHnd $node;
      print ("\n  Joint: " + $node );

      float $pos[] = `xform $spaceFlag -query -translation $node`;
      float $rot[] = `xform $spaceFlag -query -rotation $node`;
      float $scl[] = `xform $spaceFlag -query -relative -scale $node`;

      writeArray( $fileHnd, $pos );
      writeArray( $fileHnd, $rot );
      writeArray( $fileHnd, $scl );

      print ("\n    pos=[ " + $pos[0] + " "
             + $pos[1] + " " + $pos[2] + " ]");
      print ("\n    rot=[ " + $rot[0] + " "
             + $rot[1] + " " + $rot[2] + " ]");
      print ("\n    scl=[ " + $scl[0] + " "
             + $scl[1] + " " + $scl[2] + " ]");
      }
    }
```

```
currentTime -update false $cTime;

fclose $fileHnd;
}
```

Before examining the script, look at it in action.

1. Open the **IKChain.ma** scene.

    The scene consists of a skeleton hierarchy controlled by an IK handle.

2. Click on the **Play** button.

    The chain of joints moves from left to right.

3. In the **Script Editor**, enter the preceding script text, then execute it.

4. Execute the following. Substitute another file name if this one won't work on your machine or operating system.

    ```
    outputJoints( "joint1", "c:\\temp\\joints.txt", 1, 10, false );
    ```

    The joint information is output for all frames from frame 1 to frame 10. The transformations are output in object space. Following is the result:

    ```
    Outputting joints...
    Frame: 1
      Joint: joint1
        pos=[ -12.03069362 4.785929251 2.314326079e-007 ]
        rot=[ -2.770645083e-006 -3.756997063e-007 50.410438 ]
        scl=[ 1 1 1 ]
      Joint: |joint1|joint2|joint3|joint4
        pos=[ 7.326328636 8.071497782e-017 7.585667703 ]
        rot=[ 0 0 0 ]
        scl=[ 1 1 1 ]
    ...
    ```

    This joint information is also written to the given file.

    Now look at the script in detail. A simple utility procedure, writeArray, is defined that outputs the given array ($array) to the file ($fileHnd).

```
proc writeArray( int $fileHnd, float $array[] )
{
float $v;
for( $v in $array )
    fwrite $fileHnd $v;
}
```

The outputJoints procedure is then defined. It takes the name of the root joint in the skeleton ($rootNode), as well as the name of the output file ($filename). The range of animation is given by the $startFrame and $endFrame variables. Finally, the $outputWS variable determines whether the transformations are output in world or object space.

```
proc outputJoints( string $rootNode, string $filename,
                   float $startFrame, float $endFrame, int $outputWS )
{
```

The file is opened using the fopen command. It returns a file handle. All subsequent file calls then use this handle.

```
int $fileHnd = `fopen $filename w`;
```

If the returned file handle is zero, then the file opening failed. Notify the user of this, then return.

```
if( $fileHnd == 0 )
  {
  error ("Unable to open output file " + $filename + " for writing");
  return;
  }
```

Get a list of all the child joints.

```
string $childNodes[] = `listRelatives -fullPath -type joint
                        -allDescendents $rootNode`;
```

Create a list of all the skeleton joints by adding the root node as the first, followed by all the children. Since the stringArrayCatenate procedure needs two input arrays, the $rootNode node is put into a temporary array, $rn.

```
string $rn[] = { $rootNode };
string $nodes[] = stringArrayCatenate( $rn, $childNodes );
```

Store the current time. You'll want to return to it later.

```
float $cTime = `currentTime -query`;
```

The $spaceFlag defines in which space you'll retrieve the transformation information.

```
string $spaceFlag = ($outputWS) ? "-worldSpace" : "-objectSpace";
```

You then iterate over every frame in the given range.

```
float $t;
for( $t = $startFrame; $t <= $endFrame; $t++ )
    {
```

The current time is set to time $t. Notice that the scene isn't updated, only the time is set.

```
currentTime -update false $t;
```

The time is output to the file as well as to the screen.

```
fwrite $fileHnd $t;
print ("\nFrame: " + $t);
```

Each joint node is then iterated.

```
for( $node in $nodes )
    {
```

The node's name is output to the file and the screen.

```
fwrite $fileHnd $node;
print ("\n  Joint: " + $node );
```

The translation, rotation, and scale are retrieved for the current joint. The request for the scale has to include the -relative flag since you can't get the absolute scaling.

```
float $pos[] =  `xform $spaceFlag -query -translation $node`;
float $rot[] =  `xform $spaceFlag -query -rotation $node`;
float $scl[] =  `xform $spaceFlag -query -relative
                                  -scale $node`;
```

The transformation information is written to the file as well as to the screen.

```
writeArray( $fileHnd, $pos );
writeArray( $fileHnd, $rot );
writeArray( $fileHnd, $scl );

print ("\n    pos=[ " + $pos[0] + " "
       + $pos[1] + " " + $pos[2] + " ]");
print ("\n    rot=[ " + $rot[0] + " "
       + $rot[1] + " " + $rot[2] + " ]");
print ("\n    scl=[ " + $scl[0] + " "
       + $scl[1] + " " + $scl[2] + " ]");
   }
}
```

The current time is restored to the previous time.

```
currentTime -update false $cTime;
```

The output file is now closed. It is very important to explicitly close the file when you are finished with it.

```
fclose $fileHnd;
}
```

The fopen command is used to open a file in binary mode. It isn't possible to open a file in text mode with this command. It is important to remember this if you intend on reading the file in another application.

SCALESKELETON SCRIPT

A relatively common task is to take a skeleton and adapt it to a smaller or larger character. Simply doing a scale on a skeleton often won't give the intended result. The problem is that a scale enlarges or reduces the skeleton about the root's origin. What is really needed is that each joint be enlarged or reduced along its bone's direction. Figure 3.6 shows the result of applying a simple scale operation (scale 0.5 0.5 0.5) to the original skeleton. It is clear that the proportions haven't been maintained. Using the scaleSkeleton script, however, produces the scaling you'd expect.

The ScaleSkeleton script is surprisingly small.

```
proc scaleSkeleton( string $rootNode, float $scale )
{
string $childs[] = `listRelatives -fullPath
                    -type joint -allDescendents $rootNode`;
for( $child in $childs )
  {
  float $pos[] = `joint -query -relative -position $child`;
  $pos[0] *= $scale;
  $pos[1] *= $scale;
  $pos[2] *= $scale;
  joint -edit -relative -position $pos[0] $pos[1] $pos[2] $child;
  }
}
```

First the scaleSkeleton procedure, which takes the root node of the skeleton ($rootNode) and the scale ($scale), is defined.

```
proc scaleSkeleton( string $rootNode, float $scale )
{
```

A complete list of all the joint nodes under the root node is then created using the listRelatives command. This list includes all descendants and not just the direct children.

```
string $childs[] = `listRelatives -fullPath
                    -type joint -allDescendents $rootNode`;
```

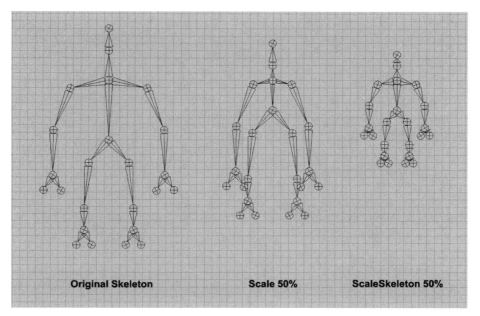

Original Skeleton   Scale 50%   ScaleSkeleton 50%

FIGURE 3.6   Incorrect and correct scaling

It is very important that the complete path to the children be used. Some of the children have the same name so aren't unique and when used in later statements would cause problems. In fact Maya would complain that the node name wasn't unique. However their complete paths (which include their ancestors) are unique, so the complete path is used.

Each of the children is then iterated over.

```
for( $child in $childs )
  {
```

The current position of the joint, relative to its parent, is then retrieved.

```
float $pos[] = `joint -query -relative -position $child`;
```

This position, $pos, is then scaled by the $scale amount. The position is the vector from the parent's center to the joint's center. This vector is therefore pointing in the same direction as the bone between the two joints. By scaling this vector, you effectively move the child joint's center closer to or farther from the parent.

```
$pos[0] *= $scale;
$pos[1] *= $scale;
$pos[2] *= $scale;
```

Finally the joint's new relative position is set.

```
joint -edit -relative -position $pos[0] $pos[1] $pos[2] $child;
```

For the case of a joint, its center is simple since a node's position relative to its parent is simply its translation.

To see an example of the procedure applied to a skeleton, complete the following:

1. Open the **Skeleton.ma** scene.

2. Define the preceding scaleSkeleton procedure.

3. Execute the following:

```
scaleSkeleton( "rootJoint", 0.5 );
```

The skeleton is now scaled proportionately by 50%.

COPYSKELETONMOTION SCRIPT

After you animate a single character, there is often a need to reapply this animation to another character. As long as the two characters share the same skeleton structure, the process of copying the animation from one to the other is relatively simple.

```
proc copySkeletonMotion( string $srcRootNode, string $destRootNode )
{
float $srcPos[] = `xform -query -worldSpace -translation $srcRootNode`;
float $destPos[] = `xform -query -worldSpace -translation $destRootNode`;

string $srcNodes[] = `listRelatives -fullPath
                        -allDescendents $srcRootNode`;
$srcNodes[ size($srcNodes) ] = $srcRootNode;

string $destNodes[] = `listRelatives -fullPath
                         -allDescendents $destRootNode`;
```

```
$destNodes[ size($destNodes) ] = $destRootNode;

if( size($srcNodes) != size($destNodes) )
  {
  error "Source skeleton and destination skeleton are
          structurely different";
  return;
  }

string $attrs[] = { "translateX", "translateY", "translateZ",
                    "scaleX", "scaleY", "scaleZ",
                    "rotateX", "rotateY", "rotateZ" };

int $i;
for( $i=0; $i < size($srcNodes); $i++ )
  {
  for( $attr in $attrs )
      {
      string $inPlugs[] = `listConnections -plugs yes
                          -destination yes
                          ($srcNodes[$i] + "." + $attr)`;
      if( size($inPlugs) )
         {
         string $tokens[];
         tokenize $inPlugs[0] "." $tokens;
         string $inNode = $tokens[0];
         string $inAttr = $tokens[1];

         string $dupInNodes[] = `duplicate -upstreamNodes $inNode`;
         connectAttr -force
                     ($dupInNodes[0] + "." + $inAttr)
                     ($destNodes[$i] + "." + $attr);
         }
      else
         {
         $res = `getAttr ($srcNodes[$i] + "." + $attr)`;
         setAttr ($destNodes[$i] + "." + $attr) $res;
         }
      }
  }
```

```
string $moveRoot;
string $parentNodes[] = `listRelatives -parent $destRootNode`;
string $found = `match "_moveSkeleton" $parentNodes[0]`;
if( size($found) )
    $moveRoot = $parentNodes[0];
else
    $moveRoot = `group -name "_moveSkeleton" -world $destRootNode`;

move -worldSpace
    ($destPos[0] - $srcPos[0])
    ($destPos[1] - $srcPos[1])
    ($destPos[2] - $srcPos[0]) $moveRoot;
}
```

Before explaining the individual sections of the script, first look at its result.

1. Open the **SkeletonMotion.ma** scene.

    The scene consists of two skeletons. The root nodes of the skeletons are **leadDancer** and **copyDancer**, respectively.

2. Click on the **Play** button.

    The **leadDancer** skeleton has some basic animation applied.

3. In the **Script Editor**, enter the preceding **copySkeletonMotion** script, then execute it.

4. Execute the following:

    ```
    copySkeletonMotion( "leadDancer", "copyDancer" );
    ```

5. Click on the **Play** button.

    The **copyDancer** skeleton now has the same animation as the **leadDancer**. Notice that the **copyDancer** now has a new parent, **_moveSkeleton**. Since the translation values are copied exactly from the **leadDancer** to the **copyDancer**, it follows that they will have the same position. Instead you'd like the **copyDancer** to move the same as the **leadDancer**, but relative to its initial position. To do this, a new transform, **_moveSkeleton**, was created and translated by the difference in the initial positions of the two skeletons. The **copyDancer** has an exact copy of the **leadDancer**'s translations, but the new parent node, **_moveSkeleton**, ensures that it is relative to its initial position.

The copySkeletonMotion procedure is defined to take the source skeleton root node ($srcRootNode) and the destination skeleton root node ($destRootNode). The animation from the source node's hierarchy is copied to the destination node's hierarchy.

```
proc copySkeletonMotion( string $srcRootNode, string $destRootNode )
{
```

The world space positions of the two root nodes are then determined. These are used later to move the new transform parent. Note that the initial position is calculated at the current time. If you'd like the initial position to happen at an absolute time, use currentTime to move to that time beforehand.

```
float $srcPos[] = `xform -query -worldSpace -translation $srcRootNode`;
float $destPos[] = `xform -query -worldSpace -translation $destRootNode`;
```

The complete list of all child joint nodes in the source skeleton is retrieved.

```
string $srcNodes[] = `listRelatives -fullPath
                     -children -type joint
                     -allDescendents $srcRootNode`;
```

The root node is also added to the list. The list now contains all the source joint nodes from the source skeleton.

```
$srcNodes[ size($srcNodes) ] = $srcRootNode;
```

The complete list of all child joint nodes of the destination skeleton is retrieved.

```
string $destNodes[] = `listRelatives -fullPath
                      -children -type joint
                      -allDescendents $destRootNode`;
```

The root node is added to the list.

```
$destNodes[ size($destNodes) ] = $destRootNode;
```

If the size of the two arrays is different, then you have a problem. This indicates that the two skeleton hierarchies are different. In this case you exit the procedure after displaying an error. Note that this isn't an exhaustive test of whether the two skeletons are structurally the same. When designing your own procedure, do more detailed checking.

```
if( size($srcNodes) != size($destNodes) )
    {
    error "Source skeleton and destination skeleton are structurely different";
    return;
    }
```

A list of all the animated parameters you want to copy is then created. If you want to copy other attributes, then simply add them to this list.

```
string $attrs[] = { "translateX", "translateY", "translateZ",
                    "scaleX", "scaleY", "scaleZ",
                    "rotateX", "rotateY", "rotateZ" };
```

You iterate over all the source joint nodes.

```
for( $i=0; $i < size($srcNodes); $i++ )
    {
```

For each joint node, you then iterate over its attributes.

```
for( $attr in $attrs )
    {
```

You retrieve the incoming connection to the current attribute.

```
string $inPlugs[] = `listConnections -plugs yes
                    -destination yes
                    ($srcNodes[$i] + "." + $attr)`;
```

If there is an incoming connection, the attribute is being controlled by another node. In most cases, though not always, this is an animation curve feeding its output into the attribute.

```
if( size($inPlugs) )
   {
```

Since there is a connection, you then take the plug and break it into pieces. A plug is of the form:

<node_name>.<attribute_name>

For example, sphere.translateX. You want to break the plug into its node name ($inNode) and attribute name ($inAttr). The tokenize command is used to do this.

```
string $tokens[];
tokenize $inPlugs[0] "." $tokens;
string $inNode = $tokens[0];
string $inAttr = $tokens[1];
```

Given the incoming node, you then duplicate it as well as any of its upstream connections. This gives use of a complete duplicate of all nodes that directly, or indirectly, feed into the attribute.

```
string $dupInNodes[] = `duplicate -upstreamNodes $inNode`;
```

Connect the new duplicate node's output attribute to the destination node's attribute.

```
connectAttr -force
            ($dupInNodes[0] + "." + $inAttr)
            ($destNodes[$i] + "." + $attr);
```

If you'd like to have both skeletons *always* to have the same animation, then don't do a duplicate but instead connect the plug directly into the destination node's attribute. This would be done as follows:

```
connectAttr -force
            ($srcNodes[$i] + "." + $inAttr)
            ($destNodes[$i] + "." + $attr);
```

If the attribute doesn't have any input connections, then it mustn't be animated or controlled externally. In that case simply copy the attribute values from the source node to the destination node.

```
    else
      {
      $res = `getAttr ($srcNodes[$i] + "." + $attr)`;
      setAttr ($destNodes[$i] + "." + $attr) $res;
      }
    }
}
```

The destination skeleton now has a duplicate of the source skeleton's animation. The destination skeleton's position will exactly match that of the source skeletons. You'd like to move the destination skeleton to its initial position by adding the **_moveSkeleton** parent. This parent **transform** node's name is stored in the $moveRoot variable.

```
string $moveRoot;
```

Get a list of parents for the destination root node.

```
string $parentNodes[] = `listRelatives -parent $destRootNode`;
```

Determine if the parent is one of the **_moveSkeleton** nodes that this procedure could have created.

```
string $found = `match "_moveSkeleton" $parentNodes[0]`;
```

If it is a **_moveSkeleton** node, then simply set the $moveRoot to the current parent.

```
if( size($found) )
    $moveRoot = $parentNodes[0];
```

If the **_moveSkeleton** node doesn't exist, then create it.

```
else
    $moveRoot = `group -name "_moveSkeleton" -world $destRootNode`;
```

The **_moveSkeleton** node is then moved to the initial position of the destination root node.

```
move -worldSpace
    ($destPos[0] - $srcPos[0])
    ($destPos[1] - $srcPos[1])
    ($destPos[2] - $srcPos[0]) $moveRoot;
}
```

3.5.5 Motion Paths

Rather than set a series of keyframes for the position and rotation of an object, it is often easier to create a curve that an object moves along. The curve defines the path the object follows. By creating a curve on a surface, you can easily set up an animation in which the object moves across the surface. It is also possible to have the object roll into and out of the turns as it moves along the curve.

1. Open the **MotionPathCone.ma** scene.

    The scene consists of a cone and curve. You'd like to set it up so that the cone moves along the path.

2. Execute the following:

    ```
    string $mpNode = `pathAnimation -curve myCurve myCone`;
    // Result: motionPath1 //
    ```

    The cone is moved to the start of the curve. Maya has created a variety of dependency nodes to make this possible.

    While it isn't necessary to know the exact details of these nodes, it is important to understand the general workflow. Since the motion path animation controls the position of the **myCone** object, the **translateX**, **translateY**, and **translateZ** attributes are driven by a **motionPath** node. Figure 3.7 is a diagram of the Dependency Graph.

    Starting from the left, the **myCurveShape** is the actual curve that the object moves along. The **motionPath1_uValue** is an animation curve node that is used to animate the *u* parameter. Both of these nodes feed into the **motionPath1** node. This node is responsible for calculating the position and rotation of the object at a given parameteric position (*u*) along the curve. In this diagram, the output

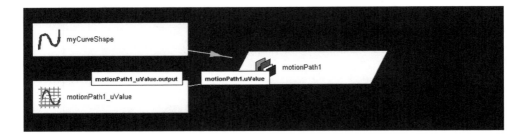

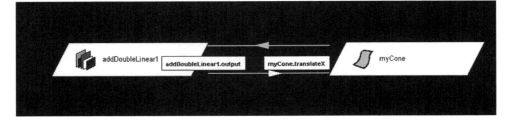

FIGURE 3.7 Dependency Graph

from the **motionPath1** node, the final *x* position, is fed into another node, **addDoubleLinear1**, which then passes it finally to the **myCone**'s **translateX** attribute. A similar flow of data happens for both the **myCone**'s **translateY** and **translateZ** attributes. The **addDoubleLinear** node is a simple node that takes two numbers and adds them together. The result of this addition is then placed in its **output** attribute. In this example the **addDoubleLinear** node has only one value, so this is output directly.

At the end of the animation range, you'd like the object to be positioned at the end of the curve. To do this you need to create another key for the *u* parameter. First the name of the motion path node is needed. Fortunately the `pathAnimation` command returns the name of the motion path node created. You have stored this in the `$mpNode` variable.

Second you need to know the parametric range of the curve, that is, the start and end parametric values of the curve's first and last control points. Execute the following to get the curve's maximum *u* extent:

```
float $maxUValue = `getAttr myCurveShape.minMaxValue.maxValue`;
```

Last you need to know the time at the end of the animation range.

```
float $endTime = `playbackOptions -query - animationEndTime`;
```

With these three pieces of information, you can now create a key.

```
setKeyframe -time $endTime -value $maxUValue -attribute uValue $mpNode;
```

This creates a key for the **uValue** attribute of the motion path node ($mpNode). The key is created at the end of the animation ($endTime), and the value is set to the maximum possible parametric value ($maxUValue) for the curve.

3. Click on the **Play** button.

The cone now moves along the curve. It is also possible to create start and end times for the path using the following statement:

```
pathAnimation -startTimeU 0 -endTimeU 48 -curve myCurve myCone;
```

However, the previous method demonstrates how to create keys at any time. You'd now like for the cone to follow the direction of the path.

4. Execute the following:

```
pathAnimation -edit -follow yes myCone;
```

5. Click on the **Play** button.

The cone now moves with its tip pointing in the direction of the path. You'd also like the cone to *bank* along the curve. When an object banks, it rotates into and out of the turns.

6. Execute the following:

```
pathAnimation -edit -bank yes myCone;
```

If you play the animation, it isn't obvious, by looking at the cone, how much it banks. Use one of the other axes to point forward so you can see the effect of the banking better. Execute the following:

```
pathAnimation -edit -followAxis x myCone;
```

The x-axis now points forward, thereby making the point of the cone face outwards. The animation now better shows the effect of the banking. To reduce the amount of banking, execute the following:

```
pathAnimation -edit -bankScale 0.5 myCone;
```

The cone now dips less into and out of the turns. Switch back to having the cone tip face forward by executing the following:

```
pathAnimation -edit -followAxis y myCone;
```

To have the cone change its shape to slither along the path, execute the following:

```
flow myCone;
```

7. Click on the **Play** button.

    The cone is now encased in a lattice that deforms the cone as it moves along the path.

3.6 GRAPHICAL USER INTERFACES

MEL can be used to create a wide variety of graphical user interfaces. In fact, the entire Maya interface is built and managed using MEL commands. These same commands are available to you, to design and build your own custom user interfaces. This section explores the different user interface elements available and how to use them.

3.6.1 Introduction

It is likely that you will need to provide a user interface to the functionality contained in your MEL scripts. In a typical development environment, the creation of user interfaces can be a long and tedious task. While Maya doesn't provide a visual means of creating and laying out your interface elements, it does provide a rich set of interface creation and management commands. Leveraging MEL's ability to execute commands immediately, you can do the prototyping of user interfaces quickly. Once the script that generates the interface is ready, it can be executed, and the new interface shown immediately. You can then go back to the script and edit the layout and interface controls as necessary.

A big gain from using MEL for all your interface needs is that you won't have to be concerned with supporting particular windowing and interface systems across different operating systems and platforms. Each operating system typically has its own windowing system with its own API and particularities. Using MEL to create interface elements frees you from writing platform-specific interface code. There is also the guarantee that, once you've written your interface in MEL, it will act and behave similarly across platforms.

The MEL commands devoted to the user interface are part of the *Extended Layer Framework* (*ELF*). MEL includes a rich set of user interface elements including windows, buttons, sliders, and so on. The following script is used to generate the window shown in Figure 3.8.

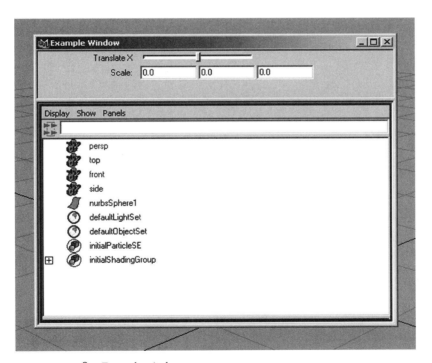

FIGURE 3.8   Example window

```
window -title "Example Window";
  paneLayout -configuration "horizontal2";
  columnLayout;
    floatSliderGrp -label "Translate X" -min -100 -max 100;
    floatFieldGrp -label "Scale:" -numberOfFields 3;
    setParent ..;
  frameLayout -labelVisible false;
    outlinerPanel;
showWindow;
```

Notice how such complex user interface elements as an outliner panel can be easily incorporated into your custom windows. The steps to creating a simple user interface are now covered.

1. Select **File | New Scene**.

2. Click on the **Edit Script** button.

3. Set the script to the following:

```
sphere -name "mySphere";
window myWindow;
columnLayout;
attrFieldSliderGrp -min 0 -max 10 -at "mySphere.sx";
showWindow myWindow;
```

4. Save the script file.

5. Click on the **Execute Script** button.

    A sphere is created, and a window named **myWindow** is displayed as shown in Figure 3.9.

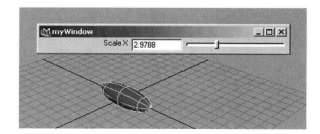

FIGURE 3.9   myWindow

6. Move the Scale X slider back and forth.

Changing the slider causes the sphere's *x* scale to change.

3.6.2 Fundamental Concepts

In order to understand how to create interfaces, you will create a simple interface and cover some of the basic interface concepts.

1. In the **Script Editor**, type the following:

```
window;
```

The result is:

```
// Result: window1
```

As with most commands, if you don't explicitly specify values for its parameters, it uses default ones. In this case, Maya created a window named **window1**. A window, by default, isn't visible, so you need to make it visible explicitly.

2. In the **Script Editor**, execute the following:

```
window -edit -visible true window1;
```

The window is now displayed. You can edit a property of an interface element by using the -edit flag. In this case the visible parameter was turned on, making the window visible. Windows contain numerous other parameters, including their position, size, whether they automatically resize, and so on.

Alternatively you could have used the following command to make the window visible:

```
showWindow window1;
```

Notice that when the window command was called, the name of the window, **window1**, was specified. All of the user interface elements are assigned a name when they are created. If you don't explicitly assign them a name, a default one is used instead. When modifying or referencing an interface element, you must include its name so that Maya knows exactly which element you are referring to. If you attempt to create a new interface element with the same name as an existing one, Maya displays an error.

3. Execute the following:

```
window -edit -widthHeight 200 100 window1;
```

The window size now has a width of 200 and a height of 100. Any of the interface element's parameters can be queried.

4. Execute the following:

```
window -query -numberOfMenus window1;
```

The result is:

```
// Result: 0 //
```

5. Close the **window1** window.

6. In the **Script Editor**, execute the following:

```
window -widthHeight 200 300 myWindow;
columnLayout myLayout;
button -label "First" myButton;
showWindow myWindow;
```

The **myWindow** is displayed. It contains a single button labeled **First**. Notice how each of the interface elements was assigned an explicit name when it was created. The window is named **myWindow**, the columnLayout is named **myLayout**, and the button is named **myButton**. Given their exact names, you can now refer to them precisely.

Before an interface element is added to the window, Maya must know how you'd like to have that element placed within the window. This is done by adding a *layout element* to the window. The layout controls how all subsequent elements are placed. There are many different ways of laying out your elements. In this case, you added a columnLayout to the window. This layout places any following elements in a single column. To see this, you add another button to the columnLayout.

7. Execute the following:

```
button -label "Second" -parent myWindow|myLayout;
```

A button labeled **Second** is added to the window. Since it was added to the columnLayout, it was automatically placed below the first button. When interface elements are added to a window, an inherent hierarchy is created. The top of the hierarchy is the window itself, **myWindow**. Under that is the layout, **myLayout**. Then under that are the two buttons. When an element is under another, it is considered the *child* of the first. The two buttons are the children of the **myLayout** element. The element with the children is referred to as the *parent*. The **myWindow** element is the parent of the **myLayout** element. Arbitrary hierarchies of elements can be created by adding children. In turn these children can become parents of other children.

Given that you now have a hierarchy of interface elements, you need to specify the complete path to refer to a specific one. The complete path to the layout is **myWindow|myLayout**. Notice that this is the same notation used for specifying the complete path to a scene object (DAG path). Notice, however, that there is no space between the element names.

Windows are always at the top of the hierarchy. As with scene objects, it is possible to have two elements with the same name as long as their full paths differ. For instance it is valid to have two layouts with the same local name **myLayout**, as long as they exist in different hierarchies. For instance **win1|myLayout** and **win2|myLayout** are two valid and different layouts.

When adding a new element, you must always specify the parent. However, this requires more work on the part of the programmer to maintain records of the names of the individual elements. In order to simplify the task of adding elements, Maya introduced the concept of the *default parent*. When no explicit parent is specified, the default parent is used. In the previous step you created a window, **myWindow**, then created a columnLayout, **myLayout**. No parent was specified for the columnLayout, yet it was automatically parented to the window.

When an interface element is created, it automatically becomes the default parent for elements of its own type. There exists an individual default parent for windows, layouts, menus, and so on. A default parent exists only for elements that can have other elements as children. Since a window can have layouts, menus, and so on as children, when it is created it automatically becomes the default window parent. When you create a layout, it becomes a child of the default parent, the window. The new layout then becomes the default layout parent. The default window parent is still the previously created window. Adding a menu element after a layout doesn't add the menu to the layout but to the last window added. As such, there are a variety of default parents depending on the type of element being created.

To set the default parent explicitly for a given interface element type, use the setParent command.

8.   Close the **myWindow** window.

9.   In the **Script Editor**, execute the following. Note that the spacing isn't important but is provided so that it is easier to determine which element is the parent and which elements are the children.

```
window -widthHeight 200 300 myWindow;
  columnLayout;
    button -label "First";
    button -label "Second";
    rowLayout -numberOfColumns 2;
      button -label "Third";
      button -label "Fourth";
      setParent ..;
    button -label "Fifth";
showWindow myWindow;
```

The window is displayed with five buttons. The first, second, and fifth are in column order, while the third and forth are in row order. The window is created first. Since it was the most recent window created, it automatically becomes the default window parent. A columnLayout is then added. Since no explicit parent is specified, it is added under the current default window parent, **myWindow**. The columnLayout, in turn, becomes the default layout parent. The next two buttons are automatically added to it. A rowLayout element is then added. Since layouts can contain other layouts as children, the rowLayout is automatically added as a child under the columnLayout. The rowLayout now becomes the new default layout parent. The next two buttons are added to it.

Before you add the last button, setParent is called with .. as its argument. This sets the default parent to the current default parent's parent. It essentially moves up one element in the hierarchy. Since the parent of the rowLayout is the columnLayout, the columnLayout becomes the new default layout parent. When the fifth button is added, it is added to the columnLayout and not the rowLayout.

Keeping track of which element is the default parent can sometimes be difficult. Adding elements to the wrong parent is a very common mistake. To avoid this, it is best to indent your commands so that you can see quickly which element is the parent. Setting it out like this won't guarantee that the right parent is used.

If your interface isn't laid out as you'd expected, be sure to check that you are adding elements to the correct parent. To determine at any time what the current parent is, use the following command:

```
setParent -query;
```

This returns a complete path to the current parent.

Once the interface elements are established, you'll want to hook them up so that when the user interacts with them they perform some useful action. The majority of the elements allow you to specify a series of MEL statements to execute when a user activates or changes an interface element.

10. In the **Script Editor**, execute the following:

```
window;
columnLayout;
button -label "Click me" -command "sphere";
showWindow;
```

A window is created with a single button labeled **Click me**. When you click on the button, a sphere is created. While this example has a single command, sphere, any number of MEL commands and statements can be used.

Some interface elements execute MEL statements based on the triggering of a certain event. The textField element is designed to let the user enter some text. It can execute MEL statements when it gains focus, the user changes the text, and the **Enter** key is pressed.

11. In the **Script Editor**, execute the following:

```
global proc myText( string $txt )
{
print ("\nThe text entered was " + $txt);
}


window;
columnLayout -adjustableColumn true;
textField -text "Change this text" -enterCommand "myText( \"#1\" )";
showWindow;
```

A window with a text field is created.

12. Change the text in the text field to something else, then press **Enter.**

The Script Editor displays the text that was just entered. When you press **Enter,** the MEL statements listed in the -enterCommand parameter are executed. Notice the use of #1 in the statement. You could have retrieved the actual text from the textField by using the statement.

```
textField -query -text <name of textField>;
```

The #1 is shorthand for the current value of the element. In this case it gives you the text. If it were a check box it would give you the on/off state. To retrieve the values for elements with multiple items, simply use #2, #3, and so on in your command statements.

3.6.3 Windows

A window is the main interface element and is most often used to hold a wide variety of other elements. A window can contain a title bar as well as minimize and maximize buttons. A window can also be positioned and resized. By default a window is invisible. This reason for this is that if you create a blank window and display it, then start adding elements, it must calculate the layout and so on for each element and then display the elements interactively. When you create an invisible window and then add elements, it displays much faster since it won't have to interactively display each element as it is added.

Now explore some of the window features in more detail.

1. Select **File | New Scene.**

2. Click on the **Edit Script** button.

3. Set the script to the following:

```
global proc showMyWindow()
{
window myWindow;
showWindow myWindow;
}

showMyWindow();
```

4. Save the script file.

5. Click on the **Execute Script** button.

The **myWindow** window is created and then displayed.

6. Click on the **Execute Script** button again.

The following error is displayed:

```
// Error: file: .../scripts/learning.mel line 3:
    Object's name is not unique: myWindow //
```

Since the **myWindow** window already exists, you can't create another window with the same name. You'd like to avoid this error message.

7. Set the script to the following, then execute it as before.

```
global proc showMyWindow()
{
if( !`window -exists myWindow` )
    window myWindow;
showWindow myWindow;
}


showMyWindow();
```

No error message is now displayed. Before creating the window, you check whether or not it already exists. This is done using the window command with the -exists flag. If the window doesn't exist, then it is created.

You'd like to now start adding other interface elements to the window. It is best to do this immediately after the window is created but before it is made visible. Since your window is already displayed, this isn't possible. While you are developing the window's interface, you'd like to start from scratch each time.

8. Set the script to the following, then execute it.

```
global proc showMyWindow()
{
// Set $developing to false when you are ready to release
int $developing = true;
if( $developing && `window -exists myWindow` )
    deleteUI myWindow;
if( !`window -exists myWindow` )
    window myWindow;
showWindow myWindow;
}


showMyWindow();
```

While the variable, $developing, is true and the window exists, it will be deleted. This allows you to create a new window each time you run the script.

9. Set the script to the following, then execute it.

```
global proc showMyWindow()
{
// Set $developing to false when you are ready to release
int $developing = true;
if( $developing && `window -exists myWindow` )
    deleteUI myWindow;
if( !`window -exists myWindow` )
    {
    window -title "My Window" -resizeToFitChildren true myWindow;
    columnLayout -adjustableColumn true;
    button -label "Change Name";
    }
showWindow myWindow;
}


showMyWindow();
```

The window is created with a button labeled **Change Name**. When the window is created, you set its -resizeToFitChildren parameter to true. This means that the window automatically resizes itself to the extents of its children. The columnLayout also has its -adjustableColumn parameter set to true so that the button extends horizontally to the width of the layout.

Unfortunately the window hasn't resized itself correctly. The reason for this is that, by default, Maya remembers the name, position, and size of a window when it is closed. If you then open this window again, the previous position and size are restored. If you'd like your window to have a different size and position, you'll need to do this explicitly using one or more of the following commands. Replace 999 with the relevant value.

```
window -width 999 windowName;
window -height 999 windowName;
window -widthHeight 999 999 windowName;
```

```
window -topEdge 999 windowName;
window -leftEdge 999 windowName;
window -topLeftCorner 999 999 windowName;
```

Alternatively you can remove the window size and position information Maya has stored for the window. This is done using the `windowPref` command. If you'd like to stop Maya from remembering every window's size and position, then turn off the **Remember Size and Position** check box in the **Preferences | Interface | Windows** section.

10. Set the script to the following, then execute it.

```
global proc showMyWindow()
{
// Set $developing to false when you are ready to release
int $developing = true;
if( $developing && `window -exists myWindow` )
    deleteUI myWindow;
if( !`window -exists myWindow` )
    {
    if( $developing )
        windowPref -remove myWindow;
    window -title "My Window" -resizeToFitChildren true myWindow;
    columnLayout -adjustableColumn true;
    button -label "Change Name";
    }
showWindow myWindow;
}


showMyWindow();
```

The window now resizes itself to the extent of the `columnLayout`. When the variable `$developing` is set to false, the user can set the size and position of the window, and it will be remembered since `windowPref -remove myWindow` will never be called.

Next, you'd like to present a dialog box when the user clicks on the **Change Name** button.

11. Set the script to the following, then execute it.

```
global proc myChangeName()
{
string $nam[] = `ls -sl`;
if( size($nam) > 0 )
    {
    string $res = `promptDialog -message "Enter new name:"
        -button "OK" -button "Cancel" -defaultButton "OK"
        -cancelButton "Cancel" -dismissString "Cancel"`;
    if( $res == "OK" )
        {
        string $newname = `promptDialog -query`;
        eval( "rename " + $nam[0] + " " + $newname );
        }
    }
}


global proc showMyWindow()
{
// Set $developing to false when you are ready to release
int $developing = true;
if( $developing && `window -exists myWindow` )
    deleteUI myWindow;
if( !`window -exists myWindow` )
    {
    if( $developing )
        windowPref -remove myWindow;
    window -title "My Window" -resizeToFitChildren true myWindow;
    columnLayout -adjustableColumn true;
    button -label "Change Name" -command "myChangeName();";
    }
showWindow myWindow;
}


showMyWindow();
```

The button now calls the myChangeName procedure when pressed. This is set up by setting the -command flag of the button to the MEL statement that is executed when the button is pressed. The myChangeName procedure determines which objects are selected. If there is at least one object selected, it displays a dialog box asking the user to enter its new name. If the user clicks on the dialog box's **OK** button, the object is renamed.

The promptDialog command is an example of a modal dialog box. This is a window like any other except that it doesn't allow you to interact with any other windows in the application until it is dismissed. Another very handy dialog box command is confirmDialog. This displays a message to have the user then confirm or deny. For example, the following command displays a dialog box and lets the user choose between Yes or No:

```
confirmDialog -message "Do you want to delete the object" -button "Yes"
    -button "No".
```

3.6.4 Layouts

There are a wide variety of layouts. Each serves a common purpose: positioning or sizing of the interface elements added to them. Complex layout schemes can be created by nesting different types of layouts.

Each window must have at least one layout. This first layout takes up all the window client area. This is the window area that doesn't include the title, menu bar, borders, and so on. The exception to this is the menuLayout, which extends itself vertically to the height of the menu bar. It won't take over the entire client area.

When you are working with a layout and don't know its type, you can use the layout command. It allows you to operate on all layouts.

```
string $layoutName = <insert name of layout here>;
layout -edit -width 200 $layoutName;
layout -query -numberOfChildren $layoutName;
layout -exists $layoutName;
```

Some of the most commonly used layouts will now be covered.

COLUMNLAYOUT

The `columnLayout` places all its children in a single column, one after another. It is possible to define the column width and row height, as well as how each child can be attached. In the following example, the column is set to a fixed width of 150. There is a space between rows of 8. When an element is added, it is stretched to fit the width of the column, but with an offset of 12 on either side. The final result is shown in Figure 3.10.

```
window;
  columnLayout -columnAttach "both" 12 -rowSpacing 8 -columnWidth 150;
    button;
    button;
showWindow;
```

FIGURE 3.10   Example of `columnLayout`

If you want the children to attach themselves to both sides and resize when the `columnLayout` does, then use this:

```
columnLayout -adjustableColumn true;
```

ROWLAYOUT

The `rowLayout` positions each of the child elements in a row. You must specify the number of columns in the row. By default this is zero, so when you attempt to add a child, you get an error similar to the following:

```
// Error: file: .../learning.mel line 4:
      Too many children in layout: rowLayout1 //
```

To correct this, simply increase the number of columns when the `rowLayout` is defined.

It is possible to set the alignment, offset, and adjustability of each individual column. In the following example, the rowLayout has three columns. The widths of the columns are 100, 60, and 80, respectively. The first column attaches its children on both sides with no offset. The result is shown in Figure 3.11.

```
window;
    rowLayout -numberOfColumns 3 -columnWidth3 100 60 80
            -columnAttach 1 "both" 0;
        button;
        button;
        button;
showWindow;
```

FIGURE 3.11   Example of rowLayout

GRIDLAYOUT

The gridLayout positions its children in a series of rows and columns. As children are added the gridLayout can automatically accommodate them by adding more rows or columns as needed. This behavior can be prevented to maintain a fixed number of rows and columns. The width and height of the cells within the grid can also be specified.

The following example uses a gridLayout with two rows and columns. Each of the individual cells has a width of 30 and and height of 60. Figure 3.12 shows the end result.

```
window;
    gridLayout -numberOfRowsColumns 2 2 -cellWidthHeight 60 50;
        button;
        button;
        button lastButton;
showWindow;
```

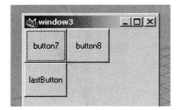

FIGURE 3.12   Example of `gridLayout`

To later reposition the individual elements in the grid, use the `-position` flag. This flag takes the name of the child element and its new position. The new position is a 1-based index counted from the first row and column position (1), then following the columns down to the next row, and so on. So to position the last button, in the previous example, in the first row and second column you would use:

```
$buttonName = <put last button's name here>;
gridLayout -position $buttonName 2;
```

FORMLAYOUT

The `formLayout` is the most flexible layout scheme, offering a great many different alignment and attachment options. It also provides absolute and relative positioning of child elements. When an element is added to a `formLayout`, it has no default position. Its position must be specified later. As such, the general procedure is to add all the child elements to the `formLayout` and then use its editing feature to finally position them.

The individual edges (left, right, top, bottom) can be aligned either to the form's extents, other controls, or a given location. In the following example, three buttons are added to a form and aligned and attached in different ways.

```
window;
   string $form = `formLayout -numberOfDivisions 100`;
   string $but1 = `button`;
   string $but2 = `button`;
   string $but3 = `button`;
   formLayout -edit
     // Button 1
     -attachForm $but1 "top" 0
     -attachForm $but1 "left" 0
```

```
        -attachForm $but1 "bottom" 0
        -attachPosition $but1 "right" 0 50
        // Button 2
        -attachForm $but2 "right" 0
        // Button 3
        -attachPosition $but3 "top" 0 5
        -attachControl $but3 "left" 5 $but1
        $form;
showWindow;
```

When the form is created, the number of divisions is given with the -numberOfDivisions flag. This defines a virtual grid to which an element's position is snapped. While the number of divisions can be set to anything, it is most often set to 100 so that positions can be given as percentages. So setting the horizontal position to 50 is like putting it at 50% along the width of the form.

```
string $form = `formLayout -numberOfDivisions 100`;
```

Three buttons are then created and automatically added to the current layout. Note that their names are stored since you will need to refer to them later.

```
string $but1 = `button`;
string $but2 = `button`;
string $but3 = `button`;
```

With the buttons added to the form, you now go about positioning and aligning them. This is done using the formLayout command with the -edit flag.

```
formLayout -edit
```

The first button has its top, left, and bottom edges aligned with the form. Its right edge is placed at 50% of the width of the form.

```
// Button 1
-attachForm $but1 "top" 0
-attachForm $but1 "left" 0
-attachForm $but1 "bottom" 0
-attachPosition $but1 "right" 0 50
```

The second button is simply aligned with the right edge of the form. Since its other edges haven't been set, it defaults to the top edge of the form and its width is whatever the original width of the button was.

```
// Button 2
-attachForm $but2 "right" 0
```

The third button is vertically positioned at 5% of the form's height. Its left edge is attached to the first button's right edge with a small offset of 5.

```
// Button 3
-attachPosition $but3 "top" 0 5
-attachControl $but3 "left" 5 $but1
$form;
```

The resulting user interface is shown in Figure 3.13. It is possible to add other layouts to a formLayout including other formLayouts. By combining layouts within layouts, you can get a lot of control over the exact position and size of each individual element.

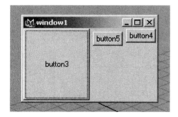

FIGURE 3.13   Example of formLayout

FRAMELAYOUT

When you need to have a region of the interface that can expand and collapse, then use a frameLayout. The frameLayout typically contains a label as well as a collapse/expand button that reduces the frame size as well as expands it to display all its children. The frameLayout has options for the label, border, margins, and so on. It is important to note that a frameLayout can have only one child, so there needs to be another layout added to the frameLayout to all the children.

In the following example, a frameLayout is created. Its only child is the columnLayout. The frameLayout is defined as collapsible, which enables the collapse/expand button. The resulting frameLayout is shown in Figure 3.14.

```
window;
  frameLayout -label "Settings" -borderStyle "etchedIn"
              -font "obliqueLabelFont" -collapsible true;
    columnLayout;
      button;
      button;
      button;
showWindow;
```

FIGURE 3.14   Example of frameLayout

TABLAYOUT

The tabLayout allows you to organize other layouts into a series of folders. Each folder has a tab button at the top so that you can select it. Once a tab is selected, the associated layout is displayed. The tabLayout, like the frameLayout, enables you to make efficient use of the same window region by reusing it among layouts.

All the children of a tabLayout must be layouts. If you attempt to add something other than a layout, an error occurs.

In the following example, a tabLayout is created and then two additional columnLayouts are added to it. Each of the columnLayouts has a simple button. Finally, the labels of the tabs are changed. Notice the use of setParent .. to set the tabLayout as the default layout parent once the button is added to the columnLayout. Figure 3.15 shows the end result.

```
window;
  string $tabs = `tabLayout`;
    string $tab1 = `columnLayout`;
    button;
    setParent ..;
  string $tab2 = `columnLayout`;
    button;
    setParent ..;
  tabLayout -edit
    -tabLabel $tab1 "Colors"
    -tabLabel $tab2 "Flavors"
    $tabs;
showWindow;
```

FIGURE 3.15   Example of tabLayout

SCROLLLAYOUT

When an interface element is too large to show within a region, a scrollLayout can be used. A scrollLayout doesn't itself provide a layout but instead displays scroll bars for a child layout. As such, another layout that holds the children elements is always added to a scrollLayout.

In this example, a scrollLayout is added to a window. A columnLayout with four buttons is then added to it. The result is shown in Figure 3.16.

```
window;
  scrollLayout ;
    columnLayout;
      button;
      button;
      button;
      button;
showWindow;
```

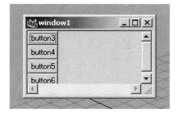

FIGURE 3.16   Example of scrollLayout

If you execute this script, then reduce the window size vertically, the vertical scrollbar becomes active and allows you to scroll down to show the hidden buttons.

MENUBARLAYOUT

The menuBarLayout is designed to contain submenus. These submenus then contain their own individual menuItems. The menuBarLayout can be used to create a main menu for a window or separate menus for layouts, as in the following example. The resulting menuBarLayout is shown in Figure 3.17.

```
window;
  menuBarLayout;
    menu -label "File";
      menuItem -label "Exit";
    menu -label "Help" -helpMenu true;
      menuItem -label "About...";
    setParent ..;
  string $tabs = `tabLayout`;
  string $tab1 = `menuBarLayout`;
    menu -label "Colors";
      menuItem -label "Red";
      menuItem -label "Green";
    menu -label "Flavors";
      menuItem -label "Vanilla";
      menuItem -label "Chocolate";
  tabLayout -edit -tabLabel $tab1 "Confectionary" $tabs;
showWindow;
```

FIGURE 3.17   Example of menuBarLayout

If you have created a window without a menu bar and then added other layouts, simply do the following to add your menu bar. This sets the default parent to the window, then the menuBarLayout is added to it.

```
setParent -topLevel;
menuBarLayout;
// ...add menus
```

3.6.5 Controls

Controls are the individual user interface elements with which the user interacts. Controls include buttons, check boxes, sliders, fields, and so on. If you don't know the exact type of the control you are working on, you can use the control command to edit and query it.

```
string $controlName = <insert control name here>;
control -edit -width 23 $controlName;
control -query -parent $controlName;
control -exists $controlName;
```

MENUS

Menus can be added to a window's main menu bar or to a menuBarLayout. The following example shows how to create a main menu bar. The -menuBar parameter is set to true when the window is created. Next a menu is added. Note that this menu can be torn off since its -tearOff flag is set to true. Three additional menu items, including a divider, are added to this menu. The final menu is shown in Figure 3.18.

```
window -menuBar true;
  menu -label "File" -tearOff true;
    menuItem -label "New";
    menuItem -divider true;
    menuItem -label "Exit";
  menu -label "Help" -helpMenu true;
    menuItem -label "About";
showWindow;
```

FIGURE 3.18   Example menu

A menu can be added to almost any layout as long as a menuBarLayout is created first. A variety of different menu items are shown in the following example. Figure 3.19 shows the completed menu.

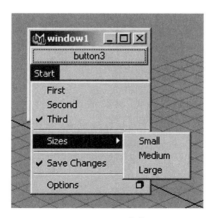

FIGURE 3.19   Detailed menu

```
window;
  columnLayout -adjustableColumn true;
    button;
    menuBarLayout;
      menu -label "Start" -allowOptionBoxes true;
        // Radio menu items
        radioMenuItemCollection;
        menuItem -label "First" -radioButton off;
        menuItem -label "Second" -radioButton off;
        menuItem -label "Third" -radioButton on;
        // Divider
        menuItem -divider true;
        // Submenu
        menuItem -subMenu true -label "Sizes";
        menuItem -label "Small";
        menuItem -label "Medium";
        menuItem -label "Large";
        setParent -menu ..;
        // Divider
        menuItem -divider true;
        // Check box menu item
        menuItem -label "Save Changes" -checkBox on;
        // Divider
        menuItem -divider true;
        // Menu item with option box
        menuItem -label "Options";
        menuItem -optionBox true -command "doOptionsBox()";
showWindow;
```

A window is created with a `columnLayout` and a single button.

```
window;
  columnLayout -adjustableColumn true;
    button;
```

Since you want your menu to be displayed inside a layout and not become the main menu, you add a `menuBarLayout`.

```
menuBarLayout;
```

The actual menu can now be added. If you intend on having option boxes in your menu, be sure to set the -allowOptionBoxes parameter to true. Otherwise you won't be able to add option boxes.

```
menu -label "Start" -allowOptionBoxes true;
```

Menu items can act like radio buttons if they are included under a radioMenuItemCollection. Also, each of the subsequent menu items must set the -radioButton flag. As with all radio buttons, only one of them can be turned on.

```
radioMenuItemCollection;
menuItem -label "First" -radioButton off;
menuItem -label "Second" -radioButton off;
menuItem -label "Third" -radioButton on;
```

A divider menu item displays a line in the menu and is used to visually separate items.

```
menuItem -divider true;
```

To create a submenu, simply create a normal menuItem but set its -subMenu parameter to true. All subsequent items are added to the submenu.

```
menuItem -subMenu true -label "Sizes";
menuItem -label "Small";
menuItem -label "Medium";
menuItem -label "Large";
```

In order to get out of the submenu, you need to move up to its parent. This is done using the setParent command.

```
setParent -menu ..;
```

Next, a check box menu item is added.

```
menuItem -label "Save Changes" -checkBox on;
```

A menu item that contains both a label and option box is created by first adding the menu item with its associated label. Another menu item has to be added, but this time with the -optionBox flag set to true. Also the -command parameter is set so that when the option box is selected the doOptionsBox procedure is called.

```
menuItem -label "Options";
menuItem -optionBox true -command "doOptionsBox()";
```

At any time during the adding of menu items, you can determine what the current menu parent is by using the following:

```
string $currentMenu = `setParent -query -menu`;
```

If you want to set the current menu, then use:

```
setParent -menu $newMenu;
```

BUTTONS

Buttons come in a variety of forms, but their basic purpose is to provide a control that the user can click to initiate some action. This action is defined as a series of one or more MEL statements.

The simplest button contains just a text label and is created using the button command. In this example, a button with the label **Press here!** is created. When the button is clicked the command is executed. Its command parameter is set to print out the text "Button pressed". The resulting button is shown in Figure 3.20.

```
window;
  columnLayout;
    button -label "Press here!"
           -command "print \"Button pressed.\\n\"";
showWindow;
```

FIGURE 3.20   Example button

To create a button that displays an image or icon, use the `symbolButton` command. The following example creates a `symbolButton` with the `sphere.xpm` icon. When the button is clicked, a sphere is created. Figure 3.21 shows the end result.

```
window;
  columnLayout;
    symbolButton -image "sphere.xpm" -command "sphere;";
showWindow;
```

FIGURE 3.21   Example of `symbolButton`

If you need a button that displays a label as well as an image, then use the `iconTextButton` command. In fact, you can define whether the text, image, or a combination of both is displayed and where they are located relative to one another. The button created in the following example has both a label and an icon. The `style` parameter is set so that the label is displayed to the right of the icon. When the button is pressed, a cone is created since its `command` parameter is set to the MEL statement "cone". The resulting `iconTextButton` is shown in Figure 3.22.

```
window;
  columnLayout -adjustableColumn true;
    iconTextButton -style "iconAndTextHorizontal"
                   -image1 "cone.xpm" -label "cone"
                   -command "cone";
showWindow;
```

FIGURE 3.22   Example of `iconTextButton`

CHECK BOXES

A check box is like a button, except that it is used to indicate whether something is turned on or off. Clicking the check box causes it to toggle its current state. If it is on, it will turn off and vice versa.

In addition to the checkBox command that creates a standard check box, there is also the symbolCheckBox command, which creates a check box with an icon, and then the iconTextCheckbox, which can have a combination of a label and an icon. Unlike a standard check box, which has a tick mark when turned on, the other check boxes are displayed as indented when turned on. The following example demonstrates the three different check box types. They are displayed in Figure 3.23.

```
window;
  columnLayout -adjustableColumn true;
    checkBox -label "Visibility";
    symbolCheckBox -image "circle.xpm";
    iconTextCheckBox -style "iconAndTextVertical"
                     -image1 "cube.xpm" -label "cube";
showWindow;
```

FIGURE 3.23   Example check boxes

RADIO BUTTONS

Radio buttons allow you to choose one item from a group. In order to know which radio buttons belong to a given group, you first need to create a radioCollection. This collection holds the radio buttons. The following example creates a radioCollection then adds three standard radio buttons to it. The final interface is shown in Figure 3.24.

```
window;
  rowLayout -columnWidth3 60 60 60 -numberOfColumns 3;
    radioCollection;
      radioButton -label "Cold";
      radioButton -label "Warm";
      radioButton -label "Hot";
showWindow;
```

FIGURE 3.24   Example of radioButtons

To determine which of the radio buttons is currently selected, use this:

```
radioCollection -query -select $radioCollectionName;
```

An icon can also be shown with each radio button. This is done using the iconTextRadioButton command in combination with the iconTextRadioCollection command. The next example shows you how to create three radio buttons with icons. Figure 3.25 shows the end result.

```
window;
  rowLayout -columnWidth3 60 60 60 -numberOfColumns 3;
    iconTextRadioCollection;
      iconTextRadioButton -image1 "sphere.xpm" -label "Cold";
      iconTextRadioButton -image1 "cone.xpm" -label "Warm";
      iconTextRadioButton -image1 "torus.xpm" -label "Hot";
showWindow;
```

FIGURE 3.25   Example of iconTextRadioButtons

TEXT

To display a single line of editable or read-only text, use the textField command. The following example creates an editable text field. It is important always to press **Enter** when you are finished editing the text. If you don't press **Enter**, the changes to the text are ignored. The textField is shown in Figure 3.26.

```
window;
  columnLayout -adjustableColumn true;
    textField -editable true;
showWindow;
```

FIGURE 3.26   Example of textField

If you need to display multiple lines of text, use the scrollField command. A scrollField element can display either read-only or editable text. To make it editable, simply set the -editable flag. The following example creates a scrollField with word wrapping. It also uses a custom font and is editable. When the user presses the **Enter** key in the element, the command parameter is executed. In this case, it calls your own myGetText procedure. Figure 3.27 shows the end result.

```
window;
  columnLayout -adjustableColumn true;
  scrollField -wordWrap true
              -text "This is a section of text that is editable"
              -font boldLabelFont
              -editable true
              -command "myGetText()";
showWindow;
```

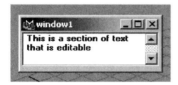

FIGURE 3.27   Example of scrollField

If you don't use the -command parameter feature, you can always retrieve the user's text using the following:

```
scrollField -query -text $scrollFieldName;
```

To display a single line of static (uneditable) text, use the text command. The text created can be aligned to the left, center, or right. Also a specific font can be used. The following window contains a text element that is centered and uses the font obliqueLabelFont. The final result is shown in Figure 3.28.

```
window;
  columnLayout -adjustableColumn true;
    text -label "Middle" -align "center"
         -font "obliqueLabelFont";
showWindow;
```

FIGURE 3.28   Example text

LISTS

To display a list of text items from which the user can select, use the textScrollList command. It is possible to configure the textScrollList so that the user can select single or multiple items. The latter is done by setting the -allowMultipleSelection parameter to true. Having selected the first item, the user can select additional items by holding down the **Ctrl** key.

The following example demonstrates how to create a textScrollList with four visible rows. The user can select multiple items. Five items are added to the list, and the fourth one is selected. Also the list is scrolled so that the item at index 4 can be seen. Figure 3.29 shows the final textScrollList.

```
window;
  columnLayout;
  textScrollList -numberOfRows 4
                 -allowMultiSelection true
                 -append "alpha"
                 -append "beta"
                 -append "gamma"
                 -append "delta"
                 -append "epsilon"
                 -selectItem "delta"
                 -showIndexedItem 4;
showWindow;
```

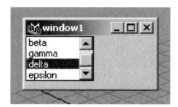

FIGURE 3.29   Example of textScrollList

The list of selected items can be retrieved using the following command:

```
textScrollList -query -selectedItem $textScrollListName;
```

To get a list of the indices of the selected items, use this:

```
textScrollList -query -selectIndexedItem $textScrollListName;
```

Note that the indices returned are base 1 and not base 0 like other MEL array indices.

GROUPS

Often you'll want to create a group of elements to display some given data. For instance you may want to display a floating-point number, then provide a slider and edit box to manipulate it, as well as a label. Fortunately Maya provides some convenience commands that allow you to create and manage whole groups of elements. The following example demonstrates how to create a float slider group. With the single command `floatSliderGrp`, a label, edit field, and slider are created. This group has the label set to **Temperature** and includes a field. It is possible to turn off the label and field. Its initial value is set to 76. The resulting `floatSliderGrp` is shown in Figure 3.30.

```
window;
  columnLayout;
    floatSliderGrp -label "Temperature"
                   -value 76
                   -field true
                   -minValue -10.0 -maxValue 100.0
                   -fieldMinValue -100.0 -fieldMaxValue 100.0;
showWindow;
```

FIGURE 3.30   Example of `floatSliderGrp`

Notice that it is possible to set the range for the slider to be different from that used for the edit box. If a value that is larger than the slider maximum is entered in the edit box, the slider's range automatically grows. However, the slider range never grows larger than the edit box's field minimum and field maximum values.

All MEL commands that create and manage groups end with Grp. Table 3.7 lists the available groups and what features they offer.

Group	Description
colorIndexSliderGrp	Scroll through a series of colors
colorSliderGrp	Edit a color with swatch or slider
floatFieldGrp	Edit floats with fields
floatSliderGrp	Edit float with a field or slider
intFieldGrp	Edit integers with fields
intSliderGrp	Edit integer with field or slider
radioButtonGrp	Collection of radio buttons
textFieldGrp	Edit text with label and field

TABLE 3.7 AVAILABLE GROUP CONTROLS

There are also extensions to some of the groups to include a button. The colorSliderButtonGrp, floatSliderButtonGrp, and textFieldButtonGrp commands all extend their equivalent <element>SliderGrp commands. The following example uses the textFieldButtonGrp command to create a text field group with a button. When you press this button, the command, which is given by the -buttonCommand parameter, is executed. Figure 3.31 shows the end result.

```
window;
  columnLayout;
    textFieldButtonGrp -label "Word" -text "incredulous"
                       -buttonLabel "Check Spelling"
                       -buttonCommand "print \"do check spelling\"";
showWindow;
```

FIGURE 3.31   Example of `textFieldButtonGrp`

IMAGES

In order to display a static bitmap image, you can use either the `picture` or `image` command. Under Windows, the `picture` command will display `.xpm` and `.bmp` files, while under Linux it will display only `.xpm` files. The `image` command can display these formats and a lot more.

Maya looks for bitmaps in the user's bitmap directory then in the *maya_install\ icons* directory. To get the current user's bitmap directory, use the following command:

```
string $imgsDir = `internalVar -userBitmapsDir`;
```

The complete path to the bitmap file can also be used if it doesn't exist in either of these two directories.

The following example uses the `picture` command to display the `sphere.xpm` image. The resulting interface is shown in Figure 3.32.

```
window;
  columnLayout;
    picture -image "sphere.xpm";
showWindow;
```

FIGURE 3.32   Example picture

Under Windows the default bitmap images (`sphere.xpm`, `cone.xpm`, and so on) are built directly into the Maya executable (`maya.exe`). On other platforms, the default bitmap images are stored in Maya's subdirectories.

The `image` command is used to display all of Maya's supported bitmap formats. The actual formats supported vary from platform to platform. To get a complete list of supported image formats for the current platform use the following:

```
global string $imgExt[];
print $imgExt;
```

Under Windows, the results are as follows:

```
als
avi
cin
eps
gif
jpeg
iff
iff
... continued
```

Note that this is a very nonstandard way of getting the bitmap formats and may not be valid for all versions of Maya.

The next example shows how to display a `.gif` image using the `image` command. Note that the full path to the file is given, since the file isn't in any of Maya's default bitmap directories. The final result is shown in Figure 3.33.

FIGURE 3.33   Example image

```
window;
   columnLayout -height 950 -adjustableColumn true;
   image -image "D:\\Temp\\Vince.gif";
showWindow;
```

PANELS

Panels can be added to a window using one of the panel commands: `outlinerPanel`, `hardwareRenderPanel`, `modelPanel`, `nodeOutliner`, `spreadSheetEditor`, and `hyperPanel`. The following example creates a window with a `modelPanel`, which displays the current viewport. The `modelPanel` is shown in Figure 3.34.

```
window;
   paneLayout;
      modelPanel;
showWindow;
```

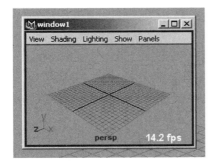

FIGURE 3.34 Example of `modelPanel`

To create a window with both the outliner and current viewport, use the following. Figure 3.35 shows the resulting interface.

```
window -width 700 -height 500;
   paneLayout -configuration "vertical2";
      outlinerPanel;
         setParent ..;
      modelPanel;
showWindow;
```

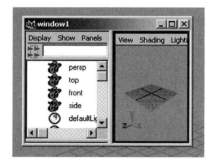

FIGURE 3.35   Example panels

In addition to the specific panel commands, you can use the general getPanel and panel commands to retrieve and set parameters of a given panel.

```
getPanel -all; // Get a list of all the panels
getPanel -underPointer; // Get the name of the panel under the cursor

panel -edit -menuBarVisible true $panelName; // Display the menu bar
panel -copy $panelName; // Create a copy of the panel
```

TOOLS

It may be necessary to include your own tool buttons. A tool button differs from a standard button in that it activates a tool rather than executes a MEL command. The following example demonstrates how to use tool buttons as well as how to group them under a toolCollection element. The results are shown in Figure 3.36.

FIGURE 3.36   Example of toolCollection

```
window;
  columnLayout;
    toolCollection;
      toolButton -tool selectSuperContext
                 -toolImage1 selectSuperContext "aselect.xpm";
      toolButton -tool moveSuperContext
                 -toolImage1 moveSuperContext "move_M.xpm";
showWindow;
```

Before you create a toolButton, a toolCollection element should be created. This holds all the subsequent toolButton elements. The toolButton command creates a tool button with a particular tool by using the -tool flag. The tool is the name of the tool context that is activated when the button is pressed.

3.6.6 Connecting Controls

Very often you'll want a user interface element or group to reflect the current value of a node's attribute. Also when the user changes the value in the interface, you'd like the node's attribute to be changed accordingly. Maya provides a series of commands that automate these tasks.

ATTRIBUTE GROUPS

Attribute groups extend on regular groups to allow you to link the value shown in the group to a node's attribute. This is done by setting the group's -attribute parameter to the name of the node and its associated attribute. In the following example, a new shader is created and its color is displayed and controlled using an attrColorSliderGrp group. The resulting group is shown in Figure 3.37.

```
string $objName = `shadingNode -asShader blinn`;
window;
  columnLayout;
    attrColorSliderGrp -attribute ($objName+".color")
                       -label ($objName + "'s color");
showWindow;
```

FIGURE 3.37 Example of attrColorSliderGrp

First, a new **blinn** shader node is created. It is important to store the new node's name, as it is needed later by the attribute group.

```
string $objName = `shadingNode -asShader blinn`;
```

Having created the window, the attribute group is created. The `-attribute` parameter is set to the node's **color** attribute. The group's label is also set.

```
attrColorSliderGrp -attribute ($objName+".color")
                   -label ($objName + "'s color");
```

Whenever the color changes, the attribute group displays the latest values. If, for example, the shader's color is changed using the Hypershade editor, the group updates automatically. When the attribute group is changed, the shader node's **color** attribute is also automatically updated. You don't have to be concerned if the node's name changes. The connection between the attribute group and the node's attribute is still maintained.

The following example creates a sphere then sets up an attribute group to control its x-axis scale. Figure 3.38 shows the resulting interface.

```
string $objName[] = `sphere`;
window;
  columnLayout;
    attrFieldSliderGrp -attribute ($objName[0]+".scaleX")
                       -min -10 -max 10
                       -label ($objName[0] + "'s x scale");
showWindow;
```

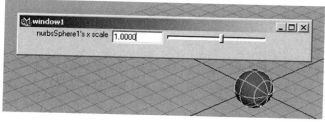

FIGURE 3.38   Group to control a sphere

The result of the sphere command is stored in the $objName array variable. The sphere command returns both the name of the sphere's **transform** node and the node that generated the sphere.

```
string $objName[] = `sphere`;
```

An attrFieldSliderGrp is created for the sphere's **scaleX** attribute. The field and slider are given a range from −10 to 10.

```
attrFieldSliderGrp -attribute ($objName[0]+".scaleX")
                   -min -10 -max 10
                   -label ($objName[0] + "'s x scale");
```

This last example demonstrated how to have the attribute group control a single value. You could create a separate attrFieldSliderGrp for each of the scale axes. Alternatively you can create a single group that controls multiple attributes. To control all of the scale values (*x, y, z*), you could do the following. Figure 3.39 shows the result.

```
string $objName[] = `sphere`;
window;
  columnLayout;
    attrFieldGrp -attribute ($objName[0]+".scale")
                 -label ($objName[0] + "'s scale");
showWindow;
```

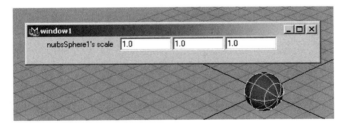

FIGURE 3.39   Example of attrFieldGrp

The `attrFieldGrp` command generates a group that can hold all the **scale**'s child attributes (**scaleX**, **scaleY**, **scaleZ**).

Sometimes an attribute does not hold its own value but instead is a connection to another attribute. For instance, a texture could be assigned to a shader's bump map. The following code sets up an attribute group that makes it very easy for the user to assign a map or navigate to an existing map. The attribute group is associated with the shader node's bump mapping attribute (**normalCamera**). The result is shown in Figure 3.40.

```
string $obj = `shadingNode -asShader blinn`;
window;
  columnLayout;
    attrNavigationControlGrp -attribute ($obj + ".normalCamera")
                             -label "Bump Map";
showWindow;
```

FIGURE 3.40 Example of `attrNavigationControlGrp`

Note that when you use the `attrColorSliderGrp` command, a navigation button is automatically shown unless you specify `-showButton false`.

NAMEFIELD

Often you'll need to display the name of an object and then let the user edit it. A `nameField` allows you to automatically display and edit the name of an object. It is always updated to hold the current name, even if the name is changed elsewhere.

The following example demonstrates how to create a `nameField`. Having first created an object, the `nameField` is then created, and its `-object` parameter is set to the name of the object. When the object name changes, the field updates. Changing the name in the field and pressing **Enter** updates the object's name. Other `nameField` controls that reference the same object also update. The resulting user interface is shown in Figure 3.41.

```
string $torusName[] = `torus`;
window;
  columnLayout -adjustableColumn true;
    nameField -object $torusName[0];
showWindow;
```

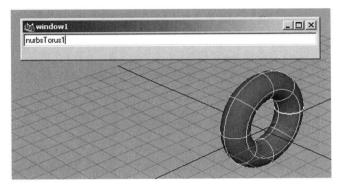

FIGURE 3.41 Example of nameField

OTHER ELEMENTS

Even if you aren't using one of the attribute groups or nameFields, it is still possible to link a node's attribute to a control. This is done using the connectControl command. In the next example, a variety of interface elements are created. Their values are then linked to a **sphere** node's attributes. The resulting interface is shown in Figure 3.42.

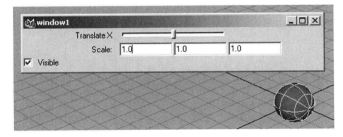

FIGURE 3.42 Example of connectControls

```
string $sphereObj[] = `sphere`;
window;
  columnLayout;
    string $fieldGrp = `floatSliderGrp -label "Translate X"
                        -min -100 -max 100`;
    connectControl $fieldGrp ($sphereObj[0] + ".translateX");

    string $grp = `floatFieldGrp -label "Scale:" -numberOfFields 3`;
    connectControl -index 2 $grp ($sphereObj[0] + ".scaleX");
    connectControl -index 3 $grp ($sphereObj[0] + ".scaleY");
    connectControl -index 4 $grp ($sphereObj[0] + ".scaleZ");

    string $check = `checkBox -label "Visible"`;
    connectControl $check ($sphereObj[0] + ".visibility");
showWindow;
```

Having created the sphere, you then create a floatSliderGrp. The sphere's **translateX** attribute is connected to the element using the connectControl command.

```
connectControl $fieldGrp ($sphereObj[0] + ".translateX");
```

From then on the group's value always displays the current value of the node's attribute. A floatFieldGrp is then created with three fields. Each of the individual fields is connected to the sphere's separate scale attributes. To connect an attribute with a specific element in a group, you need to specify its index in the group. In this case, the field for displaying the x-axis scale is the second element in the group (index 2); the first element is the label (index 1).

```
connectControl -index 2 $grp ($sphereObj[0] + ".scaleX");
```

Last, a checkBox element is created. Its value is connected to the sphere's **visibility** attribute.

```
connectControl $check ($sphereObj[0] + ".visibility");
```

The connectControl command can be used on the following elements: floatField, floatScrollBar, floatSlider, intField, intScrollBar, intSlider, floatFieldGrp, intFieldGrp, checkBox, radioCollection, and optionMenu.

3.6.7 User Feedback

In addition to providing users with an interactive interface, it is often also necessary to provide them with feedback. This feedback can be in the form of instructions, help messages, or simply showing that user input is unavailable during a complex operation.

HELP

Almost all the interface elements allow you to specify some help text. This is done using the -annotation flag. The following example creates a window with a button. This button has the annotation "This is pop-up help". When you move the cursor over the button and pause for a short time, the pop-up help displays the annotation text. The result of doing this is shown in Figure 3.43.

```
window;
  columnLayout;
    button -label "Hover over me" -annotation "This is pop-up help";
showWindow;
```

FIGURE 3.43 Example of pop-up help

Pop-up help is a fast and easy means of displaying help or other instructions related to a particular interface element. This can be combined with the helpLine interface element to instantly display the annotation. The following example creates a helpLine in a window. Annotations are added to the menu item and button. When you move the cursor over both items, the helpLine immediately displays their associated annotation text. Figure 3.44 shows the resulting helpLine element.

```
window -height 600 -menuBar true;
  menu -label "Start";
    menuItem -label "Processing" -annotation "Starts the processing";

  string $form = `formLayout`;
    button -label "Initialize" -annotation "Initialize the data";
    string $frame = `frameLayout -labelVisible false`;
      helpLine;

  formLayout -edit
    -attachNone $frame "top"
    -attachForm $frame "left" 0
    -attachForm $frame "bottom" 0
    -attachForm $frame "right" 0
    $form;

showWindow;
```

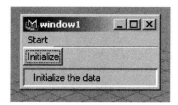

FIGURE 3.44　Example of helpLine

DISPLAYING PROGRESS

To let the user know that the computer is busy and can't accept any user input, use the waitCursor command. The mouse cursor is changed to an hourglass or equivalent image.

```
waitCursor -state on;
```

To restore the cursor, simply use the following:

```
waitCursor -state off;
```

When the computer is performing an operation, there are a variety of methods to give the user notification of this. The easiest is to use the progressWindow command.

This creates a window with a progress bar. As your operation advances, simply increment its -progress parameter. When the progress window is displayed, the mouse cursor is automatically displayed in its wait state. In the following example, a progressWindow is created, and then as the operation progresses, its status is updated. The user is free to cancel the operation at any time. The progressWindow is shown in Figure 3.45.

```
int $amount = 0;

progressWindow
    -title "Working"
    -progress $amount
    -status "Completed: 0%"
    -isInterruptable true;

while (true)
    {
    // Do step in lengthy operation here
    pause -seconds 1; // Dummy operation

    if( `progressWindow -query -isCancelled` ) break;

    $amount += 1;

    progressWindow -edit
            -progress $amount
            -status ("Completed: "+$amount+"%");
    }

progressWindow -endProgress;
```

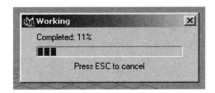

FIGURE 3.45 Example of progressWindow

First the progressWindow is created. Only one progressWindow can be displayed at a time. The minimum and maximum range can be explicitly set, but in this case you use the default values of 0 and 100. The status text is set to display the percentage of the operation's completion. By setting the -isInterruptable flag, the user can cancel the operation. If you don't want to give the user this option, then set it to false.

```
progressWindow
    -title "Working"
    -progress $amount
    -status "Completed: 0%"
    -isInterruptable true;
```

Next the operation is started. As it advances, check to see if the user has tried to cancel it. If so, stop immediately.

```
if( `progressWindow -query -isCancelled` ) break;
```

Last update the progressWindow on the completion of each step. Since you are advancing 1% at a time, the current amount, $amount, is simply displayed. The status text is also updated.

```
$amount += 1;

progressWindow -edit
                -progress $amount
                -status ("Completed: "+$amount+"%");
```

Once the operation is complete, it's very important to let the progressWindow know. Use the following to do this:

```
progressWindow -endProgress;
```

If the progressWindow isn't told that the operation has completed, it won't close its window and restore the cursor. Even if the user cancels the operation, it is important to ensure that the progressWindow is ended correctly by calling this command.

In addition to using this global progress window, it is also possible to create an individual progress bar in a window. The following code creates a window with a progress bar. This is done using the progressBar command. You can set its range and amount completed. The results are shown in Figure 3.46.

```
window;
  columnLayout;
  string $progCtrl = `progressBar -maxValue 5 -width 300`;
  button -label "Next step"
         -command ("progressBar -edit -step 1 " + $progCtrl);
showWindow;
```

FIGURE 3.46 Example of progressBar

3.7 EXPRESSIONS

As you know, any attribute can be animated in Maya by creating a series of keyframes. Expressions also allow you to animate an attribute, except that rather than setting keyframes you define the attribute's value through MEL commands. These MEL commands are evaulated at each frame, and the result is stored in the attribute to which the Expression is assigned. This technique is commonly known as *procedural animation*. This is when a program (MEL commands) controls the animation rather than it being controlled through keyframing. Expressions can be used to create complex animations with little or no manual intervention. It is a very powerful way of animating attributes, since you are completely free to use any MEL commands or statements you want. Generally, any attribute can be controlled by an Expression. As such almost any component of Maya can be procedurally animated.

Unfortunately the word *expression* now has two meanings. The first is its meaning in programming languages to be one or more programming constructs; for example, 1 + 5 is considered an expression. The second meaning is the use of MEL statements to animate attributes, which is the topic of this section. To distinguish the difference between the two, the capitalized word, *Expression,* will be used for expressions that animate attributes, and the lowercase word, *expression,* will be used as they relate to MEL programming statements.

3.7.1   Learning Expressions

This section covers how to animate objects using Expressions. Rather than get bogged down in learning syntax and so on, you dive straight in and begin using Expressions. This will allow you to quickly learn how useful and easy they are.

WIGGLE

This exercise demonstrates how to control the movement of an object using Expressions. A ball that moves across the screen is made to wiggle up and down based on an Expression.

1. Open the **Wiggle.ma** scene.

2. Press **Alt+v** or click on the **Play** button.

    A small sphere named **ball** moves across the screen.

3. Select the **ball** object.

4. Select **Windows | Animation Editors | Expression Editor...**

    The **Expression Editor** window is where you create and edit all expressions.

5. In the **Expression Name** field, type `WiggleBall`.

    It is important to give the Expression a name, since this makes it easier to find later when you have many Expressions. Currently the **ball** object is selected, so the **Attributes** section lists its attributes. The goal is to animate the ball's vertical motion, so you need to write an expression to control the **ball's translateY** attribute.

6. Click on the **translateY** attribute in the **Attribute** list.

7. In the **Expression:** area type the following:

    ```
    ball.translateY = time;
    ```

    It is possible to use an attribute's short name. For instance, you could have written:

    ```
    ball.ty = time;
    ```

    Maya automatically substitutes the long name for you afterwards. In general, it is best to use the long name, since it is clearer.

8. Click on the **Create** button to create the expression.

   If there is a syntax error or other problem with the Expression, an error message is displayed. The details of the error won't be shown in the Expression Editor. Instead open the Script Editor and try again. The complete error message is then displayed in the Script Editor. Turn on **Show Line Numbers** in the Script Editor to show exactly where in the Expression the error occurred.

9. Click on the **Play** button.

   The ball now steadily rises as the animation progresses. The ball's *y* position is now set to the current time. As you move from one frame to another, the Expression is evaluated. If the Expression gives a different result each frame, the attribute will be animated. Since the *y* position is set to the current time and it increases steadily with each new frame, the *y* position also increases.

   Notice that, unlike in standard MEL scripting, in which you need to call the currentTime command to get the current time, in Expressions you can simply use the predefined time variable. To make writing Expressions more convenient, Maya provides two predefined variables: time and frame. The time variable holds the current time, in seconds, and the frame variable holds the current frame. The frame variable is automatically calculated based on the current time and frame rate settings. These variables are read-only, so they can't be changed in an Expression.

   You'd like the *y* position to wiggle up and down rather than just move upwards.

10. Set the **Expression** text to the following:

    ```
    ball.translateY = rand(0,1);
    ```

    The ball's *y* translation is now set to the result of the rand command. This command generates a new random number each time it is called. By calling the function with the arguments 0 and 1, only random numbers between 0 and 1 are generated. As a result, the ball's **translateY** value is now random but is guaranteed never to be outside of the range of 0 to 1.

11. Click on the **Edit** button to save and apply the changes.

12. Click on the **Play** button.

    The ball now jumps up and down as the animation progresses. Unfortunately the movement is now a little too erratic. Since the rand command creates an entirely new random number each time it is called, at each frame it moves to a completely different position.

What you'd like is for the ball to move randomly but not as erratically. Fortunately there is another command, noise, that gives you some randomness, though more easily controlled.

13. Set the **Expression** to the following:

```
ball.translateY = noise( ball.translateX );
```

The ball's *y* translation is now set to the result of the noise command. The noise command generates a random number, but unlike the rand command, it generates the same random number if you call it with the same input value. In this example, the ball's *x* translation is given as input to the command. So when the ball is at the same *x* position, it generates the same random *y* position. Since the *x* position is animated, the ball moves across the screen and its new **ball.translateX** value is fed into the noise command, which in turn controls the **ball.translateY** attribute.

14. Click on the **Edit** button.

15. Click on the **Play** button.

The ball's movement isn't as wild as before, but it still isn't quite right. You'd like to make the movement a little smoother. Since the noise command creates a random number based on its input value, to create random numbers that don't vary so wildly, the input value shouldn't vary as much from frame to frame. Instead of using the ball's *x* position as is, you could use half of it instead. This means that the value passed into the noise command won't change as much, and therefore the ball's *y* position won't change as wildly.

16. Set the **Expression** to the following:

```
ball.translateY = noise( ball.translateX / 2 );
```

17. Click on the **Edit** button.

18. Click on the **Play** button.

The ball moves across the screen, but the wiggles are now less abrupt and smoother.

By using an Expression, you have indirectly stated that the ball's **translateY** value depends on the ball's **translateX** value. As such, any time you change the translateX value, the Expression is automatically evaluated and the **translateY** value updated.

19. **Zoom** out a little.

20. Click on the **Move Tool**.

21. Interactively move the ball back and forth along the x-axis.

The ball's *y* position is continually updated as you change its *x* position. The animation is driven entirely by your Expression, so you no longer have to explicitly keyframe it. One of the great features of Expressions is that once they are set up, the animation happens automatically.

FLASH

In this next example, as an object moves around, you would like it to flash on and off automatically.

1. Open the **Flash.ma** scene.

2. Click on the **Play** button.

The sphere, **ball**, moves along a path.

3. Right-click on the **ball** object, then select **Materials | Material Attributes...** from the pop-up menu.

The **siren** material is currently assigned to the **ball**.

4. In the **Attribute Editor** at the bottom, click on **Select** to select the **siren** material.

5. Select **Windows | Animation Editors | Expression Editor...**

6. Set the **Expression Name** to Flashing.

Notice that the **Selected Obj & Attr** and **Default Object** fields are set to **siren**. When an Expression is created, the currently selected object becomes the default. If you begin writing your Expression but don't give the name of a node to apply it to, Maya automatically applies it to the node listed in the **Default Object** field.

7. Set the **Expression** field to the following:

```
colorR = 1;
```

Notice that you didn't specify which object's color should be changed, but just the attribute.

8. Click on **Create**.

   The ball's color now changes to pink.

9. Set the **Expression** field to the following:

   ```
   colorR = 0;
   ```

10. Click on **Edit**.

    This time the Expression is automatically updated to use the default object, so it now reads:

    ```
    siren.colorR = 0;
    ```

    Notice also that the **Selected Obj & Attr** field is now set to to `siren.colorR`.

11. Set the **Expression** to the following:

    ```
    siren.colorR = colorG = colorB = 1;
    ```

12. Click on **Edit**.

    The Expression is automatically updated to include the default object name.

    ```
    siren.colorR = siren.colorB = siren.colorC = 1;
    ```

    While the use of the default object and default attribute can be handy for quickly typing your Expression, it is best to write the explicit name and attribute of the object you want to change. As the number and complexity of your Expressions increase, relying on this automatic substitution behavior may result in subtle bugs as an unintended name is substituted. By using the complete name and attribute, you can be sure the correct object is being used.

13. Click on the **ball** object.

    Since this is the selected object, your Expression for the material is no longer displayed.

14. In the **Expression Editor**, select **Select Filter | By Expression Name**.

Since you named your Expression Flashing, it is shown in the **Expressions** list.

15. Click on the **Flashing** item.

16. Set the **Expression** text to the following:

```
vector $pos = <<ball.translateX, ball.translateY, ball.translateZ>>;
float $dist = mag( $pos );
siren.colorR = siren.colorG = siren.colorB = $dist;
```

17. Click on **Edit**.

18. Click on the **Play** button.

The ball is now completely white. The ball's color is set to its distance from the origin (0, 0, 0). This was done by first getting its current position as a vector and then determining the length of that vector. The Expression has a problem. Color values must be within the range of 0 to 1, yet you are setting values that are greater than 1, since the distance of the object is being used. You need to have the Expression set valid color values.

19. Set the **Expression** text to the following:

```
vector $pos = <<ball.translateX, ball.translateY, ball.translateZ>>;
float $dist = mag( $pos );
siren.colorR = siren.colorG = siren.colorB = (cos( $dist ) + 1) / 2;
```

20. Click on the **Edit** button.

21. Click on the **Play** button.

The ball now flashes slowly as it moves along the path. You have used the cos command to produce an undulating wave pattern that is perfect for flashing since it gradually changes from on to off and then on again. Unfortunately, the direct result of a cosine function gives you values ranging between −1 and 1. Since you need values between 0 and 1, the result of the cosine has 1 added to it. Its values now lie between 0 and 2. This result is then scaled by half to produce the final value, which ranges between 0 and 1.

The flashing is now working, but you'd like to make it faster. To do this, you just scale the input value to the cos command. By making its input a larger number, the ball flashes faster, and by making it smaller it flashes slower. For this example, it is scaled by 3.

22. Set the **Expression** text to the following:

```
vector $pos = <<ball.translateX, ball.translateY, ball.translateZ>>;
float $dist = mag( $pos );
siren.colorR = siren.colorG = siren.colorB = (cos( $dist * 3 ) + 1) / 2;
```

23. Click on the **Edit** button.

24. Click on the **Play** button.

The ball now moves flashing rapidly.

MAGNET

This exercise covers how to create a magnet object that attracts another when it is within a certain distance.

1. Open the **Magnet.ma** scene.

2. Click on the **Play** button.

The sphere object, **magnet**, moves across the screen. The cylinder object, **metalObject**, remains stationary. You'd like to have the **metalObject** attracted to the **magnet** when it gets close.

3. Select the **metalObject**.

4. Select **Windows | Animation Editors | Expression Editor...**

5. Set the **Expression Name** to Attractor.

6. Click on the **translateX** attribute in the **Attributes** list.

7. Set the **Expression** to the following:

```
vector $magPos = <<magnet.translateX,
                   magnet.translateY,
                   magnet.translateZ>>;
vector $newPos = $magPos;
metalObject.translateX = $newPos.x;
metalObject.translateY = $newPos.y;
metalObject.translateZ = $newPos.z;
```

The **metalObject**'s position is now exactly that of the **magnet**. First, the **magnet**'s position is retrieved and stored in the $magPos vector variable. Another variable, $newPos, is defined, and it is assigned the $magPos variable. The **metalObject**'s position is then set to the $newPos vector.

8. Click on the **Create** button.

9. Click on the **Play** button.

The **metalObject** follows the **magnet**'s position exactly. You'd like the **metalObject** to attach itself to the **magnet** only when it gets within a certain distance. If it isn't within that distance, it should remain at its original location.

10. Set the **Expression** to the following:

```
vector $startPos = <<4.267, 1, -0.134>>;
vector $magPos = <<magnet.translateX, magnet.translateY,
magnet.translateZ>>;
vector $newPos;
if( frame == 1 )
    $newPos = $startPos;
else
    $newPos = $magPos;
metalObject.translateX = $newPos.x;
metalObject.translateY = $newPos.y;
metalObject.translateZ = $newPos.z;
```

The starting position of the **metalObject** has been manually recorded by looking at its value in the **Channel Box**. The $startPos vector is set to this value. When the current frame is the first frame, the **metalObject**'s position, $newPos, is set to the $startPos. When it isn't the first frame, its position is set to the $magPos vector.

11. Click on the **Edit** button.

12. Move the time slider to the first frame.

The **metalObject** moves to its initial position.

13. Move the time slider to the next frame.

The **metalObject** moves to the **magnet**'s position. With the initial and final positions for the object now decided, how do you decide when it should move from one to the other?

14. Set the **Expression** to the following:

```
vector $startPos = <<4.267, 1, -0.134>>;
vector $magPos = <<magnet.translateX, magnet.translateY,
magnet.translateZ>>;
vector $newPos;
if( frame == 1 )
    $newPos = $startPos;
else
    {
    vector $curPos = <<metalObject.translateX,
                        metalObject.translateY,
                        metalObject.translateZ >>;
    float $dist = mag( $curPos - $magPos );
    if( $dist < 5 )
        $newPos = $magPos;
    else
        $newPos = $curPos;
    }
metalObject.translateX = $newPos.x;
metalObject.translateY = $newPos.y;
metalObject.translateZ = $newPos.z;
```

The current position is taken from the **metalObject** and stored in the $curPos variable. Next the distance from the **metalObject** to the **magnet** is calculated using the **Expression** mag($curPos - $magPos). This is the length of the vector between the two positions. If the distance is less than 5, the **metalObject** is moved to the **magnet**'s position; otherwise it remains at its current position.

15. Click on the **Edit** button.

16. Click on the **Play** button.

You're almost there. The only remaining problem is that the cylinder actually penetrates the sphere rather than stick to its surface. Since you can determine the radius of the **magnet** sphere and the radius of the **metalObject** cylinder, you can calculate where to position the **metalObject** so that it just touches the sphere.

17. Set the **Expression** to the following:

```
vector $startPos = <<4.267, 1, -0.134>>;
vector $magPos = <<magnet.translateX, magnet.translateY,
magnet.translateZ>>;
vector $newPos;
if( frame == 1 )
    $newPos = $startPos;
else
    {
    vector $curPos = <<metalObject.translateX,
                       metalObject.translateY,
                       metalObject.translateZ>>;
    float $dist = mag( $curPos - $magPos );
    if( $dist < 5 )
        {
        $offset = makeNurbCylinder1.radius + makeNurbSphere1.radius;
        $newPos = <<$magPos.x + $offset, $magPos.y, $magPos.z>>;
        }
    else
        $newPos = $curPos;
    }
metalObject.translateX = $newPos.x;
metalObject.translateY = $newPos.y;
metalObject.translateZ = $newPos.z;
```

The distance the metalObject has to be positioned away from the magnet is calculated in the $offset vector. The metalObject's position is offset along the x-axis by that amount.

18. Select the **metalObject**.

19. In the **Channel Box**, click on the **makeNurbSphere1** item listed under **Inputs**.

20. Move to a frame where the **metalObject** is attracted to the **magnet**.

21. Interactively change the **Radius** attribute.

The **metalObject** remains stuck to the **magnet** as the radius changes. If the radius increases so much that the **metalObject** is greater than 5 units away, it will no longer stick. If you'd like to correct this, change the Expression so that it calculates the distance between the surfaces of the objects rather than their centers.

3.7.2   Expression Guidelines

Once you understand how Expressions work and how to create them, the real work is defining which formula or equations you need to write in order to animate an attribute in a particular way. Fortunately, almost all the MEL commands and procedures can be used in an Expression. You can even define and use your own procedures. This section covers the use of Expressions in more detail, including any restrictions and caveats you should be aware of.

ATTRIBUTE ASSIGNMENT ONLY

An Expression's purpose is to set an attribute's value based on some MEL statements. The Expression should do nothing else. In particular, an Expression should not directly or indirectly change the topology of the Dependency Graph; it shouldn't create or break connections, create or delete nodes, and so on. Doing so leaves the Dependency Graph in an inconsistent state. Therefore all MEL commands that significantly alter the Dependency Graph should be avoided.

Once an Expression has been run, there is no way to undo any of the commands it issued. A normal MEL script is run and then can be immediately undone if necessary. An Expression can be run at any time. If the user requests the attribute the Expression controls, it runs. If the time slider is changed, the Expression runs. Since there is no defined "start, run, end" path for an Expression, there is no way to undo its actions.

If you had an Expression, for example, that created a new sphere each frame, simply rewinding to the first frame won't remove all the spheres it has created previously and return the scene to its original state. Playing the animation again causes the Expression to create another series of spheres. Likewise, an Expression that deleted objects doesn't restore them when the animation is rewound. As such, avoid all MEL commands that create or delete objects.

Only MEL commands that don't directly or indirectly change the Dependency Graph should be used. It should be clear from the command's description whether this is the case. If not, save your scene before letting a potentially dangerous Expression evaluate.

SUPPORTED ATTRIBUTE TYPES

In an Expression, only attributes of type, `float`, `int`, or `boolean`, can be accessed. An error results if you attempt to access, for instance, an attribute of type `string`, `matrix`, or any other type. The following Expression causes an error message to be displayed:

```
$wm = obj.worldMatrix;
```

Expressions don't take into account an attribute's implicit minimum and maximum values. These values are used only for the user interface. As such, you are free to set an attribute's value to any floating-point value. However, most attributes have a well-defined range of valid values. For instance, setting the colorR attribute to 10 is invalid since the range of color component values is between 0 and 1. It is important to bear this in mind, since an error message will be displayed when you assign to an attribute a value that is outside its valid range.

When you refer to an object, it may be necessary to use its complete DAG path. This is particulary important when two objects in the scene have the same name but different parents. Take, for example, a scene with two **box** objects. The first is a child of the **objA** transform node, and the second is a child of the **objB** transform node. Their complete paths are **objA|box** and **objB|box**, respectively. If the following Expression is used, an error results:

```
box.translateX = 1;

// Error: More than one attribute name matches.
        Must use unique path name:  box.translateX //
```

The complete path of the **box** object is needed to avoid any ambiguities. Changing the Expression to the following corrects this:

```
objA|box.translateX = 1;
```

Note that there are no spaces before or after the vertical line character (|).

AVOID SETATTR AND GETATTR COMMANDS

To retrieve and set an attribute's value, the getAttr and setAttr commands must be used. For example, the following sets and then gets the **box.scaleX** attribute:

```
setAttr box.scaleX (rand(100) * 0.5);
float $sx = `getAttr box.scaleX`;
```

For convenience, you can directly retrieve and set attributes in an Expression using the member access operator (.). Recall that this is similar to how the *x, y, z* components of a vector are accessed. The previous code would be written as follows if used in an Expression.

```
box.scaleX = rand() * 0.5;
float $sx = box.scaleX;
```

In fact, using setAttr and getAttr in an Expression can result in unexpected results. This is because both these commands can bypass the usual Dependency Graph evaluation mechanism. Calling them from inside an Expression produces an undefined result. As such, both commands should be avoided entirely.

CONNECTED ATTRIBUTES

If your Expression attempts to set the value of an attribute that is the destination of a connection, an error results. If, for instance, in the following Expression the **scaleX** attribute is already animated (driven by an animation curve node), then an error message is displayed.

```
sphere.scaleX = 23;

// Error: Attribute already controlled by an expression,
          keyframe, or other connection: sphere.scaleX
```

To correct this, you first need to break the connection to the **scaleX** attribute. Use the disconnectAttr command to do this. Once broken, the Expression is free to control the **scaleX** attribute.

AUTOMATIC DELETION

In certain situations your Expression could be deleted without your even knowing. When you create an Expression, Maya actually creates an *expression* node. This is a Dependency Graph node with connections to the attributes the Expression controls. The **expression** node actually stores your Expression. Maya can decide to delete the **expression** node if it thinks it is no longer being used. Say you had a scene with a **box** object, then created the following Expression:

```
box.translateX = 2;
```

If you then delete the **box** object, Maya also deletes its associated **expression** node and, thereby, your Expression. The reason for this is that with the **box** object now gone, the **expression** node doesn't have any connections coming into it. The **expression** node, like many others, is designed to automatically delete itself when this happens. Similarly, if you have an Expression that refers to multiple objects and these are all deleted, the **expression** node also is deleted since all its output connections have been removed. For instance, animation curve nodes automatically delete themselves when they aren't used to animate any attributes.

This node behavior is designed to prevent the existence of *orphaned nodes*. These are nodes that don't have any input or output connections. They simply exist in the scene but don't do anything.

In most cases this automatic deletion behavior causes no problems since your Expression no longer had any effect anyway. If you want to prevent problems, however, simply have the Expression control a *dummy* attribute on a node that you know won't be deleted. For example, create a group node **dummyNode**, then add a float attribute, **dummy**, to it as follows:

```
group -empty -name dummyNode;
addAttr -shortName dmy -longName dummy
        -attributeType "float" dummyNode;
```

Finally, set your Expression to the following:

```
dummyNode.dummy = 1;
... // Other expression statements
```

As long as the **dummyNode** object and its associated **dummy** attribute exist, your Expression won't be automatically deleted.

3.7.3 Debugging Expressions

Due to when and how Expressions are evaluated, they have some particularities and restrictions on how you write and debug them. This section covers some of these issues.

ERROR CHECKING

When an Expression is written in the Expression Editor and it contains a syntax error, the error's complete details aren't shown. Open the Script Editor to see the complete details of the error. Note also that if you have a working Expression and then go and change it, you should be sure to check for errors. If the new changes cause an error, the new expression won't be used. Instead the previous expression will still exist, and it will be what is evaluated. Only when the expression is free of syntax errors does it replace the previous expression. If you have made changes to an expression but it's operating as before, then check for this.

TRACING

Since an Expression is executed automatically when the attributes it affects need updating, you don't have direct control over when it will be executed. Also the results of expressions aren't displayed like commands issued from the Command Line or Script Editor. In order to trace the execution of an Expression, the best method is to use `print` statements. Use the `print` command to display information about what statement is being executed, as well as the current values of variables.

For example, if you had assigned an Expression named **Centered** that placed the current object in the center of two others, then its execution and variables could be traced as follows:

```
print ("\nExecuting Centered at frame " + frame);
obj.translateX = objA.translateX + 0.5 * (objB.translateX -
    objA.translateX);
obj.translateY = objA.translateY + 0.5 * (objB.translateY -
    objA.translateY);
obj.translateZ = objA.translateZ + 0.5 * (objB.translateZ -
    objA.translateZ);
print (" x=" + obj.translateX + " y=" + obj.translateY + " z=" +
    obj.translateZ );
```

When you animate or move **objA** or **objB**, the Expression would be automatically executed. The updated **obj** position will be printed as follows:

```
Executing Centered at frame 8 x=-12.90351648 y=-0.6519004166 z=1.691102353
Executing Centered at frame 8 x=-12.97169705 y=-0.6322368845 z=1.677296334
Executing Centered at frame 8 x=-13.07624005 y=-0.5929098204 z=1.643959307
Executing Centered at frame 8 x=-13.2126012 y=-0.5535827562 z=1.61634727
....
```

To see the complete results of the `print` statements, open the **Script Editor**. Since you may not always want to have tracing on, you could define a global variable to control this feature:

```
global int $doTracing = false;
```

Then in your Expression, you can print messages based on whether $doTracing is turned on.

```
if( $doTracing )
    print ("\nExecuting Centered at frame " + frame);
obj.translateX = objA.translateX + 0.5 *
                 (objB.translateX - objA.translateX);
obj.translateY = objA.translateY + 0.5 *
                 (objB.translateY - objA.translateY);
obj.translateZ = objA.translateZ + 0.5 *
                 (objB.translateZ - objA.translateZ);
if( $doTracing )
    print (" x=" + obj.translateX + " y=" + obj.translateY +
           " z=" + obj.translateZ );
```

DISABLING

If you are debugging multiple Expressions, it is often useful to disable some so you can concentrate on others in detail. To disable an Expression, open it in the Expression Editor, then turn off the **Always Evaluate** check box. The Expression still exists, but simply won't be evaluated.

BROKEN CONNECTIONS

An Expression can get input from one object's attribute in order to control another object's attribute. It is quite possible that this input object is somehow deleted. In this case the Expression can't evaluate correctly. If an Expression uses an attribute that has subsequently been deleted, Maya displays it in the Expression using a special notation. Take, for instance, the following Expression:

```
obj.translateX = box.scaleX;
```

Suppose the **box** object was then deleted. Maya automatically changes the expression to the following:

```
obj.translateX = .I[0];
```

When an attribute is missing, Maya substitutes its name with .I[x], where x is its internal index. The .I indicates that it was an *input attribute*. This is an attribute that was being used as input to the Expression. Similarly, there are *output attributes*. These are the attributes being controlled by the Expression. If, in the previous example, the **obj** object had been deleted rather than the **box**, Maya would set the expression to the following:

```
.O[0] = box.scaleX;
```

The `.0` indicates that an output attribute is now missing. Whenever this occurs, you must manually edit the Expression so that it refers to a valid attribute.

OBJECT RENAMING

Maya automatically handles the situation in which an object that you were referring to in an Expression changes its name. However, your Expression, as shown in the Expression Editor, may need to be reloaded to show the new updated name. Simply click on the **Reload** button. The Expression is then displayed with the object's new name.

3.7.4 Particle Expressions

A particle is simply a point. Often it is animated to move around. Each particle has an individual position, velocity, and acceleration. It can also have a mass. While an understanding of physics and how forces apply to objects will greatly benefit your writing of Expressions for particles, it's still possible to control particles with a basic knowledge of mathematics.

1. Open the **ParticleGrid.ma** scene.

   The scene consists of an array of stationary particles.

2. Select the **particles** object.

3. Open the **Attribute Editor.**

4. Click on the **particlesShape** tab.

5. Scroll down to the **Per Particle (Array) Attributes** section.

6. Right-click in the field next to **position**, then select **Creation Expression...** from the pop-up menu.

7. Set the **Expression:** text to the following:

   ```
   particlesShape.position = <<1,0,0>>;
   ```

8. Click on **Create.**

9. Go to the first frame.

   All the particles seem to have disappeared. What has actually happened is that they all now have the same position (1, 0, 0).

   In the Expression Editor, notice that the **Particle:** option is set to **Creation.** You have just defined the *creation expression* for the particles. The creation expression is called at the first frame. This expression is used to define the initial settings for the particles. In this example, all the particle positions have been initialized to the same point.

In order to see the effect of the creation expression, it is important that you be at the first frame.

10. Set the **Expression** text to the following:

```
particlesShape.position = sphrand( <<4, 0, 4>> );
```

11. Click on **Edit**.

The particles are now placed in a circle. The sphrand function generates random positions inside a sphere. The extent of the sphere's width (*x*), height (*y*), and depth (*z*) are defined by the vector passed into the sphrand command. In this instance, the sphere has been reduced to a flat circle since the *x* and *z* radii are 4 while the *y* radius is 0.

12. Move to some other frame.

13. Move back to the first frame.

The particle positions change. Each time you move back to the first frame, the particle positions change. While you want particles to have a random position, you don't want them to be completely different each time you move to the start frame. When you first render the particles, they will be in one set of locations. If you then went to the start frame again, they would be initialized to a new set of locations. The first render wouldn't match the second render, even though you are rendering the same frame. When you are doing multilayer composites, this simply won't do. It is very important that the particles be initialized to a consistent set of random locations.

Even though the sphrand function generates completely random numbers, it does so based on an initial number. This number is used to initalize the random number generator used internally by the sphrand command. This number is commonly referred to as the *seed*. All numbers that the sphrand command generates are, therefore, relative to this intial number. By setting the initial number, you can guarantee that the sphrand command produces a consistent series of random numbers. This is done using the seed command.

So it follows logically that the seed command be called just before the sphrand command. Unfortunately the creation expression is called once for each particle, so the seed command is called the same for each particle. What is really wanted is for the seed to be initialized once for all the particles. Since this is impossible in the creation expression, the seed command is called using an alternate methodology.

14. Set the **Expression** text to the following:

```
seed( particleId );
particlesShape.position = sphrand( <<4, 0, 4>> );
```

15. Click on **Edit**.

16. Move to some other frame.

17. Move back to the first frame.

The particle positions are now random but consistent at the first frame. The particleId is a unique index assigned to each individual particle. The creation expression is run once for each of the particles. As such, the particleId is updated with the current particle's ID before the expression is called. By seeding the random number generator based on this ID, you can guarantee that a call to sphrand will have been initialized to the same value.

It is also possible to position the particles in a more structured manner using the particleId.

18. Set the **Expression** to the following:

```
int $nRows = sqrt(particlesShape.count);
float $spacing = 0.5;
float $x = (particlesShape.particleId % $nRows) * $spacing;
float $z = trunc(particlesShape.particleId / $nRows) * $spacing;
particlesShape.position = <<$x, 0, $z>>;
```

19. Click on **Edit**.

The particles are now evenly spaced in a grid. The first step is to get the actual number of particles. This value is kept in the **particleShape**'s **count** attribute. Taking the square root of the count gives the number of rows and columns needed to create a square layout, that is, $nRows * $nRows particles. The $spacing variable defines the distance between each particle.

The $x and $z positions are calculated using the particle's ID. Since the ID ranges from 0 to **count**–1, you can divide that range into strips, each $nRows in length. These are then multiplied by the $spacing amount to determine their final position.

In addition to creation expressions, particles also support *runtime expressions.* These expressions are evaluated on all frames other than the start frame. So the creation expression will be evaluated on the start frame, then on all later frames (> start frame) the runtime expression will be evaluated.

20. Click on the **Runtime** radio button next to the **Particle:** prompt.

An empty Expression field is shown. Your creation expression is still there. You can toggle between the creation and runtime expressions by clicking on their associated radio buttons. A particle shape stores both the creation and runtime expressions internally, so you don't have to create separate Expressions.

21. Set the **Expression** field to the following:

```
particles.velocity = <<0,1,0>>;
```

22. Click on **Edit**.

23. Click on the **Play** button.

The particles gradually move upward. By setting the velocity of the particles, they can be moved in a particular direction. In this case, they are all moving up 1 unit along the y-axis, each frame.

Notice that it wasn't necessary to create a new Expression for the **velocity** attribute that is being changed. A particle shape node has just one creation expression and one runtime expression. Unlike regular Expressions, where you can have one Expression per attribute, particle Expressions allow all their attributes to be accessed from the creation and runtime expressions.

24. Set the **Expression** to the following:

```
vector $pos = particlesShape.position;
particlesShape.velocity = <<0, sin( $pos.x ),0>>;
```

25. Click on **Edit**.

26. Click on the **Play** button.

The particles now move up and down, as if they were on a series of longitudinal waves.

27. Set the **Expression** to the following:

```
vector $pos = particlesShape.position;
particlesShape.velocity = <<0,sin( mag($pos) ),0>>;
```

28. Click on **Edit**.

29. Click on the **Play** button.

The particles now move up and down, as if they were on a series of radial waves.

An object is now created that when moved near a particle results in the particle being pushed upward.

30. Minimize the **Expression Editor** window.

31. Select **Create | Locator** from the main menu.

32. Name the locator transform **updraft** node.

33. Animate the **updraft** node, in x and z, so that it moves across the particles.

34. Maximize the **Expression Editor** window.

35. Select **Select Filter | By Expression Name** from the menu.

36. Click on the **particleShape** expression.

37. Set the **Expression** to the following:

```
vector $draftPos = <<updraft.translateX, updraft.translateY,
    updraft.translateZ>>;
vector $partPos = particlesShape.position;
float $dist = mag( $partPos - $draftPos );
vector $v = particlesShape.velocity;
if( $dist <= 2 )
    $v = <<0,2,0>>;
particlesShape.velocity = $v;
```

38. Click on **Edit**.

39. Click on the **Play** button.

Any of the particles within two units of the **updraft** locator are driven up in the air. This is done by setting their velocity to (0, 2, 0). If a particle is further than 2 units away, it simply maintains its current velocity.

CREATION AND RUNTIME EXPRESSION EVALUATION

The creation expression is evaluated when the current time is less than or equal to the particle's **startFrame** time. So if the particle's **startTime** is set to 10, then the creation expression is evaluated for all frames from 0 to 10. At frame 11 and all later frames, the runtime expression will be evaluated. The runtime expression is always evaluated after the **startFrame** time.

More precisely, the creation expression is evaluated on every particle whose **age** attribute is 0. When a particle's **age** isn't 0, the runtime expression is evaluated. The **age** attribute is a read-only array of doubles. This is where Maya stores the current age of each of the individual particles. Since a particle can be born at any time, their ages can differ. As such, the creation expression is evaluated for those individual particles whose **age** is 0. Those particles whose **age** is greater than 0 have the runtime expression evaluated.

Fortunately it is possible to visualize the age of each particle. With the **particleShape** selected, open the **Attribute Editor**. In the **Render Attributes**, set the **Particle Render Type** to **Numeric**. Click on the **Current Render Type** button. Set the **Attribute Name** field to **age**. The particles now display their current age.

PER OBJECT AND PER PARTICLE ATTRIBUTES

It is important to understand that particles are actually stored in a **shape** node. This **shape** node is of type `particle`. Since it is a node like any other, all its attributes can be animated using Expressions, as you would expect. However, particles are special in that you could write an Expression to control not just the entire **shape** node, but also each individual particle. As such, a distinction is made to attributes that are shared between all particles and attributes that are individual to each particle. An attribute that is common to all particles is referred to as a *per object attribute.* By changing this attribute, all particles are affected. An attribute that allows you to define per particle values is referred to as a *per particle attribute.*

1. Open the **ParticleGrid.ma** scene.

2. Select **Shading | Smooth Shading All**.

3. Select the **particles** object.

4. Open the **Attribute Editor**.

5. Select the **particlesShape** tab.

6. Scroll down to the **Add Dynamic Attributes** section.

7. Click on the **Color** button.

8. Turn on the **Per Object Attribute** option, then click on **Add Attribute**.

   In the **Render Attributes** section, there are now three additional attributes (**Color Red**, **Color Green**, **Color Blue**).

9. Set the **Color Red** attribute to **1**.

   All the particles are displayed in red. Since the newly added color attribute is a per object attribute, it is applied to all the particles. Changing the attribute affects all particles. If you want to control the colors of the particles individually, you need to create a per particle color attribute.

10. In the **Add Dynamic Attributes** section, click on the **Color** button.

11. Turn on the **Per Particle Attribute** option, then click on **Add Attribute**.

    The **rgbPP** attribute is now listed in the **Per Particle (Array) Attributes** section.

12. Right-click on the field next to **rgbPP**, then select **Creation Expression...** from the pop-up menu.

13. Set the **Expression** text to the following:

```
particlesShape.rgbPP = <<rand(1),rand(1),rand(1)>>;
```

14. Click on **Create**.

    The particles now have random colors. Since a per particle attribute, **rgbPP**, was created, it automatically overrides the per object attributes, **colorRed, colorGreen, colorBlue**. To remove either a per object or per particle attribute, simply use the **Delete Attributes** feature.

15. Click on the **Select** button at the bottom of the **Attribute Editor**.

    The **particlesShape** node is now selected.

16. Select **Attributes | Delete Attributes...** from the **Attribute Editor** menu bar.

    A list of newly added attributes is listed.

17. Select the **rgbPP** attribute.

18. Click on the **OK** button.

    The per particle attribute has now been deleted. The particles are once again displayed in red, since they are no longer overriden by a per particle attribute. The per object color attributes are now in effect. They too can be removed from the node by using the **Delete Attributes** method.

When a particle shape is first created, Maya creates attributes only for the most common particle properties. It is then up to you to add the other per object and per particle attributes that you need.

19. In the **Add Dynamic Attributes** section, click on the **General** button.

20. Click on the **Particles** tab.

The list contains all the per particle attributes you can add to the node. Notice that at the end of the list there are the **userScalarPP** and **userVectorPP** attributes. You can use these to define your own custom attributes that you want to associate with the particles.

VECTOR COMPONENTS

While an expression can freely read and assign vectors, it can't read or assign *components* of vectors. You'll have noticed in the earlier example that the **particleShape's** **position** attribute was set as follows:

```
particlesShape.position = <<1,0,0>>;
```

Since the **position** attribute is a vector, what would have happened if the components, *x*, *y*, and *z*, had been accessed directly?

```
particlesShape.position.x = 1;
...
```

This results in the following error:

```
// Error: Attribute not found or variable missing
        '$': particlesShape.position.x //
```

The following statement also generates a similar error.

```
float $x = particlesShape.position.x;
```

The reason neither of these work is that the dot operator (.) is used to access both a node's attributes as well as a vector's components. The attribute access takes precedence over the vector component access when you use the dot operator, so in the previous statement, Maya is trying to find an attribute named **x** in the **position** attribute, rather than trying to access its *x* component. If you want to access any of the components of a vector attribute, then you first put the attribute's values into a local vector variable.

```
vector $v = particlesShape.position;
```

You are then free to use the dot operator (.) to access the vector's components, since Maya now knows that you are implicitly referring to a vector.

```
float $x = $v.x;
```

Likewise, when you assign a value to a vector attribute, you can't do it one component at a time. Only an entire vector can be assigned, so to change just the *x* component of the position, you would need to do this:

```
vector $v = particlesShape.position;
$v.x = 34;
particlesShape.position = $v;
```

3.7.5 Advanced Expressions

This section covers some of the more advanced uses of Expressions.

COMBINING EXPRESSIONS WITH KEYFRAME ANIMATION

What if you wanted to create an animation that combined hand-animated keyframes with Expressions? The realistic animation of an airplane is one such candidate. Direct control over the general movement of the airplane would be supplemented with some added turbulence. The direct control can be done using standard keyframing, while the turbulence can be done with an Expression. Unfortunately, Maya provides no direct means of combining these two techniques, so indirect methods need to be used instead.

1. Open the **Plane.ma** scene.

2. Click on the **Play** button.

   A small plane flys across, then out of the screen.

3. Select **Window | Outliner...**

4. Click on the **plane** item in the list.

5. Display the **Channel Box**.

The Channel Box indicates that the **plane**'s translation and rotations have already been animated. Some automatic vertical turbulence should be added to this animation. You'd also like to be able to go back and change the original key-frame animation and have the turbulence update automatically.

6. Open the **Attribute Editor**.

7. Right-click in the **TranslateY** box.

A small pop-up menu is displayed. It shows that the **plane_translateY.output** attribute is connected into this attribute. The **translateY** attribute needs to be controlled by the Expression. The Expression takes the original animation and perturbs it slightly to simulate the turbulence. The connection from the current animation curve to the **translateY** attribute needs to be broken.

Unfortunately, when you remove all the output connections from an animation node, it is automatically deleted. There is no way to change this behavior. In order to prevent the deletion, there must always be one connection for its output. A new attribute in the **plane** node is created, then the animation is connected to it before breaking the original connection. This ensures that the animation node isn't automatically removed, since it is always this newly formed connection.

8. Open the **Script Editor**.

9. Execute the following:

```
addAttr -longName "animTranslateY" -attributeType "float" plane;
```

The **animTranslateY** attribute is added to the **plane** node.

10. Execute the following:

```
connectAttr plane_translateY.output plane.animTranslateY;
disconnectAttr plane_translateY.output plane.translateY;
```

The animation output is now connected to the new attribute, **animTranslateY**.

11. Execute the following:

```
expression -string "plane.translateY = plane.animTranslateY"
            -name "Turb";
```

An expression named **Turb** is created. It sets the plane's **translateY** to take the value of the new **animTranslateY** attribute. Since the original animation curve is feeding the **animTranslateY** attribute, the plane's **translateY** is now indirectly taking the animated values.

12. Click on the **Play** button.

The plane moves exactly as before; however, the final **translateY** value now comes from an expression and not from the animation curve. The expression directly outputs the result of the animation curve. Some turbulence is now added.

13. In the **Script Editor**, execute the following:

```
expression -edit -string "plane.translateY = plane.animTranslateY +
    noise( plane.translateX / 3, plane.translateZ / 3  );" Turb;
```

The plane's height is now determined by the original animation plus some turbulence introduced by using the noise command. The noise command is called with the plane's *x* and *z* position, reduced by a factor 3.

14. Click on the **Play** button.

The plane is now getting a good amount of buffeting from the turbulence. Extending on this technique, it would be possible to automatically jolt the plane based on the location of antiaircraft gunfire.

With the plane now configured, it is possible to change the plane's keyframe animation and have the turbulence added automatically.

C ₊₊ API

4.1 INTRODUCTION

MEL clearly provides a very powerful and effective means for both automating and simplifying tasks in Maya. It may be that MEL provides all the programmable functionality you'll ever need. If however you need further access and control, you can use the C++ API. Through this API you can create your own custom Dependency Graph nodes. These can be integrated directly into Maya and work seamlessly with all other nodes. This allows you to directly implant your own functionality into the very core of Maya.

Another nonnegligible advantage of the C++ API is that the plugins you develop will often run much faster than the equivalent MEL scripts. Since the plugins are compiled and linked, the result is fully optimized for the target platform. There is no need for on-the-fly interpretation as with MEL, thereby making it much faster.

Admittedly, to exploit the C++ API fully requires a good understanding of the C++ language, though it is possible to begin creating some Maya plugins with just a minimum understanding of C++.

Following is a nonexhaustive list of all the areas and functionality in Maya that can be extended using this API.

♦ **Commands**

Custom commands can be created that have all the functionality of Maya's own built-in commands, including undo/redo, help, complete access to the scene, and any combination of command arguments. Since the command is written in C++, you are free to use any C++ functionality, including external libraries, from within your command. This is in sharp contrast with MEL procedures, which allow calls only to other MEL procedures and commands. Your own commands are treated exactly like Maya's built-in commands. As such, they can be called in any MEL statement.

♦ **Dependency Graph Nodes**

The C++ API allows you to create your own custom DG nodes. You can create a simple DG node that provides basic functionality, such as adding two points together, or a very complex one that animates an entire character. Once your node is registered with Maya, it can be created, deleted, and edited like any standard node. Connections can be made to it from other nodes, and it can connect its outputs to other nodes. Your nodes can be completely and seamlessly integrated into Maya.

In addition to the basic DG nodes, you can extend on more specialized DG nodes, such as manipulators, locators, shapes, and so on to add your own functionality. By deriving your own nodes from these specialized nodes you can reuse a lot of their existing functionality, thereby enabling you to add just the minimum necessary for your purposes.

♦ **Tools/Contexts**

There is often a need to perform a given set of interactive operations in order to complete a task. To split an edge, for example, you must select two edges then press **Enter.** This series of interactive steps is performed using a context. You are given quite a lot of freedom as to what your context can do, including how the mouse clicks and the mouse movements are interpreted. Creating your own contexts allows for the implementation of specific modeling and animation operations.

♦ **File Translators**

In order to support a wide variety of known, and unknown, file formats, Maya provides for custom file translators. These file translators control the loading and saving of Maya data. They can use any means necessary to convert the data into their own formats. There are even specific extensions for doing game translators.

♦ **Deformers**

A deformer provides a mechanism for moving a series of points. The way in which it does its deformation can be as simple or as complex as necessary. With the C++ API, you can create your own deformers that are completely free to deform many different types of objects.

♦ **Shaders**

Maya includes an extensive set of **Shading Network** nodes. These nodes can be combined in different ways to create complex shading of objects. Using the C++ API, you can create your own custom shading nodes. Like Maya's nodes, they have complete access to all the relevant shading information, including normals, positions, textures, and so on. You can even implement your very own super-sampling mechanisms.

Custom hardware shaders can also be created.

♦ **Manipulators**

While is it possible to change a node's attribute values using the Channel Box, Graph Editor, and so on, Maya does provide a visual means of changing values: manipulators. Manipulators provide a series of visual controls with which you interact to change a node's attribute. For instance the sphere manipulator allows you to move one of the manipulator points to increase the radius of the sphere. Manipulators can sometimes be more intuitive for users, since with them users can interactively move or adjust a visual control, which is often easier than typing in a specific value. While they are interactively changing the value, they will get immediate feedback as to the result.

♦ **Locators**

A locator is used to give the user a visual reference point. Locators operate exactly like any Maya object, except that they won't show up in the final render. Custom locators can be created using the C++ API. You are free to draw the locator using almost any OpenGL method, so locators can be very simple or complex in appearance.

♦ **Fields**

A field provides a volume in which various forces can be applied. A field is typically applied to particles to have them move in a particular way. Some examples of fields include gravity, drag, and turbulence. By creating your own fields you control the forces being applied to particles.

♦ **Emitters**

The purpose of an emitter is to determine when and how a series of particles is generated. Emitters control how many particles are created and in what direction and at what velocity they move. While Maya comes with an extensive set of different emitters, using the C++ API you can create your own custom emitters.

- **Shapes**

  Shape nodes hold the actual geometry data. Some examples include NURBS curves and surfaces, polygonal meshes, particles, and so on. Maya allows you to create your own custom shapes. These shapes can be completely integrated into Maya, so all the standard modeling and animation tools will work with them. Your custom shapes can be created, deleted, and edited like Maya's built-in shapes.

- **Solvers**

  Even though Maya already provides an extensive set of inverse kinematic (IK) solvers, it is possible to create your own. A custom IK solver can be created and integrated into Maya. It can then be used to control a series of bones such as the standard Maya does.

  It is also possible to define your own *spring laws*. These can be used to get complete control over how soft body dynamics are performed.

4.2 FUNDAMENTAL CONCEPTS

Before discussion of the specifics of the C++ API, it is extremely important to cover some of the fundamental concepts. Since any system provides its own particular levels of freedom and, likewise, constraints, it is important to have a good grasp of the factors that motivated its design. Understanding why the C++ API was designed the way it is gives you insights into how best to design your own plugins so that they work well within Maya's framework.

Since the design of the C++ API differs from the typical object-oriented approach, it is important to learn its differences. An understanding of the differences will help guide you in the design and implementation of your own plugins. In fact, this understanding is absolutely critical to developing efficient and effective plugins.

4.2.1 Abstracted Layer

When using the C++ API, it may seem as if you are directly manipulating Maya's objects and data structures. What you are, in fact, doing is using a layer above the actual Maya core. The API gives the programmer access to Maya's core through a well-defined set of interfaces. Maya's core consists of all the internal functions and data that is developed by Alias | Wavefront. At no time can you *directly* access Maya's core. All communication, whether it be the creation, manipulation, or deletion of data, must be done through the API. The diagram in Figure 4.1 shows the different programming layers and how they communicate with each other.

Those familar with systems or windows programming will recall that typical APIs provide a set of function calls that give them access to the underlying system. The complete API consists of the entire set of available functions. However, in Maya the API is defined through a set of C++ classes. All access to Maya's core is therefore done through each class's member functions. These member functions can create, retrieve, and manipulate Maya's data.

So why create an API on top of Maya's core? Why not give the developer direct access to Maya's internal functions and data? By creating an API on top of the core, the developer is abstracted from the actual details of Maya's current implementation. By not exposing the current implementation to the developer, Maya's engineers are free to change and improve Maya's core without having to be concerned about "breaking" code developed by external developers. As long as the API doesn't change too radically, external developers don't have continually to update their plugins when a change is made to Maya's core. This safeguards their investment in plugins that have already been developed.

The API also provides a certain level of protection from possible misuse. Since Maya maintains and controls the internal data, it can prevent an errant plugin from deleting critical data. The API can trap potentially bad calls and return an error without actually performing the call. As such, the API acts as a filter and guards against potentially dangerous operations. This isn't to say that you can't crash Maya, though these safeguards reduce the likelihood substantially.

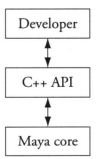

FIGURE 4.1 Programming interface

Given that you are using a layer on top of Maya's core, you may wonder if there is a speed penalty by going through this extra layer. In practice there is little penalty. Many of the C++ classes are, in fact, wrapper classes that translate very quickly into Maya's internal representation. Also, many of the API class methods have direct equivalents in the internal classes, so the translation from one to the other is fast.

4.2.2   Classes

The C++ API consists of a series of C++ classes. The majority of the classes are divided into logical hierarchies based on their type. At this stage, it isn't important to learn what each particular class is and how it works, but it is important to understand the general structure of the hierarchy and where the classes are located in this hierarchy. The complete hierarchy of Maya classes can be found in the Maya documentation:

```
maya_install\docs\en_US\html\DevKit\PlugInsAPI\classDoc\hierarchy.html
```

The Maya C++ hierarchy consists of a lot of classes. Fortunately, only a relatively small portion of them are used for the most common plugins. In practice, a core set of classes is used very often, while many of the more esoteric ones are rarely used. As such, this book doesn't cover each class in detail, but instead focuses on the most important and widely used ones.

NAMING CONVENTION

All the Maya class names start with a capital **M**, for example, **MObject**. Since Maya doesn't use C++ namespaces, this helps prevent any conflicts with other user-defined classes. Maya also differentiates classes by putting them into subclasses that are based on their functionality. While some of the classes don't follow the typical object-oriented parent-child hierarchy, they do contain common functionality and so share a common prefix. For example, you'll notice that there are many classes prefixed with **MPx**. All proxy classes are derived from this subclass. The class name prefixes are presented in Table 4.1.

DESIGN

While the C++ class hierarchy may appear to be similar in design to most object-oriented hierarchies, there are some very important differences that must be understood in order to effectively use the API. In fact, not fully understanding the differences often causes a great deal of confusion when you later design your own plugins.

TABLE 4.1 CLASS NAME PREFIXES		
Prefix	Logical Grouping	Examples
M	Maya class	MObject, MPoint, M3dView
MPx	Proxy object	MPxNode
MIt	Iterator class	MItDag, MItMeshEdge
MFn	Function set	MFnMesh, MFnDagNode

Classical Approach

First, take a look at how *typical* C++ class hierarchies are designed and then compare this to the design of the class hierarchy used in the Maya C++ API. The standard texts on object-oriented design state that the most common methodology for designing a class hierarchy is by starting with a base class. This base class defines the root of the hierarchy. While it is possible to have more than one base class, for the purposes of this explanation it is restricted to just one. This root base class is typically abstract and contains just the most common member functions and data that all derived classes share. These functions are often defined to be abstract (pure virtual functions). Classes derived from this base class implement either some or all of these member functions or possibly add their own abstract functions. The number of classes and whether they implement the functions or leave them abstract is up to the designer. Applying this design methodology to the creation of a vehicle class hierarchy could result in the hierarchy shown in Figure 4.2. The hierarchy starts with the root **Vehicle** class and then derives a set of specific vehicle classes (**Motorcycle, Car, Truck**) from it.

If you use the standard object-oriented approach, each of the classes contains both the data and the functions that operate on it. As such, each vehicle subclass would contain its own specific vehicle data. The **Car** class may, for instance, hold information about what type of wheels and how many gears there are. This data

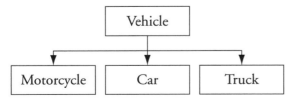

FIGURE 4.2 Vehicle class hierarchy

could be hidden away in a private or protected member, or it could be exposed as a public member. Alternatively, this data could be accessed only through member functions. Whichever approach is used, the class ultimately defines the *interface* to the data. The class decides how you can access the data. So each class, in essence, defines its own API to its functionality and data.

In order to better exploit *polymorphism,* the **Vehicle** class may define the following set of pure virtual functions:

```
virtual void drive() = 0;
virtual int numWheels() = 0;
```

The subclasses, **Motorcycle, Car,** and **Truck,** would then implement this function. Once implemented, these classes could then be used as follows:

```
Car speedy;
speedy.drive();
```

Since all the main classes are derived from **Vehicle,** you can use polymorphism to call an object's drive() function without knowing the exact type of the object. In the following example, the broom pointer can point to both the **Truck** and **Car** objects and call their drive() functions. The actual function called is the class-specific drive() function.

```
Truck t;
Car c;

Vehicle *broom = &c;
broom->drive();
broom = &t;
broom->drive();
```

Imagine that the vehicle hierarchy was the API provided to you, the developer. In order to extend the hierarchy to incorporate your own classes, you could derive them from **Vehicle** or any of the other classes. If, for example, you wanted to create a more specific type of car that is used for off-road travel, you could derive a new class, **Offroad,** from the **Car** class. The new class hierarchy is shown in Figure 4.3.

The new **Offroad** class has been seamlessly integrated into the hierarchy. It can be used with the same ease as any of the original vehicle-derived classes. Even

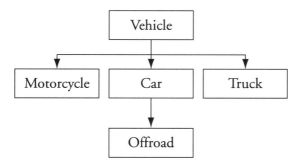

FIGURE 4.3 Extended class hierarchy

though you can add classes, you can't make changes to the original hierarchy. You can add extensions to it by deriving your own classes. It isn't possible, with this design, to add a new virtual function to the **Vehicle** or **Truck** classes. Only the original hierarchy designers can do this. If they decide to make a change to the hierarchy, then your class will be affected. The amount of work you would have to do to your class depends on the pervasiveness of their changes. Any new member functions may also need to be implemented in your class. If, for example, the following virtual function was added to the **Vehicle** class:

```
virtual bool isElectric() = 0;
```

then your **Offroad** class must provide an implementation for this function or else it can't be instantiated, since it will be an abstract class.

Maya Approach

With an understanding of the classical approach to object-oriented hierarchy design, now look at how Maya's approach differs. In order to demonstrate the difference, this same set of vehicle classes is redesigned using the Maya approach. The previous design coupled the data and the functions that operate on that data into the class. The Maya approach makes a separation between the two. So for the vehicle hierarchy, a class, **Object**, for holding data is created. This class is designed to hold many different types of data. The type of data it holds depends on which vehicle class uses it. The hierarchy of data classes is shown in Figure 4.4.

The **Object** class would contain data common to all the classes in the hierarchy, while the derived classes, **MotorcycleObj**, **CarObj**, and **TruckObj**, would contain

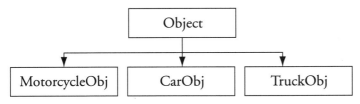

FIGURE 4.4   Data hierarchy

more specific data for a particular type of vehicle. These classes contain the data and also their own member functions to access the data.

```
virtual void drive() = 0;
virtual int numWheels() = 0;
```

Another separate hierarchy of classes is used to access and manipulate the various data classes. Maya refers to classes that operate on the data as *function sets.* In this example, you create classes that don't contain any data but that provide member functions that can operate on an **Object** object. In object-oriented terminology, these classes are known as *functors.* An entire class hierarchy of function sets is created to operate on vehicle data. Figure 4.5 shows this hierarchy.

The root of the hierarchy is the **VehicleFn** class. This class contains the same set of member functions as the original hierarchy.

```
virtual void drive();
virtual int numWheels();
```

The difference is that the class won't also contain the data that it operates on. Instead, the data will be given to the class through the **Object** hierarchy classes. The

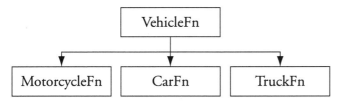

FIGURE 4.5   Function set hierarchy

MotorcycleFn class therefore operates on a **MotorcycleObj** object. The data object is attached to the function set class so that whenever a member function is called it operates on that data.

The **VehicleFn** class contains a private pointer to the data object it operates on.

```
Object *data;
```

Another member function, which allows you to specify which data object the class operates on, is added to the base **VehicleFn** class.

```
virtual void setObject( Object *obj ) { data = obj; }
```

Given this new hierarchy design, how can you perform some of the same operations as the original hierarchy? To make the car drive, the following would now be used:

```
CarObj carData;
VehicleFn speedyFn;
speedyFn.setObject( &carData );
speedyFn.drive();
```

The **CarObj** object is first created. This contains the data for the car. A **VehicleFn** function set is then created and attached to the car data. When the drive() function is called, it then operates on the **carData** object.

Since the **VehicleFn** class defines common functions for all derived classes, it can call those functions. It could be applied to the **TruckObj** object.

```
TruckObj t;
CarObj c;

VehicleFn broomFn;
broomFn.setObject( &t );
broomFn.drive();
broomFn.setObject( &c );
broomFn.drive();
```

The astute programmer will notice that the **VehicleFn** class can't know about the **CarFn** or the **TruckFn** class implementations, so calling drive() in the preceding code actually calls the **VehicleFn**'s `drive()` function rather than the **CarFn** or **TruckFn** `drive()` function. The trick is that while the function set classes define an interface for performing operations on the data, it is actually the data classes that do the real work.

As shown earlier, the data classes would define their own internal virtual `drive()` function. Under the covers, the **VehicleFn**'s `drive()` function would be implemented as follows:

```
virtual void VehicleFn::drive()
{
data->drive();
}
```

Depending on what data object you set the function set to using **setObject()**, the data's appropriate `drive()` function is called. As such, the same function set can operate on different types of data objects.

You may then wonder why they even bother having function sets when you can access the data objects directly and call their member functions. In Maya, you are *never* given access to the data class hierarchy. You are given access only to a class called **MObject**. This class knows about the hierarchy. So with the entire data hierarchy hidden from you, you must use the function set class hierarchy to operate on Maya's hidden data objects. It is through these function set classes that you access all of Maya's internal data.

So the major difference between the original hierarchy design and Maya's is that Maya exposes a function hierarchy only through its function set classes. This is unlike the original design, in which the hierarchy exposes both a data and function hierarchy.

4.2.3 MObject

While the previous section described the Maya class hierarchy in abstract terms, its actual specifics are now covered.

In the previous example, the data objects were known to you. You knew that there was an **Object**, **MotorcycleObj**, **CarObj**, and **TruckObj** class. Since you knew about the different objects, you could then access them directly. In Maya only the root **Object** class is exposed to the developer. All the other classes are hidden. In Maya, the equivalent of your example **Object** class is the **MObject** class.

All data is accessed through the **MObject** class, so this class is used for accessing all the different data types in Maya. It may appear that the **MObject** class itself holds the actual data that is being used. In reality the **MObject** is just a *handle* to another

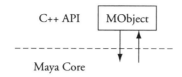

FIGURE 4.6 **MObject** interface

object inside the core. Since it is just a handle, it can be thought of as a pointer to some other internal data held within the core. Only the core can make use of the pointer. The **MObject** itself doesn't contain any data other than this pointer. This situation is shown in Figure 4.6.

Since the **MObject** effectively contains a *void pointer* (void *) to some internal data and the specifics of the internal data are never exposed, you can't convert this pointer into something meaningful in your code. Only Maya's core knows exactly what the pointer refers to. Since the class doesn't hold the data but instead a reference, when you delete or create an **MObject**, you are just deleting and creating a handle. You aren't actually deleting or creating the internal Maya data.

It is very important to understand this, since it can be the source of a lot of confusion. Maya owns the actual internal data and never gives you direct access to it. It instead gives you a handle to the data in the form of an **MObject** object. At no time can you directly delete the internal data, since deleting the **MObject** simply deletes a handle and not the actual data. Maya maintains and controls all of the internal data, whether it be nodes, attributes, or some other Maya data. You are given access to this data through the API, but at no time do you have direct control over it. The data is always accessed and manipulated through the API.

It is important to bear this in mind, since, as with any API, you are just being given an interface to some underlying structure or system. You are never given direct access. The internals of Maya are never directly exposed. An important side effect of this lack of direct access is that you, as a developer, never actually own or have any complete control over any of the Maya nodes or other objects. Maya, in fact, maintains complete and total control over all objects. This immutable fact is so important that it has to be reemphasized:

Maya owns all the data, you own none of it!

4.2.4   MFn Function Sets

With a better understanding of how Maya presents its data, now look at how you can create, edit, and delete that data. A handle is needed to the data before it can be worked on. Maya uses the **MObject** class as this handle. With an **MObject** pointing to the data, the next step is to create a function set that then operates on the data.

As mentioned earlier, all classes prefixed with **MFn** are function sets. Function sets are designed to create, edit, and delete data. To create a **transform** node, the following **MFnTransform** function set would be used:

```
MFnTransform transformFn;
MObject transformObj = transformFn.create();
```

The `transformNodeObj` contains a handle (**MObject**) to the newly created **transform** node. The member functions of the **MFnTransform** object, `dagNodeFn`, can now be called to operate on the **transform** node. Its name can be retrieved using the `name()` function.

```
MString nodeName = transformFn.name();
```

Function sets are organized into a class hierarchy based on what type of data they can operate on. All function set classes are derived from **MFnBase**. The **MFnTransform** function set's ancestors are shown in Figure 4.7.

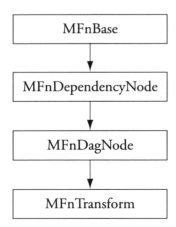

FIGURE 4.7 **MFnTransform** ancestors

Each new derived class adds new functions that can operate on more specific types of data. Since **MFnTransform** is derived from **MFnDagNode**, it can operate on all DAG node objects. Likewise, it is derived from **MFnDependencyNode**, so **MFnTransform** can operate on any dependency node. This hierarchy of functionality allows derived classes to operate on all data that their ancestors can operate on. For instance, the **MFnDagNode** class can operate on the node created by **MFnTransform**, since **MFnDagNode** is a base class of **MFnTransform**.

```
MFnTransform transformFn;
MObject transformObj = transformFn.create();
MFnDagNode dagFn( transformObj );
MString name = dagFn.name();
```

Notice how the dagFn function set could be applied to the transformObj since the **MObject** that is created points to a **transform** node that is itself derived from a **dagNode**.

So what happens when a function set is asked to operate on an **MObject** that it isn't designed to? The **MFnNurbsSurface** function set is designed to work on NURBS surfaces. The **MFnPointLight** function set operates on point lights. What would happen if the **MFnNurbsSurface** function set were asked to operate on a point light object?

```
MFnPointLight pointLightFn;
MObject pointObj = pointLightFn.create();

MFnNurbsSurface surfaceFn( pointObj );
double area = surfaceFn.area();
```

The surfaceFn is asked to operate on the pointObj data by having this data passed into its constructor. When the area() function is called, Maya checks to see that the data object it is operating on is indeed a NURBS surface. If it isn't, Maya returns an error. Since the object is a point light and not a NURBS surface, an error is returned. In this case, the error isn't checked, so the program continues. The value of the area variable is therefore invalid. Error checking and reporting are covered in a later section.

How does Maya know what type of data an **MObject** is referring to? The **MObject** class contains a member function, apiType(), that returns the type of object. Each function set class can determine if it is compatible with a given object by calling this function. The **MObject**'s similar function, hasFn(), can also be used.

CUSTOM FUNCTION SETS

In the original example, the **Offroad** class was added to the class hierarchy. This was done by simply deriving from the **Car** class. The necessary **Vehicle** and **Car** member functions then had to be implemented in this new class. Since Maya separates the data from the functions, this approach does not work in Maya.

Intuitively, you may consider simply deriving a new function set from an existing one. This new function set would reimplement the functions that it wants to override. Say, for example, you wanted to implement a new NURBS geometric type of your own design. Even though it would be a new type and include its own features, it would have some features in common with Maya's current NURBS implementation. You could potentially derive a new function set class, **MFnMyNurbs**, from the existing **MFnNurbsSurface** class. With this new function set class, it should be possible to operate on your new NURBS shape.

Unfortunately this won't work. Rather than create a new NURBS type, you have in fact simply created a new NURBS function set that can still operate only on existing NURBS surfaces. Recall that an **MObject** points to some data that only Maya knows about. The different **MFn** function sets operate on these **MObjects**. The engineers and designers of Maya know exactly to which data the **MObject** refers and so can manipulate it. Since the exact details of the data pointed to by the **MObject** isn't known to outside developers, there is no way that you can access this data in any meaningful way. Even deriving the new function set class doesn't give you any more access than you had before. As such, the new class can call only the functions that its base class already implemented. You couldn't provide your own functions, since you can't operate on the actual real data. Since the actual Maya data can't be accessed, there is no point in deriving from function sets.

4.3   DEVELOPING PLUGINS

To add your own custom nodes, commands, and so on to Maya, you need to create a plugin. A plugin is a dynamically linked library. Maya loads the plugin (library) at run time to integrate your new functionality.

Under Windows, plugins are standard dynamic link libraries with the special file name extension .mll rather than the usual .dll extension. Under the various Unix environments, plugins are dynamic shared objects with the file name extension of .so. In reality, any file name extension can be used, but using these standard extensions ensures better consistency.

It is assumed that you have installed the Maya development kit. You may recall that this was one of the optional packages available during the installation. The development kit includes all the necessary headers and library files for creating plugins. If it is installed correctly, you should have the following directories under the main `maya` directory:

```
maya_install\include
maya_install\libs
maya_install\devkit
```

If these are missing, you will need to install them before continuing.

When a new version of Maya is released, it may require a change in the plugin development environment. This may mean that a new version of the compiler is needed or that plugins should now be placed in another directory. These and a multitude of other requirements may change from one version to the next. Since the development environment is very specific to a particular version of Maya, any instructions that this book gives may not apply to future versions. Rather than provide obsolete information, the complete instructions for developing plugs for the various platforms are available at the book's companion website, *www.davidgould.com*.

The website includes the most up-to-date instructions for developing plugins for Windows, Irix, Linux, Mac OS X, and any later platforms that run Maya. Having the instructions available online means that they can be quickly updated and amended to ensure that you have the precise set of instructions for the particular version of Maya for which you are developing.

4.3.1 Plugin Development under Windows

For those developing under Windows, this section contains instructions for developing Maya 4.*x* plugins. As mentioned earlier, these instructions may not apply to later versions of Maya, so please consult the companion website for more recent instructions. Maya is supported under Windows NT 4.0, Windows 2000, and Windows XP. Later versions of Windows that are derived from any of these versions should work.

To develop Maya plugins, you'll need a copy of Microsoft Visual C++ 6.0 or later. Be sure to apply the latest Microsoft Visual C++ service packs. If you are familiar with creating Windows DLLs, then creating a plugin should be relatively easy, since it uses exactly the same process.

Be sure to complete the following sections in order, since later sections assume that the previous section has been completed.

SETUP

If Microsoft Visual C++ was already installed when you installed Maya, the **Maya Plug-in Wizard** should have been automatically installed. This wizard does a lot of the plugin setup work for you. It asks you about a series of options, then generates all the necessary workspace, project, and source code files. While it is possible to set up a plugin without it, using the wizard is far more convenient. To create the Hello World plugin, complete the following:

1. Open Microsoft Visual C++.

2. Select **File | New**.

3. In the **New** dialog box, click on the **Projects** tab.

4. Click on the **Maya Plug-in Wizard** from the list of possible project types.

5. Set the plugin name in the **Project name:** field to HelloWorld.

6. Set the directory where you'd like to keep the plugin development files in the **Location:** field.

7. Click on **OK**.

8. In the next dialog box, select which version of Maya you'll be targeting.

9. If you've installed the development kit to a custom directory, set the **Location of the Developer Kit** to **custom location**. Ensure that the location is the parent directory of the devkit directory. For example, if the devkit is a subdirectory under the C:\Maya4.0 directory, then put c:\Maya4.0 in the location field and not c:\Maya4.0\devkit.

10. Set the **Vendor Name** field to your name.

11. Click on the **Next** button.

12. Leave the plugin type to **Mel Command**.

13. Set the **Maya type name** field to helloWorld.

14. Click on the **Finish** button.

   If you clicked on **Next** rather than **Finish**, you could have set the output plugin file name and also specified which other Maya libraries to link in. Most often the default settings are fine, so there is no need to change anything on this page.

15. A listing of all the new project files is then displayed.

16. Click on **OK**.

17. Click on the **Fileview** tab in the **Workspace** area on the left.

18. Expand the **HelloWorld Files** item.

19. Expand the **Source Files** item to reveal the helloWorldCmd.cpp file name.

20. Double-click on the helloWorldCmd.cpp item to open it.

21. Under the line #include <maya/MSimple.h>, add the following:

```
#include <maya/MGlobal.h>
```

22. Change the following line:

```
setResult( "helloWorld command executed!\n" );
```

to:

```
MGlobal::displayInfo( "Hello World\n" );
```

23. Save the helloWorldCmd.cpp file.

24. Build the plugin by selecting **Build | Build helloWorld.mll** from the main menu or by pressing **F7**.

    The resulting plugin file, helloWorld.mll, will be located in the Debug subdirectory. This subdirectory is under the directory that you specified earlier as the plugin location.

    The plugin file has now been built. It is now ready for use in Maya.

EXECUTION

The next step is to run Maya, then load your new plugin.

1. Open Maya.

2. Select **Windows | Settings/Preferences | Plug-in Manager** from the main menu.

3. Click on the **Browse** button.

4. Locate the directory that contains your plugin file, `helloWorld.mll`.

5. Select the `helloWorld.mll` file.

6. Click on the **Load** button.

    After a short pause Maya will have loaded the plugin. In the **Other Registered Plugins** section you should see a listing with `helloWorld.mll` and the **loaded** check box selected. This indicates that the plugin is currently loaded.

7. Close the **Plug-in Manager** window.

8. Press the back quote (`) key or click in the **Command Line** field.

9. Type in `helloWorld`, then press **Enter**.

    The words `Hello World` are displayed in the Command Feedback line.

    You've now successfully created, loaded, and executed your first Maya plugin.

EDITING

Now that the initial plugin has been created, you'll inevitably want to edit the source code.

1. Return to Visual C++.

2. In the the `helloWorld.cpp` file, change the following line:

    ```
    MGlobal::displayInfo( "Hello World\n" );
    ```

    to:

    ```
    MGlobal::displayInfo( "Hello Universe \n" );
    ```

3. Save the `helloWorld.cpp` file.

4. Rebuild the plugin by pressing **F7** or selecting **Build | Build helloWorld.mll** from the main menu.

    During compilation, the following error is displayed.

```
------------------Configuration: HelloWorld - Win32 Debug------------
Compiling...
helloWorldCmd.cpp
Linking...
LINK : fatal error LNK1168: cannot open Debug\helloWorld.mll for
    writing
Error executing link.exe.

helloWorld.mll - 1 error(s), 0 warning(s)
```

The plugin file `helloWorld.mll` can't be written to disk. What has happened is that Maya still has the previous `helloWorld.mll` file loaded. As long as this file is loaded in Maya, it can't be overwritten. The plugin must be unloaded prior to recompiling.

5. Return to Maya.

6. Select **Windows | Settings/Preferences | Plug-in Manager...** from the main menu.

7. Click on the **loaded** check box to the right of the `helloWorld.mll` item. This unloads the plugin.

8. Leave the **Plug-in Manager** window open.

9. Return to Visual C++.

10. Build the plugin again by pressing **F7** or selecting **Build | Build helloWorld.mll** from the main menu.

    This time the build should complete successfully.

11. Return to Maya.

12. In the Plug-in Manager window, click on the **loaded** check box next to the `helloWorld.mll` item. This reloads the plugin.

13. Click in the **Command Line**.

14. Type `helloWorld`, then press **Enter**.

    The words, `Hello Universe`, are printed in the **Command Feedback** line.

The process of editing and recompiling a plugin is the same as with any software development. The difference in Maya is that you must ensure that your plugin is unloaded before linking. Once the plugin has been recompiled, you can load it again.

DEBUGGING

Debugging in Visual C++ can be done interactively.

1. Close Maya.

2. Return to Visual C++.

   When the helloWorld project was created, the wizard automatically created two configurations: a debug and a release configuration. The debug configuration is used by default. This configuration ensures that the plugin contains debugging information. The steps for setting the active configuration are now covered, even though the project should be already set to the debug configuration.

3. Select **Build | Set Active Configuration...** from the main menu.

4. Select **HelloWorld – Win32 Debug** from the list.

5. Click on the **OK** button.

   Once this configuration is set, you don't have to redo these last steps unless the active configuration is changed.

6. Select **Project | Settings...** from the main menu.

7. Click on the **Debug** tab.

8. Next to the **Executable for debug session:** field, click on the arrow button.

9. Select **Browse...**

10. Locate the Maya executable file, maya.exe. This typically is in the bin subdirectory under the main Maya directory.

11. Click on the **OK** button.

12. Click on the **Category:** combo box.

13. Select the **Additional DLLs** from the drop-down list.

14. Click in the **Modules...** list.

    An editable field appears.

15. Click on the ... button.

    The **Browse** dialog box is displayed.

16. Set the **Files of type:** to **All Files(*.*)**

17. Locate the `helloWorld.mll` plugin file. It is in the `Debug` subdirectory of the main `helloWorld` project.

18. Click on the **OK** button.

19. Click on the **OK** button to close the **Project Settings** dialog box.

    The project is now set up to begin debugging. These steps have to be completed only once per project.

20. In the `helloWorld.cpp` file, click anywhere in the following line of text:

    ```
    MGlobal::displayInfo( "Hello Universe\n" );
    ```

21. Press **F9** to set a breakpoint.

    A red dot appears to the left of the line.

22. Press **F5** or select **Build | Start Debug... | Go** from the main menu to start debugging.

    If this is the first time the `maya.exe` program has been run in the debugger, you are told that the executable doesn't contain any debug information.

23. Select the **Do not prompt in the future** check box.

24. Click on the **OK** button.

    Maya then loads. The next steps load the plugin, as before.

25. Select **Windows | Settings/Preferences | Plug-in Manager** from the main menu.

26. Click on the **Browse** button.

27. Locate the directory that contains your `helloWorld.dll` plugin file.

28. Select the `helloWorld.dll` file.

29. Click on the **Load** button.

    After a short pause Maya loads the plugin.

30. Close the **Plug-in Manager** window.

31. Press the back quote (`` ` ``) key or click in the **Command Line** field.

32. Type in `helloWorld` and then press **Enter**.

The plugin executes and then when it reaches the breakpoint immediately returns you to Visual C++. You can now do the usual debugging tasks of checking variables, stepping through the code, and so on.

RELEASE

As mentioned in the previous section, the helloWorld project is automatically created with two configurations: debug and release. When developing and debugging the plugin, the debug configuration should be used. When you decide to finally release the plugin, the release configuration should be used. This configuration ensures that the plugin runs at maximum speed and doesn't contain any unnecessary debugging information. To use the release configuration, complete the following:

1. Select **Build | Set Active Configuration...** from the main menu.

2. Select **HelloWorld – Win32 Release** from the list.

3. Click on the **OK** button.

    The plugin has to be rebuilt using the current configuration.

4. Rebuild the plugin by pressing **F7** or selecting **Build | Build helloWorld.mll** from the main menu.

    The release version of the helloWorld.mll file is located in the Release subdirectory.

4.3.2 Initialization and Uninitialization

Since a plugin is a dynamic link library, plugins must provide an *entry point* and *exit point*. These are the functions that are called when the plugin is first loaded (entry function) and when it is finally unloaded (exit function), respectively. Under Windows, this is typically handled by the developer's own DllMain function. In the helloWorld plugin, these entry and exit points were automatically created by using the DeclareSimpleCommand macro. This macro automatically creates the command and both the initialization and uninitialization functions for you.

HELLOWORLD2 PLUGIN

Now take a closer look at how plugin initialization and uninitialization happens. In this example, a helloWorld2 command is created that simply prints out Hello World, as before. The complete source code is as follows.

Plugin: HelloWorld2
File: HelloWorld2.cpp

```cpp
#include <maya/MPxCommand.h>
#include <maya/MGlobal.h>
#include <maya/MFnPlugin.h>

class HelloWorld2Cmd : public MPxCommand
{
public:
    virtual MStatus doIt ( const MArgList& )
    { MGlobal::displayInfo( "Hello World\n" ); return MS::kSuccess; }
    static void *creator() { return new HelloWorld2Cmd; }
};

MStatus initializePlugin( MObject obj )
{
    MFnPlugin pluginFn( obj, "David Gould", "1.0" );

    MStatus stat;
    stat = pluginFn.registerCommand( "helloWorld2",
                                    HelloWorld2Cmd::creator );
    if ( !stat )
        stat.perror( "registerCommand failed");

    return stat;
}

MStatus uninitializePlugin( MObject obj )
{
    MFnPlugin pluginFn( obj );

    MStatus stat;
    stat = pluginFn.deregisterCommand( "helloWorld2" );
    if ( !stat )
        stat.perror( "deregisterCommand failed" );

    return stat;
}
```

The first section simply creates the helloWorld2 command. This section covers some of the basics of creating a command. Section 4.4 covers the creation of commands in far greater detail. The command class contains a simple doIt() function that is called when the command is executed. As before, it simply prints out Hello World into the Command Feedback line.

```
virtual MStatusdoIt ( const MArgList& )
{ MGlobal::displayInfo( "Hello World\n" ); return MS::kSuccess; }
```

The command also contains a static creator() function that allocates a command object and returns it.

```
static void *creator() { return new HelloWorld2Cmd; }
```

Following the definition of the command are the two initialization and uninitialization functions.

```
MStatus initializePlugin( MObject obj )
MStatus uninitializePlugin( MObject obj )
```

Both these functions must be present in any Maya plugin. If they aren't included, the plugin won't link. The initializePlugin function takes an **MObject** as input. This **MObject** is a handle to Maya's internal data for plugin types.

```
MStatus initializePlugin( MObject obj )
{
```

The next line creates an **MFnPlugin** object and initializes it with the obj variable passed in. Attaching the **MFnPlugin** to the **MObject** allows you to then call the **MFnPlugin** functions that in turn operate on the **MObject**.

```
MFnPlugin pluginFn( obj, "David Gould", "1.0" );
```

The helloWorld2 command is then registered. Registering the command makes it known to Maya so it can be used. Registration includes giving the name of the command as well as its creator function. The name is the text that you use to call the command, so in this case it is simply helloWorld2. The creator function is the static function that allocates a single instance of the command. This needs to be registered with Maya, since it won't know how to create an instance of your command otherwise.

```
MStatus stat;
stat = plugin.registerCommand( "helloWorld2",
                                HelloWorld2Cmd::creator );
```

The result of the registration is then checked, and if it fails an error is displayed.

```
if ( !stat )
    stat.perror( "registerCommand failed");
```

The initialization function then returns the result:

```
return stat;
}
```

If the return status of the function is not MS::kSuccess, then the plugin exits and the dynamic library is automatically unloaded. An error message is also displayed in the Command Feedback line. It is important to note that if the initializePlugin function fails, the uninitializePlugin function won't be called. As such, all cleanup, in the event initializePlugin fails, should be done in the initializePlugin function before it returns.

The uninitializePlugin function does the reverse of the initializePlugin function. It unregisters the command that was registered in the initializePlugin function.

```
stat = plugin.deregisterCommand( "helloWorld2" );
```

The function also returns a status indicating whether or not the uninitialization succeeded. If the return status is not MS::kSuccess, then the plugin isn't unloaded. It remains loaded in Maya and isn't unloaded until Maya exits.

In this particular example a single command was registered with Maya. In practice there can be an unlimited number of registrations. In later chapters, the registration of other functionality such as custom nodes, and custom data, is covered. However, in all cases, the initializePlugin and uninitializePlugin functions simply let Maya know what new functionality the plugin provides so that it can be used in the application.

4.3.3 Errors

CHECKING

Checking for errors and consistently handling and reporting them is very important for creating robust and stable applications. Maya provides a consistent error-reporting mechanism through the use of the **MStatus** class. This class defines possible states for the result of a given operation. When an operation fails, the status is set to the appropriate state.

Almost all Maya class functions take an optional pointer to an **MStatus** object. If you supply a pointer to an **MStatus** object, then Maya sets the object to the result of the function call. The complete declaration of the **MFnDependencyNode**'s name() function is as follows:

```
MString name( MStatus * ReturnStatus = NULL ) const
```

This function can be called without checking the result as follows:

```
MString dagName;
MFnDagNode dagFn( obj );
dagName = dagFn.name();
```

To do correct error checking, it is important to determine whether the function succeeded or failed. To do this, a pointer to an **MStatus** object is passed to the name() function.

```
MStatus stat;
dagName = dagFn.name( &stat );
if( !stat )
    MGlobal::displayError( "Unable to get dag name" );
```

The result of the function call is stored in the **stat** object. It is checked to determine whether it is set to a failure; if so, an appropriate action can be taken. In this example an error message is displayed. This example shows the most commonly used error-checking methodology in plugins.

There are a variety of ways to check the resulting **MStatus**. In addition to the if(!stat) used previously, the error() function can be used.

```
if( stat.error() )
    ... // error
```

The exact status can be retrieved from the object and compared against a particular status code. To test whether the status is set to the MS::kSuccess code, use the following:

```
if( stat.statusCode() != MS::kSuccess )
    ... // error
```

or more simply:

```
if( stat != MS::kSuccess )
    ... // error
```

Unfortunately, the error-reporting mechanism that Maya uses puts a lot of the emphasis on the developer to be vigilant in checking for errors. More often than not, the developer has to check the result of *every* Maya function called. This can become tiresome, and many programmers tend to be sporadic with their checking. However, it is extremely important to maintain consistent error checking throughout your plugin. In a series of function calls that don't check for failed calls, having a single check makes it very difficult to pinpoint where the error occurred. Bugs and runtime issues are resolved a lot faster if every piece of code is checked.

To help make writing error-checking code easier, the following macros can be used:

```
inline MString MyFormatError( const MString &msg, const MString
                              &sourceFile, const int &sourceLine )
{
    MString txt( "[MyPlugin] " );
    txt += msg;
    txt += ", File: ";
    txt += sourceFile;
    txt += " Line: ";
    txt += sourceLine;
    return txt;
}


#define MyError( msg ) \
    { \
    MString __txt = MyFormatError( msg, __FILE__, __LINE__ ); \
    MGlobal::displayError( __txt ); \
    cerr << endl << "Error: " << __txt; \
    } \
```

```
#define MyCheckBool( result ) \
    if( !(result) ) \
      { \
      MyError( #result ); \
      }

#define MyCheckStatus( stat, msg ) \
    if( !stat ) \
      { \
      MyError( msg ); \
      }

#define MyCheckObject( obj, msg ) \
    if( obj.isNull() ) \
      { \
      MyError( msg ); \
      }


#define MyCheckStatusReturn( stat, msg ) \
    if( !stat ) \
      { \
      MyError( msg ); \
      return stat; \
      }
```

You notice that these macros include the source file and line number in the error message. They also automatically output the error message to the standard error stream. The macros can be used as follows:

```
MObject dagObj = dagFn.object();
MyCheckObject( dagObj, "invalid dag object" );
```

Another example includes the following:

```
MStatus stat;
dagName = dagFn.name( &stat );
MyCheckStatusReturn( stat, "Unable to get name" );
```

It is important to note that many of the examples in this book don't do consistent error checking. The reason for this is that this book attempts to not overload or obfuscate the code. With all the error checking removed, the core concepts are presented more clearly to the reader. It is due to this goal of maintaining simplicity and brevity that the example code contains very minimal error checking. When developing plugins, however, the exact opposite should be done. Everything should be checked, and this should be done in a consistent manner. Your plugins will be more robust and stable as a result.

REPORTING

The **MStatus** class also provides some additional functions for error reporting. The errorString() function returns a string corresponding to the current error code. The perror() function allows you to print an error message to the current stderr stream. An example use of these functions is as follows:

```
if( stat.error() )
    stat.perror( MString("Unable to get name. Error: ") +
        stat.errorString() );
```

Like MEL, the C++ API has warning and error-reporting functions. The general method for reporting error messages is to use the **MGlobal**'s static displayError() function, as follows:

```
MGlobal::displayError( "object has been deleted" );
```

The error message is displayed in red in the Command Feedback line. To display a warning, use the displayWarning() function.

```
MGlobal::displayWarning ( "the selected object is of the wrong type" );
```

The warning message is displayed in magenta in the Command Feedback line. It is also possible to display general information by using the displayInfo() function.

```
MGlobal::displayInfo( "select a light, then try again" );
```

While there are a variety of ways of notifying the user of errors and warnings, the MGlobal::displayError() and MGlobal::displayWarning() are the ones that should be consistently used. They still work when Maya is run in batch mode, without an interface. If you want to display the result of an **MStatus** comparison, then use the **MStatus**'s errorString() function combined with the MGlobal:: displayError() function.

```
if( !stat )
  {
  MGlobal::displayError( MString("Unable to get name. Error: ") +
                                 stat.errorString() );
  return stat;
  }
```

Don't use pop-up windows to display errors or warnings. You can't know that your command isn't being called many times, so displaying a pop-up window each time may only frustrate the user. Also, the windows won't appear when Maya is being run in batch mode, so there will be no error reporting for the user to see.

Also, outputting errors and warnings to the standard error stream should really be used only for debugging. Users won't be able to see these errors when they are running Maya with the graphical interface. You should design your plugin so that this debugging and testing information isn't displayed in the final release version.

The **MGlobal** class also provides some error-logging features. While they aren't always used, you may find them handy. Refer to the **MGlobal** class for a complete list.

INTEGRATION

When you begin writing your own plugin functions, it is often best to adopt the Maya error-reporting mechanism. Your classes will then work in a consistent manner with other Maya C++ API classes. At its simplest you can provide an additional status pointer in your functions, in the same way that Maya does. The following function demonstrates how to do this:

```
int myNumPoints( points *data, MStatus *returnStatus = NULL );
```

In the function you simply have to check whether the pointer is valid and, if it is then returned, whether the function succeeded or failed.

```
int myNumPoints( points *data, MStatus *returnStatus )
{
int num = 0;
MStatus res = MS::kSuccess;
if( data )
  num = data->nElems();
else
  res = MS::kFailure;
if( returnStatus )
  *returnStatus = res;
return num;
}
```

Some Maya functions don't take a pointer to an **MStatus** object but instead return an **MStatus**. The following example demonstrates this:

```
MStatus myInitialize()
{
bool ok;
... // do initialization
return ok ? MS::kSuccess : MS::kFailure;
}
```

Consistently designing your functions to return **MStatus**, either directly or through a pointer, ensures that your functions behave like Maya's. That way the error-checking and reporting approach you put in place will be consistent throughout your plugin. It also means that other programmers that read or use your code won't have to use different error-checking and reporting schemes.

4.3.4 Loading and Unloading

As mentioned earlier, a plugin must be loaded into Maya before its functionality is made available. Likewise, when a plugin is no longer need, it can be unloaded. Also, when a plugin is being recompiled, it must be unloaded from Maya.

Since the tasks of loading and unloading a plugin are done so often, it is best to try to automate them. The following instructions detail how you can create two shelf buttons for unloading and loading a plugin.

1. Open Maya.

2. In the **Script Editor**, type the following, but don't execute it. Set the `$pluginFile` string to the complete path of the plugin you are developing.

```
{
string $pluginFile = "c:\\helloWorld\\Debug\\helloWorld.mll";
if( `pluginInfo -query -loaded $pluginFile` &&!
    `pluginInfo -query -unloadOk $pluginFile`)
  file -f -new;
unloadPlugin helloWorld.mll;
}
```

Notice that the MEL statements are enclosed in parentheses. This is to create a temporary block so that any variables created are local and therefore don't pollute the global namespace.

The `pluginInfo` command is called with `-query -unloadOK` flags to determine whether the plugin can be successfully unloaded. The most common reason that a plugin can't be unloaded is that one of its commands or nodes is still being used in the scene. Even if you delete the nodes, they can still exist in Maya's undo queue. In this case, the easiest solution is to create a new scene. This manually removes all commands and nodes. This is done using the `file -f new` statement. Lastly, the plugin is actually unloaded using the `unloadPlugin` command.

3. Select the text, then drag it to the **Shelf**.

    A shelf button is created. This shelf button is referred to as the **Unload** button.

4. In the **Script Editor**, type the following, but don't execute it. Once again, set the `$pluginFile` variable to the path of the plugin you are developing.

```
{
string $pluginFile = "c:\\helloWorld\\Debug\\helloWorld.mll";
loadPlugin $pluginFile;
}
```

The plugin is simply loaded using the `loadPlugin` command.

5. Select the text, then drag it to the **Shelf**.

    A shelf button is created. This shelf button is referred to as the **Load** button.

With these two shelf buttons set up, the process of loading and unloading your plugin is a lot faster. They can be used as follows:

♦ Write the plugin.

♦ Click on the **Load** button.

♦ Test the plugin.

♦ Click on the **Unload** button.

♦ Edit the source code and recompile.

♦ Click on the **Load** button.

♦ Test the plugin.

♦ .... Repeat.

In addition to the method mentioned previously, you can have your plugin loaded automatically when Maya starts by doing the following:

1. Set the **auto load** check box for the plugin in the **Plug-in Manager**.

2. Include the path to the plugin directory in the MAYA_PLUG_IN_PATH environment variable, or use a maya.env file to set the MAYA_PLUG_IN_PATH environment variable.

3. Restart Maya, and your plugin loads automatically.

4.3.5 Deployment

If you need to make your plugin available to a wider number of users, then you need to decide on a deployment scheme. The method for deploying plugins will most likely be the same as that used for deploying scripts.

1. If you have a work environment in which all the users can access a central server, the task of deployment is greatly simplified. Simply create a shared directory on a server, for example, \\server\mayaPlugins. This example uses the UNC (Universal Naming Code) format, but use whatever path format your network requires.

   If you don't have a central server but instead each user has his or her own local machine, then create a directory on each machine, for example, c:\mayaPlugins.

This directory is referred to as the *plugin_directory.*

2. Copy the plugin binary files to this directory.

3. On each of the users' machines, set the MAYA_PLUG_IN_PATH environment variable to include the path to the server's directory.

```
set MAYA_PLUG_IN_PATH=$MAYA_PLUG_IN_PATH;plugin_directory
```

Alternatively you could update each user's maya.env file to contain the environment variable setting:

```
MAYA_PLUG_IN_PATH=$MAYA_PLUG_IN_PATH;plugin_directory
```

While it is possible to store your plugins directly to the *maya_install*\plugins directory, this isn't advisable. It is always best to keep your plugins separate from the standard Maya plugins. This prevents confusion and helps to localize and update your plugins.

UPDATING

If a user is already running Maya when you deploy your plugins, the user won't automatically use the latest version. In fact, most operating systems don't allow you to overwrite the old plugin file since Maya is still using it. To correctly update, the user either needs to quit Maya then restart or to unload then reload the plugin. If the scene contains data specific to the plugin, then it won't unload. At that point the easiest thing to do is to restart Maya.

4.4 COMMANDS

When writing MEL scripts, you will most likely be using a lot of Maya's commands. Through the C++ API it is possible to add your own custom commands that can be used exactly like Maya's native commands. Like Maya's commands, they can be called from MEL scripts or anywhere a command can be called. At its barest minimum, a command is simply a function that gets called when the command is executed. In the previous section, the helloWorld command was created. When the command was executed, it simply printed out Hello World.

This section covers the creation of more-complex commands. Commands can include a lot more features, such as taking multiple inputs (arguments), providing help, and working with Maya's undo and redo mechanism.

4.4.1 Creating Commands

In order to understand how to create more-complex commands, a command named posts is covered in detail. It takes a curve and generates a number of posts (cylinders) along the curve. Figure 4.8 shows the original "guide" curve. The second figure, Figure 4.9, shows the result of executing the posts command.

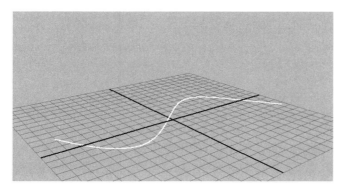

FIGURE 4.8 Guide curve

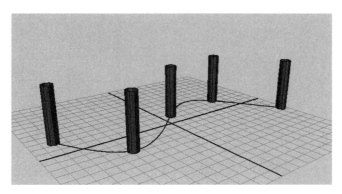

FIGURE 4.9 Resulting cylinders from post command

4.4.2 Posts1 Plugin

This section begins with a simple version of the posts command and progressively builds on it. As such, the first version of the command is named posts1.

1. Open the **Posts1** workspace.

2. Compile it, and load the resulting posts1.mll plugin in Maya.

3. Open the **PostsCurve.ma** scene.

4. Select the curve.

5. In the **Command Line**, type the following, then press **Enter**.

```
posts1
```

Five cylinders are created along the curve.

The source code for the command is now covered in detail.

Plugin: Posts1
File: postsCmd1.cpp

```cpp
class Posts1Cmd : public MPxCommand
{
public:
    virtual MStatus doIt ( const MArgList& );
    static void *creator() { return new Posts1Cmd; }
};

MStatus Posts1Cmd::doIt ( const MArgList & )
{
    const int nPosts = 5;
    const double radius = 0.5;
    const double height = 5.0;

    MSelectionList selection;
    MGlobal::getActiveSelectionList( selection );

    MDagPath dagPath;
    MFnNurbsCurve curveFn;
    double heightRatio = height / radius;
```

```
    MItSelectionList iter( selection, MFn::kNurbsCurve );
    for ( ; !iter.isDone(); iter.next() )
        {
        iter.getDagPath( dagPath );
        curveFn.setObject( dagPath );

        double tStart, tEnd;
        curveFn.getKnotDomain( tStart, tEnd );

        MPoint pt;
        int i;
        double t;
        double tIncr = (tEnd - tStart) / (nPosts - 1);
        for( i=0, t=tStart; i < nPosts; i++, t += tIncr )
            {
            curveFn.getPointAtParam( t, pt, MSpace::kWorld );
            pt.y += 0.5 * height;

            MGlobal::executeCommand( MString( "cylinder -pivot ") +
                pt.x + " " + pt.y + " " + pt.z + " -radius 0.5
                -axis 0 1 0 -heightRatio " + heightRatio );
            }
        }

    return MS::kSuccess;
}


MStatus initializePlugin( MObject obj )
{
    MFnPlugin pluginFn( obj, "David Gould", "1.0" );
    MStatus stat;
    stat = pluginFn.registerCommand( "posts1", Posts1Cmd::creator );
    if ( !stat )
        stat.perror( "registerCommand failed");
    return stat;
}
```

```
MStatus uninitializePlugin( MObject obj )
{
    MFnPlugin pluginFn( obj );
    MStatus stat;
    stat = pluginFn.deregisterCommand( "posts1" );
    if ( !stat )
        stat.perror( "deregisterCommand failed" );
    return stat;
}
```

The first step is to define the new command class, **Post1Cmd**. This class is derived from **MPxCommand**. All commands are derived from this class.

```
class Posts1Cmd : public MPxCommand
{
public:
        virtual MStatus doIt ( const MArgList& );
        static void *creator() { return new Posts1Cmd; }
};
```

The only two functions that need to be implemented are doIt and creator. The doIt function is a virtual function that is called when the command is executed. This function does the real work of the command. It performs whatever operation the command should do to produce its result.

The creator function is used to create an instance of the command. You'll notice that it is a static function, so it can be called without needing an instance of the class. In fact, there is no requirement that it be a static member function of the class or even named creator. The creation function is simply a standard function that returns an allocated instance of the command.

```
static void *creator() { return new Posts1Cmd; }
```

This function is registered with Maya in the initializePlugin function so that Maya knows how to create an instance of the command. When Maya is asked to execute the command, it first allocates an instance of the command using the creator function. Maya then calls the instance's doIt function. Each time you execute a command, Maya repeats these steps. This means that a new instance of the command is created each time a request is made to execute the command. The reason for this behavior is related to Maya's undo/redo mechanism. This mechanism is explained shortly.

Since the `doIt` function does all the real work, it is now covered in greater detail. The first section initialized the number of posts and their radius and height.

```
MStatus Posts1Cmd::doIt ( const MArgList & )
{
        const int nPosts = 5;
        const double radius = 0.5;
        const double height = 5.0;
```

A list of currently selected objects is then created. The `selection` object is used to hold the list of objects.

```
MSelectionList selection;
MGlobal::getActiveSelectionList( selection );
```

Unfortunately the **cylinder** primitive doesn't allow you explicitly to set its height. Instead a cylinder's height is based on its `heightRatio` value. This is the ratio of the height of the cylinder to its width. The `heightRadio` is calculated based on the desired height and radius of the cylinder.

```
double heightRatio = height / radius;
```

The list of selected objects is iterated over. This is done using an **MItSelectionList** object. Since the command is interested only in NURBS curves, a *filter* is specified that excludes all other objects that aren't a NURBS curve. The `iter` object is initialized with the `selection` object that you set up earlier.

```
MItSelectionList iter( selection, MFn::kNurbsCurve );
```

Iterating over the NURBS curves is then done with the following loop. Since the iterator traverses all the selected NURBS curves, you can apply the `posts1` command to multiple curves and it creates cylinders for each.

```
for ( ; !iter.isDone(); iter.next() )
    {
```

In order to identify the current NURBS curve, its complete DAG path is retrieved.

```
iter.getDagPath( dagPath );
```

The NURBS curve function set, **MFnNurbsCurve**, is attached to the DAG path. This specifies that all further function set operations will be applied to the object given by the DAG path.

```
curveFn.setObject( dagPath );
```

A NURBS curve is a parametric primitive. The curve can be evaluated at a given parametric value, *t*, resulting in a point that lies on the curve. The value *t* typically ranges from 0 to 1; however, it is possible that the curve has an arbitrary parametric range. The following code gets the start and end of that range:

```
double tStart, tEnd;
curveFn.getKnotDomain( tStart, tEnd );
```

The command creates `nPosts` number of posts along the length of the curve. The parametric range is divided into the number of desired posts. Because there needs to be a post at the start of the curve, as well as its end, the curve is made to have `nPosts-1` divisions.

```
double tIncr = (tEnd - tStart) / (nPosts - 1);
```

The next step is really the core of the function. For each step in the value *t*, a post is planted along the curve.

```
for( i=0, t=tStart; i < nPosts; i++, t += tIncr )
    {
```

The `getPointAtParam` function returns a point on the curve, given a parametric value. In this instance, the point is requested to be in world coordinates (`MSpace::kWorld`) rather than the default object coordinates (`MSpace::kObject`). The reason for this is that the posts should be placed in their final world position, irrespective of the transformation hierarchy of the curve.

```
curveFn.getPointAtParam( t, pt, MSpace::kWorld );
```

By default, the pivot point of a cylinder is at its center. Since the base of the cylinder should rest on the curve, the pivot point needs to be moved up by half the height.

```
pt.y += 0.5 * height;
```

Now with all the various parameters to the command prepared, the necessary MEL commands can be executed to do the actual cylinder creation. The `cylinder` command is used to create the cylinder with the given pivot (`-pivot`), radius (`-radius`), and height ratio (`-heightRatio`). A MEL statement can be executed from C++ by using the `MGlobal::executeCommand` function. It takes a string containing the MEL statements to be executed.

```
MGlobal::executeCommand( MString( "cylinder -pivot ") + pt.x + " " + pt.y
    + " " + pt.z + " -radius " + radius + " -axis 0 1 0 -heightRatio " +
    heightRatio );
}
```

In fact, it is quite common to see the execution of MEL statements inside a C++ plugin. There are many times when doing so makes more sense than trying to perform the same operation with many C++ API calls. There are also some MEL commands that don't exist in the C++ API, so you'll have no choice but to execute the MEL commands.

4.4.3 Adding Arguments

The `posts1` command is quite good, but it doesn't let you specify a different number of cylinders along the curve or the radius and height of each cylinder. Currently those parameters are set to fixed values inside the `doIt` function. The next command, `posts2`, extends the current command to allow for the various parameters to be set on the command line.

1. Open the **Posts2** workspace.

2. Compile it, and load the resulting `posts2.mll` plugin in Maya.

3. Open the **PostsCurve.ma** scene.

4. Select the curve.

5. In the **Command Line**, type the following, then press **Enter**.

```
posts1 -number 10 -radius 1
```

Ten cylinders are created along the curve. Each of the cylinders is now wider than before.

Notice that the height of the posts is the same as before. Since the height wasn't specified, the command uses a default value. The specific changes to the command are now covered.

4.4.4 Posts2 Plugin

Plugin: Posts2
File: posts2Cmd.cpp

```
...
MStatus Posts2Cmd::doIt ( const MArgList &args )
{
    int nPosts = 5;
    double radius = 0.5;
    double height = 5.0;

    unsigned index;
    index = args.flagIndex( "n", "number" );
    if( MArgList::kInvalidArgIndex != index )
        args.get( index+1, nPosts );

    index = args.flagIndex( "r", "radius" );
    if( MArgList::kInvalidArgIndex != index )
        args.get( index+1, radius );

    index = args.flagIndex( "h", "height" );
    if( MArgList::kInvalidArgIndex != index )
        args.get( index+1, height );
...
```

Since the only major change is at the start of the doIt function, just that portion is covered. The doIt function itself hasn't changed. It still takes a reference to an **MArgList** as its only input. In the previous command, posts1, this function argument was simply ignored. The **MArgList** class used to hold the list of arguments that are passed to a command. From this class the parameter *flags* and *values* can be retrieved. The flags are the parameter names specified with a dash character before them. The -radius flag specifies the radius parameter. The argument following the flag is typically the value to assign to the parameter. In this case it is 1.

Notice that the parameters (number, radius, height) are no longer fixed values. Instead they are initialized to their respective default values. In the event that one of the parameters isn't explicitly set on the command line, its default value is used. In the current example, the height parameter wasn't specified on the command line, so it uses the default value of 5.0.

```
int nPosts = 5;
double radius = 0.5;
double height = 5.0;
```

Since almost all parameters have a default value, specifying a value for them on the command line is optional. As such, the existence of a parameter flag must be checked for. The flagIndex function returns the index of the argument containing a given flag. Flags come in two forms: short and long. Either form can be used, so to test for the **number** parameter flag, both "n" and "number" were given to the flagIndex function.

```
index = args.flagIndex( "n", "number" );
```

If the flag hasn't be set on the command line, then the index is set to MArgList::kInvalidArgIndex.

```
if( MArgList::kInvalidArgIndex != index )
```

If the flag is valid, then the argument following the flag is retrieved. This argument is at index+1. The value is stored in the appropriate variable.

```
args.get( index+1, nPosts );
```

The same steps are completed for all the remaining flags. If flags have been set, their values are taken from the command line. Otherwise the default value is used.

Those familiar with the C language constructs argc and argv will now notice the similarities in functionality provided by the **MArgList** class. It must be noted, however, that the first argument in **MArgList** is the first argument to the command and not the name of the command, as it is with argv.

In this example the number of command parameters is relatively small, so it was easier just to check for each parameter flag individually. More sophisticated commands can have many more parameters, so using the **MArgList** class can become rapidly cumbersome. Maya provides another more advanced mechanism for parsing argument flags and getting their values.

4.4.5   Posts3 Plugin

The `posts2` command is now altered to make use of the **MSyntax** and **MArgDatabase** classes. Both these classes give greater flexibility in the number and type of parameters that can be used. Also they provide better argument type checking. In fact, they are the preferred classes to use when writing robust commands. The **MArgList** class is therefore rarely used and, when it is, only for simple commands.

♦   Open the **Posts3** workspace.

Plugin: Posts3
File: posts3Cmd.cpp

The **Posts3Cmd** class is based on the **Posts2Cmd** class. The following static function was added. Its job is to return an **MSyntax** object for the command.

```
static MSyntax newSyntax();
```

The **MSyntax** class provides a convenient means for specifying all the possible parameters to your command. The following code defines a set of flags, in both short and long form, that the command will accept.

```
const char *numberFlag = "-n", *numberLongFlag = "-number";
const char *radiusFlag = "-r", *radiusLongFlag = "-radius";
const char *heightFlag = "-h", *heightLongFlag = "-height";
```

The data types of the flags' arguments are then specified. Using the `addFlag` function, it is possible to add up to six different types of data that follow the flag. In this example the **number** parameter accepts a single `long`, while both the **radius** and **height** parameters accept a single `double`.

```
MSyntax Posts3Cmd::newSyntax()
{
    MSyntax syntax;
    syntax.addFlag( numberFlag, numberLongFlag, MSyntax::kLong );
    syntax.addFlag( radiusFlag, radiusLongFlag, MSyntax::kDouble );
    syntax.addFlag( heightFlag, heightLongFlag, MSyntax::kDouble );
    return syntax;
}
```

The start of the doIt function is as before.

```
MStatus Posts3Cmd::doIt ( const MArgList &args )
{
    int nPosts = 5;
    double radius = 0.5;
    double height = 5.0;
```

The doIt function now makes use of the **MArgDatabase** class to parse and separate the different flags and their values. The **MArgDatabase** object is initialized with syntax() and the **MArgList** object. The syntax() function returns the syntax object for the given command. In this case, it is the prepared **MSyntax** object from the newSyntax() function that is returned from the syntax() function.

```
MArgDatabase argData( syntax(), args );
```

Each flag is checked in turn to see if it has been set. If it has, then its value is retrieved from the command line and the associated variable is set.

```
if( argData.isFlagSet( numberFlag ) )
    argData.getFlagArgument( numberFlag, 0, nPosts );

if( argData.isFlagSet( radiusFlag ) )
    argData.getFlagArgument( radiusFlag, 0, radius );

if( argData.isFlagSet( heightFlag ) )
    argData.getFlagArgument( heightFlag, 0, height );
...
```

In order for Maya to know that you will be using your own custom **MSyntax** object, you need to signal this. In `initializePlugin`, the `registerCommand` function is called with an additional parameter, the `newSyntax` function.

```
...
    stat = pluginFn.registerCommand( "posts3",
                                     Posts3Cmd::creator,
                                     Posts3Cmd::newSyntax );
...
```

While it may not be completely apparent from this example that the **MSyntax** and **MArgDatabase** are worth using, in practice they offer a lot more functionality than **MArgList**. The **MSyntax** class allows you to specify that certain object types can be used as parameters. The current selection can be automatically included in the list of command arguments when using the **MSyntax** class. Overall, it is a far more robust and powerful means of parsing, extracting, and verifying arguments to your command.

4.4.6 Providing Help

Almost all of Maya's commands support some form of assistance. This assistance is usually in the form of some help text that explains what the command does and what its parameters are. This basic help functionality is provided through the `help` command. This command prints out a short, concise help description for any given command.

♦ In the **Script Editor,** type the following, then execute it.

```
help sphere;
```

The result is as follows:

```
// Result:
```

```
Synopsis: sphere [flags] [String...]
Flags:
   -e -edit
   -q -query
  -ax -axis                     Length Length Length
 -cch -caching                  on|off
  -ch -constructionHistory      on|off
   -d -degree                   Int
 -esw -endSweep                 Angle
  -hr -heightRatio              Float
   -n -name                     String
 -nds -nodeState                Int
 -nsp -spans                    Int
   -o -object                   on|off
   -p -pivot                    Length Length Length
  -po -polygon                  Int
   -r -radius                   Length
   -s -sections                 Int
 -ssw -startSweep               Angle
 -tol -tolerance                Length
  -ut -useTolerance             on|off
//
```

A complete list of all the command's flags and their acceptable data types is displayed. In addition to working for Maya's built-in command, the help command can be used on commands that you write.

AUTOMATIC HELP

As long as you provide an **MSyntax** object, which is the case since the new newSyntax() function has been added, the help command can determine what flags and values your command accepts. It automatically generates a listing of those flags and values.

1. Open the **Posts3** workspace.

2. Compile it, and load the resulting posts3.mll plugin in Maya.

3. In the **Script Editor**, type the following, then execute it.

```
help posts3;
```

The following help text is displayed:

```
// Result:

Synopsis: posts3 [flags]
Flags:
   -h -height  Float
   -n -number  Int
   -r -radius  Float

//
```

POSTS4 PLUGIN

In addition to the quick help that is automatically provided by the `help` command, you can also create and display your own help text. In the following example a help flag, `-h/-help`, is added to the command. The **height** parameter's short form flag was renamed from `-h` to `-he` in order to prevent any conflicts. A parameter's short form flag can have up to three characters.

1. Open the **Posts4** workspace.

2. Compile it, and load the resulting `posts4.mll` plugin in Maya.

3. In the **Script Editor**, type and then execute the following:

```
posts4 -h;
```

The following help text is displayed:

```
// Result:
The posts4 command is used to create a series of posts
(cylinders) along all the selected curves.
It is possible to set the number of posts, as well as
their width and height.
For further details consult the help documentation.
For quick help instructions use: help posts4 //
```

Implementing your own custom help requires just a few simple additions to the existing command.

Plugin: Posts4
File: Posts4Cmd.cpp

A new help flag is added.

```
const char *helpFlag = "-h", *helpLongFlag = "-help";
```

In the newSyntax() function, the new flag is added to the **MSyntax** object.

```
syntax.addFlag( helpFlag, helpLongFlag );
```

The help text that will be displayed is then defined:

```
const char *helpText =
"\nThe posts4 command is used to create a series of posts
    (cylinders) along all the selected curves."
"\nIt is possible to set the number of posts, as well as
    their width and height."
"\nFor further details consult the help documentation."
"\nFor quick help use: help posts4";
```

You are free to set the help text to anything you'd like. It is important however to remember that the automatic help should be a succinct, shorthand help, so keep it small. The custom help can include any additional information that you feel is necessary. If the help instructions are much longer or need specialized images or animations, then it is best simply to point the user to the relevant documentation.

The last required change is the addition of several lines to the doIt() function. As with the other flags, the help flag is tested to see if it is set. If it is, then the result is set to the help text defined earlier. The command then returns immediately, indicating its success.

```
if( argData.isFlagSet( helpFlag ) )
  {
  setResult( helpText );
  return MS::kSuccess;
  }
```

Commands can return a variety of results. When calculating the length of a curve, a command returns a single distance value. When querying the translation of a transform node, a series of three doubles is returned, one for each of the axes (*x*, *y*, *z*). The number and type of the results are defined by the command. In this example, the posts4 command returned a string containing the help text.

Since the command returned a string, you can store this in a variable. The following MEL statements store the result of asking the command for help:

```
string $text = `posts4 -h`;
print $text;
```

Since the help text is now stored in the $text variable, you could, for example, store it in a file or display it in a window.

4.4.7 Undo and Redo

A very important topic that needs to be understood when you write commands is that your command must be compatible with Maya's undo and redo mechanism. This compatibility is extremely important for your command to work seamlessly in Maya. In fact, a command that changes the scene in some way but doesn't provide a way to undo those changes is actually illegal. Such a command can cause Maya's state to be undetermined if the user attempts to undo it.

1. Open the **Posts4** workspace.

2. Compile it, and load the resulting posts4.mll plugin in Maya.

3. Open the **PostsCurve.ma** scene.

4. Select the curve.

5. In the **Command Line**, type and then execute the following:

   posts4

6. Select **Edit | Undo** from the main menu.

   Nothing happens. Since the posts4 command doesn't include support for undo or redo, the command can't be undone.

MAYA'S UNDO/REDO MECHANISM

Maya supports the ability to undo a series of commands through its undo mechanism. When a MEL command is executed, the state of the scene is likely to be changed in some way. Undoing the command is the same as reversing those changes and thereby returning the scene to the scene state before the command was executed. As such, Maya's undo mechanism allows you to undo the operations of a series of commands.

Undo Queue

Maya maintains a queue of the most recently run commands. The size of this queue defines the number of commands that can be undone.

1. Select **Window | Settings/Preferences | Preferences...** from the main menu.

2. Click on the **Undo** item in the **Settings** section.

3. Ensure that **Undo** is set to **On**.

4. Set the **Queue** setting to **Finite** and the **Queue Size** to **30**.

If the **Queue** is set to **Infinite**, then there is no limit to the number of commands that can be undone. However, this setting increases Maya's memory usage since Maya must store every one of the commands executed from the beginning of the session in case you request that they be undone later. Setting the queue to a reasonable, but finite, size is the best compromise between memory usage and the need to undo a series of commands.

Assume that the undo queue was set to hold three commands, that is, the **Queue Size** was set to 3. The queue is initially empty. Figure 4.10 shows the empty queue. The last command points to the last command executed. The queue head is the front

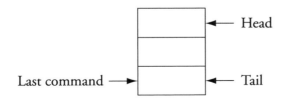

FIGURE 4.10 Empty undo queue

of the queue, while the queue tail is the end of the queue. As with any queue, items are added to the tail of the queue and eventually make their way to the head.

Now see the result of executing a few MEL commands.

```
sphere;
move 10 0 0;
scale 0.5 0.5 0.5;
```

The resulting undo queue is shown in Figure 4.11.

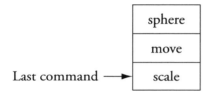

FIGURE 4.11   Full undo queue

The sphere command is added to the tail of the queue. The move command is added next. The sphere command moves up one slot making room for the move command. The scale command is then added to the tail, pushing the other two items up one slot. The undo queue is now full.

What happens to the undo queue if another command is executed?

```
rotate 45;
```

The rotate command is added to the tail of the queue, pushing all the other items up one slot. Since there is no empty space at the head of the queue the sphere command is removed from the queue. When the queue is full, the oldest item in the queue is the first to be removed. Figure 4.12 shows the undo queue after the rotate command is executed.

A consequence of being removed from the queue is that the command is now deleted. As such, the sphere command is deleted. It is now impossible to undo the sphere command, since it no longer exists in the undo queue. It may be clear now that setting the size of the undo queue affects how many commands can be undone. It is impossible to undo more commands than are currently available in the undo queue.

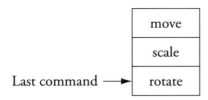

FIGURE 4.12 Undo queue after rotate command

What happens if you now select undo? The rotate command is undone. The last command is set to the scale command. If the user, once again, selects undo, the scale command is undone and the last command is set to the move command. The resulting undo queue is shown in Figure 4.13.

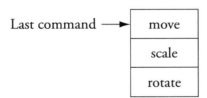

FIGURE 4.13 Undo queue after two undos

The scene is now in the state it was before the scale and rotate commands were executed. Since you can undo commands, it follows logically that you should also be able to redo commands. If users decided that they didn't want to undo the scale, they would simply select redo. The scale command would be redone, and the last command would be set to the scale command. Figure 4.14 shows the result.

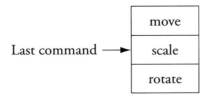

FIGURE 4.14 Undo queue after redo

You can continue redoing commands for as many commands as remain in the queue. Instead of redoing, another command is executed:

```
cylinder;
```

Since the last command, scale, is midway in the undo queue and a new command has been executed, all the subsequent commands are removed. Therefore, the rotate command is removed. If the queue were larger, all commands after the rotate command would also be removed. The cylinder command is then added to the end of the queue. The resulting undo queue is shown in Figure 4.15.

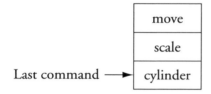

FIGURE 4.15   Undo queue after cylinder command

It is important to understand the reason the later commands were deleted. Remember that the undo queue can hold only one possible history path. When several undos were done until you reached the scale command, you moved up a history path. If the queue actually allows more than one path, when the cylinder command is executed, a branch in the history is created. There would now be two possible paths to follow after the scale command. One branch would result in the original rotate command, and the other branch would result in the cylinder command. Since there is no mechanism to support multiple branching, the previous branch is simply pruned when a new command is executed. The consequence of this is that the earlier commands can no longer be redone. They have been pruned away, and only the last executed command exists.

It is also important to note that the undo queue exists during the current Maya session. The undo queue isn't saved with the scene, so it isn't possible to undo operations to a file that has been saved and loaded again. When a new scene is loaded, the undo queue is completely emptied.

MPXCOMMAND SUPPORT FOR UNDO/REDO

With a better understanding of how the undo queue works, look at how commands can be designed to support undo and redo. When Maya executes a command, an instance of the command is allocated. This is done by calling the command's creator function. The command object's doIt function is then called. This function performs the real work of the command.

What happens if the user then requests to undo the command? In addition to the doIt function, the **MPxCommand** class also contains several other member functions to support undoing. These functions are as follows:

```
virtual MStatus undoIt();
virtual MStatus redoIt();
virtual bool isUndoable() const;
```

In the previous command examples, none of these functions were implemented, since the **MPxCommand** class provided its own default implementation. The default implementation of the isUndoable function returns false. This effectively means that the command can't be undone. As such, the undoIt and redoIt functions would never be called.

Since the previous commands weren't undoable, how did they work with Maya's undo mechanism? Here are the series of steps that Maya performed when the command, say posts1, was executed.

1. An instance of the posts1 command is created using the creator function.

2. The command object's doIt function is then called to do the work of the command.

3. Maya then calls the isUndoable function to determine whether the command is undoable. Since the command returns false, it isn't undoable, so it isn't placed in the undo queue but is instead deleted immediately.

4. As a result of the deletion, the command object's destructor is then called.

Why did the command object get immediately deleted after it was executed? Since the command can't be undone, it can't be put into the undo queue. What would have happened if the command was undoable? In order for the command to be undoable, the isUndoable function would have to be implemeted to return true. When the command was then executed, the following would happen:

1. An instance of the posts1 command is created using the creator function.

2. The command object's doIt function is called.

3. The isUndoable() function is then called to determine if the command is undoable. Since it now returns true, the command is placed into the undo queue.

Notice, in this case, that the command object wasn't deleted. The object now sits in the undo queue. What if the user now selects undo? Maya looks at the last command in the undo queue and calls its undoIt function. This function should undo any changes the command made. As such, the undoIt should restore Maya to exactly the same state it was in prior to the command being called. The scene, for example, will now be the same as if the command had never been executed. If the user continues to select undo, the undoIt function is called on each successive command object in the queue. This can be continued until there are no more command objects in the undo queue.

It is important to note that command objects still exist after their undoIt function has been called. They aren't deleted, because the user may decide to redo any of them. If redo is selected, the most recently undone command object's redoIt function is called. This is the equivalent of reexecuting the command. As a result, the redoIt function should provide the same functionality as the doIt function. In fact, doIt and redoIt can be considered synonymous.

UNDOABLE AND NONUNDOABLE COMMANDS

Since it is possible to design a command without support for undoing, how do you decide if you need to support undoing? The answer is quite simple.

If the command changes Maya's state in any way,
it *must* provide undo and redo!

It is possible to write a command that treats the Maya state as read-only. For instance, you could write a command that simply counted the number of spheres in the scene. This command won't alter Maya's current state, so it doesn't need to provide support for undoing. Maya has a particular name for commands that don't support undoing: *actions*. Actions are commands that when executed don't create, modify, or change the Maya state, so they can be called anytime without concern. Any command whose `isUndoable` function returns `false` is considered an action.

This doesn't mean that you can't write a command that accidently alters Maya's state and that doesn't support undoing. In this case, you must change the command so that it is undoable.

POSTS5 PLUGIN

Since the previous `posts` commands altered the state of Maya, they really should include undo and redo functionality.

1. Open the **Posts5** workspace.

2. Compile it, and load the resulting `posts5.mll` plugin in Maya.

3. Open the **PostsCurve.ma** scene.

4. Select the curve.

5. In the Command Line, type and then execute the following:

    ```
    posts5 -number 7 -radius 1
    ```

    Seven cylinders are created along the curve.

6. Select **Edit | Undo** or press **Ctrl+z** to undo.

    The `posts5` command is undone. As a result, the newly created cylinders are removed.

7. Select **Edit | Redo** or press **Shift+z** to redo.

    The command is reexecuted, which results in seven new cylinders.

Now look at how the `posts` command was changed in order to support undoing and redoing.

Plugin: Posts5
File: posts5Cmd.cpp

The command class is defined as before but with the addition of some new member functions and a new data member.

```
class Posts5Cmd : public MPxCommand
{
public:
        virtual MStatus doIt ( const MArgList& );
        virtual MStatus undoIt();
        virtual MStatus redoIt();
        virtual bool isUndoable() const { return true; }

        static void *creator() { return new Posts5Cmd; }
        static MSyntax newSyntax();

private:
        MDGModifier dgMod;
};
```

The member functions undoIt, redoIt, and isUndoable have been added. You'll notice that the isUndoable function has been implemented and now returns true to indicate that undoing is supported. The most significant addition is the new member, dgMod. It is an **MDGModifier**. The **MDGModifier** class is used to create, remove, and alter nodes in the Dependency Graph. While this can be done using other classes, the biggest benefit of the **MDGModifier** class is that it automatically provides undo and redo for all its operations. This saves you from having to implement this yourself.

As each of the **MDGModifier** functions for editing the Dependency Graph is called, the class keeps a record of it. In fact, when one of these functions is called, the operation it should have performed is simply recorded. The class contains two additional functions, doIt and undoIt. Only when the doIt function is called are all the recorded operations actually executed. Likewise, when the undoIt function is called, all the recorded operations are undone. It follows logically that the undoIt function can be called only after the doIt function; otherwise there would be nothing to undo.

When the posts5 command is executed, its doIt function is called. Its doIt function has been changed. The call to MGlobal::execute has been replaced with a call to the **MDGModifier**'s commandToExecute function.

```
...
dgMod.commandToExecute( MString( "cylinder -pivot ") + pt.x + " " + pt.y +
    " " + pt.z + " -radius " + radius + " -axis 0 1 0 -heightRatio " +
    heightRatio  );
...
```

The series of calls to commandToExecute results in a corresponding series of operations being recorded. At this point the commands haven't actually been executed, only recorded. The very last line of the doIt function has an important change. The function now calls redoIt.

```
...
return redoIt();
}
```

The redoIt function now does the actual work of the command. Since executing a command (doIt) is the same as reexecuting it (redoIt), there is no need to write two separate functions that perform the same operation. Instead, the actual command operations are put in the redoIt function, and the doIt function simply calls it. The redoIt function is defined as follows. The function makes a call to the **dgMod**'s doIt function. Since all the Dependency Graph operations have been recorded by the **dgMod** in the command's doIt function, to actually execute them the **dgMod** 's doIt function is called.

```
MStatus Posts5Cmd::redoIt()
{
    return dgMod.doIt();
}
```

Similarly, the undoIt function is defined as follows:

```
MStatus Posts5Cmd::undoIt()
{
    return dgMod.undoIt();
}
```

The **MDGModifer** is also responsible for undoing all its recorded operations. This example demonstrates the best approach to designing undoable commands. The doIt function should just prepare and record all the operations needed by the command. This information should be stored away in the class. The doIt function should simply call the redoIt function to do the actual work. The redoIt function takes the recorded information and then executes the operations. The undoIt function should take the recorded information and undo anything performed during the redoIt function.

In this particular example, a series of DG nodes (cylinders) were created, so the undo operation simply had to remove the cylinders. In a more complex command, you may need to record far more information in advance, such as the control points of a mesh before they are deformed or some other relevant information. In fact, all information necessary to return Maya to its previous state before the command was executed must be recorded. For complex operations, the recording of the data that is about to be altered can be quite burdensome. Unfortunately this can't be avoided.

When you design a command that isn't an action, it is very important to consider how you will support undoing and redoing. Often a command that hasn't been designed to handle undoing is difficult to change later into an undoable command. Designing the command with this in mind from the very start often means that you won't have to make large changes to incorporate it later. Once implemented, you can be assured that your command will operate seamlessly with Maya's undo/redo mechanism.

4.4.8   Edit and Query

In a previous section, the posts command was extended to include a few custom flags that allowed the specification of such parameters as the height and radius of the posts. Once a command is executed, the current values of the parameters are used. It may be necessary to tweak these parameters later. For many parameters, it is important that the user be able to query their current values as well as to set new values. To enable this, a command can be called in a variety of *modes*. When a command is executed to create something, it is run in *creation mode*. When a command is executed to retrieve the value of a parameter, it is operating in *query mode*. When a command is executed to change an existing parameter, it operates in *edit mode*. Most commands support one or more of these modes.

These various modes aren't actual real states. A command doesn't really change states. A command is free to do anything it wants at any time. The various modes are simply a convention used to describe when certain operations can and can't be performed. Since the operations of creating, editing, and querying are so common, they have been given their own convention that all commands should follow. The standard convention is that if a command supports querying and editing, it adds the query and edit flags. These are defined in their short and long forms as -q/query and -e/edit, respectively.

The sphere command can be called in a variety of modes.

1. Create a new scene by selecting **File | New Scene**.

2. In the **Script Editor**, execute the following:

```
sphere -radius 2;
```

A NURBS sphere is created with a radius of 2. Since the sphere command is neither being queried nor edited, it is being executed in the creation mode. As a result, a new sphere object is created.

The sphere's radius is now increased.

3. Execute the following:

```
sphere -edit -radius 10;
```

The sphere's radius is now larger. In this instance, the sphere command was executed in edit mode. The command didn't create a new sphere but instead altered the attributes of the existing sphere.

4. Execute the following to query the current radius of the sphere:

```
sphere -query -radius;
```

The result is then displayed.

```
// Result: 10 //
```

The sphere command has been executed in query mode. It neither creates a new sphere nor edits an existing one but instead returns the current value of the requested parameter.

When you call the `sphere` command with the `-query` flag, it returns a result. This result can be stored in a variable and used later. It is important to note that you can't query multiple parameters at the same time. It isn't valid, for example, to ask for the sphere's `radius` and the `startSweep` at the same time, since only one value can be returned at a time from the command.

```
// Could return radius or startSweep?
sphere -query -radius -startSweep;
```

When you want to query multiple parameters, simply break the requests into multiple command calls, each with a single query, as follows:

```
sphere -query -radius;
sphere -query -startSweep;
```

It is possible, however, to edit multiple parameters with the same command call.

```
sphere -edit -radius 2 -startSweep 20;
```

It isn't possible to mix modes in a single command call. Therefore, it isn't possible to run a command in both edit and query modes. Multiple executions of the command must be done, with separate edits and queries.

CLOCK PLUGIN

In order to demonstrate a more complex example of querying and editing, the implementation of the `clock` command is covered. This command sets the hands of a 3D clock based on a provided time. Figure 4.16 shows an example of the `clock` command applied to a 3D clock.

1. Open the **Clock** workspace.

2. Compile it, and load the resulting `clockCmd.mll` plugin in Maya.

3. Open the **Clock.ma** scene.

4. Select the two hand objects, **hour_hand** and **minute_hand**.

5. In the **Script Editor**, execute the following:

```
clock -edit -time 745;
```

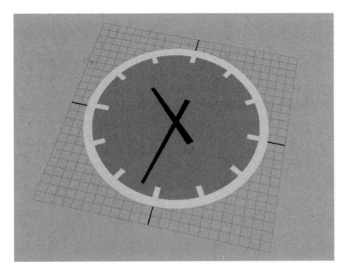

FIGURE 4.16   3D clock controlled by the clock command

The hour and minute hands are rotated to the given time, 7:45. Time is specified to the command with the hour first then the minutes: *hhmm*. For example 2:31 is represented as 230 while 3:00 is represented as 300.

6. Execute the following:

```
clock -e -time 1018;
```

The hands rotate to the given time: 10:18. Notice that the short form (-e) of the edit flag was used.

Without knowing the time in advance, you may want to query the current time of the clock.

7. Execute the following:

```
clock -query -time;
```

The result of the query is displayed.

```
// Result: 1018 //
```

This command implements both undo and redo.

8. Execute the following:

```
undo;
```

The hands are returned to the previous time.

9. Execute the following:

```
redo;
```

The hands are set, once again, to the new time.

The source code to the `clock` command will now be covered in detail.

Plugin: Clock
File: clockCmd.cpp

The command is implemented in the **ClockCmd** class. As with all Maya commands, it is derived from **MPxCommand**. As demonstrated earlier, it supports both undo and redo. The class also contains some additional members and methods. These are explained as they are used in the command.

```
class ClockCmd : public MPxCommand
{
public:
        virtual MStatus doIt ( const MArgList& );
        virtual MStatus undoIt();
        virtual MStatus redoIt();
        virtual bool isUndoable() const;

        static void *creator() { return new ClockCmd; }
        static MSyntax newSyntax();

private:
        bool isQuery;
        int prevTime, newTime;
        MDagPath hourHandPath, minuteHandPath;

        int getTime();
        void setTime( const int time );
};
```

As before, the command defines which parameters it accepts and what values these parameters can take. The clock command has only one parameter flag, time, which is given as -t/-time.

```
const char *timeFlag = "-t", *timeLongFlag = "-time";

MSyntax ClockCmd::newSyntax()
{
    MSyntax syntax;

    syntax.addFlag( timeFlag, timeLongFlag, MSyntax::kLong );
```

In addition to adding the time flag, the syntax object also specifies that it accepts both the query and edit flags. This is done by calling the **MSyntax**'s enableQuery and enableEdit functions. The command syntax object now supports three flags: time, query, and edit.

```
    syntax.enableQuery(true);
    syntax.enableEdit(true);

    return syntax;
}
```

The command's doIt function is a little more involved, since undoing and redoing have to be handled manually. To perform the undo, you must know the current state of the object that is about to be changed by the command. With this state stored away, the command can restore the object to its original state when the user selects undo. Likewise, exactly which state is going to be changed must be known. This is important for both executing (doIt) and reexecuting (redoIt) the command.

Since the command really has only one parameter, time, this is what is stored. The current time is stored in the prevTime class variable. This is the value that is used when the command is undone. The new time value is stored in the newTime class variable. This is the value that is used when you execute or reexecute the command.

```
int prevTime, newTime;
```

The doIt function takes the command parameters and stores them away. It also records in the isQuery class variable whether the command is being run in query or edit mode.

```
bool isQuery;
```

Since the command doesn't create anything, it won't need to support creation mode. The new time is also recorded if the command is in edit mode. Finally the currently selected clock hand objects are also recorded in the `hourHandPath` and `minuteHandPath` class variables.

```
MDagPath hourHandPath, minuteHandPath;
```

The various operations of the `doIt` function will now be explained.

```
MStatus ClockCmd::doIt ( const MArgList &args )
{
    MStatus stat;
```

The **MArgDatabase** is initialized as before. Notice that if its initialization fails, then the command also fails. Its initialization fails if any of the command arguments are invalid.

```
MArgDatabase argData( syntax(), args, &stat );
if( !stat )
    return stat;
```

The `isQuery` member is then set. The **MArgDatabase** class has a convenience function, `isQuery()`, that returns `true` if the query flag was set on the command line. Setting this effectively puts the command in query mode. Since the **clock** command doesn't create anything, it runs only in two possible modes: query or edit.

```
isQuery = argData.isQuery();
```

If the command is running in edit mode, then it retrieves the value of the `newTime` member.

```
if( argData.isFlagSet( timeFlag ) && !isQuery )
    argData.getFlagArgument( timeFlag, 0, newTime );
```

This next section of code iterates over all the selected objects and retrieves their names. When it finds objects named either **hour_hand** or **minute_hand**, their DAG paths are stored.

```
// Get a list of currently selected objects
MSelectionList selection;
MGlobal::getActiveSelectionList( selection );

MDagPath dagPath;
MFnTransform transformFn;
MString name;

// Iterate over the transforms
MItSelectionList iter( selection, MFn::kTransform );
for ( ; !iter.isDone(); iter.next() )
  {
  iter.getDagPath( dagPath );
  transformFn.setObject( dagPath );

  name = transformFn.name();
  if( name == MString("hour_hand") )
    hourHandPath = dagPath;
  else
    {
    if( name == MString("minute_hand") )
      minuteHandPath = dagPath;
    }
  }
```

If the clock hand objects weren't found, then the command emits an error message.

```
// Neither hour nor minute hand selected
if( !hourHandPath.isValid() || !minuteHandPath.isValid() )
  {
  MGlobal::displayError( "Select hour and minute hands" );
  return MS::kFailure;
  }
```

The current time, as represented by the two hand positions, is then determined.

```
prevTime = getTime();
```

If the command is in query mode, then simply set the result to the current time, then return.

```
if( isQuery )
  {
  setResult( prevTime );
  return MS::kSuccess;
  }
```

If the command is in edit mode, then call the redoIt function to do the editing work.

```
  return redoIt();
}
```

The undoIt and redoIt functions simply call the setTime member function. The undoIt function sets the clock hands to the previous time, while the redoIt function sets them to the new time.

```
MStatus ClockCmd::undoIt()
{
  setTime( prevTime );
  return MS::kSuccess;
}

MStatus ClockCmd::redoIt()
{
  setTime( newTime );
  return MS::kSuccess;
}
```

The getTime function calculates what time is currently shown by the position of the clock hands. While an exact understanding of the math isn't necessary, it is important to note that the function gets the hour_hand object and then determines what rotation it has about the y-axis. The amount of rotation determines what the current time is. The time is then formatted as *hhmm* and returned.

```
int ClockCmd::getTime()
{
    // Get the time from the rotation
    MFnTransform transformFn;
    transformFn.setObject( hourHandPath );
    MEulerRotation rot;
    transformFn.getRotation( rot );

    // Determine the time and format it
    int a = int(-rot.y * (1200.0 / TWOPI));
    int time = (a / 100 * 100) + int( floor( (a % 100) *
        (6.0 / 10.0) + 0.5 ) );

    return time;
}
```

The setTime function rotates the **hour_hand** and **minute_hand** objects to reflect the given time.

```
void ClockCmd::setTime( const int time )
{
    MFnTransform transformFn;

    // Calculate the hour and minutes
    int hour = (time / 100) % 12;
    int minutes = time % 100;

    // Rotate the hour hand by the required amount
    transformFn.setObject( hourHandPath );
    transformFn.setRotation( MEulerRotation( MVector( 0.0, hour *
        (-TWOPI / 12) + minutes * (-TWOPI / 720.0), 0 ) ) );

    // Rotate the minute hand by the required amount
    transformFn.setObject( minuteHandPath );
    transformFn.setRotation( MEulerRotation( MVector( 0.0, minutes *
        (-TWOPI / 60.0), 0 ) ) );
}
```

The `isUndoable` function contains an important change. It normally returns `true` for any command that supported undo. Recall from the previous section that a command that isn't undoable is considered an action. An action, when executed, won't change the state of Maya. When the `time` parameter is being queried, this is effectively what is being done. The parameter is only being queried, so Maya's state isn't being changed. As such, the `isUndoable` function returns `false` when the command is operating in query mode; otherwise it returns `true`, since it will then be running in edit mode.

```
bool ClockCmd::isUndoable() const
{
    return isQuery ? false : true;
}
```

What happens if the command doesn't return `false` when in query mode? As with all undoable commands, the command object is added to the undo queue. When the command is undone, nothing happens, since undoing a query doesn't result in anything being restored. Nothing has been changed, so there is nothing to be undone. As such, returning `true` when in query mode can be considered benign. However, since the command object is added to the undo queue, a lot of queries result in the undo stack being filled unnecessarily. In general, it is best that the `isUndoable` function return `true` when it actually has something to undo and `false` otherwise.

4.5 NODES

By creating your own commands and using MEL, you can already access a great deal of Maya's power. However, even these methods don't allow you to add your own pieces to the underlying Maya engine, the Dependency Graph. In order to create your own parts and have them included in this machinery, you'll need to create a node. The node is integrated directly into the Dependency Graph, so it becomes a seamless part of the general scene. It is possible to create a variety of different nodes, each with its own particular way of processing or creating data.

4.5.1 GoRolling Plugin

In order to provide a general understanding of how to write a node and then integrate it into Maya, a simple node will be covered. This node will show you how to control the rotation of a wheel. When animating wheels, it is easiest for the animator

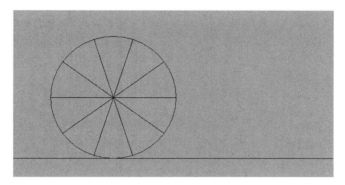

FIGURE 4.17 Wheel that automatically rotates

to define the start and end location of the object. The animator then has to set rotation keys for the wheel so that it rolls as it moves along. As you can imagine, this last step can be completely automated. A custom node is developed that automatically rotates the wheel based on its position. The animator can use this new node by simply moving the wheel, and its rotation happens automatically. In Figure 4.17 the wheel object that automatically rotates as a result of the new node is shown.

The complete project involves creating both a command as well as a node. The command, goRolling, will be responsible for creating the node, **RollingNode**, inserting it into the DG, and making all the necessary attribute connections. The node handles the actual rotation of the object.

1. Open the **GoRolling** workspace.

2. Compile it, and load the resulting GoRolling.mll plugin in Maya.

3. Open the **GoRolling.ma** scene.

4. Click on **Play**.

   The wheel moves along the ground, but it doesn't rotate.

5. Select the **rim** object.

6. Open the **Attribute Editor**.

   Notice that the rim's translation is currently animated, while its rotation isn't.

7. In the **Script Editor**, execute the following:

    ```
    goRolling;
    ```

    In the Attribute Editor, you can see that the **Rotate Z** is now animated.

8. Click on **Play**.

    The wheel now rotates as it moves.

9. Click **Stop**, then select the **Move Tool**. With the **rim** object still selected, move it along in the *x* direction (red arrow). Move the rim back and forth to see how the wheel automatically rotates wherever you translate it. Now take a closer look at what is happening under the covers.

10. Open the **Hypergraph**.

11. With the **rim** transform node selected, click on the **Up and Downstream Connections** button.

    The Hypergraph shown in Figure 4.18 is displayed.

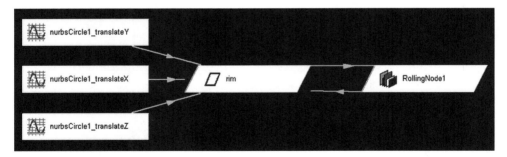

FIGURE 4.18   Hypergraph after executing goRolling command

This view shows that the rim's translations, **translateX**, **translateY**, and **translateZ**, are controlled by three animation curves, **nurbsCircle1_translateX**, **nurbsCircle1_translateY**, and **nurbsCircle_translateZ**, respectively. This is the standard setup for animating any attribute.

The new addition is the **RollingNode1** node. There are two connections from the **rim** node to the **RollingNode1** node. It may not be easy to see these, since they are drawn almost one on top of the other. There is also one connection going back from the **RollingNode1** node to the **rim** node. These connections are shown more clearly in Figure 4.19.

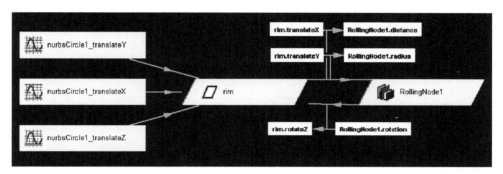

FIGURE 4.19   Node connections

From this diagram, it is easier to deduce what is happening. The value of the **rim**'s *x* translation attribute, **translateX**, is being fed into the **RollingNode1**'s **distance** attribute. The **distance** attribute defines how far the object has traveled. In this instance, this is simply the distance the object has moved along the x-axis, which equates directly to the **rim**'s **translateX** value.

Since the rim shape was created from a circle, its **transform** node, **rim**, is located at its center. Consequently its distance along the y-axis, **translateY**, is equivalent to the radius of the wheel. The **rim**'s **translateY** value is therefore fed into the **RollingNode**'s **radius** attribute. So the **rim**'s **translateX** and **translateY** are being used as the inputs to the **distance** and **radius** values, respectively, in the **RollingNode**. Taking these two input values, the **RollingNode1** node calculates a single output value, **rotation**. The **rotation** output is fed back into the **rim** node's **rotateZ** attribute. The **rim**'s **rotateZ** value is now the result of the **RollingNode1**'s rotation calculation.

When the wheel was moved back and forth, this changed the **translateX** value, which in turn changed the **RollingNode**'s **distance** input value. The node then recomputed a new **rotation** value that was subsequently fed into the **rim**'s **rotateZ** value. The end result is that as the **rim** moves along the x-axis, its *z* rotation changes.

The details of the **RollingNode** node will now be explained. The **GoRolling** project defines a custom command, `goRolling`, and a custom node, **RollingNode**.

Plugin: GoRolling
File: GoRollingCmd.h

The goRolling command is used to create a new **RollingNode** and connect it to the currently selected objects. The posts command demonstrated how to create cylinder nodes. The goRolling command also creates nodes, but it now creates connections between those nodes. The goRolling command is designed to handle both undo and redo to ensure that its effects can be removed if requested. The class declaration is straightforward and follows logically from the format of the previous commands.

```
class GoRollingCmd : public MPxCommand
{
public:
        virtual MStatus doIt ( const MArgList& );
        virtual MStatus undoIt();
        virtual MStatus redoIt();
        virtual bool isUndoable() const { return true; }

        static void *creator() { return new GoRollingCmd; }
        static MSyntax newSyntax();

private:
        MDGModifier dgMod;
};
```

The command contains a single **MDGModifier** member, dgMod, that is used to create the **RollingNode** node as well as the necessary connections. The **MDGModifier**, as before, simplifies the task of providing undo and redo.

Plugin: GoRolling
File: GoRollingCmd.cpp

The main work is completed in the doIt function.

```
MStatus GoRollingCmd::doIt ( const MArgList &args )
{
    MStatus stat;
```

A list of the currently selected objects is created.

```
MSelectionList selection;
MGlobal::getActiveSelectionList( selection );
```

All the transform nodes are then iterated over by specifying the `MFn::kTransform` filter.

```
MDagPath dagPath;
MFnTransform transformFn;
MString name;

// Iterate over all the transforms
MItSelectionList iter( selection, MFn::kTransform );
for ( ; !iter.isDone(); iter.next() )
    {
    iter.getDagPath( dagPath );
    transformFn.setObject( dagPath );
```

For each of the **transform** nodes, the following tasks are completed. A new **RollingNode** node is created by using the **MDGModifier**'s `createNode` function.

```
MObject rollNodeObj = dgMod.createNode( "RollingNode" );
```

An **MFnDependencyNode** function set, `depNodeFn`, is attached to the newly created node object. Using `depNodeFn`, the contents of the node can be accessed.

```
MFnDependencyNode depNodeFn( rollNodeObj );
```

A node's attributes are accessed by getting its *plugs*. Plugs are explained in more detail later, but for now they can be considered a mechanism for getting a node's attribute values. The **translateX** plug is obtained from the **transform** node, and the **distance** plug is obtained from the **RollingNode** node. The **MDGModifier**'s `connect` function is then used to make a connection from one plug to the other.

```
dgMod.connect( transformFn.findPlug( "translateX" ),
               depNodeFn.findPlug( "distance") );
```

This same steps are repeated to connect the **translateY** plug to the **radius** plug.

```
dgMod.connect( transformFn.findPlug( "translateY" ),
               depNodeFn.findPlug( "radius" ) );
```

Finally the **RollingNode**'s **rotation** plug is connected to the transform's **rotationX** plug.

```
dgMod.connect( depNodeFn.findPlug( "rotation" ),
               transformFn.findPlug( "rotateZ" ) );
}
```

The `redoIt` function is then called to do the real work now that the **MDGModifier,** `dgMod`, has been set up with all the required Dependency Graph operations.

```
    return redoIt();
}
```

The `redoIt` function simply calls the **MDGModifer**'s `doIt` function, which performs all the requested operations.

```
MStatus GoRollingCmd::redoIt()
{
return dgMod.doIt();
}
```

Undoing the command is, once again, simplified by using the **MDGModifier** class, which provides automatic undoing.

```
MStatus GoRollingCmd::undoIt()
{
return dgMod.undoIt();
}
```

With the command now complete, the custom node is covered.

Plugin: GoRolling
File: RollingNode.h

A custom node is created by deriving from the **MPxNode** class. A node is quite different from a command. It doesn't have any `doIt` function but instead provides a few functions, the most important of which is the `compute` function. This function does all the real work of data processing, and is therefore considered the "brains" of the node.

```
class RollingNode : public MPxNode
{
public:
    virtual MStatus compute( const MPlug& plug, MDataBlock& data );

    static  void *creator();
    static  MStatus initialize();
};
```

The following static member variables are another important addition to the node. These variables contain definitions for the node's attributes. There is one variable for each of the node's input and output attributes.

```
    static MObject distance;
    static MObject radius;
    static MObject rotation;

    static MTypeId id;
};
```

Plugin: GoRolling
File: RollingNode.cpp

Each type of node in Maya, irrespective of whether it is native or custom, has a unique identifier so that Maya knows how to create it, as well as store and restore it from disk. The **MTypeId** class is used for this identifier.

When Maya needs to reload a node from disk, it needs to know which node stored the data. To identify the node that created the data, the node's identifier is stored with the data. During retrieval Maya loads the node identifier and then creates a new node of the type indicated by the identifier. The node then loads its data from disk.

From this description it is clear that if two different types of nodes have the same identifier, then Maya could create the wrong node when the data is restored from disk. This is particularly important for binary Maya files since they store only the node's identifier and not the node's class name. If a node is stored to a binary file with a given identifier and you later change its identifier, then Maya won't be able to read the restored node data from the file. The node's new identifier won't match the one stored on disk, so Maya won't be able to locate the owner of the original data. Therefore, if you store your nodes to a binary Maya file, make sure never to later change the nodes' identifiers. This isn't necessarily a problem for ASCII files, since the node's type is stored and not its identifier.

It is, therefore, important that you ensure that each new node has a unique identifier. What happens if you get Maya files from another person who happens to use similar identifiers for his or her own custom nodes? This would result in the same data-loading problem mentioned earlier. In order to prevent nodes having similar identifiers, Alias | Wavefront provides developers with a unique set of identifiers that they can use. These numbers are assigned to you so no one else in the world will have the same one. If this protocol is strictly followed, every node ever created will have a unique identifier. As a result, there should never be any problems sharing files from different companies or individuals who use custom nodes.

So before you start development, it is generally a good practice to ask Alias | Wavefront for a set of unique identifiers. For details on becoming a registered developer and getting identifiers, visit the Alias | Wavefront website, *www.aliaswavefront .com.*

If for whatever reason you can't get unique identifiers for your nodes before development starts, you can use some temporary "internal development only" identifiers. These identifiers are to be used only temporarily while you await the final identifiers. Therefore, they should never be used in nodes that will be used outside your development environment. You can use any of the temporary identifiers in the range of 0 to 0x7FFFF. For the **RollingNode** example, the arbitrary temporary identifier, 0x00333, has been used.

```
MTypeId RollingNode::id( 0x00333 );
```

It is important to replace this number with a correctly allocated identifier as soon as possible. While this may not seem important while you are developing the node, it can cause a great deal of problems if it is stored to a Maya scene file and then the identifier is later changed. This can happen quite easily if testers create Maya files with your node during beta testing and then you change the node identifier when you release the final plugin. All files created during the beta testing now won't load the node's data.

The next section of code defines the node's attribute specifiers. At this point they are just defined. They will be initialized later.

```
MObject  RollingNode::distance;
MObject  RollingNode::radius;
MObject  RollingNode::rotation;
```

The compute function is defined next. It takes two arguments; the first is an **MPlug** that specifies which plug (node's attribute) needs to be recomputed, and the second is an **MDataBlock** that holds the current data for the node.

```
const double PI = 3.1415926535;
const double TWOPI = 2.0 * PI;


MStatus RollingNode::compute( const MPlug& plug, MDataBlock& data )
{
MStatus stat;
```

A node can have any number of output attributes. Since only output attributes are computed and they may not all need updating, Maya calls the compute function with each output attribute individually. As such, you must check which of the output attributes is being requested to update. Since this node has only one output attribute, **rotation**, only it is checked for.

```
if( plug == rotation )
    {
```

When a request is made to recompute the **rotation** attribute, the set of current input attributes is first retrieved. These values are retrieved from the node by calling the **MDataBlock**'s inputValue function. This function treats the node's attribute as read-only. You can then retrieve its values but can't write to it. Similarly there is an outputValue function that allows you to write to an attribute but not read it. Even though Maya makes no distinction between input and output attributes, by having separate input and output functions, the data can be retrieved and maintained more efficiently.

You need to specify which of the attributes you want to retrieve. In this case, the **distance** and **radius** attributes are needed. The inputValue function returns an **MDataHandle** object. This is used to access the actual attribute data.

```
MDataHandle distData = data.inputValue( distance );
MDataHandle radData = data.inputValue( radius );
```

The steps to getting an attribute's values may seem convoluted, but there are very good reasons, which are explained in detail in the section covering the

MDataBlock class. With the **MDataHandle** object, the input attribute's data can now be retrieved. Since the attributes are known to each hold a double, the asDouble function is used.

```
double dist = distData.asDouble();
double rad = radData.asDouble();
```

The result of the computation is stored in the **rotation** attribute. A handle to this attribute is needed. This handle is created by calling the **MDataBlock**'s outputValue function. This returns a **MDataHandle** object that can be used to write to an attribute.

```
MDataHandle rotData = data.outputValue( rotation );
```

The **rotation** attribute is calculated from the input **distance** and **radius** attributes. The result is stored in the **rotation** attribute by using the **MDataHandle**'s set function.

```
rotData.set( -dist / rad );
```

In the next step, the plug is set to be clean. This lets Maya know that the plug has been recomputed and holds the new correct value.

```
data.setClean( plug );
}
```

The **MPxNode** class itself contains many attributes. Since the **RollingNode** is derived from the **MpxNode**, it automatically inherits these attributes. Rather than have the derived class, **RollingNode**, handle the recomputation of these inherited attributes, the compute function simply has to return MS::kUnknownParameter when it finds an attribute that it doesn't know about. Maya then calls the base class's compute function and sees if it can recompute the attribute. This way, derived classes have to compute only the attributes that they explicitly introduce. All other attributes are handled by their direct or indirect base classes.

```
else
    stat  = MS::kUnknownParameter;
```

The `compute` function returns an **MStatus** indicating whether computation was successful.

```
return stat;
}
```

Like commands, nodes also have a function to create an instance of themselves. The `creator` function is a static function that simply creates a new instance of the node.

```
void *RollingNode::creator()
{
return new RollingNode();
}
```

The `initialize` function is also static. It is called only when the node is first registered. Registration of the node is detailed in the next source code file.

```
MStatus RollingNode::initialize()
{
```

The job of the node's `initialize` function is to set up all the node's attributes. Since the node's attributes, **distance**, **radius**, and **rotation**, are all static members, there is one copy of them shared by all instances of the node. The reason for this is that the attributes don't actually hold the data for each individual node. Instead they act as a blueprint for the creation of the attribute data that each node will use. Technically, a node's attribute data is stored in an **MDataBlock** and is retrieved and set using an **MPlug**. In the context of the C++ API, an attribute is just a specification for creating a node attribute. In the C++ API, an attribute is created and edited using an **MAttribute** and its derived classes.

Maya supports a wide variety of attributes including simple numeric types such as `bool`, `float`, and `int`, as well as more complex compound attributes. These attributes use the simple types and combine them in more complex ways. The **RollingNode** node requires only some simple floating-point values as input. The **distance** attribute is defined in the following code. The attribute is created by calling the `create` function. This attribute is stored as a single `double`. This is indicated to the **MFnNumericAttribute** by using the indicator `MFnNumericData::kDouble`. It has a long and short name, "distance" and "dist", respectively. The attribute's default value is 0.0. The resulting attribute object is stored in the distance static member. The **distance** attribute should be created using the **MFnUnitAttribute** class, but a double suffices for this example.

```
MFnNumericAttribute nAttr;
distance = nAttr.create( "distance", "dist",
                         MFnNumericData::kDouble, 0.0 );
```

The **radius** attribute is created in a similar fashion.

```
radius = nAttr.create( "radius", "rad", MFnNumericData::kDouble, 0.0 );
```

The last attribute is the **rotation** attribute. It is different from the input attributes in that it holds an angle. An angle in Maya can be represented in many different ways. It can for example be given in radians or degrees. In fact, an angle is considered a unit. Since an angle can have multiple representations, it can't be stored in a simple double. Instead, it is specifed using an **MFnUnitAttribute** object. This class is designed to handle different types of Maya units, including time, angles, and so on.

```
MFnUnitAttribute uAttr;
rotation = uAttr.create( "rotation", "rot",
                         MFnUnitAttribute::kAngle, 0.0 );
```

Now that all the attributes have been created, they can be added to the node by calling the **MPxNode**'s addAttribute function.

```
addAttribute( distance );
addAttribute( radius );
addAttribute( rotation );
```

In order for Maya to know how the attributes affect each other, you must explicitly state this using the **MPxNode**'s attributeAffects function. This sets up a dependency between the attributes, thereby defining which attributes are considered input and which output. Changing the input attribute causes a direct reaction in the attributes it affects. When the **distance** or **radius** attribute changes, the **rotation** attribute needs to be recomputed. This relationship is formally expressed by using the attributeAffects function as follows.

```
attributeAffects( distance, rotation );
attributeAffects( radius, rotation );
```

The initialization was successful.

```
return MS::kSuccess;
}
```

Notice that no error checking was done. This is because the example code is designed to be simple and brief. In a real plugin, you would do error checking on each of the function calls, and if any of them fail, an **MStatus** indicating failure would be returned.

With the command and node now completed, you need to notify Maya that they both exist. Once they are registered with Maya, they can be used in the scene.

Plugin: GoRolling
File: pluginMain.cpp

As always, the initializePlugin and uninitializePlugin functions must be present in order for Maya to load and unload the plugin. These functions have been extended to include better error checking. The registration process is completed as follows:

```
MStatus initializePlugin( MObject obj )
{
    MStatus stat;
    MString errStr;
    MFnPlugin pluginFn( obj, "David Gould", "1.0", "Any");
```

The command is registered, as before, using the **MFnPlugin**'s registerCommand function.

```
stat = pluginFn.registerCommand( "goRolling",
                                 GoRollingCmd::creator );
if ( !stat )
    {
    errStr = "registerCommand failed";
    goto error;
    }
```

The registration of the node is slightly different. You must provide a name for the node's type as well as its unique identifier. A creator function also needs to be specified. Last the node's initialize function must also be given.

```
stat = pluginFn.registerNode( "RollingNode",
                              RollingNode::id,
                              RollingNode::creator,
                              RollingNode::initialize );


if ( !stat )
    {
    errStr = "registerNode failed";
    goto error;
    }


return stat;
```

The initialize function is called just once to set up the blueprints for all the node's attributes. This is done when the node is first registered.

If any errors occur, an error message is displayed.

```
    error:

    stat.perror( errStr );
    return stat;
}
```

Deregistering the command and node is done in the unitializePlugin function.

```
MStatus uninitializePlugin( MObject obj)
{
    MStatus stat;
    MString errStr;
    MFnPlugin pluginFn( obj );
```

As in the previous command examples, the command is deregistered using the **MFnPlugin**'s deregisterCommand function. The function is given the name of the command to deregister.

```
stat = pluginFn.deregisterCommand( "goRolling" );
if ( !stat )
    {
    errStr = "deregisterCommand failed";
    goto error;
    }
```

The node is deregistered by passing the node's identifier to the **MFnPlugin**'s deregisterNode function. Since each node's identifier is unique and was used earlier to register the node, Maya can deregister the node given its identifier.

```
stat = pluginFn.deregisterNode( RollingNode::id );
if( !stat )
    {
    errStr = "deregisterNode failed";
    goto error;
    }
```

```
return stat;
```

If there is an error during the uninitializePlugin function, an error message is displayed.

```
    error:

    stat.perror( errStr );
    return stat;
}
```

This example demonstrates that creating a new custom node is relatively simple. Once the node is registered it can be created and inserted into the Dependency Graph like any other node. Maya handles all the data retrieval and storage for the node. It also handles all attribute connections and so on. In fact all the node really has to do is to ensure that it recomputes its output attributes when Maya requests them.

4.5.2   Melt Plugin

A slightly more complex node will now be presented. This node simulates the effect of an object melting. More precisely, it deforms the object so that it gives the impression that the object is being heated from below. It then begins to slowly melt and spread.

The original objects are shown in Figure 4.20. The result of applying the melting is shown in Figure 4.21.

This project creates a command and a node both named **melt**. The command iterates over all the selected NURBS surfaces. A **melt** node is inserted into the shape's

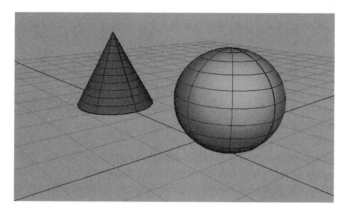

FIGURE 4.20   Original objects

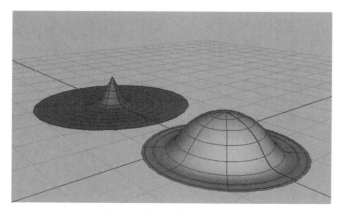

FIGURE 4.21   Objects after melting

construction history. The construction history concept will be explained shortly. The **melt** node's job is to deform the original surface to make it appear as if it were melting. The amount of melting is defined by the **melt** node's **amount** attribute. The **melt** command automatically animates the **melt** node's **amount** attribute so that the object melts over the current animation time range.

1. Open the **Melt** workspace.

2. Compile it, and load the resulting `Melt.mll` plugin in Maya.

3. Open the **Melt.ma** scene.

4. Select both the **nurbsCone1** and **nurbsSphere1** objects.

5. In the **Script Editor**, execute the following:

```
melt;
```

6. Click on the **Play** button.

    Both objects slowly melt downward and then begin spreading outward.

The `melt` command creates a `melt` node and inserts it into each of the object's construction histories. In order to understand what is being done, the **sphere** object is looked at in detail. Before the application of the `melt` command, the sphere appears as in Figure 4.22.

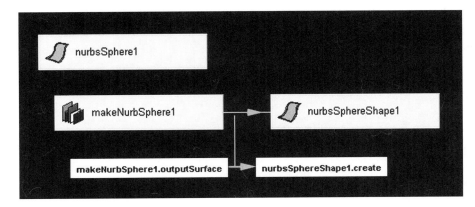

FIGURE 4.22   Standard sphere

The entire sphere consists of both the **shape** node, **nurbSphereShape1**, and the **transform** node, **nurbSphere1**. The actual NURBS surface results from the **makeNurbSphere1** node. This node generates a NURBS surface in the shape of a sphere. This same methodology is used for other NURBS primitives such as the cylinder and torus, which use a **makeNurbCylinder** and **makeNurbTorus** node, respectively.

The surface is output through the **makeNurbsSphere1**'s **outputSurface** attribute. This is then fed into the **nurbsSphereShape1**'s **create** attribute. Therefore, the **nurbsSphereShape1** node holds the final NURBS surface. It is also the responsibility of the **shape** node to display its shape. As such, the **nurbsSphereShape1** node displays the resulting NURBS surface in the scene.

In the previous examples, the node attributes were relatively simple. Many were just single `double` values. This node uses a more complex attribute that holds an entire NURBS surface. This NURBS surface attribute can be stored in the node and be connected to other nodes. The NURBS surface is effectively passed from one node to another through the connection.

When the `melt` command is executed, a **melt** node is created. This node is inserted into the sphere's construction history. The construction history is the series of nodes that together define the final shape. They do this by generating some data and then processing it, each in turn, resulting in the final shape being produced at the very end. The original sphere had only a **makeNurbSphere1** node in its construction history. When the melt node was inserted, it went in between the **makeNurbsSphere1** node and the final **nurbsSphereShape1** node. The new DG is shown in Figure 4.23. Notice the new **melting2** node.

The construction history of the NURBS sphere consists of the **makeNurbSphere1** node followed by the **melting2** node. The **makeNurbSphere1**'s **outputSurface** now feeds into the **melting2**'s **inputSurface** rather than directly into the **nurbsSphereShape1** node. The **melting2** node can now modify the surface before passing it into the **nurbsSphereShape1** node. All that has changed is that the **melting2** node now sits in the middle of the two previous nodes. The surface is fed into the node so it can change the surface before finally passing it into the **shape** node as before.

The **melt** node has an **amount** attribute that defines the amount of melting. The `melt` command automatically animates this attribute for you. In order to do this, an **animCurve** node is created and then connected to the **melting2** node's **amount** attribute. Fortunately this animation curve node doesn't have to be created manually, but instead Maya creates it automatically.

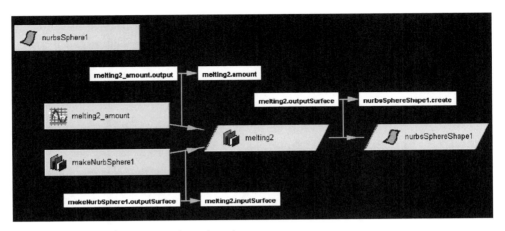

FIGURE 4.23 After inserting the **melt** node

Plugin: Melt
File: MeltCmd.cpp

The melt command is responsible for creating the necessary nodes and then connecting them. It also handles the animating of the **amount** attribute. The doIt function, once again, is assigned the task of setting up the command, while the redoIt function does the actual work.

```
MStatus MeltCmd::doIt ( const MArgList &args )
{
    MStatus stat;

    MSelectionList selection;
    MGlobal::getActiveSelectionList( selection );
```

In order to animate the **amount** attribute, the start and end range of the current animation needs to be known. Keyframes at those times will be created later.

```
MTime startTime = MAnimControl::minTime();
MTime endTime = MAnimControl::maxTime();
```

All the currently selected NURBS surfaces are iterated over. This means that the `melt` command can be applied to any number of NURBS surfaces. To let the **MItSelectionList** know that it should iterate only over NURBS surfaces, the `MFn::kNurbsSurface` filter is used.

```
MItSelectionList iter( selection, MFn::kNurbsSurface );
for ( ; !iter.isDone(); iter.next() )
    {
```

Only the NURBS surface shape nodes are needed from the selected objects.

```
MObject shapeNode;
iter.getDependNode( shapeNode );
```

An **MFnDependencyNode** function set is used to get a plug to the **shape** node's **create** attribute. This attribute holds a NURBS surface.

```
MFnDependencyNode shapeFn( shapeNode );
MPlug createPlug = shapeFn.findPlug( "create" );
```

The `melt` command inserts the new **melt** node between the current **makeNurbsSphere1** node and the **nurbSphereShape1** node, and you need to determine where the incoming connection to the **create** attribute comes from. If you didn't get the source of the connection, you couldn't later connect it into the new **melt** node. To get the source of a connection, the **MPlug**'s `connectedTo` function is used. It generates an array of plugs that are the source of the connection. Since there can be only one input connection to any attribute, why the need for an array? The `connectedTo` function is also used to query all the destination plugs of an attribute. Since an attribute can be fed into multiple destination attributes, an array is needed.

```
MPlugArray srcPlugs;
createPlug.connectedTo( srcPlugs, true, false );
```

Since it is known that there can be only one input connection to the **create** attribute, it must be the first element in the array. A truly robust plugin would check whether there are any elements in the array. This could happen, so it should be checked for, even though this example does not.

```
MPlug srcPlug = srcPlugs[0];
```

A new **melt** node is then created. To create a node, its unique identifier can be used. This is a more robust and error-proof method of specifying a particular node type. It is possible to use a node's type name, but this isn't as robust.

```
MObject meltNode = dgMod.createNode( MeltNode::id );
```

Plugs to the node's **inputSurface** and **outputSurface** attributes are then created.

```
MFnDependencyNode meltFn( meltNode );
MPlug outputSurfacePlug = meltFn.findPlug("outputSurface");
MPlug inputSurfacePlug = meltFn.findPlug("inputSurface");
```

The new **melt** node can now be connected to the existing nodes. Before establishing the new connections, the existing connection must be broken. This means that the connection between the **makeNurbsSphere1** and the **nurbSphereShape1** nodes must be broken. The **MDGModifer**'s disconnect function is used to do this. Its first argument is the source plug and its second is the destination plug. Combined, the two plugs uniquely identify a particular connection.

```
dgMod.disconnect( srcPlug, createPlug );
```

The various plugs are now connected.

```
dgMod.connect( srcPlug, inputSurfacePlug );
dgMod.connect( outputSurfacePlug, createPlug );
```

The new **melt** node has now been successfully inserted. An unfortunate consequence of using the **MDGModifier** is that it doesn't actually create nodes until its doIt function is called. Before its doIt function is called, the DG operations have simply been recorded but not executed. Therefore, it isn't possible to know ahead of time what the exact name of a new node will be. The node's name is determined when it is created. Each node must have a unique name so if a node already exists with the given name, Maya will automatically assign the new node a unique name. A number is appended to the given name to make a unique name. However, in the next section the exact name of the new node is needed in advance. In order to do this, a unique name must be assigned to the new node. Admittedly, the name encoding that is used isn't entirely robust, but it serves the purpose for this example. The **melt** node is renamed to the pregenerated name.

```
static i = 0;
MString name = MString("melting") + i++;
dgMod.renameNode( meltNode, name );
```

The next step is to set a keyframe for the **melt** node's **amount** attribute. At the start of the time range, the attribute's value is set to 0.0, and at the end of the time range, it is set to 1.0. This results in an object that starts as a solid on the first frame and then completely dissolves by the end of the last frame.

It is possible to create an **animCurve** node manually and connect it up to the **amount** attribute. Keyframes can then be set by using an **MFnAnimCurve** function set on the **animCurve** node. However, this is a simpler method. The MEL command, setKeyframe, can do all the hard work. The MEL statements are prepared in advance, then passed to the **MDGModifier**'s commandToExecute function. This first call to setKeyframe sets the first keyframe for the **amount** attribute.

```
MString cmd;
cmd = MString( "setKeyframe -at amount -t " )
                + startTime.value()
                + " -v " + 0.0 + " " + name;
dgMod.commandToExecute( cmd );
```

A similar command is used to generate a keyframe for the last frame.

```
    cmd = MString("setKeyframe -at amount -t ")
                    + endTime.value()
                    + " -v " + 1.0 + " " + name;
    dgMod.commandToExecute( cmd );
}
```

Finally the redoIt function is called to do the real work.

```
    return redoIt();
}
```

In the redoIt function, all the operations recorded in the **MDGModifier** object are executed by calling the **MDGModifier**'s doIt function.

```
MStatus MeltCmd::redoIt()
{
    return dgMod.doIt();
}
```

Similarly, undoing all the operations is handled by the **MDGModifier** in the undoIt function.

```
MStatus MeltCmd::undoIt()
{
    return dgMod.undoIt();
}
```

With an understanding of how the command created the **melt** node and connected it up, you are ready to cover the **melt** node. Recall that this node does the actual "melting" of the original surface.

Plugin: Melt
File: MeltNode.cpp

The **MeltNode** class is derived from the **MPxNode** class, as are all custom DG nodes. A temporary node identifier has been assigned to the node class.

```
const MTypeId MeltNode::id( 0x00334 );
```

The node has just three attributes. The **inputSurface** and **outputSurface** attributes are NURBS surfaces, while the **amount** attribute is a floating-point number.

```
MObject MeltNode::inputSurface;
MObject MeltNode::outputSurface;
MObject MeltNode::amount;
```

The compute function is where the actual melting takes place. Since the node has only one output attribute, **outputSurface**, it has to check only for this one.

```
MStatus MeltNode::compute( const MPlug& plug, MDataBlock& data )
{
    MStatus stat;

    if( plug == outputSurface )
        {
```

Handles to all the attributes are obtained.

```
MDataHandle amountHnd = data.inputValue( amount );
MDataHandle inputSurfaceHnd = data.inputValue( inputSurface );
MDataHandle outputSurfaceHnd = data.outputValue( outputSurface );
```

The **amount** attribute is known to be a `double`, so the **MDataHandle**'s `asDouble` function is used to retrieve it.

```
double amt = amountHnd.asDouble();
```

It is very important to use the correct `as...` function, since using the wrong one could cause Maya to crash. As such, it is important to know in advance the type of data that a given attribute holds.

The **inputSurface** attribute is a NURBS surface. It is retrieved using the **MDataHandle**'s `asNurbsSurface` function. This function returns an **MObject** to the NURBS surface data.

```
MObject inputSurfaceObj = inputSurfaceHnd.asNurbsSurface();
```

Maya stores the more complex data types, such as NURBS surfaces, as special geometry data. In order to be able to create and store this kind of data, you need to use the appropriate **MFnGeometryData** function set. In this case, the appropriate function set is the **MFnNurbsSurfaceData** class. Using this function set, the NURBS surface data is created.

```
MFnNurbsSurfaceData surfaceDataFn;
MObject newSurfaceData = surfaceDataFn.create();
```

With a place to store the new surface, the original input surface can be copied to the new output surface.

```
MFnNurbsSurface surfaceFn;
surfaceFn.copy( inputSurfaceObj, newSurfaceData );
```

The output surface is now an exact duplicate of the original input surface. The output surface can now be deformed, without affecting the input surface. The first step is to attach the **MFnNurbsSurface** function set to the data. This function set can be used to access and change the NURBS surface data.

```
surfaceFn.setObject( newSurfaceData );
```

All the surface control vertices (CVs) are retrieved and stored in an array using the **MFnNurbsSurface**'s `getCVs` function.

```
MPointArray pts;
surfaceFn.getCVs( pts );
```

It is possible to get and set individual surface CVs using the **MFnNurbsSurface**'s getCV and setCV functions, but it is often easier to put them all into a single array and then operate on that array. This reduces the number of function calls and is thereby faster.

The vertical extents of the NURBS surface is now calculated. After this step, the **minHeight** and **maxHeight** variables hold the minimum (base) and maximum (top) *y* extent of the surface, respectively.

```
double minHeight = DBL_MAX, maxHeight = DBL_MIN, y;
unsigned int i;
for( i=0; i < pts.length(); i++ )
    {
    y = pts[i].y;
    if( y < minHeight )
        minHeight = y;
    if( y > maxHeight )
        maxHeight = y;
    }
```

The distance that all the CVs will move is calculated next. It is computed as a percentage of the vertical range of the NURBS surface. An **amount** of 1 corresponds to the entire vertical range, while 0.5 corresponds to half that distance. This means that when the **amount** is set to 1, all the CVs at the top of the object will be moved to the base. When it is 0.5, they will be halfway down.

```
double dist = amt * (maxHeight - minHeight);
```

All the CVs in the NURBS surfaces are then iterated over.

```
MVector vec;
double d;
for( i=0; i < pts.length(); i++ )
    {
    MPoint &p = pts[i];
```

Each point is moved down vertically by the required distance.

```
p.y -= dist;
```

Those points that are now under the original base are treated specially.

```
if( p.y < minHeight )
    {
```

Their distance under the base is calculated.

```
d = minHeight - p.y;
```

A 2D vector is calculated from the x and z coordinates of the CV. This is the vector from the object's center to the CV, looking from the top viewport.

```
vec = MVector( p.x, 0.0, p.z );
```

The length of this vector is then calculated.

```
double len = vec.length();
```

This length is used to determine how far the CV should spread out. If the CV is very, very close to the center of the object, then it shouldn't move. This ensures that the spreading calculation doesn't result in numerical inaccuracy and divide-by-zero errors. This also ensures that shapes such as spheres, tori, and so on do not have a hole in their underbody, since these points won't be moved.

```
if( len > 1.0e-3 )
    {
```

The new length of the vector is calculated by taking the vertical distance traveled under the base and then moving the CV horizontally by that same distance. This simulates the effect of the CV moving down to the base and then spreading out. The new vector is calculated based on this new length.

```
double newLen = len + d;
vec *= newLen / len;
```

The CV's *x* and *z* coordinates are now set to the new position.

```
p.x = vec.x;
p.z = vec.z;
}
```

The vertical height of the CV can't ever go below the original base.

```
    p.y = minHeight;
    }
}
```

Now that all the new positions for the CVs have been calculated, the NURBS surface is updated.

```
surfaceFn.setCVs( pts );
```

Since the NURBS surface has been changed, it is very important that Maya be notified of this. The **MFnNurbsSurface**'s updateSurface function must always be called after any changes are made to the surface.

```
surfaceFn.updateSurface();
```

The output NURBS surface attribute is now set to the new NURBS surface data.

```
outputSurfaceHnd.set( newSurfaceData );
```

Since the attribute has now been recomputed, the plug is marked as clean.

```
    data.setClean( plug );
}
```

If another attribute that this node didn't define is being asked to recompute, return the MS::kUnknownParameter so that the base class can handle it.

```
else
    stat = MS::kUnknownParameter;
```

Finally, return the success or failure of the function call.

```
    return stat;
}
```

The node's `initialize` function sets up the node's attributes.

```
MStatus MeltNode::initialize()
{
    MFnNumericAttribute nAttr;
    MFnTypedAttribute tAttr;
```

The **amount** attribute is defined to be a single `double` value.

```
amount = nAttr.create( "amount", "amt",
                        MFnNumericData::kDouble, 0.0 );
```

Since the **amount** attribute is animated, it must be made *keyable*. When an attribute is keyable, you can set keyframes for it. Attributes, by default, aren't keyable. Setting an attribute to keyable also makes it visible in the Channel Control.

```
nAttr.setKeyable( true );
```

The **inputSurface** and **outputSurface** attributes use the **MFnTypedAttribute** class for their creation. This class is used to create more complex attributes, such as NURBS surfaces.

```
inputSurface = tAttr.create( "inputSurface", "is",
                        MFnNurbsSurfaceData::kNurbsSurface );
```

Any attribute is visible by default. Since the input surface attribute is manually connected by the `melt` command, it is best to avoid having it displayed. Even if an attribute is hidden, it is still possible to disconnect and reconnect this attribute using the Connection Editor.

```
tAttr.setHidden( true );
```

The **outputSurface** attribute is created in a similar manner to the **inputSurface** attribute.

```
outputSurface = tAttr.create( "outputSurface", "os",
                        MFnNurbsSurfaceData::kNurbsSurface );
```

The **outputSurface** is the direct result of taking the **inputSurface** and **amount** attributes and calculating a new surface. The new surface is derived from the inputs and thus can be re-created with just the input. Since this new surface can always be regenerated from these input attributes, there is no need to store it in the Maya scene file. Not saving the attribute saves disk space, which can be important for scenes with lots of complex surfaces.

```
tAttr.setStorable( false );
```

Like the **inputSurface** attribute, the **outputSurface** attribute should be displayed in any of the main editing windows.

```
tAttr.setHidden( true );
```

All the attributes are then added to the node.

```
addAttribute( amount );
addAttribute( inputSurface );
addAttribute( outputSurface );
```

Both the **amount** and **inputSurface** attributes directly affect the **outputSurface** attribute. This dependency is specified using the **MPxNode**'s attributeAffects function.

```
    attributeAffects( amount, outputSurface );
    attributeAffects( inputSurface, outputSurface );

    return MS::kSuccess;
}
```

While this example was more complex than the previous, the basic principles didn't change. The node still specified which attributes it contained and what their types were. It specified that certain attributes affected others. Even when a more complex data type (NURBS surface) was used, there weren't any large changes needed to support it.

4.5.3 GroundShadow Plugin

This project covers the creation of a command and node, named **groundShadow**, that generates interactive ground shadows. Given a point light source and a set of objects, the plugin generates the projected shadows of the objects onto the ground. Since it operates as a node that creates its output dynamically, the light position can be moved, and the resulting shadows are automatically regenerated. Also if the geometry of any of the objects is altered, the projected shadows are automatically updated.

Figure 4.24 shows the object's that will cast shadows. The resulting shadows, from the **groundShadow** plugin, are shown in Figure 4.25.

An important addition to this example is the use of an attribute that can accept different types of geometry. In the previous example, a single type of geometry, NURBS surface, could be operated on. The way the attribute is set up, a polygonal mesh could be used, for instance. This project shows you how to set up an attribute that takes different types of geometry.

1. Open the **GroundShadow** workspace.

2. Compile it, and load the resulting `GroundShadow.mll` plugin in Maya.

3. Open the **GroundShadow.ma** scene.

4. Select **Shading | Smooth Shading All**.

5. Select **Lighting | All Lights**.

6. Click on the **Play** button.

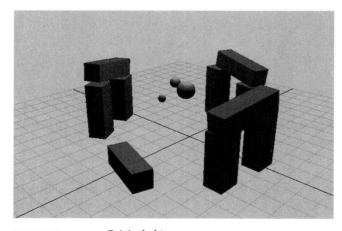

FIGURE 4.24 Original objects

FIGURE 4.25   Shadows cast onto the ground

The single point light moves across the scene while the small spheres rotate around each other.

7. Select all the objects including the point light.

8. In the **Script Editor**, execute the following:

```
groundShadow;
```

Ground shadows are created for all the selected objects.

9. Unselect all the objects.

10. Click on **Play**.

The ground shadows interactively change when the light moves.

The groundShadow command is responsible for creating the various geometry and **groundShadow** nodes, as well as connecting their attributes together.

The groundShadow command functions by taking all the selected objects and determining which of them are geometry nodes. A geometry node contains some form of geometry, including NURBS surfaces, curves, polygonal meshes, and so on. A shadow node is created for each of the selected geometry objects. A shadow node is an exact duplicate of the original geometry. The only difference is that the geometry is flattened and distorted to create a flat object in the shape of the shadow. The **groundShadow** node is responsible for performing this distortion.

Plugin: GroundShadow
File: GroundShadowCmd.h

The **GroundShadowCmd** class is derived from the **MPxCommand** class.

```
class GroundShadowCmd : public MPxCommand
{
public:
    virtual MStatusdoIt ( const MArgList& );
    virtual MStatus undoIt();
    virtual MStatus redoIt();
    virtual bool isUndoable() const { return true; }

    static void *creator() { return new GroundShadowCmd; }
    static MSyntax newSyntax();
```

The main difference from previous commands is that the class contains an **MDagModifier** rather than the usual **MDGModifier**. The **MDagModifier** is an extension of the **MDGModifier** class to handle DAG nodes. It understands about the DAG hierarchy and so lets you reorganize DAG node parent-child relationships. Since this command will be creating DAG nodes and reparenting them, this class is used instead.

```
private:
    MDagModifier dagMod;
};
```

Plugin: GroundShadow
File: GroundShadowCmd.cpp

The **groundShadow**'s doIt function does all the command preparation.

```
MStatus GroundShadowCmd::doIt ( const MArgList &args )
{
MStatus stat;
MSelectionList selection;
```

It is important to note that when a new shape node is created using the C++ API, it isn't automatically assigned the default shading group, **initialShadingGroup**. As such, the new shape must be explicitly added to the group. If this isn't done, the new shape will appear without shading and use a random color, often magenta.

The first step is, therefore, to get the **initialShadingGroup** node.

```
MObject shadingGroupObj;
selection.clear();
MGlobal::getSelectionListByName( "initialShadingGroup", selection );
selection.getDependNode( 0, shadingGroupObj );
```

An **MFnSet** is attached to the shading group, since shading groups are really just sets.

```
MFnSet shadingGroupFn( shadingGroupObj );
```

The currently selected objects are put in the `selection` list.

```
selection.clear();
MGlobal::getActiveSelectionList( selection );
MItSelectionList iter( selection );
```

In order to know where the light is coming from, at least one point light must have been selected. This next step iterates over the selection and determines if a point light has been selected.

```
MDagPath lightTransformPath;
MPlug pointLightTranslatePlug;
iter.setFilter( MFn::kPointLight );
for ( iter.reset(); !iter.isDone(); iter.next() )
    {
    iter.getDagPath( lightTransformPath );
```

When the path for a selected object is requested, the entire DAG path, right down to the **shape** node, is returned. Since only the shape's **transform** node is needed, the last node is popped off the DAG path. This resulting DAG path then includes all the **transform** nodes in the hierarchy above the **shape** node.

```
lightTransformPath.pop();
```

An **MPlug** is created to get the transform's **translate** attribute. This is used to determine the position of the light.

```
MFnDagNode dagNodeFn( lightTransformPath );
pointLightTranslatePlug = dagNodeFn.findPlug( "translate" );
```

Since only the first selected light is taken into consideration, the loop can now stop.

```
break;
}
```

Next, it is determined whether the light's transform path is valid. Even though the **MItSelectionList** would iterate only over point lights, if none were selected, the `lightTransformPath` would never have been set. As such, it is checked here. If it isn't, then no point light must have been selected, and you can exit with an error.

```
if( !lightTransformPath.isValid() )
    {
    MGlobal::displayError( "\nSelect a point light." );
    return MS::kFailure;
    }
```

The light's necessary information has now been retrieved. The next step is to iterate over all the selected geometric shapes and create shadow shapes for them.

```
iter.setFilter( MFn::kGeometric );
for ( iter.reset(), count=0; !iter.isDone(); iter.next(), count++ )
    {
    MDagPath geomShapePath;
    iter.getDagPath( geomShapePath );
```

The complete path to the shape is retrieved. The path is popped to remove the last item, the **shape** node, so that the path includes only the parent **transform** nodes.

```
MDagPath geomTransformPath( geomShapePath );
geomTransformPath.pop();
```

The shadow **shape** node that is created is simply a duplicate of the original shape. The duplicate function is called with the instance argument set to `false` so that a copy of the shape rather than an instance is created. Since this shape is later distorted to create a flat shadow shape, the original shape should be left untouched. If the original **shape** node were instanced, the shadow **shape** node would deform the common shape they would both share, which isn't the intention.

```
MFnDagNode geomShapeFn( geomShapePath );
MObject newGeomTransformObj = geomShapeFn.duplicate( false, false );
```

The **MFnDagNode** function set, newGeomShapeFn, is attached to the new **shape** node. The **shape** node is the first child of the parent **transform** node, so the **MFnDagNode**'s child function is used.

```
MFnDagNode newGeomShapeFn( newGeomTransformObj );
newGeomShapeFn.setObject( newGeomShapeFn.child(0) );
```

When the new shape is created, it is placed under a new **transform** node. You'd like the new **shape** node to reside under the original shape's parent **transform** node. Setting it up this way ensures that if the original shape moves, the shadow shape also moves, since they share the same parent transform hierarchy.

```
dagMod.reparentNode( newGeomShapeFn.object(), geomTransformPath.node() );
```

As mentioned earlier, Maya doesn't automatically assign a new **shape** node the default shading group, so it must be done manually. Assigning a **shape** node to a shading group consists of simply adding it to the set using the **MFnSet** addMember function.

```
shadingGroupFn.addMember( newGeomShapeFn.object() );
```

The **groundShadow** node is created next. It is responsible for distorting the shadow shape to appear as the shadow.

```
MObject shadowNode = dagMod.MDGModifier::createNode(
                                         GroundShadowNode::id );
assert( !shadowNode.isNull() );
MFnDependencyNode shadowNodeFn( shadowNode );
```

Plugs for the various attributes are then set up for the **groundShadow** node.

```
MPlug castingSurfacePlug = shadowNodeFn.findPlug( "castingSurface" );
MPlug shadowSurfacePlug = shadowNodeFn.findPlug( "shadowSurface" );
MPlug lightPositionPlug = shadowNodeFn.findPlug( "lightPosition" );
```

The **groundShadow** node and command are designed to support two different types of geometry: polygonal meshes and NURBS surfaces. Each geometry type has different input and output plugs. For a mesh node, the input geometry comes into the node through its **inMesh** attribute, while a NURBS surface has its input geometry come in through the **create** attribute. To retrieve the right attribute based on the geometry type, the outGeomPlugName and inGeomPlugName strings are set up. To determine the **shape** node's type, the **MDagPath**'s apiType function is used.

```
MString outGeomPlugName, inGeomPlugName;
switch( geomShapePath.apiType() )
    {
    case MFn::kMesh:
        outGeomPlugName = "worldMesh";
        inGeomPlugName = "inMesh";
        break;

    case MFn::kNurbsSurface:
        outGeomPlugName = "worldSpace";
        inGeomPlugName = "create";
        break;
    }
```

A plug is initialized to the geometry shape's associated output attribute.

```
MPlug outGeomPlug = geomShapeFn.findPlug( outGeomPlugName );
```

It is important to remember that the output geometry attribute isn't just a single output but instead an array of outputs. There exists a different output for each instance of the shape, so a shape that has been instanced three times has three elements in its output geometry array. To determine to which of the instances the currently selected object corresponds, the **MDagPath**'s instanceNumber function is called. This returns the instance number of the selected object. This number directly corresponds to the instance's index in the output geometry array.

```
unsigned int instanceNum = geomShapePath.instanceNumber();
```

At this point, the outGeomPlug plug is pointing to the output geometry's parent attribute, the array. You want it to point to a particular element in the array. This is done using the **MPlug**'s `selectAncestorLogicalIndex` function. This sets the plug to point to the array element with the given index.

```
outGeomPlug.selectAncestorLogicalIndex( instanceNum );
```

The input geometry plug, `inGeomPlug`, is set the geometry node's input attribute.

```
MPlug inGeomPlug = newGeomShapeFn.findPlug( inGeomPlugName );
```

The **MDagModifier** member is set up to connect the various attributes. The position of the point light is fed into the **shadow** node's light position attribute. The exact attributes of the **GroundShadowNode** are described in the next section. The output geometry is fed into the **shadow** node's casting surface attribute. This is the surface that generates the shadow. The result of the **shadow** node is another surface that is distorted to represent the final flat shadow. This resulting surface is fed into the input geometry attribute of the duplicated shape. This is the shadow shape that is displayed in the scene.

```
dagMod.connect( pointLightTranslatePlug, lightPositionPlug );
dagMod.connect( outGeomPlug, castingSurfacePlug );
dagMod.connect( shadowSurfacePlug, inGeomPlug );
}
```

If none of the objects are either meshes or NURBS surfaces, then the function exits with an error.

```
if( count == 0 )
    {
    MGlobal::displayError("\nSelect one or more geometric objects.");
    return MS::kFailure;
    }
```

With the **dagMod** object now set up, its `redoIt` function can be called to perform the actual work.

```
return redoIt();
}
```

The `redoIt` and `undoIt` functions are similar in form to the previous commands. The only difference is that the **MDagModfier** class is used in place of the usual **MDGModifier** class.

```
MStatus GroundShadowCmd::redoIt()
{
return dagMod.doIt();
}


MStatus GroundShadowCmd::undoIt()
{
return dagMod.undoIt();
}
```

The **groundShadow** node takes some input geometry and produces some output geometry. The node also takes the light's position as input. Taking into account the light position and input geometry, the node computes where the shadow of the geometry would lie on the ground plane. The resulting output geometry is simply a flat, distorted version of the original input geometry. This flattened geometry is displayed as the object's shadow. An additional extra that hasn't been discussed is the **groundShadow** node's **groundHeight** attribute. You can change this to set the ground plane to a new height.

Plugin: GroundShadow
File: GroundShadowNode.h

The **GroundShadowNode** class is a standard DG node, so it is directly derived from the **MPxNode** class. It contains all the usual member functions. Its attributes are covered in the next section.

```
class GroundShadowNode : public MPxNode
{
public:
    virtual MStatus compute( const MPlug& plug, MDataBlock& data );

    static   void *creator();
    static   MStatus initialize();

    static const MTypeId id;

public:
    static MObject lightPosition;
    static MObject castingSurface;
    static MObject shadowSurface;
    static MObject groundHeight;
};
```

Plugin: GroundShadow
File: GroundShadowNode.cpp

The node's attributes are first defined. The **lightPosition** attribute is the position of the light source in the scene. The **castingSurface** attribute is the original object's surface. The **shadowSurface** attribute holds the resulting shadow surface. The **groundHeight** attribute contains a single floating-point value for the height of the ground plane.

```
MObject GroundShadowNode::lightPosition;
MObject GroundShadowNode::castingSurface;
MObject GroundShadowNode::shadowSurface;
MObject GroundShadowNode::groundHeight;
```

The compute function is responsible for taking the input attributes (**lightPosition**, **castingSurface**, and **groundHeight**) and creating the final shadow surface in the **shadowSurface** attribute.

```
MStatus GroundShadowNode::compute(const MPlug& plug, MDataBlock& data)
{
MStatus stat;
```

This node's only output attribute is the **shadowSurface** attribute, which it is checked for.

```
if( plug == shadowSurface )
    {
```

MDataHandle objects to all the input and output attributes are set up.

```
MDataHandle groundHeightHnd = data.inputValue( groundHeight );
MDataHandle lightPositionHnd = data.inputValue( lightPosition );
MDataHandle castingSurfaceHnd = data.inputValue(castingSurface);
MDataHandle shadowSurfaceHnd = data.outputValue( shadowSurface );
```

A copy of the original casting surface is made and put into the shadow surface handle, shadowSurfaceHnd. At this point the shadow surface is an exact duplicate of the casting surface.

```
shadowSurfaceHnd.copy( castingSurfaceHnd );
```

The next section of code initializes variables that are used later in the calculation of the final shadow geometry. The height of the ground plane is first retrieved.

```
double gHeight = groundHeightHnd.asDouble();
```

The position of the light source is stored in the **Mvector**'s lightPoint.

```
MVector lightPoint( lightPositionHnd.asDouble3() );
```

The *normal* to the ground plane points directly upward, that is, in the direction of the y-axis.

```
MVector planeNormal( 0.0, 1.0, 0.0 );
```

A point is created that is known to lie on the ground plane.

```
MVector planePoint( 0.0, gHeight, 0.0 );
```

The dot product between the normal and the point is calculated.

```
double c = planeNormal * planePoint;
```

Each point in the shadow surface geometry is now distorted. The distortion is the result of projecting the points from the light location onto the ground plane.

```
MPoint surfPoint;
double denom, t;
MItGeometry iter( shadowSurfaceHnd, false );
for( ; !iter.isDone(); iter.next() )
    {
```

The position of the geometry in world space coordinates is retrieved.

```
surfPoint = iter.position( MSpace::kWorld );
```

An imaginary line between the surface point and the light source is then created. The new position of the surface point is where this line intersects the ground plane.

```
denom = planeNormal * (surfPoint - lightPoint);
    if( denom != 0.0 )
        {
        t = (c - (planeNormal * lightPoint)) / denom;
        surfPoint = lightPoint + t * (surfPoint - lightPoint);
        }
```

The surface point's position is updated to the projected position.

```
iter.setPosition( surfPoint, MSpace::kWorld );
}
```

The output surface attribute has now been updated.

```
data.setClean( plug );
}
```

If the attribute that Maya is requesting to be recomputed isn't known to this node, the appropriate status code is returned.

```
else
    stat = MS::kUnknownParameter;

return stat;
}
```

The `initialize` function sets up the blueprints for the node's attributes.

```
MStatus GroundShadowNode::initialize()
{
```

The **lightPosition** attribute is simply a position. It is stored as three doubles.

```
MFnNumericAttribute nAttr;
lightPosition = nAttr.create( "lightPosition", "lpos",
                             MFnNumericData::k3Double, 0.0 );
nAttr.setKeyable( true );
```

The **groundHeight** attribute is just a single distance value. Since it is a distance unit, the **MFUnitAttribute** class is used.

```
MFnUnitAttribute uAttr;
groundHeight = uAttr.create( "groundHeight", "grnd",
                             MFnUnitAttribute::kDistance, 0.0 );
uAttr.setKeyable( true );
```

The **castingSurface** attribute is of type **MFnGenericAttribute**. This attribute allows you to define a variety of different data types that it will accept. In this case the attribute should accept both meshes and NURBS surfaces.

```
MFnGenericAttribute gAttr;
castingSurface = gAttr.create( "castingSurface", "csrf" );
gAttr.addAccept( MFnData::kMesh );
gAttr.addAccept( MFnData::kNurbsSurface );
gAttr.setHidden( true );
```

Since the **shadowSurface** attribute is the result of deforming a copy of the **castingSurface** attribute, it must support the same type of data as the **castingSurface** attribute. It is therefore the same attribute type as the **castingSurface**.

```
shadowSurface = gAttr.create( "shadowSurface", "ssrf" );
gAttr.addAccept( MFnData::kMesh );
gAttr.addAccept( MFnData::kNurbsSurface );
gAttr.setHidden( true );
```

Since this is an output attribute, it can be regenerated from the node's inputs, so it doesn't have to be stored in the Maya scene file.

```
gAttr.setStorable( false );
```

All the node's attributes are now added.

```
addAttribute( groundHeight );
addAttribute( lightPosition );
addAttribute( castingSurface );
addAttribute( shadowSurface );
```

When any of the attributes, **groundHeight**, **lightPosition**, or **castingSurface**, change, the **shadowSurface** attribute is affected. This relationship is next defined.

```
attributeAffects( groundHeight, shadowSurface );
attributeAffects( lightPosition, shadowSurface );
attributeAffects( castingSurface, shadowSurface );

return MS::kSuccess;
}
```

4.5.4 Attributes

All node attributes are defined using a class derived from **MFnAttribute**. Depending on what type of attribute you'd like to create, the appropriate **MFnAttribute** derived class is used.

Unfortunately Maya uses the same term, *attribute,* to mean two slightly different things. This creates two different perspectives. From a user's perspective, each node has a series of attributes. The user changes and animates these attributes. From a programmer's perspective, attributes are somewhat different. This section refers to the term *attribute* as it is understood from the programmer's perspective.

In the C++ API, the **MFnAttribute** and all its derived classes can be intuitively thought of as a template or blueprint for how a piece of data in the node should be created. The most important distinction from the user's perspective is that the attribute doesn't actually hold any data. It simply provides a specification for the data. Given this specification, the actual data is created.

For instance, an **MFnAttribute** derived class defines the name and type of the data within the node. It also specifies whether the data should be stored to disk and whether its value can be changed (read/write). An attribute defines the specification for a single piece of data. For instance, an attribute may specify that the node is going to contain a float named **amplitude**. When the node is created, it prepares a slot for a float and gives it the name **amplitude**. Each node has its own unique **amplitude** data value. If you change the **amplitude** value in one node, it doesn't affect the **amplitude** value in other nodes.

Maya takes the information defined in the attribute and then uses it to actually create the data that exists inside each of the individual nodes. Since an attribute is the blueprint, it follows logically that it is defined only once. By convention attributes are defined in the node's static member function called initialize, though you are free to use any function.

CREATING ATTRIBUTES

An attribute is created inside the initialize function. It is then registered with the node by using the **MPxNode**'s addAttribute function. The following example creates an attribute, **days**, that is registered with the node.

```
class MyNode : public MPxNode
{
...
  static MStatus initialize();
  static MObject daysAttr;
};

MObject MyNode::daysAttr;

MStatus MyNode::initialize()
{
MFnNumericAttribute numFn;
daysAttr = numFn.create( "days", "d", MFnNumericData::kLong );

addAttribute( daysAttr );

return MS::kSuccess;
}
```

This same basic format is used for all attributes. The main difference is that, depending on the type of attribute, a different **MFn...Attribute** class will be used.

COMPOUND ATTRIBUTES

A compound attribute is used to group other attributes. The grouped attributes are considered *children* of the compound attribute, which is itself considered the *parent*. In this example a compound attribute, **player**, is created with two child attributes, **age** and **homeruns**.

```
class MyNode : public MPxNode
{
...
  static MStatus initialize();
  static MObject playerAttr;
  static MObject ageAttr;
  static MObject homeRunsAttr;
};

MObject MyNode::playerAttr;
MObject MyNode::ageAttr;
MObject MyNode::homeRunsAttr;

MStatus MyNode::initialize()
{
```

The child attributes are defined as usual.

```
MFnNumericAttribute numFn;
ageAttr = numFn.create( "age", "a", MFnNumericData::kLong );
homeRunsAttr = numFn.create( "homeruns", "hr", MFnNumericData::kLong );
```

The compound attribute uses the **MFnCompoundAttribute** class. It is created like any attribute.

```
MFnCompoundAttribute compFn;
playerAttr = compFn.create( "player", "ply" );
```

The child attributes are then added to the compound attribute.

```
compFn.addChild( nameAttr );
compFn.addChild( homeRunsAttr );
```

Last all the attributes, both child and parent, are added to the node. It is important to note that when you add a compound attribute all its children aren't automatically added. The children must be explicitly added.

```
addAttribute( ageAttr );
addAttribute( homeRunsAttr );
addAttribute( playerAttr );

return MS::kSuccess;
}
```

DEFAULT VALUES

Each attribute has a default value. This is the value with which the attribute is initialized. Depending on the particular class, you will have the option of setting the default through the function set's create function or using an appropriate default setting function.

For example, for attributes that use enumerated types (**MFnEnumAttribute**), the default is set in the create function as follows. This sets the attribute's default to 0.

```
MFnEnumAttribute enumFn;
attr = enumFn.create( "days", "d", 0 );
...
```

The **MFnNumericAttribute** class is used to create numeric attributes. Its default can be set using the create function or its setDefault member function. The following demonstrates how to use the latter method:

```
MFnNumericAttribute numFn;
attr = numFn.create( "active", "act", MFnNumericData::kBoolean );
numFn.setDefault( false );
```

If the user never changes an attribute's value, it retains its default value. If an attribute's value is the same as its default, it won't be stored to disk. Since the value is no different from the default, there is no need to store it. Its value can be simply initialized to the default rather than to a value on disk. This reduces the size of the scene files stored to disk.

An important consequence of this is that if you later change the default values for your attributes, those attributes that used the previous default values automatically use the new defaults. This may not always be what you intended. This may "break" existing scenes, since those attributes that used the default now have a different value. The best way to avoid this is to decide early in the node's development what an attribute's default will be. By fixing on a default value before any Maya scenes are created using the node, you won't encounter this problem.

ATTRIBUTE PROPERTIES

An attribute has various properties. These properties define, for instance, whether you can change the attribute's value or make connections to it. Table 4.2 lists the common properties that all attributes share.

TABLE 4.2 COMMON ATTRIBUTE PROPERTIES		
Property	Description	Default
Readable	Can be the source of connections	true
Writable	Can be the destination of connections	true
Connectable	Can be connected	true
Storable	Is stored to scene files	true
Keyable	Can be animated	false
Hidden	Is hidden	false
UsedAsColor	Treat values as colors	false
Cached	Value is cached	true
Array	Is an array	false
IndexMatter	Index shouldn't change	true
ArrayDataBuilder	Uses array data builder to set value	false
Indeterminant	Determines if it can be used in an evaluation	false
DisconnectBehavior	Behavior after disconnection	kNothing
Internal	Is internal to the node	false
RenderSource	Overrides rendering sampling information	false

The following section covers some of the most important properties in greater detail.

Readable and Writable

An attribute has a *readable* and *writable* flag. By default, both these flags are set to true. Interestingly enough an attribute's value can always be retrieved, irrespective of whether its readable flag is set. The readable flag defines whether the attribute can be used as the source of a connection. If it is set to false, then you won't be able to create a connection from the attribute to another attribute. The isReadable and setReadable functions are used to retrieve and set the readable flag, respectively.

An example using these functions is as follows:

```
MFnMessageAttribute msgFn;
attr = msgFn.create( "controller", "ctrl" );
bool isread = msgFn.isReadable(); // Returns true
msgFn.setReadable( false );
```

When an attribute doesn't have its writable flag set to true, you can't change its value using the setAttr command. It also can't be used as the destination in a connection, which means that you can't create a connection from another attribute to this attribute. The following example demonstrates the various writable flag retrieval and setting functions:

```
MFnMessageAttribute msgFn;
attr = msgFn.create( "controller", "ctrl" );
bool iswrite = msgFn.isWritable (); // Returns true
msgFn.setWritable ( false );
```

Connectable

As mentioned previously, the readable and writable flags determine whether you can use the attribute as the source and destination of a connection, respectively. However, the connectable flag ultimately determines if any connection can be made. If the readable flag is set to true, but the connectable flag is set to false, then you won't be able to use the attribute as the source of a connection. Both flags must be set to true for this to work. As such the connectable flag is used in combination with the readable and writable flags to determine what types of connections are valid.

This example shows how to retrieve and set the connectable flag.

```
MFnMatrixAttribute mtxFn;
attr = mtxFn.create( "xform", "xfm", MFnMatrixAttribute::kDouble );
bool iscon = mtxFn.isConnectable(); // Returns true
mtx.setConnectable( false );
```

Keyable

When an attribute is keyable, you can animate it by setting keyframes. By default, an attribute isn't keyable. Consequently it isn't shown in the Channel Box. The isKeyable and setKeyable functions are used to retrieve and set the keyable flag, respectively.

```
MFnMatrixAttribute mtxFn;
attr = mtxFn.create( "xform", "xfm", MFnMatrixAttribute::kDouble );
bool canKey = mtxFn.isKeyable(); // Returns false
mtx.setKeyable( true );
```

Storable

The storable flag determines whether an attribute's values are stored to disk. By setting this to false, the attribute won't be stored. By default, an attribute is storable.

Certain attributes don't necessarily have to be stored to disk. These attributes include those that have their value computed from other attributes: output attributes. The values of these attributes are derived from other input attributes. Since they are derived, they can be reconstructed from the input attributes. As such, there is no need to store them to disk, since they can be reconstructed. While it isn't illegal to store these attributes, they use disk space unnecessarily. So when you know that an attribute is an output attribute—that is, it is used as the dependent attribute in an attributeAffects function call—it doesn't have to be stored to disk. The following example demonstrates this:

```
MFnNumericAttribute numFn;
widthAttr = numFn.create( "width", "w", MFnNumericData::kDouble );

sizeAttr = numFn.create( "size", "s", MFnNumericData::kDouble );
numFn.setStorable( false ); // No need to store it

attributeAffects( widthAttr, sizeAttr );
```

Array

By default, an attribute holds a single instance of its data. An attribute can be made to hold a series of data instances by making it into an array. Array attributes are also referred to as multis. By default, an attribute isn't an array. The isArray and setArray functions are used to retrieve and set the array property, respectively. In the following example, an attribute is made to hold an array of doubles:

```
MFnNumericAttribute numFn;
sizesAttr = numFn.create( "sizes", "s", MFnNumericData::kDouble );
numFn.setArray( true ); // Can no hold an array of doubles
```

The methods for accessing and adding elements to the array are discussed in a later section.

Cached

An attribute, by default, is cached. This means that a copy of the attribute data is maintained in the node's datablock. By caching an attribute's value, the `compute` function doesn't have to be continually called whenever the attribute's value is requested. This makes it faster to retrieve node attribute values. The downside to caching attributes is that it requires more memory. Caching can be turned on or off using the `setCache` function.

```
MFnNumericAttribute numFn;
sizesAttr = numFn.create( "sizes", "s", MFnNumericData::kDouble );
numFn.setCached( false ); // No longer cached
```

DYNAMIC ATTRIBUTES

The `initialize` function is where you define the various attributes of a node. Each instance of the node will use these attributes. These attributes are known as static attributes since they always exist for each instance of the node. There is no way to remove these attributes from the node.

It is also possible to create *dynamic attributes.* These are attributes that are added later as needed. A dynamic attribute can be shared between all nodes of a given type or be unique to a particular node.

To create a dynamic attribute, an attribute is first defined. It is defined in the same way as static attributes.

```
MFnNumericAttribute numFn;
MObject attr = numFn.create( "size", "s", MFnNumericData::kDouble );
```

This attribute is then added to the node by using the **MFnDependencyNode**'s `addAttribute` function. In this case, the `MFnDependencyNode::kLocalDynamicAttr` value is passed to the `addAttribute` function. This indicates that the attribute should be added to this particular node and not to all nodes of the same type.

```
MFnDependencyNode nodeFn( nodeObj );
nodeFn.addAttribute( attr, MFnDependencyNode::kLocalDynamicAttr );
```

To add an attribute to all instances, both existing and future, of a given node type, the `MFnDependencyNode::kGlobalDynamicAttr` value should be used when calling the addAttribute function. It is important to use a unique name for the attribute. If the node already has an attribute with the given name, the dynamic attribute won't be added. A dynamic attribute can be deleted later using the removeAttribute function.

```
nodeFn.removeAttribute( attr, MFnDependencyNode::kLocalDynamicAttr );
```

4.5.5 Compute Function

The compute function is where the output attributes are calculated from the input attributes. The compute function takes a reference to the **MdataBlock**, which is used to retrieve and set the various node attributes. It is extremely important to use only the **MDataBlock** to get all the information the node needs to calculate its outputs. No data from outside the **MDataBlock** should be used in the computation.

It is also extremely important to not use the MEL setAttr and getAttr commands inside of the compute function. These commands can indirectly cause the DG to evaluate. If during this evaluation the value of the same plug is requested, either directly or indirectly, an infinite loop results.

Take the following example. Although contrived, it does demonstrate the danger of using getAttr inside the compute function. An instance of the **MyNode** class is created, **myNode1**. Assume that the node has two attributes; **scores**, an array of player scores, and **average**, which gives the average score. If the value of the **average** attribute is requested, the node is asked to compute this value. When the compute function is called and executes the MGlobal::executeCommand part, an infinite loop occurs.

```
MStatus MyNode::compute( const MPlug& plug, MDataBlock& data )
{
MStatus stat;

if( plug == avgAttr )
    {
    MArrayDataHandle scoresHnd = data.inputArrayValue( scoresAttr );
    MDataHandle avgHnd = data.outputValue( avgAttr );
    MGlobal::executeCommand( "getAttr myNode1.average" );
    data.setClean( plug );
    }
else
    stat  = MS::kUnknownParameter;

return stat;
}
```

This leads to a very important rule that is key to preventing any indirect DG reevaluations when you are inside of a compute function.

Get attribute values only from the MDataBlock.

Note that while it isn't illegal to get the value of the plug that is being recomputed, there often isn't any point. Using **MPlug**'s getValue and **MDataHandle**'s asDouble won't cause an infinite loop.

```
MStatus MyNode::compute( const MPlug& plug, MDataBlock& data )
{
MStatus stat;

if( plug == avgAttr )
    {
    MArrayDataHandle scoresHnd = data.inputArrayValue( scoresAttr );
    MDataHandle avgHnd = data.outputValue( avgAttr );
    double value;
    plug.getValue( value ); // Retrieve value
    MDataHandle resInHnd = data.inputValue( resAttr );
    value = resInHnd.asDouble (); // Retrieve value
    data.setClean( plug );
    }
else
    stat  = MS::kUnknownParameter;

return stat;
}
```

You should never rely on the previous value of a plug in order to compute its current value. In fact, you can never make any assumption about the current value of a plug. Since plugs can be evaluated at different times, there is no guarantee that the plug will, for instance, hold the value it had from the previous frame.

4.5.6 Plugs

In the context of the C++ API, an attribute is simply a blueprint for creating data within a node. An attribute doesn't hold any data but instead provides a specification for how that data should be created. Given a particular instance of a node, a *plug* is used actually to access the node's data. A plug provides a mechanism for accessing the actual data for a given node. A plug is created by specifying a particular node and attribute. Using this combination, a plug refers to the actual data of a given node. Plugs are created and accessed using the **MPlug** class.

The following example creates an **MPlug** to the **translateX** attribute of the given **transform** node, `ballObj`. The **MFnDependencyNode**'s `findPlug` function is used to create a plug to a given attribute. The attribute name given can be either the long or short form.

```
MFnDependencyNode nodeFn( ballObj );
MPlug transxPlg = nodeFn.findPlug( "translateX" );
```

The `findPlug` function is also overloaded to take an attribute object registered in the node's `initialize` function. Since a direct reference to the attribute object is often available only in the node's implementation file, this is rarely used.

With the plug now created, the attribute data can now be retrieved using **MPlug**'s `getValue` function.

```
double tx;
transxPlg.getValue( tx );
```

The `getValue` function has been overloaded to retrieve many different types of data. It is therefore important to ensure that the data type being retrieved matches the attribute's data type. Since the **translateX** attribute is of type `double`, it is retrieved into a `double` variable. If you attempt to retrieve an attribute's data but with the wrong type, the result will be unpredictable. It may even cause Maya to crash. The following example demonstrates trying to retrieve the same attribute but as a `short`:

```
short tx;
transxPlg.getValue( tx ); // Unpredictable result
```

This is the most common mistake when using plugs, so be sure that the type of data you are attempting to retrieve matches the attribute's data type.

To set the value of a plug, use the `setValue` function. The following example shows how to set the plug's value to 2.3. Note the use of the explicit type case to ensure that the appropriate overloaded version of the `setValue` function is called.

```
transxPlg.setValue( double(2.3) );
```

By default, the value of an attribute is retrieved at the current time. It is also possible to retrieve its value at another time. To do this, use the **MDGContext** class. First set it to the required evaluation time, then use the call to the getValue function. In the following example, the **MTime** variable t is set to the time 1.5 seconds. This variable is then used to initialize the **MDGContext** variable ctx. This ctx variable is passed to the **MPlug**'s getValue function to retrieve the attribute value at the given time.

```
MTime t(1.5, MTime::kSeconds );
MDGContext ctx(t);
transxPlug.getValue( tx, ctx );
```

It isn't possible to use the setValue function at an alternative time. It always sets the attribute's value at the current time. To change the current time, use the **MGlobal**'s viewFrame function. Note that this function often requires the DG to update, so it should be used sparingly.

```
MTime t(1.5, MTime::kSeconds );
MGlobal::viewFrame( t );
```

To create animated values for the attribute, the MEL keyframe command should be used.

Compound Plugs

The **MPlug** class is also used to navigate compound attributes. In this next example, a plug is created for a **transform** node's **translate** attribute.

```
MFnDependencyNode nodeFn( transformNodeOj );
MPlug transPlg = nodeFn.findPlug( "translate" );
```

This transPlg variable is now referencing the **translate** attribute. This is a compound attribute containing three child attributes: **translateX**, **translateY**, and **translateZ**. To access the child, use the **MPlug**'s child function.

```
MObject transxAttr = nodeFn.attribute( "translateX" );
MPlug transxPlg = transPlg.child( transXAttr );
```

The parent of a child plug can be retrieved using the **MPlug**'s parent function.

```
MPlug parent = transxPlg.parent();
```

If you don't know the exact number and names of the children, the **MPlug**'s numChildren and child functions can be used. The child function is overloaded to take an index to the *n*th child. For instance, to iterate over all the children in a compound attribute, use the following:

```
const unsigned int nChilds = transPlg.numChildren();
unsigned int i;
for( i=0; i < nChilds; i++ )
    {
    MPlug child = transPlg.child(i);
    ... use the child plug
    }
```

Array Plugs

An array attribute contains a series of other attributes. These attributes are referred to as the elements of the array. A plug that references the array is referred to as an array plug, while a plug that references an element is an element plug.

In the following example, a custom node is created that contains an array attribute, **scores**. This attribute contains a series of long integer values.

```
class MyNode : public MPxNode
{
...
  static MStatus initialize();
  static MObject scoresAttr;
};

MObject MyNode::scoredAttr;

MStatus MyNode::initialize()
{
```

The scores attribute is created using the **MFnNumericAttribute** class.

```
MFnNumericAttribute numFn;
scoresAttr = numFn.create( "scores", "scrs", MFnNumericData::kLong );
```

The setArray function is called to indicate that the attribute is an array.

```
numFn.setArray( true );

addAttribute( scoresAttr );

return MS::kSuccess;
}
```

In order to see what elements an array contains, a utility function, printArray, is defined as follows. It prints out the contents of the array to the Script Editor.

```
void printArray( MPlug &arrayPlug )
{
MString txt( "\nArray..." );

unsigned int nElems = arrayPlug.numElements();
unsigned int i=0;
for( i=0; i < nElems; i++ )
    {
    MPlug elemPlg = arrayPlug.elementByPhysicalIndex(i);

    txt += "\nElement #";
    txt += (int)i;
    txt += ": ";
    double value = 0.0;
    elemPlg.getValue( value );
    txt += value;
    txt += " (";
    txt += (int)elemPlg.logicalIndex();
    txt += ")";
    }

MGlobal::displayInfo( txt );
}
```

The significant portions of the function are now covered. The first step in the function is to determine the number of elements in the array. This is done using the **MPlug**'s numElements function.

```
unsigned int nElems = arrayPlug.numElements();
```

The elements are iterated over.

```
for( i=0; i < nElems; i++ )
    {
```

A plug is created for each element by calling the **MPlug**'s elementByPhysicalIndex function. This returns a plug to the *i*th array element.

```
MPlug elemPlg = arrayPlug.elementByPhysicalIndex(i);
```

The value of the element plug is retrieved using the **MPlug**'s getValue function.

```
double value = 0.0;
elemPlg.getValue( value );
```

In addition to displaying the element's value, the logical index is also displayed. Logical indices are explained shortly. The logical index of the plug is given by the **MPlug**'s logicalIndex function.

```
txt += (int)elemPlg.logicalIndex();
```

To demonstrate how elements are added to an array, the following statements are used. They create a **MyNode** node and add elements to the **scores** array.

```
MObject myNodeObj = dgMod.createNode( MyNode::id );
MFnDependencyNode depFn( myNodeObj );
```

A plug to the **scores** attribute is created using the findPlug function.

```
MPlug scoresPlg = depFn.findPlug( "scores" );
```

Elements in an array have both a physical and a logical index. The physical index of an element in the array is its index into the actual array. The physical indices of the array range from 0 to numElements()-1. When an element is deleted from the array, the physical indices of some of the elements could change. The logical index to an element, on the other hand, never changes. The logical index is a means of giving an element an absolute, unchanging index, irrespective of any additions or deletions to the physical array. When you refer to an array element in MEL, you use its logical index. There is no way in MEL to get an element's physical index.

The need for physical and logical indices is that connections between attributes are made based on their logical indices. Since these indices don't change, you can be sure that deleting another element in the array won't change an element's logical index. This is unlike their physical index, which could change.

The following examples help further clarify the difference between the two types of indexing. The scorePlg plug is set to the element at logical index 0. This is done by using the elementByLogicalIndex function.

```
MPlug scorePlg;
scorePlg = scoresPlg.elementByLogicalIndex(0);
```

Its value is then set to 46.

```
scorePlg.setValue( 46 );
```

The contents of the array are then printed out.

```
printArray( scoresPlg );
```

The results are as follows:

```
Array...
Element #0: 46 (0)
```

An element has been added to the array. The elementByLogicalIndex is used to create an element at the given index. If an element already exists at the given logical index, the existing element is accessed. The first element has a physical index of 0 and a logical index of 0.

Next, the element at logical index 2 is referenced. Since it doesn't exist yet, it is created.

```
scorePlg = scoresPlg.elementByLogicalIndex(2);
```

Its value is set to 12.

```
scorePlg.setValue( 12 );
```

The array is once again printed out.

```
printArray( scoresPlg );
```

The results are as follows:

```
Array...
Element #0: 46 (0)
Element #1: 12 (2)
```

The physical array now contains two elements. As you would expect, their physical indices are 0 and 1. However the logical indices of the elements are 0 and 2. Since the second element was accessed using an index of 2 to the elementByLogicalIndex function, it is assigned the logical index of 2. Notice that there is no logical index 1. Since it hasn't been referenced yet, it hasn't been created. Since the logical indices of the array can have "missing" indices, the array can be considered to be a sparse array. While the logical indices are sparse, the physical indices are contiguous.

In the next step, the element at logical index 1 is referenced.

```
scorePlg = scoresPlg.elementByLogicalIndex(1);
```

The element's value is set to 93.

```
scorePlg.setValue( 93 );
```

The array contents are then printed out.

```
printArray( scoresPlg );
```

The results are as follows:

```
Array...
Element #0: 46 (0)
Element #1: 93 (1)
Element #2: 12 (2)
```

The element is inserted into the array at physical index 1. The logical index it uses is the one passed into the elementByLogicalIndex function. Notice that the element with logical index 2 (value of 12) now has a different physical index. It was index 1 before, and now it is index 2. This shows once again that the physical index of an element can change, while its logical index never will.

To further emphasize that the logical index doesn't necessarily correspond to the physical index, another element is added. This time it uses a logical index that is much larger than any of the others. The element is referenced using logical index 25.

```
scorePlg = scoresPlg.elementByLogicalIndex(25);
```

Its value is set to 57.

```
scorePlg.setValue( 57 );
```

The array is printed.

```
printArray( scoresPlg );
```

The results are as follows:

```
Array...
Element #0: 46 (0)
Element #1: 93 (1)
Element #2: 12 (2)
Element #3: 57 (25)
```

The array now has four elements. The physical indices range from 0 to numElements()-1. The logical indices are exactly those chosen. There are currently no elements at logical indices 3 to 24. Since logical indices are unchanging, they are the safest way to refer to array elements.

Elements are retrieved using the logical index with the **MPlug**'s elementByLogicalIndex function. As mentioned earlier, if an element exists at a given logical index, it is retrieved. If an element doesn't exist, it is created. In the following example, the element at logical index 1 is retrieved:

```
int value;
scorePlg = scoresPlg.elementByLogicalIndex(1);
scorePlg.getValue( value ); // Value of 93
```

To get a list of all the logical indices of an array, use the **MPlug**'s
getExistingArrayAttributeIndices function. This returns an array of logical indices
for all elements that exist (that are connected or that have their value set).

```
MIntArray logIndices;
scoresPlg.getExistingArrayAttributeIndices( logIndices );
```

The logIndices array now contains the values [0, 1, 2, 25]. What happens if
you attempt to retrieve a value for an element that doesn't exist? In the following
code, the value of the element at logical index 10 is retrieved:

```
MStatus stat;
scorePlg = scoresPlg.elementByLogicalIndex( 10 );
scorePlg.getValue( value );
MGlobal::displayInfo( MString("value: ") + value );
```

The result is as follows:

```
// value: 0
```

When an element doesn't exist at a given logical index, the default value for the
element is returned. This indicates that *all* logical indices are valid. When you access
an element that doesn't exist, the default value is returned. If an element does exist,
its current value is returned.

Given an element plug, it may be necessary to determine its parent array plug.
This is done using the **MPlug**'s array function.

```
MPlug arrayPlg = scorePlg.array();
```

The arrayPlg plug now refers to the **scores** array attribute.

4.5.7 Datablocks

Datablocks are where the actual node data is stored. The data isn't stored within the
node but inside one or more datablocks. It isn't necessary to understand their inner
workings and how they are networked together. Instead the **MDataBlock**,
MDataHandle, and **MArrayDataHandle** classes are used to retrieve and set node data.

The **MDataBlock** provides a convenient means of grouping all the node's data together. To access a single node attribute, use the **MDataBlock**'s `inputValue` or `outputValue` functions. If the attribute is being used as input to a computation, then use the `inputValue` function. If it is being used as output in a computation, then use the `outputValue` function. Both these functions return an **MDataHandle** instance that is then used to access the data. Similarly, when you want to access an array attribute, the **MDataBlock**'s `inputArrayValue` and `outputArrayValue` functions should be used. These both return an **MArrayDataHandle** that allows you to access the individual elements of the array.

The `input...Value` functions return a handle that can be used only for reading the data. The data is read-only. You can't write to the data using the handle they return. Similarly, the `output...Value` functions return a handle that is used for writing the data. The data is write-only. You can't read the data using the handle they return. Since attributes are classified into input (read-only) and output (write-only), these restrictions typically aren't a problem.

In this example, the **MyNode** class has two attributes: **scores**, an array of integers, and **average**, which is the average of the scores. The `compute` function therefore needs to access both an array attribute, **scores**, as well as a single attribute, **average**.

```
MStatus GroundShadowNode::compute( const MPlug& plug, MDataBlock &data)
{
MStatus stat;

if( plug == avgAttr )
    {
    MArrayDataHandle scoresHnd = data.inputArrayValue( scoresAttr );
    MDataHandle avgHnd = data.outputValue( avgAttr );
    const unsigned int nElems = scoresHnd.elementCount();
    double sum = 0.0;
    unsigned int i;
    for( i=0; i < nElems; i++ )
        {
        scoresHnd.jumpToElement( i );
        MDataHandle elemHnd = scoresHnd.inputValue();
        sum += elemHnd.asInt();
        }
    sum /= nElems;
    avgHnd.set( sum );
    data.setClean( plug );
    }
```

```
else
    stat  = MS::kUnknownParameter;

return stat;
}
```

Inside the `compute` function, the **scores** data is being used as input in the calculation of the **average** data. The **scores** data is accessed using the **MDataBlock**'s `inputArrayValue` function. This returns an **MArrayDataHandle** that can then be used to access the individual elements of the **scores** array.

```
MArrayDataHandle scoresHnd = data.inputArrayValue( scoresAttr );
```

A handle to the average data is then created by calling the **MDataBlock**'s `outputValue` function.

```
MDataHandle avgHnd = data.outputValue( avgAttr );
```

The number of elements in the **scores** array is determined using the **MArrayDataHandle**'s `elementCount` function.

```
const unsigned int nElems = scoresHnd.elementCount();
```

The individual elements are then iterated over.

```
double sum = 0.0;
unsigned int i;
for( i=0; i < nElems; i++ )
    {
```

To access a particular element, the **MArrayDataHandle**'s `jumpToElement` function is used. It takes the index of the element as its argument.

```
scoresHnd.jumpToElement( i );
```

A handle to the individual element is then created.

```
MDataHandle elemHnd = scoresHnd.inputValue();
```

The value of the element is retrieved and added to the running total.

```
sum += eleHnd.asInt( );
}
```

The average is then calculated, and the data set. Finally the plug is marked as being updated.

```
sum /= nElems;
avgHnd.set( sum );
data.setClean( plug );
```

The individual children of a compound attribute can be retrieved using the **MDataHandle**'s `child` function. Since an attribute can contain arbitrary arrays of attributes, and each of these attributes can themselves be arrays, the **MArrayDataHandle** can also return a handle to its subarrays by using the **MArrayDataHandle**'s `inputArrayHandle` or `outputArrayHandle` functions.

The **MDataHandle** and **MArrayDataHandle** classes are lightweight so they can be easily created and deleted as necessary. They simply provide a convenient interface to the underlying data that resides in the various datablocks.

4.5.8 Node Design Guidelines

Having covered how to create custom nodes and integrate them into the DG, some general guidelines for designing your own nodes are now discussed. The following are the cardinal rules of node design:

♦ Keep the node simple.

♦ Nodes should never be aware of their environment or context.

♦ A node should never use data that is external to itself.

SIMPLICITY

As you are designing and implementing nodes, it is quite easy to begin adding more and more features to a given node. As a result, the node can become feature bloated. Recalling that nodes are really building blocks used in a larger system, by keeping them simple and singular in purpose, you can reuse their functionality more easily. If a single node performs two disjointed tasks, it should be split into two separate nodes. This reduces the complexity of your nodes and maximizes their reusability.

Another important consideration is that since a node is simply a C++ class, it is easy to make the mistake of giving the class more features and functionality than is really necessary. DG nodes fulfill a very precise and specific purpose in Maya. They take input data and produce some outputs. They should never be designed to do anything more than that. So keep in mind that your node is not a general C++ class capable of anything but a specific piece in a particular system: Maya's Dependency Graph.

CONTEXT

A node should never know where it is located in the DG. In fact, the node should never know that it is even used in the DG. A node should know only its input and output attributes and how to generate them when requested.

Unfortunately, it is possible for a node to begin looking outside of itself. The C++ API provides a variety of functions that let you follow the connections from your node to other nodes. These functions let you trace connections upstream and downstream. A node could therefore determine its place in the larger DG network. Doing this, however, is extremely dangerous.

If you design your node so that it knows, for instance, that it is part of an object's construction history, it makes certain assumptions. It assumes that it is being used in a particular configuration of nodes. This is extremely dangerous, since the user can create an instance of your node and use it somewhere else in the DG network. You node will most likely produce incorrect results or may even crash, because it assumes that certain conditions exist; in this case they won't.

A node should never check whether its attributes are connected to other nodes. A well-designed node will never have to do this. Maya handles all node connections without you, the node designer, having to be concerned. Attributes are presented in the C++ API in the same fashion, irrespective of whether they are connected or not. A common mistake is to create nodes that know they are connected to one another. The nodes then attempt to communicate or share data between themselves using pointers. This is effectively trying to circumvent Maya's data passing mechanisms and is extremely dangerous. If one of the nodes is deleted or disconnected, it could cause the other node to dereference a now invalid pointer. This can result in Maya crashing.

A node should never ascertain at which particular time it is being evaluated. If you design a node to cache information based on particular times, there is a very good chance that your node won't work correctly in certain contexts. For instance, it is possible to evaluate a node's attributes at any given time. In fact, a node can be evaluated at multiple times. If you design your node based on the assumption that it being called at a given time, it won't work when other times are used.

As such, making no assumptions about when and how the node is being evaluated ensures that your nodes operate correctly.

LOCALITY

A node must never, under any circumstances, look outside of itself. This is especially important when the node is computing its outputs. A node should never use external data in its computations. It should look only at its input attributes. If there is data that a node needs in order to do its computation that isn't in its input attributes, it should be added as an input attribute. You are free to perform the computation in any way you like.

All data that flows into a node should be done strictly through the DG. Data should not come from external sources. Using external data inside a node breaks its ability to operate without context. The DG will most likely not evaluate to the correct result.

This cardinal rule is so important that it can't be emphasized enough.

A node must never look beyond its own attributes!

NETWORKS OF NODES

Since a node should have a very myopic view of the world, how do you design a system in which many interconnected nodes are needed? Since nodes can't know anything about their context, it should be the task of a custom command to create and maintain the network of nodes. The command should have all the knowledge of the context in which the nodes are created and connected. So the nodes should remain simple and singular in their purpose. The commands should be the ones aware of the context in which the nodes are used.

4.6 LOCATORS

A locator provides users with a 3D visual aid that they can move and manipulate. It is drawn in the Maya viewport but won't appear in the final rendered image. Locators can be used to create a 3D handle that users can manipulate to control some other process. For example, locators in the shape of a footprint could be used to define the steps of a character. The user would simply move the footprint locators to change where the character walked.

Maya comes with a variety of measuring tools that are implemented as locators. The **Distance Tool** creates two locators and then displays the distance between them. Linking each of the end-point locators to separate objects gives you an immediate display of the distance between them, even when they are animated. Additional measuring tools include the **Parameter Tool** and the **Arc Length Tool**, which display the parametric value of a point and the distance along the curve, respectively.

Creating a custom locator is quite simple since you need only to overwrite a few member functions in order to add your new functionality. The main member functions needing changes are draw, isBounded, and boundingBox. If you want to draw the locator in a custom color, then the color and colorRGB functions should also be implemented. Inside the draw function, you are free to draw the locator in any way you like. Almost all OpenGL functions are available for drawing. Last the bounding box functions, isBounded and boundingBox, are important if you want your locator to work correctly with the various Maya selection and view zooming tools.

4.6.1 BasicLocator Plugin

This example plugin demonstrates how to create a basic locator. This locator can draw itself in a variety of ways. It also allows the user to stretch its width and length. An example of the basic locator is shown in Figure 4.26.

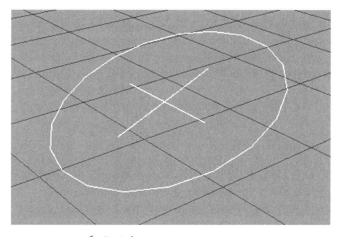

FIGURE 4.26 Basic locator

1. Open the **BasicLocator** workspace.

2. Compile it, and load the resulting `BasicLocator.mll` plugin in Maya.

3. Select **File | New Scene**.

4. Execute the following in the **Script Editor**:

```
createNode basicLocator;
```

A **basicLocator** node is created and displayed. Since the locator doesn't need to be connected to other nodes or need any particular initialization, as was the case in previous examples, the `createNode` command is a fast and easy method of creating a node instance.

5. Zoom into the locator or press **a** so you can see it more clearly.

6. Open the **Attribute Editor**.

The keyable attributes for the **basicLocator1** node are displayed.

7. Set the **X Width** to 2.

8. Set the **Disp Type** to 1.

The locator is drawn as a lozenge.

9. Set the **Disp Type** to 2.

The locator is drawn as an ellipse, since the **X Width** is twice the **Z Width**. Setting them both to the same size results in a circle being drawn. Since a locator has a parent transform node, like all DAG nodes, you can move, rotate, and scale it.

10. Experiment by moving and rotating the node.

Plugin: BasicLocator
File: BasicLocator.h

A custom locator node is created by first deriving from the **MPxLocatorNode** class. In addition to the usual `creator` and `initialize` functions, the class also implements the `draw`, `isBounded`, and `boundingBox` functions.

It has three attributes, **xWidth**, **zWidth**, and **dispType**, which define the scale of the locator's width, length, and how it will drawn, respectively.

```
class BasicLocator : public MPxLocatorNode
{
public:
    virtual void draw( M3dView & view, const MDagPath & path,
                       M3dView::DisplayStyle style,
                       M3dView::DisplayStatus status );

    virtual bool isBounded() const;
    virtual MBoundingBox boundingBox() const;

    static void *creator();
    static MStatus initialize();

    static const MTypeId typeId;
    static const MString typeName;

    // Attributes
    static MObject xWidth;
    static MObject zWidth;
    static MObject dispType;

private:
    bool getCirclePoints( MPointArray &pts ) const;
};
```

Plugin: BasicLocator
File: BasicLocator.cpp

The node draws itself in one of three fashions: triangle, lozenge, or circle. Each of these shapes can be defined by a series of interconnected lines. Rather than define different drawing functions for each type, an array of points is created. When the display type is a triangle, only three points are output. When it is a lozenge, then four points are generated, and so on. An additional point that wraps around to the first is also included. The getCirclePoints function generates this array of points. It takes into account the **xWidth**, **zWidth**, and **dispType** attributes when calculating the final positions of the points.

```
const double M_2PI = M_PI * 2.0;

bool BasicLocator::getCirclePoints( MPointArray &pts ) const
{
MStatus stat;
MObject thisNode = thisMObject();
MFnDagNode dagFn( thisNode  );

MPlug xWidthPlug = dagFn.findPlug( xWidth, &stat );
float xWidthValue;
xWidthPlug.getValue( xWidthValue );

MPlug zWidthPlug = dagFn.findPlug( zWidth, &stat );
float zWidthValue;
zWidthPlug.getValue( zWidthValue );

MPlug typePlug = dagFn.findPlug( dispType, &stat );
short typeValue;
typePlug.getValue( typeValue );

unsigned int nCirclePts;

switch( typeValue )
    {
    case 0:
        nCirclePts = 4;
        break;
    case 1:
        nCirclePts = 5;
        break;
    default:
        nCirclePts = 20;
        break;
    }

pts.clear();
pts.setSizeIncrement( nCirclePts );
```

```
MPoint pt;
pt.y = 0.0;

const double angleIncr = M_2PI / (nCirclePts - 1);
double angle = 0.0;
unsigned int i=0;
for( ; i < nCirclePts; i++, angle+=angleIncr )
    {
    pt.x = xWidthValue * cos( angle );
    pt.z = zWidthValue * sin( angle );
    pts.append( pt );
    }

return true;
}
```

Often the most complex part of a locator is its draw function. The draw function serves a dual purpose in Maya. It is called to draw the node in the current viewport. It is also used by Maya to determine whether the node is selected. When Maya is determining whether an object is the selection region or where the user has clicked, the object's draw function is called. Maya then uses the result of the drawing to determine if the object is selected. You don't have to be concerned about the second use of the draw function, since Maya handles this aspect automatically for you.

The locator can be as simple or as complex as you like. In fact almost all the OpenGL function calls are available to you during drawing. There are some restrictions, however. It is important that the draw function leave OpenGL in exactly the same state it was before the function is called. The OpenGL glPushAttrib function can make this task easier. It is used for pushing and popping the current graphics state.

When a locator's draw function is called, the current transformation has already been applied. As such, the node doesn't need to be concerned with positioning, rotation, or scaling itself. This is all handled automatically. The node simply draws itself in local object space. Also the current color is set automatically based on the current state of the node (selected, live, dormant, and so on). It is possible for the node to define a custom color for any of these states by implementing the color and colorRGB functions.

The draw function is called with several arguments. The first is the current Maya viewport in which the locator will be drawn. This is given as an **M3dView** class. The complete DAG path, **MDagPath**, to this locator node is also provided. The **M3dView ::DisplayStyle** defines the drawing mode in which the locator is to be drawn. The styles include bounding box, shaded, flat shaded, and so on. The **M3dView:: DisplayStatus** defines the current state of the node in the viewport. This status can include active, live, dormant, invisible, and so on.

```
void BasicLocator::draw( M3dView &view, const MDagPath &path,
                    M3dView::DisplayStyle style,
                    M3dView::DisplayStatus status )
{
```

Before any OpenGL drawing functions are called, the beginGL function should be called and the current OpenGL state pushed.

```
view.beginGL();
glPushAttrib( GL_CURRENT_BIT );
```

The vertices of the current display shape are then generated.

```
MPointArray pts;
getCirclePoints( pts );
```

The series of vertices are then drawn as line segments.

```
glBegin(GL_LINE_STRIP);
for( unsigned int i=0; i < pts.length(); i++ )
    glVertex3f( float(pts[i].x), float(pts[i].y), float(pts[i].z) );
glEnd();
```

A small cross is also drawn at the center of the locator.

```
glBegin(GL_LINES);
     glVertex3f( -0.5f, 0.0f, 0.0f );
     glVertex3f( 0.5f, 0.0f, 0.0f );

     glVertex3f( 0.0f, 0.0f, -0.5f );
     glVertex3f( 0.0f, 0.0f, 0.5f );
glEnd();
```

Now that drawing is finished, the current OpenGL state can be popped to restore the previous one. The endGL function should also be called to indicate that drawing is now finished.

```
glPopAttrib();
view.endGL();
}
```

The isBounded function is called when Maya needs to determine if the node knows its own bounding extents. The boundingBox function is called to retrieve the actual extents of the locator shape. It is highly recommended to implement these bounding functions. Without them, Maya has difficulty determining the exact size of the locator, so the Frame All and Frame Selection operations will result in incorrect zooming.

```
bool BasicLocator::isBounded() const
{
return true;
}
```

Since the vertices of the locator are known to be the widest and longest parts of the node, finding their bounding box equates to finding the bounding box for the node. This process is greatly simplified by the getCirclePoint function, which provides a list of all the vertices in the locator.

```
MBoundingBox BasicLocator::boundingBox() const
{
MPointArray pts;
getCirclePoints( pts );
```

The bbox default constructor initializes it to an empty volume.

```
MBoundingBox bbox;
```

Points are added using the **MBoundingBox**'s expand function. This increases the bounding box, if necessary, to include the given point.

```
for( unsigned int i=0; i < pts.length(); i++ )
    bbox.expand( pts[i] );
return bbox;
}
```

The initialize function creates the three custom attributes and adds them to the node.

```
MStatus BasicLocator::initialize()
{
MFnUnitAttribute unitFn;
MFnNumericAttribute numFn;
MStatus stat;
```

Both the **xWidth** and **zWidth** attributes are distances and so must be created using the **MFnUnitAttribute** rather than a simple double. Their minimum and default values are also specified.

```
xWidth = unitFn.create( "xWidth", "xw", MFnUnitAttribute::kDistance );
unitFn.setDefault( MDistance(1.0, MDistance::uiUnit()) );
unitFn.setMin( MDistance(0.0, MDistance::uiUnit()) );
unitFn.setKeyable( true );
stat = addAttribute( xWidth );
if(!stat)
  {
  stat.perror( "Unable to add \"xWidth\" attribute" );
  return stat;
  }

zWidth = unitFn.create( "zWidth", "zw", MFnUnitAttribute::kDistance );
unitFn.setDefault( MDistance(1.0, MDistance::uiUnit()) );
unitFn.setMin( MDistance(0.0, MDistance::uiUnit()) );
unitFn.setKeyable( true );
stat = addAttribute( zWidth );
if(!stat)
  {
  stat.perror( "Unable to add \"zWidth\" attribute" );
  return stat;
  }
```

The **dispType** attribute holds a short indicating the current drawing style. It is set up to use a minimum value of 0 and a maximum of 2.

```
dispType = numFn.create( "dispType", "att", MFnNumericData::kShort );
numFn.setDefault( 0 );
numFn.setMin( 0 );
numFn.setMax( 2 );
numFn.setKeyable( true );
stat = addAttribute( dispType );
if(!stat)
  {
  stat.perror( "Unable to add \"dispType\" attribute" );
  return stat;
  }

return MS::kSuccess;
}
```

Plugin: BasicLocator
File: PluginMain.cpp

The locator node is like any other node, so it needs to be registered during the initialization of the plugin. Registration of the node is the same as usual, with the exception that the node's type, MPxNode::kLocatorNode, needs to be given to the registerNode function. If the explicit node type wasn't used, then the default, MPxNode::kDependNode, is used.

```
...
stat = plugin.registerNode(
        BasicLocator::typeName,
        BasicLocator::typeId,
        &BasicLocator::creator,
        &BasicLocator::initialize,
        MPxNode::kLocatorNode );
...
```

The deregisterNode function is called, as usual, with the node's ID.

```
...
stat = plugin.deregisterNode( BasicLocator::typeId );
...
```

4.7   MANIPULATORS

Maya provides many different ways to adjust and change the attributes of a given node. The Attribute Editor is the most commonly used method for setting an attribute's value. For certain nodes there is a more visual means of achieving this same goal. Through the use of manipulators, the user can visually modify a given set of attributes. Depending on the type of attribute, this can be more intuitive than using the Attribute Editor or other method.

4.7.1   BasicLocator2 Plugin

To actually see a quick example of how manipulators work, the **BasicLocator2** plugin is compiled, then loaded. This plugin extends on the locator node created in the previous example to include manipulators for all its custom attributes: **xWidth**, **zWidth**, and **dispType**. The manipulators are shown in Figure 4.27.

1. Open the **BasicLocator2** workspace.

2. Compile it, and load the resulting `BasicLocator2.mll` plugin in Maya.

3. Select **File | New Scene**.

4. Execute the following in the **Script Editor**:

    ```
    createNode basicLocator;
    ```

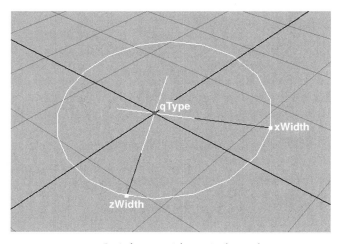

FIGURE 4.27   Basic locator with manipulators shown

A **basicLocator** node is created and displayed.

5. Select **View | Frame Selection** from the viewport panel, or press **f**.

6. Open the **Attribute Editor**.

    The editor is opened so you can see how the attribute's values are changing.

7. Select **Modify | Transformation Tools | Show Manipulator Tool**, or press **t**.

    The manipulators for the locator are displayed.

    If the manipulators aren't shown, ensure that the **basicLocator1** node is selected and not its parent transform node, **transform1**.

8. Click on the circle icon next to **Type**.

    The locator's **dispType** attribute is incremented.

9. Click on the circle icon again.

    The locator is now drawn as a circle.

10. Drag the dot next to the **X Width** text.

    The locator's **xWidth** attribute is updated. Notice in the Attribute Editor that the attribute value changes when you interact with the manipulator.

It is possible to define a manipulator node for any other Dependency Graph node. In the current example, the locator node, **basicLocator**, was defined, as well as its manipulator node, **basicLocatorManip**. The manipulator node is a special node that is created when the user selects a node and then requests its manipulator tool by choosing **Show Manipulator Tool**. Maya then creates an instance of the manipulator node. This node then goes about creating a series of base manipulators with which the user interacts. The manipulator node attaches these base manipulators to the node being edited so that a change in one of the manipulators, for instance dragging a point, results in a change to the node's attribute value. When the user exits the **Show Manipulator Tool**, the manipulator node is automatically deleted. The manipulator node can't be displayed in any of the Maya windows (**Hypergraph**, **Outliner**, and so on) or have any of its own attributes edited. It is, in essence, a temporary worker node that exists only while the node it is editing is selected. It isn't possible to create a manipulator node outside of the **Show Manipulator Tool** or user-defined context.

A manipulator node can be considered a "container" of base manipulators. A base manipulator is one of Maya's predefined interactive methods for changing an attribute. In the current example the **baseLocatorManip** manipulator contains three base manipulators: distance manipulators for both the **xWidth** and the **zWidth** attributes and a state manipulator for the **dispType** attribute. Maya current supports ten different base manipulators:

♦ **FreePointManip**

♦ **DirectionManip**

♦ **DistanceManip**

♦ **PointOnCurveManip**

♦ **PointOnSurfaceManip**

♦ **DiscManip**

♦ **CircleSweepManip**

♦ **ToggleManip**

♦ **StateManip**

♦ **CurveSegmentManip**

The complete details of each base manipulator are documented in the Maya class reference documentation. It isn't possible to define your own base manipulators, so you instead build up a more complex manipulator by using a series of base manipulators. These base manipulators are referred to as *children* of the main manipulator node.

The general steps to creating a manipulator node include deriving a new class from **MPxManipContainer**. The node then adds a series of children base manipulators. These children are associated with a given attribute in the target node that the manipulator will operate on. It is possible to define a simple relationship between a child manipulator and its associated attribute or a more complex one. This relationship is defined through the use of conversion functions. These functions define how information is translated from the manipulator to the attribute and vice versa.

Plugin: BasicLocator2
File: BasicLocator.cpp

Before delving into the specifics of the manipulator node, the original locator node must be altered slightly to let Maya know that it now has an associated manipulator node. Maya keeps an internal table of all the nodes and their associated manipulator nodes. At the end of the `initialize` function, the static `addToManipConnectTable` function is called with the ID of the node that now has a manipulator.

```
MStatus BasicLocator::initialize()
{
...
MPxManipContainer::addToManipConnectTable( const_cast<MTypeId &>
                                         ( typeId ) );
...
}
```

This is the only change necessary to the **baseLocator** node in order to have it work with the manipulator.

Plugin: BasicLocator2
File: BasicLocatorManip.h

A manipulator node is derived from the **MPxManipContainer** class.

```
class BasicLocatorManip : public MPxManipContainer
{
public:
    virtual MStatus createChildren();
    virtual MStatus connectToDependNode(const MObject & node);

    virtual void draw( M3dView & view, const MDagPath & path,
                    M3dView::DisplayStyle style,
                    M3dView::DisplayStatus status);

    static void * creator();

    MManipData startPointCallback(unsigned index) const;
    MManipData sideDirectionCallback(unsigned index) const;
    MManipData backDirectionCallback(unsigned index) const;

    MVector nodeTranslation() const;
    MVector worldOffset(MVector vect) const;

    static const MTypeId typeId;
    static const MString typeName;

    MManipData centerPointCallback(unsigned index) const;
```

```
    // Paths to child manipulators
    MDagPath xWidthDagPath;
    MDagPath zWidthDagPath;
    MDagPath typeDagPath;

    // Object that the manipulator will be operating on
        MObject targetObj;
};
```

In addition to defining a variety of member functions, which are covered shortly, the node defines DAG paths to the base manipulators it uses. These are the child manipulators with which the user interacts.

```
MDagPath xWidthDagPath;
MDagPath zWidthDagPath;
MDagPath typeDagPath;
```

The manipulator node also needs to a keep a record of which node it will be manipulating. This is the **baseLocator** node that was currently selected when the user activated the **Show Manipulator Tool**. The node being manipulated is referenced using the `targetObj` member. Notice that it is an **MObject** rather than an **MDagPath**.

```
MObject targetObj;
```

Manipulators can be applied to any dependency node, not just DAG nodes. It is therefore possible to use manipulators on any node that you define.

Plugin: BasicLocator2
File: BasicLocatorManip.cpp

Like all nodes, the **BasicLocatorManip** node must define a unique identifier. In this example, a temporary identifier is used.

```
const MTypeId BasicLocatorManip::typeId( 0x00338 );
```

It is *very* important to name the manipulator node based on the node it operates on. The name of the manipulate node must be the node name followed by **Manip**, so this manipulator node must be named **baseLocatorManip**. It is very important that the node name match exactly or the manipulator won't be associated correctly. Note that node names are case-sensitive.

```
const MString BasicLocatorManip::typeName( "basicLocatorManip" );
```

It is interesting to note that the **MPxManipContainer** contains its own static initialize function. In previous examples, the class defined its own. Since this manipulator doesn't do any special initialization beyond what is done by the base class, the manipulator node doesn't need to override this. Note, however, that if you do define your own initialize function, you should be sure to call back to the base class's initialize function. The following code shows an example of how you would do this:

```
MStatus BasicLocatorManip::initialize()
{
MStatus stat;
stat = MPxManipContainer::initialize();
... // do any extra initialization here
return stat;
}
```

Since the manipulator node is really just a container for base manipulators, the createChildren function is very important. It is used to create and add the base manipulators to the node.

```
MStatus BasicLocatorManip::createChildren()
{
MStatus stat = MStatus::kSuccess;
```

The addDistanceManip function is called to create a new distance manipulator node. The DAG path, xWidthDagPath, is used to store the path to the newly created node.

```
xWidthDagPath = addDistanceManip( "xWidthManip", "xW" );
```

The **MFnDistanceManip** function set is attached to the distance manipulator node so that you can set its various properties.

```
MFnDistanceManip xWidthFn( xWidthDagPath );
```

The distance manipulator is drawn as a start point and end point in a particular direction. The user moves the end point to set the distance. For the **xWidth** manipulator, the start point should begin at the center of the node, and the end point should run along the x-axis.

```
xWidthFn.setStartPoint( MVector(0.0, 0.0, 0.0) );
xWidthFn.setDirection( MVector(1.0, 0.0, 0.0) );
```

Another distance manipulator node is created, this time for the **zWidth** attribute. It also has its starting point at the center of the node. Its end point, however, runs along the z-axis.

```
zWidthDagPath = addDistanceManip( "zWidthManip", "zW" );
MFnDistanceManip zWidthFn( zWidthDagPath );
zWidthFn.setStartPoint( MVector(0.0, 0.0, 0.0) );
zWidthFn.setDirection( MVector(0.0, 0.0, 1.0) );
```

A state manipulator is created to interact with the **dispType** attribute. It is initialized to have a maximum of three states, which is the same as the number of states for the **dispType** attribute.

```
typeDagPath = addStateManip( "typeManip", "tM" );
MFnStateManip typeFn( typeDagPath );
typeFn.setMaxStates( 3 );
```

All the base manipulators have now been created. Notice that no association has been created between a given base manipulator and the attribute of the node it will affect. The connectToDependNode function is used for this purpose. When a node in the scene is selected and its manipulator is requested, usually through the **Show Manipulator Tool**, the connectToDependNode function is called with the selected node. It connects the base manipulators to the node's plugs. It also sets up any callbacks for placing and displaying the individual manipulators.

```
MStatus BasicLocatorManip::connectToDependNode( const MObject &node )
{
```

The targetObj is set to the node that is being manipulated.

```
targetObj = node;
MFnDependencyNode nodeFn(node);
```

An **MFnDistanceManip** function set is attached to the distance manipulator. A plug is created to the node's **xWidth** attribute.

```
MFnDistanceManip xWidthFn( xWidthDagPath );
MPlug xWidthPlug = nodeFn.findPlug( "xWidth", &stat );
```

The distance manipulator is associated with the **xWidth** plug. Any changes to the distance manipulator now affect the value of the **xWidth** attribute and vice versa.

```
xWidthFn.connectToDistancePlug( xWidthPlug );
```

When a manipulator is drawn, it is done so relative to the world origin. If the node is moved, the manipulator needs to be notified of this so that it can draw itself relative to the node's new location. This notification process is set up by using a call-back function. This function will be called any time the node moves. It can then determine the exact location of the center of the node. This center is where the distance manipulator's start point will be drawn.

In order to do this setup, a plug-to-manipulator conversion callback is needed. This callback converts the plug value into its associated manipulator value.

```
addPlugToManipConversionCallback( xWidthFn.startPointIndex(),
                (plugToManipConversionCallback)centerPointCallback );
```

Similarly, the distance manipulator's direction should follow the node's x-axis direction. Another plug-to-manipulator conversion callback is set up that provides the exact direction of the node's x-axis.

```
addPlugToManipConversionCallback( xWidthFn.directionIndex(),
                (plugToManipConversionCallback)sideDirectionCallback );
```

These same series of steps are applied to the **zWidth** plug. The start point of its distance manipulator is set to the center of the node, while its direction is set to the node's z-axis.

```
MFnDistanceManip zWidthFn( zWidthDagPath );
MPlug zWidthPlug = nodeFn.findPlug( "zWidth" );
zWidthFn.connectToDistancePlug( zWidthPlug );

addPlugToManipConversionCallback( zWidthFn.startPointIndex(),
                (plugToManipConversionCallback)centerPointCallback );

addPlugToManipConversionCallback( zWidthFn.directionIndex(),
                (plugToManipConversionCallback)backDirectionCallback );
```

The state manipulator is associated with the node's **dispType** plug. The position of the state manipulator is defined by the center of the node.

```
MFnStateManip typeFn( typeDagPath );
MPlug typePlug = nodeFn.findPlug( "dispType" );
typeFn.connectToStatePlug( typePlug );

addPlugToManipConversionCallback( typeFn.positionIndex(),
                (plugToManipConversionCallback)centerPointCallback );
```

It is extremely important that at the end of the function the finishAddingMaps function be called. It can be called only once.

```
finishAddingManips();
```

Somewhere following the finishAddingMaps function call, there must be a call to the **MPxManipContainer**'s connectToDependNode function. This lets the base class add any manipulator associations that it needs.

```
MPxManipContainer::connectToDependNode(node);

return MS::kSuccess;
}
```

Unless you want to add some custom drawing, there is no need to add your own draw function. Without it the base manipulators will still draw themselves. Include your own draw function when you want to add some additional drawing to the base manipulators or some other custom display information. In this example, some text labels are displayed next to the base manipulators in order for the user to more easily identify them.

Like the locator's draw function, the manipulator node's draw function takes an **M3dView** that contains the current view. The **MDagPath** parameter is a path to the manipulator node being drawn. The **M3dView::DisplayStyle** and **M3dView:: DisplayStatus** define the appearance and mode the node should be drawn in.

```
void BasicLocatorManip::draw( M3dView &view, const MDagPath &path,
                              M3dView::DisplayStyle style,
                              M3dView::DisplayStatus status )
{
```

Before any drawing is done, the base class's draw function must be called. This performs any drawing needed by the base class, which most often includes the drawing of the base manipulators.

```
MPxManipContainer::draw(view, path, style, status);
```

The values of the node's attributes are then retrieved.

```
MFnDependencyNode nodeFn( targetObj );
MPlug xWidthPlug = nodeFn.findPlug( "xWidth" );
float xWidth;
xWidthPlug.getValue( xWidth );

MPlug zWidthPlug = nodeFn.findPlug( "zWidth" );
float zWidth;
zWidthPlug.getValue( zWidth );
```

Preparations are made for the OpenGL drawing.

```
view.beginGL();
glPushAttrib( GL_CURRENT_BIT );
```

The text for the manipulator labeling is set up.

```
char str[100];
MVector TextVector;
MString distanceText;
```

Set the text for the manipulator labeling.

```
strcpy(str, "XWidth");
distanceText = str;
```

The next step is to determine where the label should be drawn. This will be the vector from which the label should be drawn in world coordinates if the node hadn't been moved. This is then offset by the vector to the node's center.

```
MVector xWidthTrans = nodeTranslation();
TextVector = xWidthTrans;
TextVector += worldOffset( MVector(xWidth , 0, 0) );
```

The label is drawn at the calculated position.

```
view.drawText(distanceText, TextVector, M3dView::kLeft);
```

The text label and position are calculated for the **zWidth** and **dispType** attributes. Their labels are also drawn.

```
strcpy(str, "ZWidth");
distanceText = str;
MVector zWidthTrans = nodeTranslation();
TextVector = zWidthTrans;
TextVector += worldOffset( MVector( 0, 0, zWidth ) );
view.drawText(distanceText, TextVector, M3dView::kLeft);

strcpy(str, "Type");
distanceText = str;
TextVector = nodeTranslation();
TextVector += worldOffset( MVector( 0, 0.1, 0 ) );
view.drawText( distanceText, TextVector, M3dView::kLeft );
```

The OpenGL drawing is now finished.

```
glPopAttrib();
view.endGL();
}
```

The remainder of the class functions are those responsible for determining various positions around the node. They are the plug-to-manipulator conversion callback functions. The `centerPointCallback` function returns the current center position of the node in world coordinates.

```
MManipData BasicLocatorManip::centerPointCallback(unsigned index) const
{
```

A numeric data object is needed to hold the position. This position is stored as three doubles: k3Double.

```
MFnNumericData numData;
MObject numDataObj = numData.create( MFnNumericData::k3Double );
```

The `nodeTranslation` function returns the offset of the node's center from the world origin.

```
MVector vec = nodeTranslation();
```

The position is set to this offset.

```
numData.setData( vec.x, vec.y, vec.z );
```

All the callback functions return an **MManipData** object. This object is designed to hold all the different data types that a manipulator could possibly alter.

```
return MManipData( numDataObj );
}
```

The `sideDirectionCallback` function returns the world space position of the vector (1, 0, 0) relative to the node.

```
MManipData BasicLocatorManip::sideDirectionCallback( unsigned index )
    const
{
MFnNumericData numData;
MObject numDataObj = numData.create(MFnNumericData::k3Double);
MVector vec = worldOffset( MVector(1, 0, 0) );
numData.setData( vec.x, vec.y, vec.z );
return MManipData( numDataObj );
}
```

The `nodeTranslation` function is a utility function that returns the node's current center position in world coordinates.

```
MVector BasicLocatorManip::nodeTranslation() const
{
MFnDagNode dagFn( targetObj );
MDagPath path;
dagFn.getPath(path);
path.pop();

MFnTransform transformFn( path );
return transformFn.translation( MSpace::kWorld );
}
```

The `worldOffset` function is a utility function that returns a vector that is the offset between the given vector and its world position.

```
MVector BasicLocatorManip::worldOffset(MVector vect) const
{
MVector axis;
MFnDagNode transform( targetObj );
MDagPath path;
transform.getPath(path);
```

```
MVector pos( path.inclusiveMatrix() * MVector(0, 0, 0) );
axis = vect * path.inclusiveMatrix();
axis = axis - pos;
return axis;
}
```

4.8   DEFORMERS

Deformers are not only conceptually simple to understand, they are also easy to implement. A deformer is a node that take a series of points and moves them to new locations. The deformer can't create or remove points, it can only move them around in space. The deformer is free to use any method to deform the points. The method can be as simple as moving the points by a fixed distance or as complex as using a fluid-dynamics simulation to determine their new positions. A deformer can operate on a wide variety of geometry primitives. At the lowest level, a deformer can modify lattice points, control vertices, and polygonal vertices.

4.8.1   SwirlDeformer Plugin

An example deformer, **SwirlDeformer**, will be covered in detail. The plugin creates a swirl deformer node that deforms an object by rotating the vertices based on their distance from the swirl's center. You can also set the start and end distances between which the swirl takes effect. Figure 4.28 shows the result of applying the **SwirlDeformer** to an object.

1.   Open the **SwirlDeformer** workspace.

2.   Compile it, and load the resulting `SwirlDeformer.mll` plugin in Maya.

3.   Open the **Swirl.ma** scene.

4.   Select the **nurbsPlane1** object.

5.   Execute the following in the **Script Editor**:

```
deformer -type swirl;
```

The NURBS plane is deformed by the swirl deformer. Notice that the swirl doesn't deform the entire object. This is because the swirl deformer end distance is shorter than the width of the object.

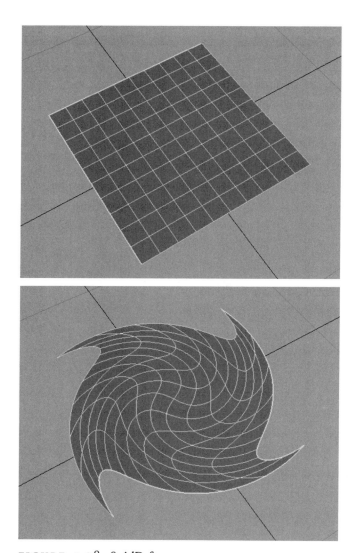

FIGURE 4.28   SwirlDeformer

6. Display the **Channel Box**.

7. Click on the **swirl1** item in the INPUTS section.

   The three main parameters are shown, **Envelope, Start Dist, End Dist**.

8. Set the **Envelope** attribute to **0.5**.

   The swirl is now less pronounced. You can interactively change the **Envelope** value to see the swirl increase and decrease in intensity.

9. Set the **Envelope** attribute back to **1.0**.

10. Set the **End Dist** attribute to **2.0**.

    The swirl now happens to a smaller area of the surface. Experiment by changing the **Start Dist** and **End Dist** to see how these attributes affect the swirl.

11. Set **Start Dist** to **0.0** and the **End Dist** to **3.0**.

    In addition to the general enveloping and distance parameters, you can define the influence of the deformer on individual vertices. This is done by changing the deformer's weighting.

12. Press **F8** to go to the **Control Vertex** level of the NURBS plane.

13. Select some vertices near the center of the plane.

14. Select **Window | General Editors | Component Editor...** from the main menu.

15. Click on the **Weighted Deformers** tab.

16. Drag down the **swirl1** column to select some vertices for editing.

17. Move the value slider at the bottom of the window.

    The weights of the selected vertices are changed, and as a result the effect of the swirl deformer is reduced or increased depending on their values.

When you create a custom deformer, Maya provides certain attributes automatically. The **envelope** attribute is common to all deformers. It defines the amount of deformation to apply.

Plugin: SwirlDeformer
File: SwirlDeformer.h

The **SwirlDeformer** class is created by deriving it from the **MPxDeformerNode** class.

```
class SwirlDeformer : public MPxDeformerNode
{
public:
    static  void *creator();
    static  MStatus initialize();
```

The major difference from other nodes is that a deformer contains a deform function and no compute function. The compute function still exists, but it is implemented in the base class. Unless you need some special computing, it is best just to implement the deform function and let the base class handle the compute function. The details of the deform function are explained in the next section.

```
virtual MStatus deform( MDataBlock &block,
                        MItGeometry &iter,
                        const MMatrix &mat,
                        unsigned int multiIndex );
```

Attributes for the start and end distance are defined. The **envelope** attribute is inherited from the **MPxDeformerNode** class.

```
private:
    // Attributes
    static MObject startDist;
    static MObject endDist;
};
```

Plugin: SwirlDeformer
File: SwirlDeformer.cpp

The major function to implement in a deformer is the deform function. It is the function that actually performs the deformation of the geometry. It is passed an **MDataBlock** that holds the datablock for the deformer node. This is the same datablock that you would normally get passed into the compute function. The second parameter is the **MItGeometry**, which is an iterator that lets you traverse all the points in the geometric object. The iterator can iterate a variety of point types including control vertices, lattice points, mesh vertices, and so on. This iterator has already been initialized to traverse only the type of points the deformer should modify.

The third parameter is the local to world transformation **MMatrix**, localToWorld. When points are given to the deformer, they are in the local space of the geometry node. If you need to do your deformations in world space, then simply transform the points using this matrix. It is important, however, to return them to local space after the deformation by using the inverse of the localToWorld matrix.

The last parameter is the geomIndex. It is possible for a deformer to deform multiple geometry nodes as well as multiple components of a single geometry node. Maya keeps track of which section of geometry you are deforming by the geomIndex.

```
MStatus SwirlDeformer::deform( MDataBlock& block,
                               MItGeometry &iter,
                               const MMatrix &localToWorld,
                               unsigned int geomIndex )
{
MStatus stat;
```

The value of the **envelope** attribute is retrieved.

```
MDataHandle envData = block.inputValue( envelope );
float env = envData.asFloat();
```

If the **envelope** value is 0, then the deformer won't have any effect on the geometry, so the function can return immediately.

```
if( env == 0.0 )
    return MS::kSuccess;
```

The start and end distance attributes are then retrieved.

```
MDataHandle startDistHnd = block.inputValue( startDist );
double startDist = startDistHnd.asDouble();

MDataHandle endDistHnd = block.inputValue( endDist );
double endDist = endDistHnd.asDouble();
```

The deformer will use the **MItGeometry** geometry iterator to traverse all the points to deform.

```
for( iter.reset(); !iter.isDone(); iter.next() )
    {
```

For each point there can be an associated individual weight. This weight is obtained by using the **MPxDeformerNode**'s weightValue function.

```
weight = weightValue( block, geomIndex, iter.index() );
```

If the point has no weight, then the deformer won't affect it, so the point is skipped.

```
if( weight == 0.0f )
    continue;
```

The current point is retrieved.

```
pt = iter.position();
```

The perpendicular distance of the point from the y-axis is calculated.

```
dist = sqrt( pt.x * pt.x + pt.z * pt.z );
```

If the point is closer than the start distance or farther than the end distance, then the deformer won't affect the point.

```
if( dist < startDist || dist > endDist )
    continue;
```

The closer a point is to the center of the deformer, the greater its rotation. The distFactor is the result of calculating the strength of this rotation. It has a value between 0 and 1.

```
distFactor = 1 - ((dist - startDist) / (endDist - startDist));
```

The rotation angle for the point is then determined. It is a result of distFactor scaled by the **envelope** value and the point's particular weight. It is multiplied by the equivalent of a full rotation, expressed in radians.

```
ang = distFactor * M_PI * 2.0 * env * weight;
```

If there is no rotation, then the point is skipped.

```
if( ang == 0.0 )
    continue;
```

The point is rotated about the y-axis by the ang amount.

```
cosAng = cos( ang );
sinAng = sin( ang );
x = pt.x * cosAng - pt.z * sinAng;
pt.z = pt.x * sinAng + pt.z * cosAng;
pt.x = x;
```

The point is now updated to use its new deformed position.

```
        iter.setPosition( pt );
    }

return stat;
}
```

The deformer node has two new attributes, **startDist** and **endDist**, in addition to those that come from the base class. The initialize function defines these attributes and adds them to the node.

```
MStatus SwirlDeformer::initialize()
{
MFnUnitAttribute unitFn;
startDist = unitFn.create( "startDist", "sd",  MFnUnitAttribute::kDistance );
unitFn.setDefault( MDistance( 0.0, MDistance::uiUnit() ) );
unitFn.setMin( MDistance( 0.0, MDistance::uiUnit() ) );
unitFn.setKeyable( true );

endDist = unitFn.create( "endDist", "ed", MFnUnitAttribute::kDistance );
unitFn.setDefault( MDistance( 3.0, MDistance::uiUnit() ) );
unitFn.setMin( MDistance( 0.0, MDistance::uiUnit() ) );
unitFn.setKeyable( true );

addAttribute( startDist );
addAttribute( endDist );

attributeAffects( startDist, outputGeom );
attributeAffects( endDist, outputGeom );

return MS::kSuccess;
}
```

Plugin: SwirlDeformer
File: PluginMain.cpp

The only minor modification to the `initializePlugin` function is that when you register the deformer node, the type must be set to `MPxNode::kDeformerNode`.

```
...
stat = plugin.registerNode( SwirlDeformer::typeName,
                            SwirlDeformer::typeId,
                            SwirlDeformer::creator,
                            SwirlDeformer::initialize,
                            MPxNode::kDeformerNode );
...
```

The deregistration process in `uninitializePlugin` is the same as for other nodes.

4.8.2   Dependency Graph Changes

As well as understanding how to write a deformer, it is important to understand how Maya uses the deformer node in the DG. When you debug your deformer, it is important to understand where your deformer node sits in the grander scheme of general Maya deformation.

The MEL `deformer` command generated a number of Dependency Graph changes. Before the deformation is applied to the NURBS plane, the DG appears as in Figure 4.29. This is the standard construction history setup for a NURBS plane.

After the `deformer -type swirl` statement is executed, the NURBS plane appears as shown in Figure 4.30. Some parts have been removed for simplicity, but the major nodes and their connections are shown.

The **makeNurbPlane1** node now feeds into the **nurbsPlaneShapeOrg** node. This node is an exact duplicate of the NURBS shape, **nurbsPlaneShape1**, before the deformer was applied. This shape then feeds into a tweak node, **tweak1**. Whenever you first apply a deformer to an object, Maya creates a duplicate and connects it to a new tweak node. This allows you to go back and tweak the object. Any tweaks to the original object are applied and followed by any deformations. The output from the tweak node is a potentially deformed shape. Since no tweaking has been done to the original NURBS plane shape, the tweak node passes the geometry from the shape to the swirl node, **swirl1**, without change. The **swirl1** node is

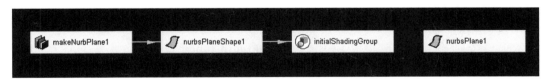

FIGURE 4.29   NURBS plane before deformation

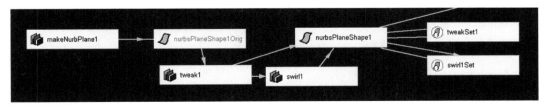

FIGURE 4.30   NURBS plane after deformation

an instance of the **SwirlDeformer** deformer node. It deforms the geometry passed into it. The resulting deformed geometry then is fed into the final NURBS shape, **nurbsPlaneShape1**. This last shape holds the final geometry and displays it on screen.

Whenever a deformer node is created, a **set** node is also generated. The **set** node contains a list of those objects, and possibly their components, to which the deformer should be applied. In this case the **tweakSet1** and **swirl1Set** set nodes have been created for the **tweak1** and **swirl1** deformation nodes, respectively.

Maya automatically handles reordering your deformer node if the user requests it. Also, if the deformer node is deleted, Maya automatically deletes any extraneous nodes, as well as reconnects the deformation chain. Maya also ensures that geometry isn't duplicated unnecessarily from one deformer node to the next. Essentially, one copy of the geometry is successively passed from the first to last deformer. Each deformer passes its deformation to the geometry. The geometry at the end is the result of applying each deformer in turn to the original geometry.

4.8.3   Accessories

For many types of deformers, it is often useful to add one or more accessories. An accessory is a node that the deformer creates either to enable the user to better visualize the deformer attributes or to allow the user to directly manipulate them. For example, the **twist** deformer includes a **twistHandle** node. This allows the user to visualize the various twist parameters, including the start and end angles, as well as the upper and lower bounds.

4.8.4   SwirlDeformer2 Plugin

This plugin demonstrates how to write an accessory that gives further control over the swirl deformer. In particular it creates a locator that is used to define the center and direction of the swirl. Used in this fashion, the accessory locator is commonly referred to as a *handle*. As such the locator is referred to as the **swirlHandle**. Figure 4.31 shows the result of applying the **SwirlDeformer** to a nurbs plane. The **swirlHandle** was then rotated causing the swirl to happen along the rotated direction.

1.   Open the **SwirlDeformer2** workspace.

2.   Compile it, and load the resulting SwirlDeformer2.mll plugin in Maya.

3.   Ensure that the SwirlDeformer.mll plugin is unloaded.

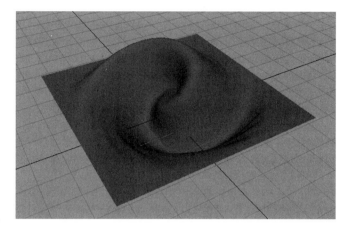

FIGURE 4.31 **SwirlDeformer** with a rotated handle

4. Open the **Swirl.ma** scene.

5. Select the **nurbsPlane1** object.

6. Execute the following in the **Script Editor:**

```
deformer -type swirl;
```

The swirl deformer is applied to the plane as before.

7. Select the **swirlHandle** object.

8. In the **Channel Box,** set the **swirlHandle's Rotate X** to **25.**

The swirl is now applied at an angle relative to the handle. Experiment by changing the **swirl1** node's **End Dist** attribute to see better how the angle has affected the swirl.

Adding one or more accessories to an existing deformer node is relatively simple. Note that in this example one of Maya's predefined locators was used. It is possible to create your own custom locator to use as a handle. It is also possible to add your own custom manipulators to the deformer node. Many of Maya's standard deformers demonstrate all these features.

Plugin: SwirlDeformer2
File: SwirlDeformer.h

The **SwirlDeformer2** class is defined in the same way as the **SwirlDeformer** class. In order to add accessories to the node, the original **SwirlDeformer** class was modified to include some new functions and a new attribute. The following functions derived from the **MPxDeformerNode** class were implemented. They are explained shortly.

```
virtual MObject &accessoryAttribute() const;
virtual MStatus accessoryNodeSetup( MDagModifier &cmd );
```

An additional matrix attribute, **deformSpace**, that contains the current transformation matrix of the handle object was added.

```
static MObject deformSpace;
```

Plugin: SwirlDeformer2
File: SwirlDeformer.cpp

The new **deformSpace** matrix attribute is added to the node in the initialize function.

```
MStatus SwirlDeformer::initialize()
{
MFnMatrixAttribute mAttr;
deformSpace = mAttr.create( "deformSpace", "dSp" );
```

Since the matrix is the transformation matrix of the handle, there is no need to store it.

```
mAttr.setStorable( false );
...
```

The deform function is modified to incorporate the new **deformSpace** matrix attribute.

```
MStatus SwirlDeformer::deform( MDataBlock& block,
                               MItGeometry &iter,
                               const MMatrix &localToWorld,
                               unsigned int geomIndex )
{
```

This attribute is retrieved from the data block like the other attributes. The inverse of the matrix is also calculated.

```
...
MDataHandle matData = block.inputValue( deformSpace );
MMatrix mat = matData.asMatrix();
MMatrix invMat = mat.inverse();
...
```

The only major change to the deformation method is that the points are first transformed into the local space of the handle accessory. The deformation is then done in that space before being converted back into the original object space. Converting to the handle space is done by transforming the point by the inverse of the handle's matrix.

```
...
pt = iter.position();
pt *= invMat;
...
```

Once the deformation is complete, the points are converted back to the original local space by transforming the handle's matrix.

```
...
pt *= mat;
iter.setPosition( pt );
...
```

When the deformer node is created, the accessoryNodeSetup function is called to create any accessory nodes that the deformer might need. The function is passed an **MDagModifier** so that new nodes can be created and added to the DG.

```
MStatus SwirlDeformer::accessoryNodeSetup( MDagModifier &dagMod )
{
```

A new locator node is created.

```
MObject locObj = dagMod.createNode( "locator", MObject::kNullObj, &stat );
if( !stat )
    return stat;
```

The locator is renamed to something more intuitive.

```
dagMod.renameNode( locObj, "swirlHandle" );
```

The **deformSpace** matrix attribute of the deformer node is controlled by the transformation matrix of the locator node by connecting the **matrix** attribute of the locator transform into the deformer node's **deformSpace** attribute. Whenever the locator is transformed, the **deformSpace** attribute is automatically updated.

```
MFnDependencyNode locFn( locObj );
MObject attrMat = locFn.attribute( "matrix" );
stat = dagMod.connect( locObj, attrMat, thisMObject(), deformSpace );

return stat;
}
```

If the user were to delete the deformer's handle object, the deformer node should also be deleted and vice versa. Fortunately Maya handles this automatically as long as you tell it which of the deformer node's attributes the accessory is affecting. Only one of the affected attributes has to be given. When the deformer's handle object is deleted, the connection to this attribute is deleted, and Maya then deletes the deformer node as well. Likewise, if the deformer node is deleted, the deformer handle object also is deleted.

```
MObject &SwirlDeformer::accessoryAttribute() const
{
return deformSpace;
}
```

4.9 ADVANCED C++ API

This section covers some of the more advanced C++ API topics.

4.9.1 General

REFERENCING NODES

Since an **MObject** is essentially a void pointer to some internal Maya data, it is very important that you don't hold on for too long. In fact, the **MObject** is valid only while the piece of data it is referencing still exists. If that data is deleted for some reason, the **MObject** is not notified and so continues to use what is now an invalid pointer. If the **MObject** is now used, it will most likely cause Maya to crash due to the invalid pointer being dereferenced. If you need to keep a reference to a DAG node, use an **MDagPath** instead. For general DG nodes, use their name. Since a node's name can change, it is important to keep your name reference updated. An **MNodeMessage** can be set up that will notify you when a given node's name changes. This is done by using the **MNodeMessage**'s addNameChangedCallback function.

PROXIES

When you define your custom commands and nodes, it may appear that they are the ones actually used in the DG. In reality they are just proxies. All the Maya classes that start with **MPx** define proxy objects.

Say, for instance, you created your own **MyNode** class that is derived from **MPxNode**. When Maya creates an instance of the **MyNode**, it in fact creates two objects. One is an internal Maya object that holds your **MyNode**. Your node isn't used directly in the DG. It is the internal Maya object that sits in the DG, which simply keeps a reference to your MyNode. This is why all the **MPx** derived classes are referred to as proxies. The real node is Maya's internal object.

In fact, you can get a pointer to your node from a DG node by using the **MPxNode**'s userNode function. This returns a pointer to the instance of your class that the internal Maya node is using.

Since a user-defined node is composed of two pieces, you have to be careful about what you do in the constructor. In the constructor of the **MyNode** class, you can't call any of the **MPxNode** member functions. This applies to all classes that are directly or indirectly derived from **MPxNode**. The reason for this restriction is that connection between the internal Maya node object and the instance of the **MyNode** isn't made until the instance is fully constructed. So during the construction of

MyNode, the **MPxNode** functionality isn't available. It is available only after the **MyNode** is created, since only then is the connection between the two established.

To make the construction of custom nodes easier, the **MPxNode** defines a virtual function, postConstructor, that you can implement in your node. This function is called when the connection between the two objects is created, so you are then free to call any **MPxNode** member function. As such, the **MyNode**'s constructor should be very minimal, and the postConstructor function should do most of the initialization work. Of course, if the **MyNode**'s constructor never needs to use any **MPxNode** functions, it won't have to implement the postConstructor and so will do all its initialization in its own constructor.

NETWORKED AND NONNETWORKED PLUGS

An often confusing Maya topic is that of networked and nonnetworked plugs. In practice, it isn't necessary to understand the distinction between the two. In fact, how they differ is an implementation issue relating to how Maya keeps connection information between connected attributes. As such, this topic is often redundant for developers. Plugs can be used without the developer ever knowing whether they are networked or nonnetworked. Even though understanding them may not impact your development, they can give you further insight into Maya's internal working.

When a plug is referencing a particular node's attribute, it needs to know only the node and the attribute. From these two pieces of information, it can find the node's specific attribute data. For array attributes, an additional piece of information is needed: the element index. With the addition of the element index, the plug can now locate the node's specific array element data. Since Maya allows attributes to be arbitrarily nested, a plug actually contains a complete path to a given attribute. This path contains indices for array plugs from the root plug to the particular attribute being referenced. To get the complete attribute path for a given plug, use the **MPlug**'s info function.

A plug can also serve another purpose in Maya. It can be used to store connection information between connected attributes. It can also store other state information. To make the process of connecting attributes and storing other state information easier, Maya maintains, for each node, an internal plug tree. This tree contains plugs for the node's connected attributes. The DG makes use of this internal plug tree to traverse connections between node attributes. A plug that exists in this internal tree is referred to as a networked plug. A plug that doesn't exist in a plug tree is referred to as a nonnetworked plug. It follows logically that all attributes that are connected will have an associated networked plug.

When an attempt is made to create a plug to an attribute, Maya first looks to see if there is an existing plug to the attribute in the internal plug tree. If there is, this networked plug is returned. If no plug exists, then a nonnetworked plug is created. In both cases, you can use the resulting plug in exactly the same way. The same **MPlug** member functions can be called, irrespective of whether the plug is networked or nonnetworked.

If you need to know if a plug is networked or not, then the **MPlug**'s isNetworked function can be used. In the following example, a plug to the **transform** node's **translate** attribute is created. The **MPlug**'s isNetworked function returns true if the plug is networked or false if it isn't.

```
MFnDependencyNode nodeFn( transformObj );
MPlug transPlg = nodeFn.findPlug( "translate" );
bool isNet = transPlg.isNetworked();
```

4.9.2 Dependency Graph

CONTEXTS

A context defines the reason a DG is evaluated. The context of a DG evaluation can be set to many different states. The context can be set to "normal" to indicate that the DG is evaluated at the current time. It can also be set to "at specific time," indicating that the DG should be evaluated at a particular time. The context can also be set to other states, such as "for an instance" or "during inverse kinematics." These later states are internal to Maya, so you can't set or query them directly.

The **MDGContext** is the class used to access and set contexts. It can be initialized with a particular time or another context. In the following example, the context is initialized with a time that is set to frame 12.

```
MTime t( 12, MTime::kFilm );
MDGContext ctx( t );
```

The **MPlug**'s getValue function can be used to retrieve the value of an attribute. By default it retrieves the value of the attribute at the current time. The context for the current time is indicated by the **MDGContext**'s fsNormal static member. The prototype for the **MPlug**'s getValue function for floats is given by the following:

```
MStatus getValue( float&, MDGContext &ctx=MDGContext::fsNormal ) const
```

Notice that it sets the reference to the context to the `fsNormal` object. You can test if a context is the current time by using the **MDGContext**'s `isNormal` function. Unless you explicity give a context, plugs are evaluated at the current time. The following example evaluates a plug at an alternate context.

```
MTime t( 500, MTime::kMilliseconds );
MDGContext ctx( t );
MFnDependencyNode depFn( transformObj );
MPlug transxPlg = depFn.findPlug( "translateX" );
double tx;
tansxPlg.getValue( tx, ctx );
```

DATABLOCKS

Datablocks are where the node's attribute data is stored. A datablock, as its name suggests, is a block of memory. When a node is defined, it also defines all the attributes it contains. The actual amount of memory needed by certain attributes can be worked out in advance. For simple fixed-size attributes, such as char, `boolean`, `float`, `2long`, `short`, `3double`, and so on, the memory requirements can be calculated. The memory needed by all these attributes is added up. A chunk of memory of this size is allocated to hold all the datablock data. This is more efficient than allocating separate memory for each of the individual attributes. For all attributes that don't have a fixed size, such as arrays, meshes, and so on, separate memory is allocated. The datablock contains a pointer to the separate memory rather than including it directly inside the datablock memory.

An example will help to further demonstrate. Given is a custom node, **makePyramid**, that generates a polygonal mesh in the shape of pyramid. It has four attrbutes: **width**, **height**, **geom**, and **capBase**. The node is shown in Figure 4.32 with the corresponding data types for each attribute.

A datablock is created for the node as shown in Figure 4.33. The datablock contains a context, which will be explained shortly. All the simple attributes, **width**, **height**, and **capBase**, can be stored in the contiguous memory block. The **geom** attribute has a variable-size data type, `mesh`, so is stored outside of the datablock. A pointer to the mesh is stored in the datablock.

When a node is initially created, it doesn't actually have a datablock. When one of its attributes changes from its default value or a connection is made, the node's datablock is then automatically allocated.

makePyramid

width (double)

height (double)

geom (mesh)

capBase (boolean)

FIGURE 4.32   **makePyramid** node

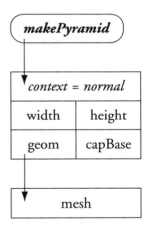

FIGURE 4.33   Datablock for **makePyramid**

A node can actually contain multiple datablocks. Each datablock has associated with it a context. The context defines a particular time instant at which the node is evaluated. Typically there is just a single context, referred to as the *normal context.* This is the context for the current time. A node could be evaluated at different times and under different circumstances and so can have multiple datablocks for each of these individual contexts. Figure 4.34 shows the **makePyramid** node with two datablocks. The first datablock holds the node data when it is evaluated at the current

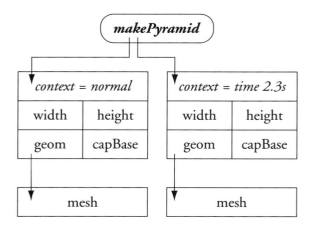

FIGURE 4.34   Multiple datablocks

time (normal). The second datablock holds the node data when the node is evaluated at 2.3 seconds.

Since most nodes are evaluated at the current time, they often contain just a single datablock. The extra datablocks are created and deleted as needed. A node can force the creation of a datablock at a given time by using the **MPxNode**'s forceCache function. To get the context for a given datablock, use the **MDataBlock**'s context function.

The **MDataHandle** and **MArrayDataHandle** classes are simple objects that understand the memory layout of the datablock. For simple data types that can be stored directly in the datablock, they can efficiently access the data. For data that resides outside the datablock, they use the pointer to dereference the associated data.

PROPAGATION FLAGS

As mentioned in the introductory chapter, when an attribute is changed, all attributes that it affects, including output connections, have their dirty bit set. The dirty bit is propagated to all direct and indirect attributes that the changed attribute affects. In a complex network, even this simple propagation of dirty bits can take some time. To reduce this overhead, a *propagation flag* is associated with each plug. If the propagation flag is set to true, then when a plug receives a dirty bit message, it sets its dirty bit and then it propagates this message to other plugs. If the propagation flag is false, then it won't pass the dirty bit message onward. The propagation flag effectively prevents propagating of dirty bit messages for plugs that should already have been set. If a given plug is marked as dirty, it can be assumed that it has propagated this message to all other affected plugs. So if you mark it as dirty again, it won't need to propagate again.

In most cases this methodology works just fine. There may be cases where a plug is not marked dirty, yet the plugs connected upstream are. In this case their dirty bit message hasn't been correctly propagated to the last plug. It will never recompute, since it is marked as clean. It will never be told that it is dirty, since the propagation flag of the incoming plug is set to false.

If this ever occurs, there is fortunately a way to correct this. Use the dgdirty command to set all the plugs of a node as either clean or dirty. It will force a propagation of the dirty bit message to all affected nodes, irrespective of their current propagation flag setting.

```
dgdirty $nodeName;
```

To mark all the plugs as clean, use the following:

```
dgdirty -clean $nodeName;
```

HANDLING PASS-THROUGH

All custom nodes are derived, either directly or indirectly, from **MPxNode**. This node contains several attributes, but the one most important to developers is the **nodeState** attribute. This attribute is accessible from Maya's interface by doing the following:

1. Select the node.
2. Open the **Attribute Editor**.
3. Expand the **Node Behavior** frame.
4. Beside the **Node State** prompt, select a new setting from the drop-down list.

Internally, the **nodeState** attribute is an enumerated data type with four values.

♦ 0 (normal)

♦ 1 (pass-through)

♦ 2 (blocking)

♦ 3 (internally disabled)

The **nodeState** attribute defines whether or not the node should compute its output attributes. Typically, the **nodeState** is set to 0(normal), so it computes its output attributes. By setting the **nodeState** to 1(pass-through), the node passes through its inputs to its outputs without doing any computation on them. This state is listed in the Attribute Editor as hasNoEffect.

When developing a node, you need to decide if you'll support the pass-through state. The decision is really based on whether the concept of pass-through is valid for the given type of node. Deformers should support this state. When the **nodeState** is set to pass-through, they should just put the input geometry into the output geometry without doing any deformation on it.

The following code shows how to change the **SwirlDeformer** plugin to support the node state. Before performing the deformation, the function checks whether the **nodeState** attribute is set to 1 (pass-through). If it is, it returns immediately, without doing the deformation.

```
MStatus SwirlDeformer::deform( MDataBlock& block, MItGeometry &iter,
                               const MMatrix &localToWorld,
                               unsigned int geomIndex )
{
MStatus stat;

MDataHandle stateHnd = data.inputValue( state );
int state = stateHdn.asInt();
if( state == 1 ) // Pass through
  return MS::kSuccess;

MDataHandle envData = block.inputValue( envelope );
float env = envData.asFloat();
...
```

CYCLIC DEPENDENCIES

It is possible to create cyclic dependencies. This is when one node feeds into another node and this node then feeds into the first. It is possible to have other intermediate nodes between the two, but the most important property is that if you walk from the first node through its outgoing connections, you eventually return to the same node.

The DG actually handles cyclic dependencies, though the results may not always be what you expect. The result most often depends on which of the nodes is evaluated first. Since the result isn't deterministic, it is best to avoid cyclic dependencies entirely.

ADDITIONAL RESOURCES

To help you continue your learning of Maya programming, a wide variety of online and offline resources is available.

Online Resources

The Internet contains an enormous variety of computer graphics programming resources. While it is possible to locate information about a given topic using your favorite web search engine, there are some sites that have specific Maya programming information.

COMPANION WEBSITE

The official companion site to this book is located at *www.davidgould.com*. A list, though not exhaustive, of the information available at the site includes:

♦ MEL scripts and C++ source code for all the examples in the book

♦ Additional example MEL scripts

♦ Additional example C++ API source code

♦ Errata for this book

♦ Continually updated glossary

♦ Updated list of other relevant websites and online resources

ADDITIONAL WEBSITES

Of particular note are the following websites that provide specific Maya programming information and forums.

Alias | Wavefront

www.aliaswavefront.com

This is the complete reference site for the Maya product. It contains the latest product development news, example scripts, and plugins. If you intend on creating commercial plugins, then be sure to look at the Alias | Wavefront Conductors program. This is a program by which Alias | Wavefront provides development and marketing support to developers who are going to commercialize their products. There is even support for developers who'd like to distribute their plugins as shareware or freeware.

Highend3D

www.highend3d.com

Best known for its in-depth coverage of the major animation and modeling packages, the Highend3D site is also a great repository of MEL scripts and plugins. It also hosts the Maya Developers Forum, where you can ask questions of other developers.

Bryan Ewert

www.ewertb.com/maya

This site contains a large number of MEL and C++ API tutorials and examples. The MEL basics are covered as well as some of the more advanced topics. The "How To" sections are interesting for developers needing a fix to a particular problem.

Maya Application

The Maya product ships with an extensive collection of Maya programming documentation and examples. Also, don't forget that you can often learn how Maya performs a given set of tasks by turning on **Echo All Commands** in the Script Editor. This can be a great starting guide if you want to do something similar.

DOCUMENTATION

In particular, the MEL and C++ API reference material will be a constant source of important programming information. All the documentation can be accessed from within Maya by pressing **F1** or by selecting **Help** from the main menu. Please note that the following links may depend on which version of Maya and which language you are using.

Learning MEL

maya_install\docs\en_US\html\UserGuide\Mel\Mel.htm

maya_install\docs\en_US\html\InstantMaya\InstantMaya\InstantMaya.htm

(Scroll to the bottom for the Expressions and MEL tutorials.)

Learning C++ API

maya_install\docs\en_US\html\DevKit\PlugInsAPI\PlugInsAPI.htm

For general programming reference material, refer to the **Reference Library** section of the **Master Index**. For specific programming references, visit the following.

MEL Reference

maya_install\docs\en_US\html\Commands\Index\index.html

maya_install\docs\en_US\html\Nodes\Index\indexAlpha.html

C++ API Reference

maya_install\docs\en_US\html\DevKit\PlugInsAPI\classDoc\index.html

maya_install\docs\en_US\html\Nodes\Index\indexAlpha.html

EXAMPLES

The standard Maya product comes with a large number of example MEL scripts and C++ plugins.

MEL Examples

Since Maya's interface is written entirely in MEL, the scripts it uses are provided with the application. There is no better insight into learning how to write professional MEL scripts than by looking at the scripts written by the Maya software engineers. You will find a host of scripts in the following directory, as well its subdirectories:

maya_install\scripts

I strongly recommend perusing them to see how well-designed scripts are written. Please note however that all the scripts provided are the copyright of Alias | Wavefront and cannot be used for derived works. Instead, study them and learn from their example, but don't be tempted to copy and use them as is.

Also be careful when you are reviewing the scripts that you don't accidentally change them. Since they are used by Maya, any changes may cause the system to become unstable and potentially to crash. For this reason, it is best to make a copy of the scripts beforehand.

C++ API Examples

The C++ API example directories include source code for plugins and stand-alone applications as well as motion-capture servers. The examples are located at:

maya_install\devkit

MEL FOR C PROGRAMMERS

For those familiar with C programming, it may come as no surprise that when you first look at a MEL command or script you note a great deal of similarity with the syntax used in the C programming language. In fact MEL is sometimes colloquially referred to as "C with $ signs." While this isn't entirely devoid of truth, there are some important exceptions that differentiate the two languages.

Following is a list of the important differences:

♦ Since MEL is designed for fast prototyping and also to be more accessible to less-sophisticated programmers, it does away with many of the lower-level system responsibilities that a C programmer is burdened with. One of these responsibilities is the allocation and deallocation of memory. MEL conveniently provides dynamic arrays so that you aren't required to create routines for expanding and shrinking array sizes. MEL handles the allocation and cleanup for you, thereby simplifying the code and reducing the risk of memory-related problems such as segmentation faults or memory leaks.

♦ MEL does not provide pointers. All variables, except arrays, are passed by value into procedures. All arrays are passed by reference.

♦ MEL assigns default values to local variables if you don't explicitly initialize them.

♦ Variables defined in the outermost scope are local by default unless you explicitly define them to be global by using the `global` keyword. This is the inverse of the scoping rules in C, where a variable defined in a unit is global by default unless you explicitly declare it to be `static`.

♦ The `float` type in MEL is the equivalent of a `double` in C. While the exact precision of this type is machine dependent, it is typically greater than the type used for C's `float`.

- MEL's `int` type is machine dependent, but most likely a signed integer, 32 bits in length.

- MEL comes with a built-in string type, `string`. A variety of operations can be automatically performed on it including concatenation.

- There are no bitwise operators (`|`, `&`, `!`, `~`, and so on) in MEL.

- MEL doesn't support type casting. You can't, for instance, convert an integer to a float using (`float`). To convert from one type to another, simply assign the type to the destination variable. For example, to convert an integer to a float, use the following:

```
int $intA = 23;
float $fltA = $intA; // Converted to float
... use $fltA in operation
```

Note that not all types can be assigned to other types.

Conversion from a string to a number is very simple. Unlike with C, you can simply assign a string to a numeric variable. This works as long as the string contains a valid number.

```
string $v = "123";
int $num = $v; // $num is now 123
```

- Boolean constants include `true`, `false`, `on`, `off`, `yes`, `no`. They have the standard numeric value of 1 for `true` and 0 for `false`. As in C, any statement that doesn't evaluate to 0 is considered `true`.

- Procedures can be defined inside blocks. However, it isn't possible to define a procedure inside of another procedure.

- Procedures can't have default values assigned to their arguments. The following is therefore illegal:

```
proc myScale( string $nodeName = "sphere", float $factor = 1.0 )
{
...
```

♦ Procedures can't be overloaded. If a procedure with the same name is defined, it overrides, rather than overloads, any previous definitions.

♦ Unlike C, it is valid to use strings in a `switch` statement. The following example demonstrates this:

```
string $name = "box";
switch( $name )
  {
  case "sphere":
    print "found a sphere";
    break;

  case "box":
    print "found a box";
    break;

  default:
    print "found something else";
    break;
  }
```

♦ In addition to all the standard flow control constructs (`for`, `while`, `do-while`, `switch`) MEL also has the `for-in` loop construct, which is exactly like a standard `for` loop except that it can be written more succinctly.

Unlike with C, it isn't possible to define a variable in the `for` loop construct. For instance the following is invalid in MEL:

```
for( int $i=0; ...
```

The variable has to be defined beforehand as follows:

```
int $i;
for( $i=0; ...
```

FURTHER READING

Computer graphics encompasses a wide variety of disciplines. However, the foundation of all computer graphics is, undoubtedly, mathematics. In particular, discrete mathematics, linear algebra, and calculus provide the major foundation for almost all computer graphics theory and practice. In addition to mathematics, a solid understanding of programming practices helps you in developing efficient and robust programs.

With a good understanding of both mathematics and programming, you'll have a solid base on which to learn the particular techniques and methods used in computer graphics. Even though the field is continually evolving, there are many computer graphics principles that once learned will hold you in good stead for all future work.

Below is a nonexhaustive list of books that provide a good grounding in their respective areas. Within each section, books are listed in order from basic to advanced.

Mathematics

Selby, Peter, and Steve Slavin. *Practical Algebra.* New York: John Wiley and Sons, 1991.

Thompson, Silvanus P., and Martin Gardner. *Calculus Made Easy.* New York: St. Martin's Press, 1998.

Mortenson, Michael E. *Mathematics for Computer Graphics Applications.* New York: Industrial Press, 1999.

Lengyel, Eric. *Mathematics for 3D Game Programming and Computer Graphics.* Hingham, Mass.: Charles River Media, 2001.

Programming

GENERAL

Deitel, Harvey M., and Paul J. Deitel. *C: How to Program,* 3d ed. Upper Saddle River, N.J.: Prentice Hall, 2000.

Knuth, Donald E. *The Art of Computer Programming,* 3 vols. Boston: Addison-Wesley Publishing Co., 1998.

Cormen, Thomas H., Charles E. Leiserson, Ronald L. Rivest, and Clifford Stein. *Introduction to Algorithms,* 2d ed. Cambridge: MIT Press, 2001.

C++ LANGUAGE

Liberty, Jesse. *Sams Teach Yourself C++ in 21 Days Complete Compiler Edition,* 4th ed. Indianapolis: Sams Technical Publishing, 2001.

Deitel, Harvey M., and Paul J. Deitel. *C++: How to Program,* 3d ed. Upper Saddle River, N.J.: Prentice Hall, 2000.

Stroustrup, Bjarne. *The C++ Programming Language,* special 3d ed. Boston: Addison-Wesley Publishing Co., 2000.

Meyers, Scott. *Effective C++: 50 Specific Ways to Improve Your Programs and Design,* 2d ed. Boston: Addison-Wesley Publishing Co., 1997.

Bulka, Dov, and David Mayhew. *Efficient C++: Performance Programming Techniques.* Boston: Addison-Wesley Publishing Co., 1999.

Computer Graphics

GENERAL

Foley, James D., Andries van Dam, Steven K. Feiner, and John F. Hughes. *Computer Graphics: Principles and Practice in C,* 2d ed. Boston: Addison-Wesley Publishing Co., 1995.

Watt, Alan H. *3D Computer Graphics,* 3d ed. Boston: Addison-Wesley Publishing Co., 1999.

Glassner, Andrew S. *Graphics Gems I.* San Francisco: Morgan Kaufmann Publishers, 1990.

Also see *Graphics Gems II, III, IV, V.*

MODELING

Rogers, David F. *An Introduction to NURBS, with Historial Perspective.* San Francisco: Morgan Kaufmann Publishers, 2001.

Warren, Joe, and Henrik Weimer. *Subdivision Methods for Geometric Design: A Constructive Approach.* San Francisco: Morgan Kaufmann Publishers, 2001.

ANIMATION

Parent, Rick. *Computer Animation: Algorithms and Techniques.* San Francisco: Morgan Kaufmann Publishers, 2002.

IMAGE SYNTHESIS

Watt, Alan, and Mark Watt. *Advanced Animation and Rendering Techniques.* New York: ACM Press, 1992.

Glassner, Andrew S. *Principle of Digital Image Synthesis.* San Francisco: Morgan Kaufmann Publishers, 1995.

Ebert, David S., et al. *Texturing and Modeling.* San Diego: Academic Press, 1998.

Shirley, Peter. *Realistic Ray Tracing.* Natuk, Mass.: A K Peters Ltd., 2000.

Blinn, James. *Jim Blinn's Corner: A Trip Down the Graphics Pipeline.* San Francisco: Morgan Kaufmann Publishers, 1996.

GLOSSARY

action An action is a MEL command that doesn't alter or change Maya's state. An action often queries the scene without changing it.

affine transformation A transformation that involves a linear transformation followed by a translation.

animation controller Many 3D packages have specific functionality for animating objects. In 3dsmax they are referred to as controllers. In Softimage, they are fcurves. In Maya, the standard animation controls are the **animCurve** nodes. They allow you to create and edit a curve that then controls a parameter over the range of the animation.

ANSI This an abbreviation of the American National Standards Institute. The institute is involved in defining standards for many computer languages, including C and C++.

API Abbreviation of *application programming interface.* A system provides a programmer with an API. This API defines the complete methods by which a programmer can access and control the given system.

argument An argument to a command or procedure is simply a value given to the command or procedure as input to perform its operation.

array An array is a list of items.

ASCII Abbreviation of American Standard Code for Information Interchange. This is a system for encoding characters using 7 bits.

assignment Assignment consists of storing a value into a variable. The assignment operator (=) is used to store values, for example, $a = 2.

attribute This is particular property of a node. For instance, the **makeNurbsSphere** node has a **radius** attribute. When you change this attribute, the sphere changes in size.

axis An axis is a direction. A 3D object has three axes: x, y, z.

black box When the exact operations of a given system aren't known outside the system, it is referred to as a black box. This means that its inner workings can't be seen.

boolean Booleans are used to denote the result of a logical operation. A boolean can be either true or false.

breakdown key This is a key that depends on keys before and after it. A breakdown key automatically maintains its position relative to the other keys when they are moved.

C++ This is an object-oriented programming language based on the C language.

Cartesian coordinates A coordinate system that defines positions based on their projection onto a series of orthogonal axes.

case sensitive When an operation is case sensitive, it makes a distinction between two names that don't have the same case. For instance, the names *bill* and *Bill* will be considered different in a case-sensitive system.

child This is something that has a parent.

class In C++, a class is the basic construct for defining a self-contained object. Classes have their own member functions and data.

class hierarchy Using standard object-oriented design methods, most complex systems are broken into a hierarchy. At the root (top) is a class with very basic functionality. Other classes (children) are derived from this class to add more specific functionality. As this process continues, you end up with a tree hierarchy of classes.

command A command is used to perform a particular operation. The sphere command, for example, is used to create and edit spheres. Commands are used throughout Maya to perform almost all its various operations.

command modes A single command can operate the following variety of modes: creation, edit, and query. When a command is executed in a given mode, it performs a restricted set of operations. When in query mode, it retrieves values. When in creation mode, it creates things.

comment This is some descriptive text that a programmer includes in the source code so that other people can read and understand what the programmer is doing. It is a means of documenting the functionality of a program. A *multiline comment* is a comment that spans more than one line of text.

compile-and-link Compiled languages like C and C++ need to have the source code compiled and linked into machine code in order to run. This is in contrast to scripting languages such as MEL, which interpret instructions and execute them immediately.

component This is the individual values of a vector, point, or other item. A point has three components: x, y, z.

compound attribute This is an attribute that consists of other attributes that are compounded into another more complex attribute.

compute function This is the function in a node that does the calculation of a node's output attributes. The compute function takes the input attributes and then calculates the final values for the output attributes.

concatenation This is the process of linking one or more items into a chain.

connection When the value of one attribute feeds into another, a connection is established between the two. It is possible to make and break connections freely.

context When the compute function of a node is called, the context defines when, in time, the node is being recalculated.

creation expression An expression that is run when a particle's age is 0, that is, when it is just born.

creation mode This is the mode a command runs in when it is called to create objects or nodes.

cross product The cross product of two vectors is another vector that is perpendicular to the two. It is often used to determine the direction of a vector that is normal to a surface.

curveAnim node These are curve animation nodes. These nodes hold an animation curve that you can edit and modify to animate a particular parameter. These nodes can do standard keyframing and driven-key animation.

DAG Abbreviation for *directed acyclic graph*. This is a technical term for a hierarchy in which none of the children can themselves be their own parents. If you walked from the first node in the hierarchy to the very last, you would never see the same node twice.

DAG path This is the complete path to a given node. The path lists the node and all its ancestor nodes.

data flow model A conceptual model in which data flows through a series of nodes from the first node to the last. Data is modified by each subsequent node.

data type Defines what type of information a variable can hold. Example data types include `string`, `int`, and `float`.

default parent If no explicitly interface element is specified, an element will be added to the default parent. There is a default parent for almost all element types.

deformer A deformer takes one or more points and moves them to new locations.

dependency node A general Dependency Graph node. All Maya nodes are dependency nodes.

dependent attribute This is an output attribute. When an attribute depends on other attributes for its final value, it is considered a dependent attribute. The `MPxNode::attributeEffects` function is used to set this dependent relationship between attributes.

DG Abbreviation for *Dependency Graph*. The DG consists of all the Maya nodes and their connections.

dirty bit This is a flag that an attribute contains to indicate whether it needs to be updated.

dirty bit propagation This is the process whereby a dirty bit message is passed through the DG from one node to another. The message eventually passes from the first attribute to all other attributes that this one affects.

dot product The dot product is simply the result of multiplying all the components of two vectors together and adding the results: `dot product(a,b) = a.x * b.x + a.y * b.y + a.z * b.z`. The dot product is often used to calculate the cosine of the angle between two vectors.

double In C++, this is a data type for storing numbers with decimal digits. It often, though not always, has a higher precision than the `float` data type.

driven key Whereas, in animation, a key is defined by its position in time, a driven key allows you to define a key relative to another attribute.

dynamic attribute This is an attribute that is added to a particular node. This attribute isn't shared by all nodes of the same type but is unique to a given node.

dynamic link library This is a library of programming functionality that is loaded into memory only when needed.

edit mode This is the mode a command runs in when its parameters are being changed.

ELF Abbreviation of *extended layer framework*. This is the framework used in MEL to define interfaces. Interfaces are designed by creating layouts to which controls are then attached. The framework supports arbitrary nesting of layouts and controls.

entry point This is the function that is called when a dynamic link library is loaded into memory.

exit point This is the function that is called when a dynamic link library is unloaded from memory.

Expression In the context of Maya, an Expression is a series of MEL commands that control one or more node attributes. This allows you to programmatically control attributes.

filter Given a large set of items, a filter defines a restricted set.

flag A flag is used to indicate whether something is on or off. It is used as a means of signaling.

float This is the data type for storing numbers with decimal digits. The size of a `float` in MEL is not necessarily the same as in C++.

floating-point A *floating-point number* is used by computers to store numbers with decimal digits. The term refers to the fact that the decimal point can change.

forward kinematics/FK This is the case in which an animator must explicitly define the orientations of all the joints.

function In the C and C++ programming languages, a function defines how to perform a particular operation. A function can, for instance, add two numbers or rotate an object or perform just about any operation. Functions are *called* to execute them.

function set Under Maya's scheme of separating the data from the functions that operate on them, a function set is a C++ class that provides the programmer with access to the data. A function set can be used to create, edit, and query the data without having to know its specific details.

functors A class that implements a set of functions but doesn't provide its own data.

global This defines the scope of variables or procedures. If they are made global, they can be accessed from anywhere.

group In Maya, a group is simply a **transform** node that becomes the parent of all the nodes in the group. The group is all the children of the **transform** node.

GUI Abbreviation of *graphical user interface*. This is the system of windows, dialog boxes, and other user interface elements with which you interact when you use Maya.

handle Something the system gives you in order to later access an object.

hierarchy Any system in which there is a parent-child relationship.

identity matrix A transformation matrix that doesn't have any effect when applied to a point. Technically, the matrix is composed of all 0s with just the diagonal having 1s.

IK solver Maya allows you to write your own inverse kinematic systems. An IK solver determines the orientations of intermediate joints.

initialization This is the value assigned to a variable when it is first defined.

input attribute This is an attribute that provides input to a node. The input attribute's value is often used by the compute function to calculate the value of one or more output attributes.

instance An instance of an object is an exact duplicate of the object. An instance is really an object that shares the exact properties of the original. It always stays the same as the original, no matter what changes are made to the original.

int This data type is used to store whole numbers or integers.

in-tangent The in-tangent defines the speed at which the animation curve approaches a key.

interface The specific communication methods through which you communicate with a system. The graphical user interface provides a set of graphical elements that you use to communicate your intentions to the underlying system.

interpreted language   This is a computer language in which the source code is interpreted and run immediately. This is different from a compiled language, in which the source code must first be compiled, then linked, before it is run. Interpreted languages tend to be slower than compiled languages, though they are often better for rapid prototyping.

inverse kinematics/IK   Through inverse kinematics an animator can control a series of joints by simply placing the last one. All the intermediate joints are calculated by the computer.

joint   A joint is like a bone. Joints can be connected to create appendages. Joints are often what the animator moves to control a character.

keyable   An attribute that can be animated by keyframing is *keyable*.

keyframe animation   In a keyframe animation you define the animation for a parameter by specifying its exact value at a given set of times. The computer can then work out by interpolation what the value should be between the keys.

keystroke   This is when a key on the keyboard is pressed.

layout element   A layout element is placeholder for other elements. The layout determines the final positioning and sizing of other elements added to it.

library   In the context of C++, a library is a repository of functionality that can be used in other programs. A library for handling files allows you to create, open, and edit files. By using a library in your program, you don't have to develop the technology yourself.

local   This defines how procedures or variables can be accessed. By making them local, they can be accessed only within the script file or current block.

local space   This is the coordinate space in which an object is first defined. In this space no transformations have been applied to the object.

locator   A locator is a 3D shape that is displayed in Maya. However, it won't show up in the final render.

loop   In a loop an operation is repeated several times.

manipulator   This is a visual control with which the user can change an attribute in 3D.

matrix   A matrix is a series of rows and columns of numbers. Matrices are used in computer graphics to transform points.

MEL Abbreviation of Maya Embedded Language. This is Maya's interpreted scripting language. It is very close to the C language in syntax but is easier to learn and allows you to write programs to access and control Maya quickly.

mesh A mesh is a series of polygons grouped to form a surface.

modal A modal dialog box prevents you from using the main application until it is dismissed.

namespace A namespace is where a set of names reside. Since they are all in the same set, the names must be different from each other. If you have names that are the same, a *namespace conflict* results.

node A node is the fundamental building block of Maya's Dependency Graph. Nodes contain attributes that a user can change. They also contain a `compute` function that automatically calculates certain attributes.

noise This is a pseudorandom number. For consistent inputs, it generates consistent, though random, numbers.

normal A normal is a vector that is perpendicular to a surface.

NURBS Abbreviation for *nonuniform rational B-spline*. This is a mathematical representation for smooth curves and surfaces.

object space *See* **local space**.

operator An operator is a shorthand method for defining an operation between one or more values. The addition operator is written using the plug sign (+). Other operators include multiply (*), division (/), and so on.

orphaned node A node that was previously connected to other nodes but has since lost all its connections.

output attribute This is an attribute that holds the result of a computation. One or more input attributes are fed into the node's `compute` function that then create an output value that is stored in an output attribute.

out-tangent The out-tangent defines the speed at which the animation curve leaves a key.

parametric space A position defined by parametric coordinates (u, v) rather than explicitly using Cartesian coordinates (x, y, z). This space is relative to the surface of an object and moves when the surface moves.

parent A parent is something that has one or more children. Since a parent can also have a parent, its children can have indirect parents. These are parents (grandparent, great-grandparents, and so on) above their direct parents.

parent attribute In a compound or array attribute, this is the topmost attribute. It is the parent of all the child attributes under it.

particles A particle defines a point in space. Particles are often animated and controlled by applying forces and other physics to them.

per object attribute A single attribute that is used by all particles.

per particle attribute Each particle will receive its own individual attribute.

pipeline In the context of a production studio, the pipeline includes all the various steps that go into making a film. Starting with modeling, then progressing to animation, lighting, and then finally rendering, the pipeline often consists of separate specialized departments.

platform A platform is a particular computer configuration. It includes the operating system and other specific components (CPU and so on). Example platforms include Irix, Linux, and Windows.

plug A plug identifies a particular node's attribute. It is used to access a specific node's attribute values.

plugin A plugin is a program that is integrated into another application. The program *plugs into* the application. Plugins often provide additional functionality that isn't available in the application.

point A point defines a position. In Maya, points are defined in Cartesian coordinates: x, y, z.

polymorphism With regards to an object-oriented programming language, such as C++, polymorphism refers to an object's ability to behave differently depending on its type. This provides a powerful means for making extensions to objects.

postinfinity This is any frame after the last key in an animation curve.

precedence In a programming language, the precedence of an operator determines in what order it is evaluated. An operator with a higher precedence is evaluated before another with a lower precedence. For instance multiplication has a higher precedence than addition.

preinfinity This is any frame before the first key in an animation curve.

procedural animation This is animation that is controlled by a program.

procedure A procedure is a means of defining a particular operation in MEL and is used to perform some operation and often return a result. This is conceptually the same as the C language's function.

propagation flag A flag that determines whether a dirty bit message will be propagated to output connections.

pseudocode Pseudocode is a shorthand way of describing a computer program. Rather than use the specific syntax of a computer language, more general wording is used. Using pseudocode makes it easier for a nonprogrammer to understand the general workings of the program.

push-pull model A conceptual model in which data is both pushed and pulled through a series of nodes. This model is more efficient than the data flow since only nodes that need updating are updated. Maya's Dependency Graph works on this principle.

query mode This is the mode a command runs in when its parameters are being queried.

random number A number that is determined entirely by chance.

redo When an command is undone, it can be reexecuted by choosing to redo it.

render To take the scene information models, lights, camera, and so on and make a final image.

root This is the fictitious node that is the parent of all other nodes in the scene. There is the concept of a root node so that the entire scene can be thought of as a tree, starting at the root.

rotate/rotation Rotating an object is the same as spinning it around. This changes its orientation. The point about which it rotates is called the *rotation pivot*. A wheel has its rotation pivot in its center.

runtime expression An expression that is run when a particle is older than zero.

scale Scaling an object means resizing it. A scale is uniform if the object is resized evenly. With nonuniform scaling, an object can be made wider, higher, or deeper without keeping its original proportions.

scene The scene consists of all the Maya data. It includes all the models, their animation, effects, settings, and so on.

scope The scope of a variable defines whether or not it can be accessed. If a variable has global scope, it can be accessed everywhere. If it has local scope, it can be accessed only in the block in which it is defined and all inner blocks.

script A text file that contains MEL statements.

scripting language A scripting language differentiates itself from other typical languages in that it is usually simpler to learn and use as well as not needing to be compiled. The language is interpreted at runtime, so you can execute instructions immediately.

seed A number used to initialize a random number generator.

set A set is simply a list of items. When an object is put into a set, it is made a part of the list.

set-driven keys Set-driven keys are used to define a relationship between one parameter and another. Unlike keyframes, which assume that you are using time, a set-driven key can use any parameter (driver) to drive another parameter. The relationship is defined by editing a curve.

shader A shader defines the final surface properties of an object. For example, a shader can define the color, reflectivity, and translucency of a surface.

shape This is the general term for all 3D data that can be displayed in Maya. Shapes include curves, surfaces, and points.

shape node A node that holds a shape, such as a polygonal mesh, curve, NURBS surface, or particles.

sibling A sibling is a child that shares the same parent.

skeleton A hierarchy of joints that define the inner structure of a character.

skinning This is the process whereby a model is wrapped around a skeleton. When the skeleton moves, the model moves correspondingly. The model effectively forms a skin over the skeleton joints.

sourcing This is the process whereby a MEL script is loaded into Maya and then executed.

space A space is a particular frame of reference for an object. Specifically, it defines the transformations that are applied to an object to put it into the frame of reference.

spring A spring provides a means of describing and calculating the elasticity, mass, damping, and so on between two points.

spring laws These define how a set of springs react given a set of forces.

string This is a series of characters; text.

structured programming This is a design approach whereby complex systems are broken down into smaller, more manageable pieces.

tangent In the context of an animation curve key, tangents define how values are interpolated between successive keys. By changing a key's tangents you can make the animation faster or slower between keys.

time node The **time** node is used to store time. It has a single attribute, **outTime**, that holds the time. While the **time1** node holds the current time, it is possible to create additional **time** nodes.

tool A tool defines a set of specific steps that must be completed in order to perform an operation. Tools often require the user to select something with the mouse before the operation can be completed.

transform node A DAG node used to specify the position, orientation, and size of a shape.

transformation hierarchy A single transformation positions, orients, and sizes a given object. By putting the transformations into a hierarchy, you can have a series of transformations applied to an object. An object that has parent transformations is also affected by those transformations.

transformation matrix A transformation matrix is a shorthand way of describing the positioning, rotating, and sizing of an object. When a transformation matrix is applied to an object, it often is in a different place, orientation, and size afterwards. The *inverse* of a transformation matrix restores the object to its original place, orientation, and size.

translate/translation Translating an object is the same as moving it.

translator In Maya, a translator is a piece of software that can translate data from one format into a format that Maya can understand. A translator may, for example, take a Softimage file and convert it to a Maya file. Translators are also referred to as importers and exporters since they can take information into and out of Maya.

tree This is the metaphor used to describe hierarchies.

truncate Truncating is when something is removed to make it compatible with something smaller. A decimal number can often be truncated to an integer by removing the decimal digits.

tweak This refers to the general process of editing something. When you tweak an object, you are simply changing it. Before a scene is final, it often undergoes a lot of tweaking.

tweak node A tweak node is used by Maya to store all the individual moves to some geometry's points.

underworld This is a parametric space (u, v) rather than a Cartesian space (x, y, z). Parametric positions are guaranteed to always "stick" to the underlying parametric object (NURBS curve or surface).

undo To remove the effect of a command, it can be undone. Undoing a command restores Maya to the state it was before the command was executed.

vector A vector defines a direction. Vectors can also have a magnitude that defines their length. A vector that has a length of 1 is called a *unit vector.*

void pointer A generic pointer that can point to an object of any type.

world space The space in which all the objects in the scene are displayed. The world space is the result of applying all of an object's parent transformations.

INDEX

ABOUT THE AUTHOR

WITH OVER A DECADE of experience in the computer graphics industry, David Gould has pursued the dual paths of programmer and artist. This rare ability to combine both the technical and artistic has won him many awards and credits. He has played a key role in the development of an eclectic mix of technology, including an award winning laser rendering system for Pangolin. He developed software for controlling the Kuper motion-control rig, as well as the Monkey stop-motion puppet. He personally developed Illustrate!, the market leading toon and technical illustration renderer. This renderer is used by NASA, British Aerospace, Walt Disney Imagineering, and Sony Pictures Entertainment, among others.

David's career has spanned a wide variety of companies and continents. In Paris, he supervised the production of 3D stereoscopic scientific films, including the award winning film, *Inside the Cell*. In London, he developed a patented facial animation system. Further broadening his experiences, he worked in New York in the post-production industry, where he contributed to many high-profile commercials.

While at Walt Disney Feature Animation, Los Angeles, David developed cutting-edge animation and modeling technology for use in the production of their animated feature films. He diversified further by joining Exluna, Berkeley, the software company founded by former Pixar rendering researchers, including Larry Gritz. While there, he played an active role in the design and development of Entropy, the Renderman-compatible renderer, as well as other products. David continued his rendering development efforts while at NVIDIA, in Santa Clara, California, by aiding in the design of their future 3D graphics chips. He has since joined Weta Digital, New Zealand, to work on the Lord of the Rings film trilogy. His varied roles in production, including shader development, lighting, and CG effects, reflects his broad range of talents.